Melissa Deener

Mental Health

Social Work Practice in Canada

Cheryl Regehr and Graham Glancy

OXFORD
UNIVERSITY PRESS

OXFORD
UNIVERSITY PRESS

8 Sampson Mews, Suite 204, Don Mills, Ontario M3C 0H5

www.oupcanada.com

Oxford University Press is a department of the University of Oxford. It furthers the University's objective of excellence in research, scholarship, and education by publishing worldwide in

Oxford New York
Auckland Cape Town Dar es Salaam Hong Kong Karachi
Kuala Lumpur Madrid Melbourne Mexico City Nairobi
New Delhi Shanghai Taipei Toronto

With offices in
Argentina Austria Brazil Chile Czech Republic France Greece
Guatemala Hungary Italy Japan Poland Portugal Singapore
South Korea Switzerland Thailand Turkey Ukraine Vietnam

Oxford is a trade mark of Oxford University Press in the UK and in certain other countries

Published in Canada by Oxford University Press

First Published 2010

Library and Archives Canada Cataloguing in Publication

Regehr, Cheryl
Mental health social work practice in Canada / Cheryl Regehr and Graham Glancy.

Includes bibliographical references and index.

ISBN 978-0-19-542971-8

1. Psychiatric social work—Canada—Textbooks.
2. Mental illness—Diagnosis—Canada—Case studies.
3. Mental illness—Treatment—Canada—Case studies.
I. Glancy, Graham II. Title.

HV690.C2R43 2010 362.2'04250971 C2009-904785-3

Cover image: istockPhoto/urbancow

5 6 – 14 13 12

Oxford University Press is committed to our environment.
This book is printed on paper that contains and minimum of 50% post-consumer waste.

Printed in the United States of America.

Contents

Preface

- Sarah, age 26, was sexually abused as a child between the ages of 10 and 15 by her stepfather. At age 15 Sarah disclosed the abuse to her mother, who called her a whore and threw her out of the house. As an adult, Sarah struggles with alcohol use and is frequently in and out of relationships with men, all of which at first seemed perfect but then ended in a crisis. Sarah has periods of intense despair where the memories of her abuse and her mother's rejection overwhelm her. Sarah cuts herself at times of extreme distress and has made several attempts on her life.

- Tom is a 19-year-old male admitted to the local general hospital psychiatric unit. He is the third child born to middle-class, first-generation immigrant parents. Recently, his parents became concerned because he was burning pieces of paper in his room, which he said would keep the aliens away. He barricaded the door of his room; it took a local police officer to persuade him to go to the hospital where he was admitted for assessment on an involuntary basis. On admission his speech was difficult to understand because of the severity of his thought disorder. He reported that aliens had been taking thoughts out of his head and had been constantly occupying his room, whispering. Tom was diagnosed as suffering from schizophrenia.

- Stefan is a 38-year-old married accountant. His father had episodes of severe depression and, although Stefan is not sure of the details, he believes that his grandfather committed suicide. Stefan always felt a little down every winter. He felt that it had been a little bit worse every year. This year his depression was so severe that he could not go to work and reported that he woke up every morning at 4 a.m. and could not get back to sleep. He had no appetite, felt nauseous all the time, and had lost 10 pounds. He complained of feeling worthless and felt guilty about letting his father down and being a failure in life.

- Bill and Jean worked together for 28 years in a family-owned business. They were known as the perfect couple. As Bill approached his seventies he had increasing difficulty remembering names and phone numbers; gradually this forgetfulness extended to his long-term memory. Bill began to have difficulty finding words that he would previously have used in everyday conversations, and eventually he forgot how to use familiar objects such as the kettle. At times he would become confused, especially in the evening, becoming agitated and fearful. Their son and their family practitioner suggested that Bill should consider a long-term care facility, but Jean felt it her duty to look after him, for better or for worse. On one evening Bill thought he heard a stranger come into the house and when Jean tried to calm him, Bill became increasingly upset and pushed Jean out of the way, hitting her with his cane.

Approximately 20 per cent of Canadians will experience a mental illness at some point in their lives. Thus, mental illness and mental health problems affect the lives of almost all individuals, families, and communities throughout Canada. Social workers are ideally suited to assist individuals and their families adapt to and overcome challenges associated with mental illness because of our focus on multiple levels of influence and multiple targets of intervention. Social workers are concerned with and trained to work with individuals and their families, drawing on client strengths to attain optimal functioning. Social workers assist individuals who are experiencing mental health problems to evaluate the challenges they face and the opportunities available to them and to facilitate the processes of making choices. Social workers support affected family members, assist families to deal with issues associated with mental health conditions and to develop creative ways to manage change.

Social workers add to the understanding of other members of the interprofessional team by focusing on the social and community contexts as contributing factors to the experience of mental illness. This includes the family and social environment in which the client lives; opportunities and challenges that exist within the community; systemic forms of oppression that influence the individual, including factors affected by race, gender, sexual orientation, ability, and social class; and social policies that influence choices. Social workers are able to advocate for changes in the environment through mobilizing and accessing community resources or working to change policies and practices that undermine mental health.

Traditionally, the dominant model of mental health focused on a deficit-based approach that had clear assumptions about normality and pathology. Overall, treatment programs and policies were designed around the assumption of chronicity, that is, people having a persistent and long-lasting condition, and mental health facilities were thought to be required to provide long-term care. However, practitioners and policymakers have now progressed in putting consumer choice and recovery at the forefront of mental health policy. This has contributed to a recovery model for mental health practice and an inherent belief that individuals can and do recover from severe mental illness. Social workers have integral roles to play in this recovery process.

This book is intended to provide a guide that will allow social work students to understand the nature of mental health issues, become aware of the Canadian legal and policy framework in which mental health treatment is provided, and learn about evidence-based social work practices that will best assist individuals and families struggling with mental health challenges.

Reviewers

We with to thank the following reviewers, whose thoughtful comments and suggestions have helped to shape this text:

Karen Schwartz, Carleton University
Gail Baikie, Dalhousie University
Rick Enns, University of Calgary
Rick Sin, McMaster University
Rohan Maitzen, Dalhousie University

Research Assistants

In the process of writing this book the following individuals identified, gathered, edited, and synthesized vast amounts of information:

Kamla Brewer
Christine Hayos
Elizabeth Ferris
Jennifer Robinson
Daniel Buchman
Adam McKie
A special thanks to Annabel Pitts for compiling the terms in the glossary.

Funding Assistance

The research contained in this book was generously supported by:

The Sandra Rotman Chair in Social Work Practice.

Dedication

This book is dedicated to Kaitlyn and Dylan.

Chapter 1

The Context of Mental Health Social Work Practices in Canada

Objectives:

- To outline the nature of mental health and mental illness in Canada
- To outline the role of social work in mental health
- To describe the role of social work on the interdisciplinary team
- To discuss ethical guidelines for social work practice in mental health
- To outline the recovery model for mental health practice
- To consider the application of evidence-based practice to mental health social work

The Canadian Association of Social Workers (CASW) (2001) suggests that mental health encompasses: psychological and social harmony and integration; quality of life and general well-being; self-actualization and growth; effective personal adaptation; and the mutual influences of the individual, the group, and the environment. Social work skills and knowledge are ideally suited to the practice of mental health because of our focus on multiple levels of influence and multiple targets of intervention. Social workers are concerned with and trained to work with individuals and their families, drawing on client strengths to attain optimal functioning. In addition, social workers focus on social dimensions of well-being and consider opportunities and barriers in the environment. Social workers are able to advocate for changes in the environment through mobilizing and accessing community resources or working to change policies and practices that undermine mental health (see Box 1.1).

Mental illness is an issue that touches all segments of Canadian society and all people within our country. The Canadian Alliance on Mental Illness and Mental Health (2006), a coalition of non-governmental organizations and professional bodies, provides the following statistics regarding the impact of mental illness in Canada.

Box 1.1 The Definition of Mental Health

Mental Health is the capacity of the individual, the group and the environment to interact with one another in ways that promote subjective well-being, the optimal development and use of mental abilities (cognitive, affective, and relational), the achievement of individual and collective goals consistent with justice, and the attainment and preservation of conditions of fundamental equality.

(Canadian Association of Social Workers, 2001)

- Approximately 20 per cent of Canadians will experience a mental illness at some point in their lives.
- It is estimated that mental illnesses alone cost our health care system as much as $7 billion a year, second only to cardiovascular disease.
- Five of the ten leading causes of disability in Canada relate to mental illness; the World Health Organization (WHO) predicts that depression will be the leading cause of workplace disability by 2020.
- Each year nearly four thousand people in Canada will die of suicide, which is nearly 40 times the number who died of AIDS in 2003. Suicide is the second leading cause of death among 10 to 19 year olds.
- Delirium occurs in up to 50 per cent of elderly people in acute care health settings.

Despite these facts, Canada has not had a national mental health strategy, and mental health has been described as the orphan of the health care system. We are far below other Western nations in our focus on mental health services and on mental health promotion. On the other hand, however, much has been done with regard to our understanding of mental illness. Biological research is furthering our understanding of some factors in the etiology, or origin, of specific mental illnesses, which is not only contributing to more effective medical interventions, but has also moved us away from blaming individuals with mental illness and their families for their own misfortune. The WHO and certain governments, such as the Government of Canada, have come to recognize the social determinants of health and mental health that provide a basis for advocating for basic human rights as adequate housing, food, income, education, and employment. Research is moving forward in determining effective psychosocial treatments for assisting clients with mental health problems and their families to regain control and enhance their own lives. Clearly, there are important roles for social workers in the area of mental health to identify problems, assist clients, advance knowledge, and create systemic change.

The Role of Social Work in Mental Health

In 1952, Mort Teicher, the first chief social worker at the Toronto Psychiatric Hospital (now the Centre for Addiction and Mental Health) wrote an article for *Canadian Welfare* entitled 'The Role of a Psychiatric Social Worker' (Teicher, 1952a). At that time he indicated:

The job of a social worker falls into two broad categories:

1. Intake: The social worker helps the patient and his relatives express feelings about the hospital and clinic services (they may have to work through feelings of anger, shame, and panic before they can really use treatment). The social worker then assesses the family's attitude towards the patient and the extent to which both patient and family are able and willing to participate in treatment.
2. Continued service: The social worker helps the patient to move into and use the psychiatric hospital or clinic and helps him find his way in the community after discharge (as cited in Skelton, 1996, p. 240).

Mora Skelton, who was the first social worker hired at Toronto Psychiatric Hospital (TPH) in 1947, indicates that at that time social workers were hired to work on discharge planning and rehabilitation in order to reduce recidivism (or relapse) and readmission. As a member of the multidisciplinary team, the social worker focused on the world in which the client lived, the world in which he or she had become mentally ill and to which he or she would return upon discharge. This analysis included the attitudes of relatives, job pressures (or the pressures of no job), finances, and housing (Skelton, 1996). Social workers at that time also played an important role with respect to patient advocacy and social justice. For instance, Mort Teicher (1952b) wrote an article entitled 'Let's Abolish the Social Service Exchange' that shifted social policy throughout North America with respect to patient confidentiality. Social service exchange was the name of a central database where agencies and hospitals would (without the client's consent) send names of clients who had accessed services in order to share information regarding a patient or client. Therefore, any former client of the psychiatric hospital obtaining services in the community would have a notation that they had been treated by TPH. Teicher, concerned about the stigma that this created for the client, was outraged; after many attempts at publication, his article was finally published in *Social Work Journal*. Despite the firestorm of letters and objections that followed, policy and practices were changed.

Skelton's description of social work in mental health in the 1940s and 1950s shows it as remarkably similar to today's role. The Canadian Association of Social Workers (2001) identify three broad areas of social work practice in mental health:

1. *Prevention:* reducing the incidence of mental illness and dysfunction through modifying stressful environments and strengthening individual, family, and community coping.
2. *Treatment:* reducing the impact of mental illness through early assessment, intervention, and treatment.
3. *Rehabilitation:* reducing the lingering effects of mental illness through the provision of retraining and rehabilitation.

The Ontario Association of Social Workers (OASW) (2006) conducted a survey in which 339 social workers in mental health described the duties in which they engaged (Calderwood, O'Brien, and MacKenzie Davies, 2007). Five major responsibilities emerged from the findings in order of prevalence: 1) assessment and referral (87 per cent of respondents engaged in this activity); 2) supportive counselling (83 per cent); 3) crisis intervention (73 per cent); 4) advocacy (60 per cent); and 5) psychotherapy (53 per cent). Activities related to education, discharge planning, addictions counselling, outreach, administration, research, and teaching of the activities of daily living were each identified by 20 to 50 per cent of respondents. On the basis of this survey, OASW developed the list of professional services offered by social workers in the mental health field (see Box 1.2).

Box 1.2 Specific Aspects of Social Work Practice in Mental Health

- **Psychosocial assessment:** perform a comprehensive assessment of individuals, families, groups, and communities based on identified needs, strengths, and coping; assess formal and informal support networks; recommend an action plan
- **Counselling and psychotherapy:** apply a therapeutic approach based on bio-psycho-social-spiritual and environmental factors
- **Individual and family psychoeducation**: provide education and promote awareness of mental health, and mental illness issues and services
- **Case management and discharge planning:** coordinate interdisciplinary services for a specific client, family, or group; advocate for equitable access to services; assist individuals and families to prepare for transitions; engage in relapse prevention
- **Supervision:** provide clinical supervision to students, volunteers, and employees
- **Consultation:** provide a social work perspective with interprofessional teams; provide consultation to colleagues
- **Community capacity-building:** participate on boards/committees and develop partnerships with the community; identify gaps in services and advocate for resources
- **Program management/administration:** ensure accountability and monitor clinical and systemic outcomes; oversee programs; contribute to organizational development
- **Teaching:** provide or facilitate workshops, courses, and presentations
- **Program, policy, and resource development:** analyze, please, and establish standards of practice; participate in or lead quality improvement initiatives
- **Research:** contribute to the development of best practices through discipline-specific or interdisciplinary research
- **Social action:** advocate for improvements to systems, policies, funding structures, and services; support self-help and self-advocacy associated with mental health and mental illness

Reprinted with permission of the Ontario Association of Social Workers.

Social work practice in mental health is highly diverse and offers many career opportunities. Of particular note, 83 per cent of social workers responding to this survey reported that they believed they were having a significant impact on the delivery of mental health services.

Social Work and the Interprofessional Team

The interprofessional team is 'a fully integrated practice by a team of professionals from a diverse background of disciplines. Each member of the team has an integrated knowledge of the other team members' roles, and all work from an equally valued team mandate. . . . When two or more professions purposely interact in order to learn with, from, and about each other . . . to improve effectiveness and the quality of care' (Gilbert, 2008). Interprofessional teams are found at the policy- and program-planning level of practice where other members of the team are economists, political scientists, and management professionals. Teams are found at the community level and at the direct practice level where other members are from other health disciplines such as medicine, nursing, occupational therapy, and psychology.

The role of social work within the context of the interdisciplinary mental health team is well recognized. According to statistics provided by the National Association of Social Workers (NASW) in the United States, social workers provide 60 per cent of mental health services in that country, whereas psychiatrists provide 10 per cent, psychologists provide 23 per cent, and psychiatric nurses provide 5 per cent (NASW, 2009). In direct service mental health practice, there is some overlap with other professionals, for instance, in the areas of assessment and some individual interventions. However, social work provides specific expertise in building partnerships among individuals, families, and professionals; collaborating with communities to build supportive environments; advocacy for services and resources; challenging and changing social policies to address poverty, employment, housing, and social justice; and supporting the development of preventative programs (CASW, 2001).

The US Department of Labor defines the role of social work in the context of mental health: 'Mental health and substance abuse social workers assess and treat individuals with mental illness or substance abuse problems. Such services include individual and group therapy, outreach, crisis intervention, social rehabilitation, and teaching skills for everyday living. They also help plan for supportive services to ease clients' return to the community' (US Department of Labor, 2009). There is evidence to suggest that other members of the team also value the role of social work in mental health. Toseland and colleagues (1986) interviewed members of interdisciplinary mental health teams who represented seven different professions, and social workers were reported as having a high degree of influence, second only to psychiatrists.

Interestingly, much of the literature on interprofessional teams focuses on the challenges various professions experience in working together (Faulkner Schofield and Amodeo, 1999; Reese and Sontag, 2001). Challenges identified include lack of knowledge of the expertise of other professions; role blurring; conflicts arising from differences in professional values and theory bases; lack of respect; and power differentials. It is useful for social workers to be aware that these challenges are experienced by all professional groups involved in the team and are by no means unique to social work. Further, social work group skills can be highly effective in assisting the team during times of crisis or conflict to come to effective resolutions that are in the best interests of clients and client groups.

An Ethical Framework for Social Work in Mental Health

Social work practice in Canada must be conducted in accordance with the Canadian Association of Social Workers' *Code of Ethics* (CASW, 2005). Six core areas of social work values are considered:

1. *Respect for the inherent dignity and worth of persons.* In mental health practice, this principle requires that social workers battle issues of stigma in mental health and show respect for clients regardless of the challenges they are encountering. This value also requires that social workers respect and advocate for client self-determination and their right to make choices based on voluntary and informed consent. As will be noted in Chapters 2 and 3 on mental health policy and legislation, client freedom of choice is sometimes limited by other factors. Social workers have an obligation to be informed of the legislated circumstances in which this arises and provide full information regarding options to clients and their families.
2. *Pursuit of social justice.* Social workers advocate for equal access to public services, treatments, and resources for their clients. Because individuals with mental health challenges are sometimes disadvantaged with regard to self-advocacy, this is of particular importance.
3. *Service to humanity.* Social workers place the needs of clients above self-interest when working in a professional capacity and work to promote justice. Social workers seek a greater good in working with disadvantaged clients and groups.
4. *Integrity in professional practice.* Social workers promote social work values in the organizations in which they work. They are honest, reliable, and diligent in their practice and set professional boundaries for the best interest of the client.
5. *Confidentiality.* Social workers respect the privacy and confidentiality of clients and only disclose information when there is consent or when legislation requires otherwise. As such, social workers must be very aware of the legislative requirements related to disclosure in the interests of client safety and public safety (see Chapters 3 and 12).
6. *Competence in professional practice.* Social workers provide the highest quality service possible and continuously strive to increase their knowledge and skills. They contribute to the development of the professional knowledge base through research and to the training of others in the profession.

Social work practice in mental health, as in other areas of practice, therefore, has a broad ethical base that incorporates core values such as justice, respect for dignity, and an obligation to work with disadvantaged groups. This has implications for the nature of practice and the theories and values on which it is based. Social workers also have an obligation to ensure confidentiality and integrity and thus must be aware of the policy and legal framework in which they work. Finally, social workers have an obligation to ensure that they practise competently, based on established knowledge. This requires social workers to remain current about best practices and research that would support competent practice.

A Recovery Model for Mental Health and Social Work Values

Traditionally, the dominant model of mental health focused on a deficit-based approach that had clear assumptions about normality and pathology (Williams and Collins, 1999). Overall, treatment programs and policies were designed around the assumption of chronicity, that is, people having a persistent and long-lasting condition (Carpenter, 2002), and mental health facilities were thought to be required to provide long-term care (as described in Chapter 2). Psychosocial programs focused on areas of family dysfunction, poor social supports, life skill deficits, educational/vocational problems, and non-compliance with treatment. Program success was thus measured by whether the program was able to prevent relapse and readmission, while ignoring the experiences of people dealing with mental health problems in their daily lives (Williams and Collins, 1999). However, practitioners and policymakers have now progressed in putting consumer choice and recovery at the forefront of mental health policy. This has contributed to a recovery model for mental health practice and an inherent belief that individuals can and do recover from severe mental illness, with hope playing an integral part in the recovery process (Carpenter, 2002; Salyers and Tsembersi, 2007). Deegan (1996), one of the early proponents of the recovery model, describes the model as a conspiracy of hope – a refusal to succumb to the images of despair often associated with a diagnosis of mental illness. The US-based President's New Freedom Commission on Mental Health (2003) in its report on this model began with the statement: 'We envision a future when everyone with a mental illness will recover . . . a future when everyone with a mental illness at any stage of life has access to effective treatment and supports – essentials for living, working, learning and participating fully in the community' (p. 1).

The recovery model is based on several fundamental components: self-direction, individualized and person-centred approaches, empowerment, holistic views, non-linearity, strengths-based, peer support, respect, responsibility, and hope (Sowers, 2005). In this model, the mental health professional works in full partnership with clients and families, developing individualized treatment plans where consumers choose what treatment will be provided, by whom, and when. Recovery itself is not viewed as an end, but as a process that will have ups and downs, successes and setbacks (Carpenter, 2002). The recovery model is premised on the value that everyone has growth potential and services need to focus on enhancing growth and improving progress (Farka et al., 2005). Finally, the recovery model is premised on the belief that a broad set of systems must work together to create opportunities for growth that include integrated services and a broad range of community supports to optimize social, educational, vocational, income, and housing opportunities. The principles espoused by the consumer (or client) advocates in this area are highly consistent with social work practice (Deegan, 1996; CMHA, 2008):

- Positive relationships and the support of others are central to recovery and independence.
- Meaningful daily activity, that is, being able to live, work, and play in our communities, helps develop self-respect, maximizes strength, and promotes health.
- Spirituality assists with mobilizing inner healing capacity.
- Personal growth involves a personal process of overcoming disability despite its continued presence.
- Medications are one tool among many that people can use in their recovery process; people can move from *taking* medications to *using* them as part of their recovery process.
- People need opportunities to learn a variety of skills that will assist them in managing their lives and symptoms; mental health professionals must ensure that skill-building opportunities exist.
- Self-determination is a desired outcome—creating an internal locus of control, personal efficacy, power, and responsibility.

A model for social work in mental health must incorporate the concept of recovery and include realistic optimism for the future of clients. Such a model carries with it the expectation of improvement in functioning and the active involvement of the client in working towards that (Williams and Collins, 1999). This model captures the ethics and values of social work and provides an important role for social workers in mental health, both in relation to their clients and families and in relation to others on the mental health team.

Psychiatric Medications and Social Work Practice

As indicated in the aspects of the preceding recovery model, medications are frequently included as one aspect of mental health care. In mental health practice, there are six primary groups of medications: antidepressants; antipsychotics that are used to treat psychoses, schizophrenia, and mania; mood stabilizers that are used primarily to treat bipolar disorder; anxiolytics for reduction of anxiety; stimulants; and hypnotics for assisting with sleep. Although people experiencing any mental health problem may be prescribed medication, people suffering from certain problems, such as schizophrenia or bipolar disorder, will almost always be prescribed medication. Therefore, social workers in mental health will undoubtedly have clients who are taking psychotropic medications or are in the process of deciding whether to take this medication.

Bentley, Walsh, and Farmer (2005) conducted a random sample survey of 994 members of the US NASW to examine the roles and activities of social workers with respect to psychiatric medications. Eighty per cent of those responding indicated that they very frequently or often discussed a client's feelings about taking medication; 91 per cent indicated that they felt competent to do this; and 96 per cent felt this was an appropriate role for social workers. Other activities frequently engaged in by social workers in this study included making referrals to physicians for medication assessment (71.9 per cent); discussing with clients the desired combined effects of medication and psychosocial treatment (70.1 per cent); discussing a medication problem with a client (61.2 per cent); discussing the pros and cons of taking medication (51.6 per cent); and discussing adverse side effects (51.4 per cent). Based on this research, Bentley and Walsh (2006) suggested that social workers in mental health be prepared to ask and reflect on the following questions when working with clients on medication: Why is medication (and specifically this medication) being prescribed for my client? What are the desired effects and what are the possible negative effects? Is there a long-range plan for this medication? When will it be altered, discontinued? How might the client's use of this medication affect other interventions that I am providing? and most importantly, What are my client's views about taking medication?

A growing body of literature addresses the meanings that clients ascribe to medications. This is critical for our work with clients for a number of reasons. First, the response of any person to medication is complex, and in addition to biology, psychological and social factors play a significant role in the outcome of psychopharmacological treatments. For instance, in one review, placebo effects were postulated to account for over 75 per cent of the efficacy of antidepressant medications (Mintz, 2005). People differ in their beliefs about the nature and uses of medication, but also in the degree to which they believe that they personally are sensitive or susceptible to the effects of medication – both the positive effects and adverse effects (Horne, et al., 2004). There is a complex interaction between these pre-existing beliefs or expectancies and medication response. Other psychological factors influencing response to medication include readiness for change, a person's general sense of control and specific sense of control over taking the medication, and the client's alliance with the person prescribing the medication (Bradley, 2003; Floersch, 2003). Longhofer and colleagues (2003), in interviewing 90 adults who were being treated for schizophrenia or schizo-affective disease, demonstrated that clients had very individualized views about the causal effects of the medication and often suggested that the effects of the medication were mediated by other factors in their environment – such as the current state of their significant relationships. Similarly, in reporting on research involving youth who were on psychiatric medications, Floersch reported on the divergent ways in which the effects were interpreted. He concluded that social workers committed to self-determination must ask clients about their experiences on medications and encourage self-monitoring and self-assessment as keys to medication management and decision-making.

Social workers in mental health will inevitably be working with clients who are prescribed medication. Therefore, they must possess knowledge about commonly used medications and their effects in order to work effectively with clients. Social workers must also be aware that clients will have diverse views and beliefs about medication that may or may not be consistent with the worker's own views. With these factors in mind, the social worker's role with clients on medications can include several elements:

- Social workers can explore with clients and their families the meaning that they ascribe to medications and how the use of medications may impact their self-image or the view that others may have of them (Bradley, 2003).
- Social workers can provide clients and families with sources of information about medications including their purpose, effectiveness, and side effects.
- Based on an understanding of both the meaning that the client ascribes and the benefits and negative aspects of medication, social workers can assist clients in making informed decisions about their own treatment and recovery plan.
- Social workers can assist clients and families to advocate for themselves with respect to questions or concerns around medications, or can advocate for clients directly by consulting with and collaborating with other members of the team. For instance, if the client finds the medications helpful to some degree, but is troubled by some side effects, what might be done to alter the medication regime so that it does not interfere with life goals?

Evidence-Based Social Work: An Ethical Responsibility?

Laura Myers and Bruce Thyer (1997) raised the controversial question 'Should social work clients have the right to effective treatment?' They argued that providing effective treatments is an ethical responsibility of social workers and that education programs and codes of ethics for social workers should reflect this ethical duty. Their position was in no way widely accepted at the time and critiques of the position included many concerns. The evidence-based practice (known as EBP) model, originally developed in medicine, was viewed by some as inconsistent with values of social workers, in particular with the profession's mission, values, and diverse service populations. Evidence-based practice was viewed by some as reductionistic, undermining one of social work's most distinctive strengths that lies in the holistic view of a person in the environment (Witkin, 1998). It was seen to be a cookbook approach that involved extracting best practices from the scientific literature and simplistically applying them to clients without regard to who the clients are, their personal motivations and goals, or other potentially complicating life situations (Regehr, Stern, and Shlonsky, 2007). Critics also fear that evidence-based practice ignores the social worker's expertise—experience and judgment—and may 'undermine traditional professional practice' (Webb, 2001, p. 58). Concerned social work writers linked the increasing emphasis on accountability and evidence-based practice to economic and resource issues and raise concerns whether evidence-based practice is necessarily in the best interests of clients or whether it is merely a means for cost containment. Similar concerns have been raised in medicine (Porta, 2004; Saarni and Gylling, 2004). Although these criticisms may be true to a greater or lesser extent, many factors make evidence-based practice consistent with good social work practice: 1) the obligation to provide our clients with services that are most likely to assist them and least likely to cause harm; 2) the obligation to provide informed consent; and 3) current legal definitions regarding expertise and competence.

Although social workers have always strived to provide the best interventions for clients, dominant treatment methods have at times been detrimental. One clear example of this is the role social workers played in the removal of Aboriginal children from their homes to be placed in residential schools in Canada. It has been observed that social workers were some of the strongest supporters of the residential school system, and when a joint House of Commons and Senate committee recommended closure of all residential schools in 1948, the social work profession joined with the churches in lobbying against such action. Social workers sat on admissions committees for the residential schools; in Saskatchewan by the 1960s more than 80 per cent of Aboriginal children who were in residential schools had been placed there by social workers (Blackstock, Brown, and Bennett, 2007). The negative aspects of residential schools, including abuse, inadequate education, and shockingly high death rates are now well known.

A second example of harmful practice is in the area of family interventions with schizophrenia. In the 1950s as part of a trend to look for family problems as the cause of mental health problems, communications within the family and family dynamics were targeted as the cause of schizophrenia. This led to coining the term 'schizophrenogenic mother' (Bateson et al., 1956; Sluzki et al., 1967). Eventually these concepts led to an entire form of therapy, strategic family therapy, which focused on changing family interactions and in particular the mother's behaviour, thereby curing schizophrenia or at least reducing relapse (Haley, 1976). More recently, however, increased knowledge regarding the biological basis for the disease (see Chapter 7) has discredited this theory as mother-blaming without justification. Nevertheless, many social workers attended major training events in which the model was taught and large numbers of well-meaning social workers then imposed the model on families. Although not all areas of practice have been subject to research, there is both qualitative and quantitative data available on client experiences and the outcomes of many forms of intervention. Any intervention must be subject to the individual scrutiny of social workers. Has the intervention been tested and does it work? Are clients satisfied with the intervention? If there is no data available, how intrusive is the intervention and what are the possible negative effects that may result in using this intervention?

A second issue surrounds ethical obligations to obtain informed consent. The notion of informed consent is consistent with the long-standing commitment of social work to the value of self-determination, which is the right of clients to participate fully in decisions made about them. The doctrine of informed consent in its most expansive form can be said to have two goals: 1) to promote individual autonomy; and 2) to encourage rational decision-making. Valid informed consent has five elements:

1. The information provided is adequate for clients to be able to weigh the risks and benefits of the proposed action.
2. Clients have been told the foreseeable risks and benefits of the proposed action.
3. Clients are competent to provide consent.
4. Consent is given voluntarily and without coercive influence.
5. Clients have been told they have the right to refuse or withdraw consent (Regehr and Antle, 1997).

Early legal decisions regarding disclosure of information to patients maintained that valid consent was based on the 'reasonable physician' standard, that is, information that the average, reasonable physician felt was adequate and appropriate in order for a patient to make a decision about whether to consent to any given treatment. In the United States and Canada, this was replaced by the 'reasonable patient' standard (*Canterbury v. Spence*, 1972; *Hopp v. Lepp*, 1980). As a result, disclosure now must include all information that an objective, reasonable person, in the patient's situation, would consider important in reaching a decision to accept or refuse the proposed treatment, including all *material* risks of that treatment and the risks of available options. However, in the absence of evidence, can we, in fact, as social workers describe the possible risks and benefits to a client? Clearly, we were not able to do this in the cases of 'schizophrenogenic mothers' and Aboriginal children admitted to residential schools.

Legal definitions regarding expertise and competent practice have changed dramatically in recent years. Since 1923 the standard for expertise in the courts in the United States (and by default in Canada) was based on the concept of general acceptance (*Frye v. United States*, 1923); that is, is the method of treatment 'generally accepted' by members of the profession? In 1993, the US Supreme Court ruled on an important case regarding the admissibility of expert evidence (*Daubert v. Merrell Dow Pharmaceuticals*, 1993). It cited four factors to assess whether a particular test used to support expert evidence has a reliable foundation. These factors were: 1) whether the theory or technique can and has been tested; 2) whether the theory or technique has been subject to peer review and publication; 3) whether the error or potential rate of error has been identified and whether standards exist; and 4) whether this theory or technique has been generally accepted. In 2000, the Supreme Court of Canada explicitly adopted the criteria in *Daubert v. Merrell Dow Pharmaceuticals* in the case of *R. v. J.(J.-L.)* (1999). These changes in law clearly suggest that the courts require social workers and all other expert witnesses to take into consideration all materials, guided by the available evidence in their field of inquiry.

How can we institute a model of evidence-based social work that balances the multiple dimensions of social work values and responsibilities? Evidence-based practice in medicine originally was defined as 'the conscientious, explicit and judicious use of current evidence in making decisions about the care of individual patients' (Sackett et al., 1996, p. 71). More simply defined, it is the use of treatments for which there is sufficiently persuasive evidence that they will attain the desired outcomes (Rosen and Proctor, 2002). Proctor and Rosen (2004) suggest that evidence-based practice has three assertions: 1) intervention decisions based on empirical, research-based support; 2) critical assessment of empirically supported interventions to determine their fit to and appropriateness for the practice situation at hand; and 3) regular monitoring and revision of the course of treatment based on outcome evaluation.

In general, decision-making that uses evidenced-based methods is achieved in a series of steps (Wilson et al., 1995; Gibbs and Gambrill, 2002). The first step is to evaluate the problem to be addressed and formulate answerable questions; for example, What is the best way to assist an individual with these characteristics who suffers from depression? The next step is to gather and critically evaluate the evidence available. A decision needs to be made about which intervention strategy is the best approach. Finally, it is necessary to monitor and evaluate the outcome of the intervention.

Regehr, Stern, and Shlonsky (2007) provide a model for deciding which intervention to implement that includes: 1) client wishes (whether an individual, family, group, or community); 2) practitioner expertise (whether a clinician, manager, or policymaker); 3) agency mandate and constraints; and 4) the broader ecological context. This model is shown in Figure 1.1.

Regehr and colleagues argue that evidence-based practice, by definition, facilitates the very best qualities of social work when a social worker involves clients in a collaborative process to consider the available evidence or lack of evidence. The practitioner fosters self-determination as the client is empowered to contribute to an informed decision about treatment planning in light of his or her goals, values, and situation; at the same time, the practitioner must take into consideration his or her own skills, resources, and agency context. Although less has been written about evidence-based practice at the policy level, the basic tenets remain the same, with social work professional values underpinning a process that encourages transparency and collaborative decision-making while recognizing the economic and political exigencies that operate.

This type of approach to evidence-based practice would support the notion of other writers that a recovery orientation and evidence-based practice are not opposed to one another (Sowers, 2005). Farkas and colleagues (2005) argue for the integration of evidence-based practice into recovery programs. They define recovery programs that focus on the notion that individuals and families can move beyond mental illness and lead meaningful lives in their own communities. They identify four key components: 1) person orientation (a focus on the individual not the disease); 2) person involvement (people's right to full partnership treatment/program planning, implementation, and evaluation); 3) self-determination/choice (regarding goals, outcomes, and preferred services); and 4) growth potential (a focus on the potential to recover). These authors contend that there is evidence to support that client outcomes improve when clients have opportunities

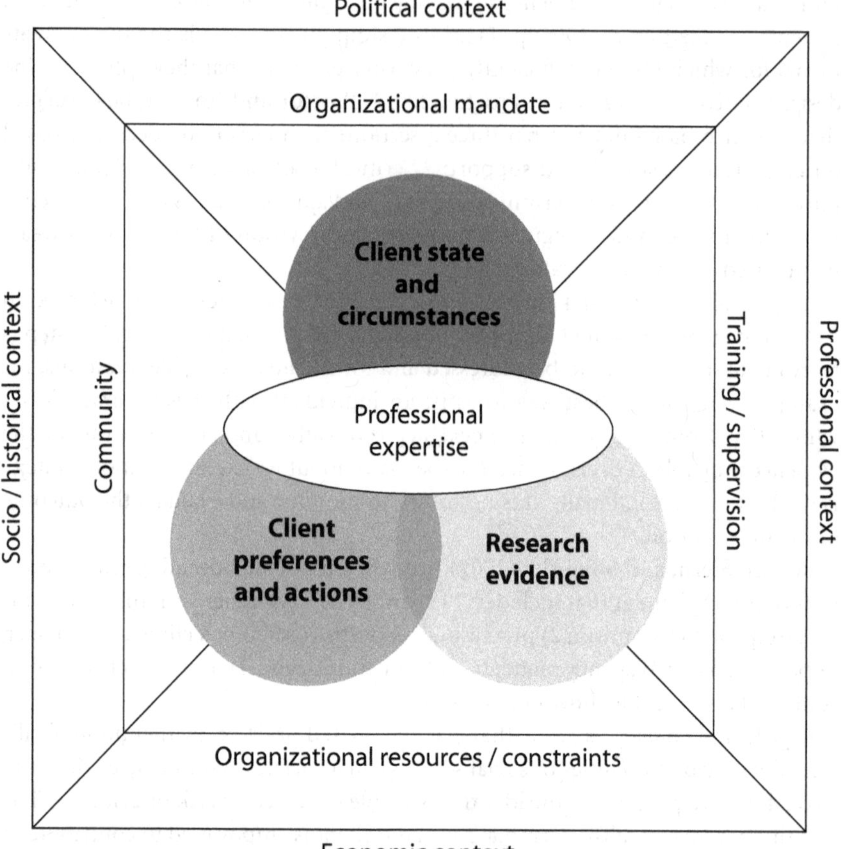

Source: 'Operationalizing Evidence-Based Practice: The Development of an Institute for Evidence-Based Social Work', Regehr, Stern, and Shlonsky. *Research on Social Work Practice.* 2007; 17: 408–16.

Fig. 1.1 A Comprehensive Model of Evidence-Based Practice

for meaningful involvement as opposed to when they are coerced into receiving treatment. Further, involving clients in the process of quality assurance and evaluation increases the validity of research findings regarding efficacy of interventions. However, at times, the basic premises of specific evidence-based approaches may need to be examined. For instance, Assertive Community Treatment, an evidence-based model described in Chapter 9 and used with individuals who suffer from schizophrenia, has particular elements that could undermine the recovery model. As one example, the unlimited time in which services are offered if presented in a rigid manner, may suggest that clients cannot manage without support. Further, team members' involvement in readmission to hospital may undermine self-determination of clients (Salyers and Tsemberis, 2007). Thus, in order to integrate the evidence-based approach with a recovery model that incorporates elements of consumer choice, processes may need to be adapted or modified. This must be conducted at a policy level, an organizational and programmatic level, and at the direct practice level.

Multiple Levels of Influence: A Social Work Perspective in Mental Health Practice

The unique perspective of social work in the practice of mental health focuses on multiple levels of influence. Social workers have key roles to play in assisting individuals and their families adapt to and overcome challenges associated with mental illness. As members of interprofessional health teams, social workers seek to assist others in understanding the social and community context in which mental illness occurs and the way in which these larger systems contribute to the development of illness and exacerbate or ameliorate the challenges in adapting to illness. As experts in family processes, social workers assist families to deal with issues of grief and loss associated with mental health conditions and to develop creative ways to manage change and support affected family members. In addition, social workers assist individuals who are experiencing mental health problems to evaluate the challenges they face and the opportunities available to them and to facilitate the processes of making choices, dealing with adversity, and when possible, recovering from illness. Further, social workers participate in the modification and development of relevant and effective programs, service systems, and policies in the areas of mental health and health in general.

In order to do this, social workers must be knowledgeable in a broad span of issues. This book is intended to provide a foundation for social work practice in mental health. We begin with Chapters 2 and 3 that consider the policy and legislative framework in which mental health programs are developed and mental health practice occurs. This larger framework creates both opportunities and limitations for clients; only with a thorough understanding can social workers articulate the systemic challenges that clients face and advocate for change. Mental health law deals with highly complex issues related to treatment of individuals who may not have the ability to make decisions about their own care or who may be a danger to themselves or others. Legislation in this area covers such issues as decisions regarding consent to treatment, substitute decision-making, and involuntary commitment. Social workers are called upon to instruct patients regarding their rights; instruct families regarding their ability to ensure that treatment is or is not provided to an ill loved one; provide assessments regarding the potential consequences of treatment decisions for provincial review boards; and provide assessments regarding the capacity to consent. Each of these roles requires an understanding of the laws pertaining to consent and treatment, essential elements of consent and capacity, and the process of review through provincially appointed boards.

Social work assessments in mental health address biological factors; individual cognitive and psychodynamic factors; family systems issues; cultural, religious, and community considerations; and the sociopolitical and legislative environment in which mental health problems are experienced. In addition, social workers working in the area of mental health must be familiar with the *Diagnostic and Statistical Manual of Mental Disorders* (DSM) and be knowledgeable about the use of multiaxial assessments in order to communicate effectively with others on the multidisciplinary team (APA, 2000). Further, social workers must be familiar with mental status examinations and suicide risk assessments as critical components of mental health assessment. Knowledge of the *DSM* does not imply uncritical acceptance of all aspects of the manual and the framework on which it is based. However, as we discuss in Chapter 4, critical analysis should be based on a thorough understanding of the text. In this way, if social workers disagree with formulations provided by other members of the health care team, they are able to present their points in a credible manner, based on knowledge of the concepts used by others and expertise in other ways of formulating the issues.

Finally, each type of mental health problem presents with a different symptom picture, a different etiology, and different challenges for individual clients and their families. As a result, the most effective treatment approaches vary widely from one mental health problem to another.

Each chapter on specific mental health problems begins with a case example that illustrates the lived experience of individuals. Next, each chapter addresses the research and literature on the nature of the problem, its presentation and prevalence. Finally, evidence-based treatments are reviewed that include community-based interventions, family interventions, group interventions, individual interventions, and medication. In each of these categories of mental health challenges, this book advocates that optimal social work practice in mental health involves a biopsychosocial approach to assessment and intervention that is based on the best current available evidence.

Summary

Social workers bring to the practice of mental health a broad perspective that includes an awareness of biological, psychological, and social influences on mental health and well-being. The unique contributions that they bring to the multidisciplinary team, however, is the focus on how these factors intersect with other issues in the person's life. This includes the family and social environment in which the client lives; opportunities and challenges that exist within the community; systemic forms of oppression that influence the individual, including factors affected by race, gender, sexual orientation, ability, and social class; and social policies that influence choices. Social work interventions are based on this broad awareness.

Social work practice is governed by ethical principles, which are codified in our code of ethics. These ethical principles require that we are respectful of all persons with whom we work; that we serve humanity through the pursuit of social justice; that we practise with integrity, including ensuring that our clients have a right to privacy and confidentiality; and that we practice competently and provide the best-quality services available. These best-quality services must be based on a combination of the best available knowledge in the area, professional expertise, and judgment, a consideration of the agency and external context, and above all, client values and consent.

Key Terms

Chronicity
Etiology
Evidence-based practice
Holistic
Informed consent
Interprofessional
Psychotropic medications
Readmission
Recidivism
Recovery model
Relapse
Schizophrenogenic
Social determinants of health
Substitute decision-making
WHO

Discussion Questions

1. What is the unique role of social work in mental health practice?
2. What are the possible positive and negative aspects of using an evidence-based approach to social work practice in mental health?
3. What should the role of social work be with respect to medications?
4. How does the recovery model fit with social work values and ethics?
5. Are there inherent conflicts between the recovery model and evidence-based practice?

Suggested Readings and Weblinks

Canadian Alliance on Mental Illness and Mental Health (2006), *Framework for Action on Mental Illness and Mental Health: Recommendations to Health and Social Policy Leaders of Canada for a National Action Plan on Mental Illness and Mental Health* (accessed at http://www.camimh.ca/frameworkforaction.htm).

Canadian Association of Social Workers (CASW) (2005), *Code of Ethics* (Ottawa: CASW).

Canadian Mental Health Association (CMHA) (2008), *Back to Basic: Enhancing our capacity to promote consumer participation and inclusion: Discussion Guide on Recovery* (accessed at http://www.cmha.ca/data/).

Chapter 2

A Policy Framework for Mental Health in Canada

Objectives:

- To provide an overview of the legislative framework for developing mental health policy in Canada
- To provide an overview of health policy in Canada
- To describe the history and development of mental health policy in Canada

Background

The policy and legal framework within which mental health practice exists in Canada is multilayered. The Canadian Constitution defines the powers of government. The *Canadian Charter of Rights and Freedoms* protects the fundamental rights of Canadians. Federal and provincial legislatures make, alter, and repeal laws; and the judiciary and administrative bodies (such as mental health review boards) interpret and apply the law (Regehr and Kanani, 2006). Broadly speaking, social policy refers to legislation that provides overarching principles about values held by society and consequently the delivery of social programs. National policies regarding health and mental health (which falls under health policy) address such issues as payment for services and access to services. By failing to meet these federally prescribed policy requirements, provincial governments can be denied federal transfer payments in the area of health. Specific provincial legislation and case law govern actual practices in the delivery of mental health services such as involuntary commitment and treatment. These issues are discussed in Chapter 3 on mental health legislation.

Canada's democratic parliamentary system is derived from the British system of governance. Canada's first constitution, the British North America Act (BNA Act), was enacted in 1867. This Act provided for the division of legislative and economic powers between the federal government and the provinces, and it defined health care, education, employment programs, and the administration of social welfare programs as provincial responsibilities (Thomlison and Bradshaw, 2002). This division was wise in a large country such as Canada in which regions were geographically isolated from one another. Local legislators would presumably be more knowledgeable about the particular needs of people in their region and be better able to oversee the administration of services. However, taxation power was placed largely in the hands of the federal government, thus ensuring federal influence over health care and mental health care, based on the ability to allocate resources.

In 1982, the Constitution Act, part of the Canada Act, 1982, declared the Constitution of Canada to be the supreme law of Canada. The Constitution sets out the basic principles of democratic government and defines the three branches of government: 1) the executive, which includes the prime minister and other ministers, that is responsible for administering and enforcing laws and that answers to the legislature; 2) the legislature that has the power to make, alter, and appeal laws; and 3) the judiciary that interprets and applies the law (see Figure 2.1). The Constitution also affirms Canada's 'dual' or 'federal' legal system that divides legislative and judicial powers between the federal government and the provinces/territories. Under the Constitution the federal government has jurisdiction to make laws concerning Canada as a whole, including matters involving, but not limited to, trade, entry of persons into Canada, national defence, and criminal justice. In contrast, the provinces and territories retained power in areas such as education, child welfare, and health (Regehr and Kanani, 2006).

When the Constitution came into force in 1982, a fundamental part of it was the *Canadian Charter of Rights and Freedoms*, which enshrined protection of the fundamental human rights of Canadians in the Constitution. Since the *Charter* is entrenched in the Constitution, it applies to and takes precedence over all federal and provincial legislation. In general, Canadian laws, the Canadian government,

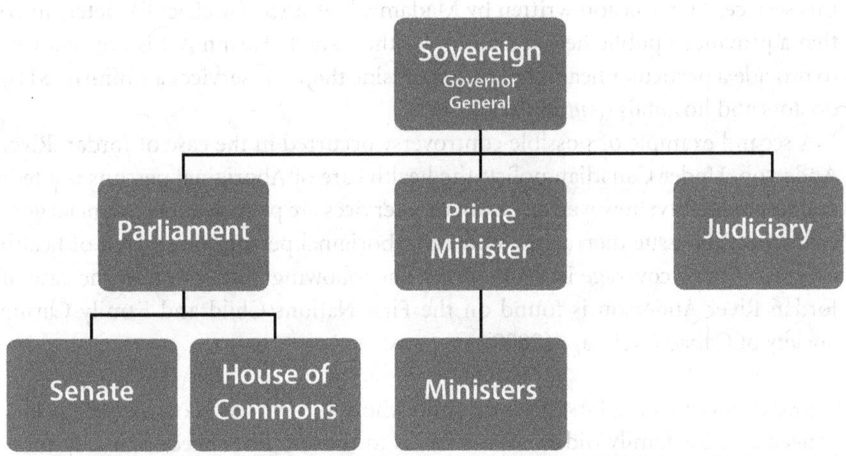

Figure 2.1 The Three Branches of Government in Canada

and bodies created, supported, or connected to the Canadian government, may not violate the guaranteed rights of Canadians under the *Charter*. A law may only infringe *Charter* rights if the limits placed on these rights can be shown to be reasonable, prescribed by law, and justified in a free and democratic society. The idea is that the interests of society must be balanced against individual interests to see if limiting individual rights would be justified. Rights under the *Charter* include fundamental freedoms (freedom of religion), democratic rights, mobility rights, legal rights, equality rights, language rights, minority language education rights, and Aboriginal rights (Regehr and Kanani, 2006).

When considering the manner in which policy and service responsibility in health and mental health is divided between the provincial and federal governments, it is not surprising that conflicts erupt. In June 2004, the Supreme Court of Canada heard an appeal in the case of *Auton (Guardian ad litem of)* v. *British Columbia (Attorney General)* that questioned whether the BC government's refusal to fund a particular type of autism therapy was contrary to the *Canadian Charter of Rights and Freedoms*. The case involved four children with autism whose parents sought funding for an intensive applied behaviour analysis (ABA) therapy known as Lovaas therapy that cost between $45,000 and $60,000 per year per child. Although the provincial government did fund some programs for children with autism through the Ministry of Health, the Ministry of Children and Families, and the Ministry of Education, it did not fund ABA therapy for a number of reasons, including the high cost of the therapy and the controversy surrounding the treatment's success. This treatment was funded in some other provinces to varying degrees, but in British Columbia the cost was borne by the families. The case was first heard in the Supreme Court of British Columbia, which found the province liable for the costs of services under the *Charter of Rights and Freedoms*. The case was appealed by the Attorney General of British Columbia to the Supreme Court of Canada. The unanimous judgment of the Supreme Court allowed the BC Attorney General's appeal and declared that the province did not have to fund this service. The decision written by Madam Chief Justice McLachlin determined that a province's public health plan under the Canada Health Act is not required to provide a particular health treatment outside the 'core' services administered by doctors and hospitals (*Auton*, 2004).

A second example of possible controversy occurred in the case of Jordan River Anderson. Under Canadian policy, the health care of Aboriginal persons is a federal responsibility; however, all health care services are provided by provincial governments. The issue then arises, how can Aboriginal persons be assured of health care when their coverage is at question? The following description of the case of Jordan River Anderson is found on the First Nations Child and Family Caring Society of Canada webpage (2008).

> Jordan was a young First Nations child who was born with complex medical needs. As his family did not have access to the supports needed to care for him at their home on reserve they made the difficult decision to place Jordan in child welfare care shortly after birth. Jordan remained in hospital for the

> first two years of his life as his medical condition stabilized. During this time the First Nations child and family service agency, First Nations community, and family worked together to locate a medically trained foster home and to raise money to refit a van for Jordan's safe transportation. Shortly after Jordan's second birthday, doctors said he could go to a family home. This decision should have been a time of celebration but for federal and provincial governments it was a time to begin arguing over which department would pay for Jordan's at home care. The jurisdictional dispute would last over two years during which time Jordan remained unnecessarily in hospital. The costs they argued over ranged from some higher cost items such as renovations to the home for a wheelchair ramp to low cost items such as showerheads. The community initially tried to mediate a solution between the governments but when this failed they turned to legal action. Shortly after Jordan's fourth birthday in hospital, the jurisdictional dispute was settled but not in time for Jordan who sadly passed away before he could live in a family home.

Stemming from this tragic situation, Jordan's Principle was established. Under Jordan's Principle, if a jurisdictional dispute arises between two government parties or between two ministries of the same government regarding payment for services guaranteed to First Nations children, the agency first contacted must pay for the services without delay or disruption. After the care of the child is assured, the paying government can seek recompense through jurisdictional dispute mechanisms. In short, this principle states, first address the medical needs of the child and worry about payment later. On 12 December 2007 Jordan's Principle was passed unanimously in the House of Commons. One month later Premier Gordon Campbell announced that the BC government supports Jordan's Principle, recognizing the culture and traditions of First Nations children, and promised to work in cooperation with First Nations across the province to bring it into effect in British Columbia.

From these two case examples, it is evident that overall guidelines provided by the federal government regarding the administration of health care in the provinces do not always provide straightforward answers and that the interpretation of responsibilities will vary significantly based on fiscal—and not clinical—considerations. When considering the issue of mental health policy and other social welfare concerns, competing demands arise. Delaney (2009) recognizes that we strive for a pluralistic society in Canada, one that benefits from many diverse worldviews that contribute to our view of the common good. Although pluralism has many benefits, such as a valuing of diverse cultures, religious views, sexual orientations, and a multiparty system, it also poses challenges in the development of social welfare policy. A major challenge is that pluralism encourages competition for political dominance of various worldviews on such issues as social welfare policy. These diverse worldviews may or may not support the notion of publicly funded programs and services in many areas that include mental health and addictions (Delaney, 2008). Further, these different views vary in their perception of the degree to which the rights and well-being of the individual are subjugated to or supersede communal rights and well-being. These issues come into sharp relief in Chapter 3 when we discuss mental health law and provisions for involuntary detainment and treatment for individuals with mental health problems.

Health Policy in Canada

Mental health in Canada falls under the umbrella of health policy and services. Andreae (2002) identifies seven core values of Canadians related to health and health care that translate nicely into Canadian values regarding mental health and mental health care. He divides Canadian values in this realm into two aspects, essential values and instrumental values. Essential values are: 1) Equity—including the equal opportunity to achieve health and well-being and equal opportunity to receive health care services according to their needs; 2) Quality—including both a right to a high quality of life and a high quality of health care; and 3) Informed choice—involving the ability of all Canadians to choose health options based on best available information. Instrumental values are: 1) the right to live in a healthy social, economic, and natural environment; 2) accountability in the health care system; 3) efficiency in the use of resources; and 4) citizen participation and citizen decision-making in their own health care and the health care of family members. These values are reflected to greater or lesser extents as we review the history of health care and mental health legislation in Canada.

Early health legislation in Canada related to public health measures in regards to communicable diseases. For instance, in 1832 the Upper Canada Sanitary Commission and Board of Health issued a directive related to quarantine of immigrants infected with cholera (Hick, 2006). In Canada's early days, health care was provided on a fee-for-service basis, leaving those who had no resources without access to health treatment. In the early to mid-1900s, insurance plans began to come into effect, including a payroll deduction plan for miners in Nova Scotia and Ontario. Hospitals and medical associations also developed plans in Ontario, Manitoba, and Nova Scotia. In 1939, Manitoba formed the first Canadian Blue Cross health insurance plan for those who could afford to pay premiums. In the 1920s, workers' groups in British Columbia and Alberta pushed for universal health care coverage, but were unsuccessful. The Great Depression, which left many destitute, became a catalyst for more widespread pressure to enact universal health care. Issues raised were that private insurance schemes were available only to those who could pay premiums or had employers who would pay premiums and that individuals with serious health problems did not qualify for coverage. In 1947 Saskatchewan instituted the first public insurance plan for hospital coverage. The federal government passed the Hospital Insurance and Diagnostic Services Act agreeing to finance 50 per cent of the cost of provincial hospital care, although notably this excluded mental health care. By 1961 all the provinces and territories had signed agreements regarding federal cost-sharing for hospital care (Government of Canada, 2008).

In 1961, under the leadership of Premier Tommy Douglas, the government of Saskatchewan began Canada's first universal health care system (Nelson, 2006).

That same year, the federal government established the Royal Commission on Health Services, chaired by Justice Emmett Hall, to study and report on the health care needs of Canadians. The 1964–65 Royal Commission on Health Services report recommended a comprehensive and universal medicare system for all Canadians, including the coverage of physician care and prescription drugs. This proposal had massive grassroots support particularly from women's groups and organized labour (Hick, 2006). In 1966, the federal government passed the Medical Care Act that extended access to government-funded health care to all Canadians. However, because health care is a provincial area of jurisdiction the Government of Canada entered into negotiations with each province individually. By 1972, each province had established its own system of free access to physician services and the federal government shared in the funding (Government of Canada, 2008). In 1979, a second Hall Commission was asked to study the operation and financing of health care in Canada and recommended the abolition of extra-billing and user fees. Then, in 1984 the Government of Canada passed the Canada Health Act, which outlined principles for funding of health care in Canada. In order to qualify for funding by the federal government for health care, the insurance plan of the province must meet the five criteria found in Table 2.1.

Table 2.1 Principles of the Canada Health Act

Public Administration	The health care insurance plans are to be administered and operated on a non-profit basis by a public authority, responsible to the provincial/territorial governments and subject to audits of their accounts and financial transactions.
Comprehensiveness	The health insurance plans of the provinces and territories must insure all insured health services and, where permitted, services rendered by other health care practitioners.
Universality	One hundred per cent of the insured residents of a province or territory must be entitled to the insured health services provided by the plans on uniform terms and conditions.
Portability	Residents moving from one province or territory to another must continue to be covered for insured health care services by the 'home' province until the new province or territory of residence assumes health care coverage. Residents temporarily absent from the country must also continue to be covered for insured health care services.
Accessibility	The health insurance plans of the provinces and territories must provide reasonable access to insured health care services on uniform terms and conditions, unprecluded, unimpeded, either directly or indirectly, by charges (user charges or extra-billing) or other means (age, health status, or financial circumstances).

In 2000, the Standing Senate Committee on Social Affairs, Science and Technology, chaired by Senator Michael Kirby, began a review of health care in Canada that took two years and heard more than four hundred witnesses. The report, released in October 2002 and entitled *The Health of Canadians—The Federal Role*, became popularly known as the *Kirby Report*. This report stressed the need for cooperation among stakeholders to reduce problems of maldistribution, undersupply, and jurisdictional competition in the area of health. It focused on three key areas: adequate human resources, appropriate public funding, and systemic reform to delivery and funding of services. The recommendations of the report included:

- Enacting a health care guarantee that would reduce wait times and ensure that patients get services within a specified period of time (the penalty for exceeding wait times was to be the requirement of the province to pay for treatment in another jurisdiction);
- Expanding public health insurance to cover catastrophic drug costs and homecare costs;
- Increasing the federal contribution to developing health care technology, evaluating system performance and outcomes, and wellness and illness prevention;
- Collecting additional federal revenue for health care and additional federal investment in health care;
- Making changes to health human resources that include: restructuring of the hospital/physician relationship; ensuring an adequate supply of graduates in various health fields; facilitating the movement of health care professionals across provinces through coordination of licensing and immigration requirements; increasing the supply of health professionals from underrepresented groups such as Aboriginal peoples; increasing the supply of health professionals in underserviced regions.

Several of these recommendations, particularly those related to human resources in health, have been enacted. For instance, recent changes have been enacted in which licensing bodies for health professions, including social work, must establish means for allowing practitioners to transfer their licensure from one Canadian province to another. For instance, in March 2007, Alberta, British Columbia, Manitoba, New Brunswick, Newfoundland, Nova Scotia, Ontario, Prince Edward Island, Quebec, and Saskatchewan entered into a Mutual Recognition Agreement on Labour Mobility for Social Workers in Canada that establishes the conditions under which a social worker registered in one Canadian jurisdiction can have his/her qualifications recognized in another Canadian jurisdiction that is a party to the agreement (Regehr and Kanani, 2009).

Before the *Kirby Report* was even released, Allan Rock, federal Minister of Health in 2001, identified a need for review of health care in Canada and subsequently Jean Chrétien formed a commission led by Roy Romanow that resulted in the report *Building on Values: The Future of Health Care in Canada*. According to Romanow:

> My recommendations are premised on three overarching themes. First, that we require strong leadership and improved governance to keep Medicare a national asset. Second, that we need to make the system more responsive and efficient as well as more accountable to Canadians. And third, that we need to make strategic investments over the short-term to address priority concerns, as well as over the long-term to place the system on a more sustainable footing (Government of Canada, 2002).

Thus, while the *Romanow Report* upheld Canadian values about universal health care particularly in the realm of catastrophic illness, there was recognition of the need for accountability and cost containment. This is in large part due to the increasing proportion of provincial budgets spent on health care. For instance, in Ontario, the top government expenditures were transportation and infrastructure in the 1940s, and education in the late fifties and early sixties, but by the late 1960s, this moved to health care. By the early 1990s health care consumed 34 per cent of the provincial budget in Ontario and 10 years later amounted to 45 per cent of the budget (McNeill and Nicholas, 2009). Part of this increased expenditure at the provincial level was related to decreased federal funding, which fell from 42 to 10 per cent between the mid-1970s and 2000 (Nelson, 2006). Clearly, such growth in cost at provincial levels was unsustainable and thus a period of cost containment followed. Of concern is that when expenditures to health are cut, mental health care is often one area that is hardest hit.

Despite significant investments in health care, it is clear that provision of funds for programs that deal with physical and mental illness alone will never be adequate. In 1999, Health Canada released a report entitled *Toward a Healthy Future: Second Report on the Health of Canadians.* This report focuses on the determinants of health, which in large part are social determinants. According to this report, the key factors that influence the health of Canadians are: income and social status, social support networks, education, employment/working conditions, social environments, physical environments, personal health practices and coping skills, healthy child development, biology and genetic endowment, health services, gender, and culture (Public Health Agency Canada, 2008). These factors are described in greater detail in Box 2.1. What is evident from Box 2.1 is that factors that can be influenced by social work intervention are key determinants of health and mental health status.

Although health care legislation also encompasses mental health, legitimate pressing concerns such as access to cancer treatments, waiting lists for life-saving surgery, and child health issues frequently take precedence over mental health, which tends to be more chronic and less dramatic than other issues in the public view. Further, stigma associated with mental health issues has tended to keep them out of the central focus. Therefore, the call for provincial and national action plans on mental health and mental illness is relatively recent.

Box 2.1 Social Determinants of Health for Canadians (Public Health Agency Canada, 2008)

Income and Social Status

There is evidence of a clear association between social and economic status and health and access to health care. Only 47 per cent of Canadians in the lowest income bracket rate their health as very good or excellent, compared with 73 per cent of Canadians in the highest income group (Health Canada, 1999).

Social Support Networks

Access to strong social support networks is associated with better health. Low levels of social support have been associated with increased mortality in a wide range of illnesses and increased morbidity in mental health.

Education and Literacy

Increased education is associated with increased access to healthy environments. For instance, the number of lost workdays decreases with increasing education (Health Canada, 1999).

Education level is associated with access to health care and mental health professionals in Canada. That is, higher educated people are more likely to access psychiatrists, psychologists, social workers, and family physicians (Steele et al., 2007).

Employment and Working Conditions

A major review done for the World Health Organization found that high levels of unemployment and economic instability in a society cause significant mental health problems and adverse effects on the physical health of unemployed individuals, their families, and their communities.

Social Environments

Social exclusion caused by racism and other factors affects both health and mental health. Members of racialized groups have differential access to economic resources, housing, and employment; consequently, this has a significant impact on health and mental health status.

Factors such as child abuse and intimate partner violence are significantly associated with health and mental health status.

Physical Environments

Contaminants in air, water, food, and soil can cause a variety of adverse health effects, including cancer, birth defects, respiratory illness, and gastrointestinal ailments.

First Nations members who live in northern communities characterized by unsafe water, inadequate housing, and other deficits have significantly higher rates of mental health concerns and suicide. Infant mortality rates among First Nations people in 1994 were still twice as high as among the Canadian population as a whole.

Box 2.1 *Continued*

Healthy Child Development	Early life experiences and *in utero* care can have long-lasting effects due to the impact on neurological development. For instance, approximately 3,000 children are born each year in Canada with Fetal Alcohol Spectrum Disorder resulting in life-long problems with cognition, kidney disorders, and mental health.
Access to Health Care	Where access to health and mental health care is limited, such as in northern and rural communities, or where access is limited by other factors, such as language or social exclusion, health and mental health suffer.
Personal Health Practices and Coping	High-risk behaviour and substance abuse are related to health and mental health outcomes. Opportunities to learn positive coping, problem-solving, and stress reduction strategies are related to better health and mental health outcomes.

Mental Health Policy in Canada: History and Reform

In the initial stages of Canada's development as a nation, people with significant mental health problems were left to fend for themselves and when they became troublesome or dangerous, they were placed in jails (BC Mental Health and Addiction Services, 2008). The records of the Colony of Vancouver Island for instance noted few cases of 'insanity' and these cases were either cared for by friends and family or sent home to their countries of origin (Yearwood-Lee, 2008). The first hospital devoted to people with mental health problems in Canada opened in New Brunswick in 1836 followed shortly by ten other mental health institutions throughout the country (Nelson, 2006).

William Lyon Mackenzie was appointed to head a committee in 1830 that was charged with the responsibility of investigating the conditions of the jails in Upper Canada. Finding that people suffering from mental health problems were confined to cells and sleeping on straw in a dungeon, the committee argued for the more humane treatment of 'lunatics'. This recommendation led to legislation in 1830 and 1833 that provided for the development of lunatic asylums in Upper Canada (Edginton, 2002). In 1850, the Toronto Lunatic Asylum was opened on the now famous 999 Queen Street site in Toronto where it quickly became filled to capacity with five hundred patients (Duffin, 2000). Over half of those admitted came from local jails, and most were destitute. Dr S.D. Clarke, the medical director of the Kingston Asylum (for whom the Clarke Institute was later named), lamented that psychiatric institutions had become a means for society to deal with the poor and were in effect large boarding homes. By 1894 the Toronto Lunatic Asylum had opened workshops as part of its 'moral treatment' and in 1904 the average working patient was employed 297 days per year.

The gold rush of 1858 resulted in a dramatic increase and shift in the population of British Columbia. The rise in population also increased the number of those suffering from mental illnesses. As in other parts of the country, these people were often housed in jail cells (Yearwood-Lee, 2008). Public outcry grew and in 1864, British Columbia opened an infirmary for women in Victoria, which had amongst its patients 'lunantics'. In 1872, the first BC asylum for the insane opened in the Victoria area in the former quarantine hospital, but within five years it became overcrowded and the 36 residents were moved to a new facility in New Westminster in 1878. By 1899 the population in the hospital exceeded three hundred. Patients included not only those with mental illnesses but also people with various disabilities. The principle causes of insanity were seen to be heredity, intemperance, syphilis, and masturbation (BC Mental Health and Addiction Services, 2008). Treatments focused on containment and moral interventions such as manual labour as a means of treatment. Indeed, mostly using patient labour, in 1905 a new hospital site was constructed, Colony Farm, which later supplied food to the Provincial Hospital for the Insane. A 1904 report stated: 'By so doing a vast saving can be effected in the general economy of the institution, as well as much health and pleasant occupation secured to the patients' (Yearwood-Lee, 2008, p. 3). This later became the new Hospital for the Mind in 1913 and housed 453 male patients. In later years buildings were added for female patients and elderly individuals. Later named Essondale, in the 1960s this facility became known as Riverview Hospital. In 1919 a hospital for the 'criminally insane' had been opened in Saanich to afford much-needed relief to the 'overcrowded wards at New Westminster and Essondale, although this relief has almost been lost sight of in the increased admissions to these places' (Yearwood-Lee, 2008, p. 3).

Reports of the facilities in British Columbia were troubling. A *Royal Commission Report on the Asylum for the Insane* produced in 1894 cited problems with cruelty and oppression whereby patients were tightly clinched in straitjackets, handcuffed, and dunked in vats of cold water with their hands and feet bound. The superintendent resigned after the report was released. In 1900 a select committee report was published on the Provincial Lunatic Asylum. This report indicated that the asylum was in very good order, but identified a concern that 25 Chinese patients who were unfit for work were in the asylum and recommended they be returned to China to lessen the financial burden on the provincial government. This sentiment continued over the years and 65 Chinese patients were repatriated in 1935 (Yearwood-Lee, 2008).

In the late-nineteenth century and early part of the twentieth century mental health was underscored by a belief in 'moral management'. For instance, Gradby Farrant, the director of the Colquitz Mental Home in British Columbia between 1920 and 1933, was renowned for cajoling residents to 'reclaim their sanity and humanity and partake in the restorative activities of physical labour' (Menzies, 1995, p. 278). He decried public ignorance about the insane and dismissed in outrage attendants caught brutalizing clients. The institution was open to a wide range of community groups including concert bands and orchestras, members of benevolent societies, the clergy, the Salvation Army, and YWCA. At the same time, two divergent models for understanding and treating mental illness came into being and attained precedence. The first was psychoanalysis, developed by Sigmund Freud in his 1900 book *The Interpretation of Dreams.* By 1911 the American Psychoanalytic Association had been founded by eight people, two of whom were from Canada. The second model was based on psychobiology, in large part due to the discovery of the causes for syphilis and viral encephalitis. The biological model spanned a number of treatments including insulin shock therapy in the 1930s, electroconvulsive shock therapy (ECT) that began in the 1940s, and prefrontal lobotomies in the 1930s and 1940s (Duffin, 2000).

It was not until the discovery of phenothiazines (major tranquillizers for the treatment of psychosis) and lithium (for the treatment of mania) in the early 1950s that mental health treatment and consequently mental health policy took an abrupt shift. The first social worker was hired by the Toronto Psychiatric Hospital (the renamed Toronto Lunatic Asylum) in 1947; a second was hired shortly thereafter. Mora Skelton (1996) recalls:

> Modest forerunners of the new look in psychiatric treatment in Ontario, we were relegated to two tiny cubbyholes on the third floor, reached by a winding wooden stair. The fire department decreed that there must be a fire escape for the third floor, but there was no way of adding one it seemed. A strong young man arrived with a rope, knotted at intervals, to be dangled from the third floor window in case of fire. However, while demonstrating how easy it would be for us and our clients to climb down to the ground outside, that strong young man fell and broke his arm. Helen and I coiled the rope in a corner and prayed for rain.

The 1960s were heralded as the period of de-institutionalization not only in Canada, but across the world (Shera et al., 2002). A community-based mental health care centre was established in Burnaby, BC, in 1957 (Yearwood-Lee, 2008). A report released that year by Mental Health Services indicated that this centre was aiming to treat individuals with mental health problems in the early stages of their illness, thereby preventing admissions to inpatient care. In 1959, proposals were drafted to the Ontario Ministry of Health for community-based treatment and the establishment of psychiatric beds in general hospitals (Hartford et al., 2003). As a result of the high cost of inpatient psychiatric treatment, the ability of new medications to relieve psychotic symptoms, and a belief in the benefits of community-based treatment over institutional care, a revolution in mental health care began. The goal was to provide services outside the hospital so that hospital care would only occur when there were acute treatment needs.

Between 1965 and 1981, the number of beds in provincial psychiatric hospitals across Canada dropped by 70 per cent from 69,128 to 20,301 (Nelson, 2006). Some of the 'deinstitutionalized' patients, specifically the elderly and those with developmental delays, went to newly established homes for special care or private nursing homes. Others were absorbed by an increase in psychiatric beds in the general hospital system. Most, however, went into the community. Although the deinstitutionalization plan was to flow money to community-based programs, only a small proportion actually did. By the late 1970s there was a shortage of housing and support systems, and many of these formerly hospitalized patients found themselves in poor-quality, unregulated boarding homes. Psychiatric ghettos developed in areas of all Canada's major cities. Meagre welfare payments received by patients were often taken and 'managed' by boarding home operators, leaving those with serious mental illnesses impoverished. After-care programs were limited and often consisted only of medication (Hartford et al., 2003; Nelson, 2006). Community care became community neglect of those with major mental health problems. A study conducted in 1981 demonstrated that of those discharged from provincial psychiatric hospitals, one-third were readmitted within six months because community supports did not exist (Goering et al., 1984).

In the 1980s it was clear that deinstitutionalization without adequate community resources doomed people with mental health problems to the revolving door of hospital care. That is, people would become ill in the community, be admitted to hospital for stabilization and short-term care, then be discharged to inadequate supports, income, and housing, and within a short period of time would again reach a crisis state requiring hospitalization. Thus, provinces across Canada embarked on an agenda of mental health reform. Plans arising from this reform had several components, including the increased investment in community-based services and the shifting of focus on existing community-based services from those highly motivated for treatment (sometimes called the worried well) to individuals with serious mental illness, which were defined by diagnosis, disability, and the duration of the illness. This focus was important to ensure that the seriously mentally ill did in fact have access to mental health services. In 1991 a report by a BC Royal Commission noted that the shift away from institutional treatment was not part of a comprehensive policy and that the mentally ill were simply being moved into communities that were unable and unprepared to provide adequate support. Further, Offord and colleagues (1994) reported that 42 per cent of people seeking mental health treatment in Ontario did not suffer from a mental disorder. Thus, the dollars that did exist for community-based care were being directed to those with the lowest level of need.

Another aspect of mental health reform involved consumer partnerships in which individuals who had experienced the mental health care system as patients were to be provided with opportunities for input into the planning and administration of programs. Consumers were encouraged to join boards of directors of institutions and community services and provide a different viewpoint; however, the system was not always receptive to this involvement and provisions to allow for meaningful involvement of consumers were not always instituted. Simultaneously, consumer self-help groups were established resulting in more concerted efforts among consumers to advocate for rights and programs. Policy shifts related to funding began to occur across the country. During the late 1980s, all provinces spent 68 per cent of their mental health budgets on institutionally based care (with the exception of Saskatchewan at 48 per cent). Between the 1980s and 1998 provincial spending on community mental health increased by 13 times (Nelson, 2006). Supportive housing programs, Assertive Community Treatment Programs, consumer support programs, and drop-in centres for persons with mental health problems were established.

Continued calls for deinstitutionalization were held despite considerable shifts during the eighties. For instance, in Ontario the influential *Graham Report* set the target that by 2003 the number of psychiatric beds in Ontario (including both provincial psychiatric hospitals and general hospitals) should be 30 per 100,000 population (Ontario Ministry of Health, 1991). This was down from 219 per 100,000 in 1965 and 58 per 100,000 in 1992. Further, Ontario was to spend 60 per cent of its mental health budget on community care by 2003, compared to 20 per cent in 1992 (Hartford et al., 2003). Although theoretically this sounded very attractive, significant concerns were raised about the viability of such a radical decline in inpatient beds without evidence of success of the model. For instance, evidence from the United States demonstrated a direct link between deinstitutionalization and homelessness (Lamb, 1998) and with increases in the number of mentally ill persons in jails (Lamb and Weinberger, 1998). This presented a considerable risk in Canada as well because the promised money for programs had not necessarily found its way to the community. Mental health spending relative to health spending in Ontario declined between 1989 and 2005 and targets for community mental health spending relative to institutional spending had not been met (Lurie, 2005).

In 2002, the Ministry of Health and Long-Term Care in Ontario (2002) released a report entitled *The Time Is Now: Themes and Recommendations for Mental Health Reform in Ontario* that described the results of nine regional task forces on mental health. The report adopted the following mission: 'To urgently seed and develop the social wisdom throughout structures, institutions and communities of Ontario for normalizing mental illness, eliminating its stigma, and creating an impetus for innovating the whole spectrum of care to restore hope and realize recovery with dignity.' The report was based on a philosophy that recovery (as defined by the individual, not service delivery professionals and systems) is possible for all people suffering from mental illness. In the end it concluded:

- that the Ontario mental health system was fragmented, with many services and supports operating independently of one another;
- that the needs of people with mental illness were not being met equitably across the province and that disparities existed related to regional, cultural, and gender differences;
- that there is a need for increased community-based services to address housing, education, employment, and income security; and
- that the system was lacking accountability and performance indicators.

The report suggested reform in a number of areas including: putting the consumer in the centre of mental health planning; increasing equity and access;

increasing accountability and research; undertaking broad-based public education; enhancing supports to families; and increasing services related to housing, income, and employment. Clearly, despite numerous attempts at mental health reform, many struggles continued to exist in the delivery of services to best meet the needs of people with serious mental illnesses.

According to *Out of the Shadows at Last,* the first national report on mental health in Canada released in 2006, Canada is the only country in the G8 group of countries (an international forum of governments including Canada, France, Germany, Italy, Japan, Russia, the United Kingdom, and the United States) that does not have a national strategy on mental health (Standing Committee, 2006). Consequently in 2007, the prime minister announced the creation of the first Mental Health Commission of Canada headed by Michael Kirby. The commission has three strategic initiatives: 1) develop a national mental health strategy; 2) conduct a 10-year antistigma campaign; and 3) build a national knowledge exchange centre. The national mental health strategy is intended to provide guidelines for mental health services in each province guided by the conceptual model provided in Figure 2.2. That is, it is based on the notion that comprehensive mental health programming must incorporate elements aimed at the social dimensions of

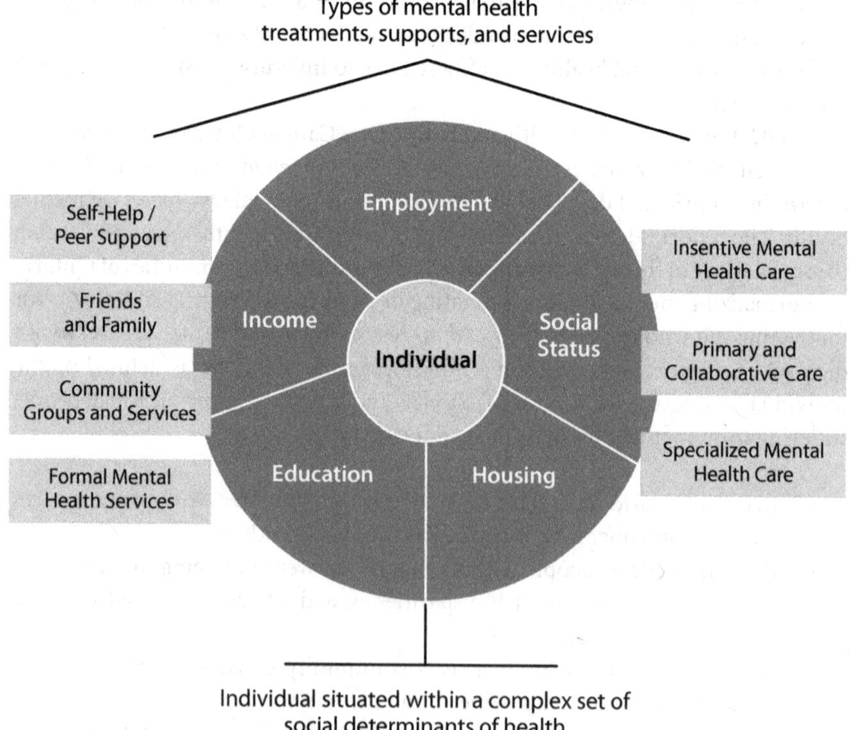

Figure 2.2 Standing Committee

mental health described earlier in this chapter including programs aimed at housing, education, and employment as well as programs enhancing social supports from family, friends, and others. Clearly, social workers have important roles to play in the planning and delivery of this national strategy.

A second aspect of the *Out of the Shadows at Last* report is the campaign against stigma (Kirby, 2008). One of the reasons previous attempts at mental health reform has failed is reluctance in the community to acknowledge mental illness and accept those with mental health problems as citizens who can actively engage as contributing members of society. The Canadian Alliance on Mental Illness and Mental Health (2006), a coalition of non-governmental organizations and professional bodies, including the Canadian Association of Social Workers, reports that many people in Canada, including many health care professionals have negative views of people suffering from mental illnesses, causing stigma not only at the societal level but also at the health care provider level. In the United States, nationally representative surveys have tracked public attitudes about mental illness since the 1950s. In the 1950s the public viewed mental illness as a stigmatized condition and displayed unscientific understandings of mental illness. By 1996, it was discovered that the public had a better understanding of mental illness and could differentiate between types of mental illness with some accuracy, but that social stigma remained essentially unchanged. In this survey, mental illness was more likely to be associated with violence than in the fifties with 31 per cent of the respondents mentioning violence in their descriptions of mental illness (Link et al., 1999). Further, individuals suffering from mental illnesses experience self-stigma which limits their participation in society and often their willingness to seek assistance. In fact, nearly two-thirds of those suffering from mental illnesses do not seek treatment (Regier et al., 1993).

Finally, the third aspect of the *Out of the Shadows at Last* report is to promote knowledge exchange. The fragmentation of our mental health systems have contributed to fragmented data-gathering. There is no coordinated system to identify needs for service, there is no clear measure of the prevalence of mental health problems, and consequently it is impossible to identify factors that contribute to morbidity (Canadian Alliance on Mental Illness and Mental Health, 2006). The formation of a central knowledge exchange on mental health will facilitate evidence-based approaches to policy and practice with the aim of enhancing services while ensuring cost effectiveness.

Summary

Mental health legislation and health legislation in Canada is complex and is driven by many factors including societal views about health and mental health, prosperity of the nation, and political priorities. Over the past two hundred years, treatment of and services for those with mental health problems have shifted dramatically from community neglect and family-based care, to institutionalization of those with mental illnesses, and now again to a community focus. However, it is not clear that current strategies for community-based care will meet their objectives. At present, poverty, inadequate housing, and lack of support services do not contribute to recovery and health. A multipronged approach that focuses on the social determinants of mental health is still a goal to be achieved.

Key Terms

Dementia
G8
Idiot
Insulin shock therapy
Lunatic
Mania
Melancholia
Out of the Shadows at Last
Phenothiazines
Pluralistic society
Prefrontal lobotomies
Psychoanalysis

Discussion Questions

1. What could the role of an individual social worker or social work as a profession be in cases such as that of Jordan River Anderson?
2. How can social workers use the social determinants of health in their practice in mental health?
3. In what ways does national policy impact the mental health of Canadians and social work practice in mental health?

Suggested Readings and Weblinks

The Standing Senate Committee on Social Affairs, Science and Technology (2002), *The Health of Canadians—The Federal Role* (Ottawa: Senate Canada) (accessed at http://www.parl.gc.ca).

The Standing Senate Committee on Social Affairs, Science and Technology (2006), *Out of the Shadows at Last: Transforming Mental Health, Mental Illness and Addiction Services in Canada* (Ottawa: Senate Canada) (accessed at http://www.parl.gc.ca).

Chapter 3

Mental Health Law in Canada

Objectives:

- To present the history of mental health law in Canada
- To discuss grounds for involuntary admission to hospital
- To discuss issues of consent in mental health treatment
- To discuss issues related to financial competence
- To identify professional duties to warn and protect
- To present limitations to the confidentiality of mental health treatment records

Case Example

Michael is a 26-year-old man who suffers from schizophrenia. During periods of psychosis he experiences disturbing auditory hallucinations of voices making demeaning comments towards him. The voices enrage him and he frequently responds to them by throwing household items such as dishes or furniture. When his parents, with whom he lives, attempt to reason with him and calm him down, he shouts at them often in very close proximity but does not physically assault them. In the past when he has been acutely ill, Michael has been admitted to hospital and treated with antipsychotic medications (see Chapter 7 for details on treatment for schizophrenia). When treated, his psychotic symptoms remit quite quickly and while he is on medication he functions quite well on a daily basis, helping somewhat around the house and working part-time in his parents' small store. However, Michael finds it difficult to remain on medication because he feels it labels him as 'crazy' and differentiates him from his siblings who completed their university education, are living independently, and are establishing careers. He maintains a belief that if he is not hampered by medication, he too will be able to return to university. Once he goes off his medication, his parents are able to identify a common pattern of decline. Michael becomes increasingly isolated and non-verbal, his hygiene deteriorates, and his concentration declines. Within a short period of time he again becomes besieged with the voices and he becomes increasingly angry. On the present occasion, as they have on previous occasions, Michael's parents desperately want the mental health professionals involved with his care to admit him to hospital, despite the fact that he refuses admission. They wish to have him treated with medications, and want to ensure that he continues treatment once he is discharged from hospital. The ability of mental health professionals to address the concerns of the parents and to respect Michael's decision not to be treated is governed by mental health legislation. The role of the social worker in these cases is frequently to provide information to both families and clients about the options available to them and to ensure that all parties are aware of their rights.

Mental Health Law

Mental health legislation in Canada, as in other parts of the world, attempts to balance three things: the civil liberties of individuals to live as they choose; the responsibility of society to ensure the safety and well-being of individuals who can't understand the consequences of their choices because of diminished capacity; and the responsibility of a society to ensure that the choices and behaviour of one individual do not compromise the safety and security of others (Regehr and Kanani, 2006). As we see in the case of Michael, above, families and others close to an individual suffering from a mental disorder often approach social workers and other mental health practitioners seeking advice on how to obtain treatment for the person even when that individual does not believe that he or she requires treatment. At times families are seeking to have the person admitted to hospital against their will, or wish to find means to ensure that their loved one will remain in treatment when in the community in order to ensure that they do not relapse. This push to ensure that people in need of assistance are not abandoned by the system must be balanced with an individual's right to determine whether or not he or she will accept treatment. Strong opinions are expressed on both sides of the issue. Psychiatric survivor groups have focused on abuses they endured as a result of involuntary admission and argue for its abolition (Capponi, 2003). Others, such as Hershel Hardin (1993), a member of the Vancouver Civil Liberties Association and a parent of a person with schizophrenia, contend that civil liberties are not respected when people are denied involuntary treatment and left as prisoners of their illnesses.

The history of mental health reform in Ontario provides an example of the struggles society has attempted to resolve through legislation. In 1813 the British House of Commons passed the Country Asylums Act, which gave local authorities the power to establish mental health institutions. In these institutions, medical superintendents controlled all aspects of the institution with the exception of admissions and discharges that were regulated by the courts (Bay, 2004). The first mental health legislation in Ontario was enacted in 1871 and was entitled An Act respecting Asylums for the Insane. This Act was intended to address the rights of individuals residing in the 'Provincial Lunatic Asylum in Toronto, the Lunatic Asylum in London, and any other public asylums.' The Act indicated that no person could be confined in an asylum except under an order of the lieutenant-governor and a certificate of three medical professionals verified by the mayor or reeve. The medical professionals were required to certify that they had examined the patient and 'after due enquiry into all the necessary facts relating to his case, found him to be a lunatic. . . . Such certificate shall be a sufficient authority to any person to convey the lunatic to any of the said asylums, and to the authorities thereof to detain him so long as he continues to be insane.' These provisions were essential because detainment was tantamount to a life sentence. Asylums provided primarily custodial care. Staffing and financing were sparse and the etiology of mental health problems and avenues of treatment largely unknown (Regehr and Kanani, 2006).

More than 60 years later, the Mental Hospitals Act, 1935, while clearly specifying a process for involuntary admission of 'mentally ill and mentally defective persons', remained relatively vague regarding the criteria for admission under involuntary conditions. Nevertheless, this Act removed the courts from the decision regarding admission, which then allowed involuntary admission based on the authorization of two physicians. This was also the first Act to allow for the fact that a patient may recover and therefore the first Act to deal with the issue of release from hospital. In part this may have been due to the development of pharmacological treatments for mental illness. However, this Act coincided with an era of community psychiatry that continued to rise in the 1940s. Mental health institutions were viewed by some as causing, not relieving, mental health problems and the goal became deinstitutionalization (Martin and Cheung, 1985). Following this trend, the revisions of the 1967 Mental Health Act sought to limit the role of medicine and reduced the grounds for involuntary admission to any person who would not enter a hospital voluntarily and suffered 'from mental disorder of a nature or degree so as to require hospitalization in the interests of his own safety or the safety of others'. These revisions to mental health legislation occurred at a time of deep distrust in the medical profession (Goffman, 1961; Szasz, 1963) and during an era of legislative activism in the interests of social reform (Bagby, 1987). However, as time progressed, there was a belief that the term *safety* was too broad and open to interpretation. Thus, the concept of safety was further limited in the 1978 Act, the year the Canadian Charter of Rights and Freedoms was passed. The new Act restricted the notion of safety to the likelihood of *serious bodily harm* to self or others or *imminent and serious impairment* due to lack of competence to care for self. However, concerns continued regarding the civil rights of people in mental health facilities and whether processes were in place to ensure proper procedures. Thus, the 1984 Act required that all certificates of involuntary admission be reviewed by the officer in charge of the facility and that the physician complete a form notifying the area director of legal aid that a certificate had been completed so a lawyer could instruct the patient about his or her right to appeal. In 1987 the Act was again modified and the initial period of involuntary admission was reduced from five days to three. Thus, at these various stages in history, there have been attempts to refine legislation to limit the possibility of abuse of power and increase the rights of those suffering from mental health problems. Paradoxically, however, this at times increases burdens and risks to families and to the community.

Involuntary Admission to Hospital

One of the central issues related to mental health legislation over the years relates to involuntary hospitalization and treatment. The criteria for involuntary admission are similar throughout Canada, but some regional differences do exist. Generally, danger is the primary criterion for involuntary admission. For example, Manitoba requires that:

> After examining a person for whom an application has been made under subsection 8(1) and assessing his or her mental condition, the psychiatrist may admit the person to the facility as an involuntary patient if he or she is of the opinion that the person
> (a) is suffering from a mental disorder;
> (b) because of the mental disorder,
> (i) is likely to cause serious harm to himself or herself or to another person, or to suffer substantial mental or physical deterioration if not detained in a facility, and
> (ii) needs continuing treatment that can reasonably be provided only in a facility; and
> (c) cannot be admitted as a voluntary patient because he or she refuses or is not mentally competent to consent to a voluntary admission.

The terminology used to define danger varies across Canada: Manitoba, as stated above, uses the term *serious harm*; Quebec uses *grave and imminent danger to himself or others*; the term in New Brunswick is *imminent physical or psychological harm*; and in other jurisdictions there are vague terms such as simply *harm* or *safety*. Regardless of the exact terminology, the courts have been attributing broad interpretations to the harm considered. For example, the Ontario term *serious bodily harm* is being increasingly interpreted to include both physical and emotional harm (Hiltz and Szigeti, 2004). Similarly, a PEI court included in the concepts of harm and safety the alleviation of distressing physical, mental, or psychiatric symptoms (Regehr and Kanani, 2006).

Additional criteria for involuntary admissions are found in some jurisdictions: British Columbia, Saskatchewan, and Manitoba require that the patient needs treatment. Saskatchewan adds that the person must be incapable of making independent treatment decisions. In other parts of Canada, the person can be competent to make treatment decisions, yet present a risk due to mental illness. In yet other jurisdictions, alternative criteria for involuntary admission have emerged. For instance, in Saskatchewan, new grounds for involuntary admission were added, namely mental or physical deterioration. Although the new grounds appear to lower the threshold for involuntary admission, some have suggested that they are actually more cumbersome, given a number of additional legislated criteria that must be met in order to rely on them (Hiltz and Szigeti, 2004).

Specific definitions of what constitutes a mental disorder vary. Ontario, Nova Scotia, and Newfoundland have relatively broad definitions that may include developmental disabilities or antisocial personality disorder. Nova Scotia specifically includes drug and alcohol addiction in the definition. Alberta, Saskatchewan, Manitoba, New Brunswick, PEI, and the territories limit the definition to substantial disorders that grossly or seriously impair functioning (Gray, Shone, and Liddle, 2000). Therefore, in those jurisdictions, the dangerous behaviour that the person is exhibiting must be due to factors such as psychosis or serious depression, not antisocial personality disorder.

Throughout Canada, a person can be admitted involuntarily to a psychiatric facility by the following means:

- A physician may complete an application for psychiatric assessment and the individual will then be transported to the psychiatric facility for assessment voluntarily or by the police.
- A judge can order a person with an apparent mental health disorder to be taken by the police to a mental health facility for psychiatric assessment.
- Family members or concerned community mental health workers can swear before a justice of the peace (a position that can generally be found in any provincial court) that a person with an apparent mental disorder is behaving in a manner that may meet the criteria for harm or danger. They are then issued an order that instructs the police to assist with transporting the individual to a psychiatric facility where a physician can complete an application for psychiatric assessment.
- A police officer may apprehend a person who is believed to meet the criteria under mental health legislation and transport them to a psychiatric facility for assessment. Police have specific guidelines for action depending on the circumstances (Hoffman and Putnam, 2004).

In these circumstances, some jurisdictions allow the individual to be detained in an approved psychiatric facility for a specified number of hours or days for the purpose of a psychiatric assessment to determine whether involuntary admission is warranted. It is important to recognize that while an individual is under detention for assessment he or she is not a patient of the psychiatric facility. Involuntary admission, by law, only occurs after the psychiatric assessment is completed and it has been determined that the individual meets the requisite criteria. Thus, in each of these cases, physicians must carry out independent assessments to determine whether the person indeed meets the criteria for involuntary admission. For practical purposes (specifically, the lack of physicians) the Northwest Territories also allows psychologists to complete certificates for involuntary admission and the Yukon Territories Act provides that nurses can perform this task.

In most jurisdictions, once it has been determined through the psychiatric assessment that the requisite criteria for involuntary admission are present, the physician files a certificate for involuntary admission with the director in charge of the facility, who, as a check and balance, reviews the same to ensure compliance with the legal requirements. In New Brunswick the final sign-off is provided by a tribunal, in Quebec by a judge, and in the Northwest Territories by a minister of the government. The time for which a person can be required to remain in hospital following involuntary admission is specified under each provincial and territorial Act.

Under the *Canadian Charter of Rights and Freedoms* (1982), involuntary patients must: 1) be informed promptly of the reasons for detention; 2) be given the opportunity to retain or instruct counsel without delay; 3) have the validity of the detention reviewed and determined. In some jurisdictions involuntary admissions may be challenged before review boards or panels, whereas in other jurisdictions recourse is only through the courts. In the mental health legislation of Ontario, for instance, patients are provided with information through a patient advocate or rights advisor and given a mechanism for appeal through the Consent and Capacity Board and secondarily through the courts. In addition to the involuntary patient, any other person on his or her behalf, the minister of health, and the officer in charge of the psychiatric facility where the patient is detained may each bring applications to the Consent and Capacity Board to review whether the legislative criteria for involuntary admission have been met (Hiltz and Szigeti, 2004). Further, court actions for malicious prosecution and false imprisonment have also been brought against mental health facilities. For instance, in the BC case of *Ketchum v. Hislop* (1984), the patient was awarded damages for procedural irregularities and the fact that the statutory requirements for admission had not been met. This occurred despite the fact that the court found that the patient both needed and benefited from treatment (Schneider, 1988).

If individuals are willing to be admitted voluntarily (that is, are capable of consent and do consent to admission) or can be admitted as informal patients (that is, are not capable of consent but consent is obtained from a substitute decision-maker) then involuntary admission will not be appropriate. In contrast to patients who have been admitted involuntarily, individuals who have been admitted voluntarily have the legal right to leave the psychiatric facility at any time. In practice, this right is often illusory. If at the time a patient wishes to leave, a psychiatric assessment reveals that the criteria for involuntary admission are met, the physician may simply detain the individual (Hiltz and Szigeti, 2004).

This issue was recently tested by the case of *Ahmed v. Stefaniu* (Glancy and Glancy, 2009). In this case, William Johannes was involuntarily admitted to hospital after his sister, Roslyn Knipe, with whom he resided, contacted her family practitioner stating that her brother, who suffered from severe paranoia, had threatened to kill her. Mr Johannes appealed his involuntary admission to the Ontario Consent and Capacity Review Board, which concluded that without treatment there was a likelihood that he would continue to deteriorate and cause harm to others. While in hospital, Mr Johannes assaulted other patients, threatened staff, physically fought with staff, and walked around the unit naked. Over the next two months he was seen by several consultants and the opinion was that he was beginning to settle and become less threatening. One evening, after threatening a nurse, Mr Johannes was assessed by Dr Stefaniu. She did not find him to be psychotic and noted that he denied any intention to harm anyone and further that he claimed to fake his symptoms. She concluded that he no longer met the criteria for being an involuntary patient and because Mr Johannes refused to remain in hospital on a voluntary basis, he was discharged to his sister's apartment. On 24 January 1997, 50 days after his discharge, Mr Johannes killed his sister. His brother-in-law, Mr Ahmed, and Ahmed's two daughters commenced legal action against Dr Stefaniu alleging professional negligence. Dr Stefaniu was found negligent in that she failed to meet the standard of care when she made the decision to change Mr Johannes' status to that of a voluntary patient. The case was appealed in 2006, but the Appeal Court dismissed the appeal and upheld the original verdict. Dr Stefaniu was held accountable for Ms Knipe's death. This decision could potentially have a chilling effect on mental health practitioners and may cause physicians to err on the side of safety when making the decision to keep people in hospital on an involuntary basis.

As indicated earlier in this chapter there has been substantial legislative reform with regard to mental health, with each subsequent revision further defining the grounds for involuntary admission, the length of involuntary admission, and the scope of control over clients by those working in psychiatric institutions. It appears that these changes have been substantive, but in practice, have the legislative reforms actually changed the procedures for involuntary admission? Page (1980) examined involuntary admission certificates following changes in the Ontario *Mental Health Acts* in 1967, 1970, and 1978 and reported no changes in the reasons provided in practice for involuntary admissions after each of the legislative revisions. Bagby (1987) and Martin and Cheung (1985) similarly concluded that changes in mental health legislation in Ontario did not have the effect of reducing involuntary admissions (see Figure 3.1). It is not clear as yet what the impact of the recent legal decision in *Ahmed v. Stefaniu* will have on decisions regarding involuntary admissions.

Despite legal decisions and legislative reforms, however, experimental analyses indicate that dangerousness and the presence of psychiatric illness are the key factors in the decision to admit patients under involuntary conditions (Bagby et al., 1991). This would suggest that other factors are at play in maintaining the admission rate despite legislative reform. One such factor is that doctors and judges continue to use a 'common-sense' perspective to assess the risk that a person with an acute mental illness may present to themselves and their families (Gray, Shone, and Liddle, 2000). Further, families and others are thought to adapt to restrictive legislative criteria by exaggerating the elements of danger and violence in order to obtain treatment. This creates a tension between the letter of the law and what is perceived as morally right by the members of society (Appelbaum, 1994). Similar histories across Canada and the rest of the Western World demonstrate the close connection between mental health legislation and prevailing societal values. Despite all the legislative changes, however, the application of legislation remains relatively stable since practitioners must always respond to the lived experiences of those with mental illnesses.

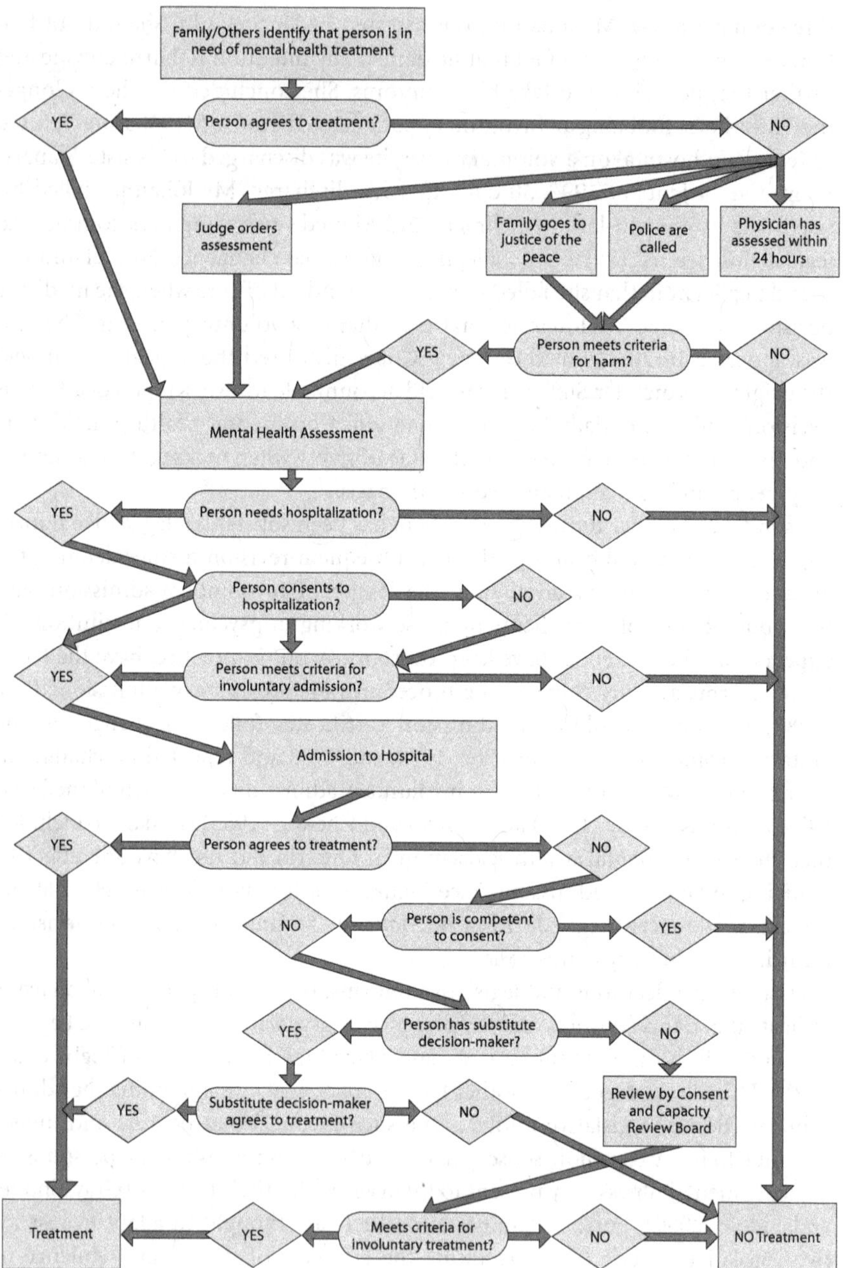

Figure 3.1 Pathways to Treatment in Ontario

Consent to Psychiatric Treatment

It is enshrined in Canadian law and in the ethical guidelines of each health discipline that before a practitioner can provide health care for a person, she or he must receive the authorization of that person. Individuals generally have the right to permit or refuse treatment. This principle has been enunciated by the Supreme Court of Canada as follows:

> Every patient has a right to bodily integrity. This encompasses the right to determine what medical procedures will be accepted and the extent to which they will be accepted. Everyone has the right to decide what is to be done with one's own body. This includes the right to be free from medical treatment to which the individual does not consent. This concept of individual autonomy is fundamental to the common law (Ciarlariello v. Schacter (1993) 2 scr 119 at 135).

Prior to the 1960s the capacity to consent to treatment by the patient and the authority of hospital personnel to treat someone was not viewed as separate from the authority to hospitalize and detain against someone's will. That is, any person admitted to hospital against their will could be treated without consent. This was in large part because admission to hospital was based on the presumption of need for treatment. For example, the 1980 Alberta Mental Health Act specifically stated that a physician may treat a patient once a conveyance and examination certificate had been issued. Similar provisions were found in Newfoundland, Saskatchewan, and New Brunswick. Legislation in British Columbia allowed for the person in charge of the mental health facility to sign consent to treatment forms for an involuntary patient (Gordon and Verdun-Jones, 1983). However, the rise in consent legislation has distinguished involuntary admission from the right to consent to treatment once in the hospital (Gray, Shone, and Liddle, 2000). Every province (except British Columbia) now has consent legislation that makes it clear that a health care professional cannot administer treatment to an individual without valid consent. For instance, the Consent to Treatment and Health Care Directives Act of Prince Edward Island states:

> Every patient who is capable of giving or refusing consent to treatment has the right
> (a) to give consent or to refuse consent on any grounds, including moral or religious grounds, even if the refusal will result in death;
> (b) to select a particular form of treatment from among those proposed by a health practitioner on any grounds, including moral or religious grounds;
> (c) to be assisted by an associate; and
> (d) to be involved to the greatest degree practicable in case planning and decision making (1996, c. 10, s. 4).

When valid consent cannot be obtained from an individual, alternative authority for consent must be sought.

There are two forms of consent: express and implied. Express consent is the oral or written expression of consent, for example, by the patient stating, 'I would like you to remove this wart from my finger.' In contrast, implied consent is derived when consent can be implied from the action or inaction of an individual. For example, consent for obtaining a blood sample is implied by the action of rolling up one's sleeve and presenting one's arm (Etchells et al., 1996). Consent to treatment must be obtained before the treatment begins. Further, once consent is provided it can be withdrawn. As stated by the Supreme Court of Canada: 'an individual's right to determine what medical procedures will be accepted must include the right to stop the procedure' (*Ciarlariello v. Schacter*, 1993). If consent has been withdrawn, medical staff are obligated to stop the procedure, although they must ensure that they do so at a stage where the patient's safety is not in jeopardy. Any treatment provided without consent may result in criminal charges of assault or civil actions of negligence or battery (the unlawful application of force to another person) (Morris, Ferguson, and Dykeman, 1999; Rozovsky, 2003). No intent to harm is necessary for a finding of battery; the lack of consent to the named intervention will be sufficient to establish the liability of the practitioner.

Elements of Consent to Treatment

It is not sufficient for a practitioner to simply obtain consent. In order for a practitioner to rely on the consent obtained, the practitioner must ensure that the consent is valid. For consent to be valid the person must have the capacity to consent; consent must be informed; and consent must be voluntary (Antle and Regehr, 2003). Treatment can be provided without consent in an emergency if a person for whom the treatment is proposed is incapable of consenting and the delay in consulting with a substitute decision-maker would result in prolonged suffering or put the patient at risk of sustaining serious bodily harm if treatment is not administered promptly. This type of situation is most easily understood in medical situations. For example, in the Nova Scotia case *Marshall v. Curry* (1933), a surgeon performed an unauthorized procedure during surgery and the court found 'where an emergency which could not have been anticipated arises . . . it is the surgeon's duty to act in order to save the life or preserve the health of the patient, and . . . in the honest execution of that duty he should not be exposed to legal liability'. It is more difficult to determine the issue of emergency in mental health situations. It may for instance be determined that it is an emergency situation when a psychotic individual is behaving in a violent manner that threatens the safety of staff—in which case he or she may be treated with medications or placed in physical restraints.

Capacity to Consent

In order to have the capacity to consent, people must be able to understand information that is provided to them and how that information applies to their specific situation. The PEI Act, for instance, states that a patient is capable to consent to treatment if he or she is able: a) to understand the information that is relevant to making a decision concerning the treatment; b) to understand that the information applies to his or her particular situation; c) to understand that the patient has the right to make a decision; and d) to appreciate the reasonably foreseeable consequences of a decision or lack of a decision.

Capacity is not viewed as a blanket status—it is specific to a particular procedure and particular time frame. Thus, a person may be incapable of consenting to some treatments but able to consent to others. For example, a person may be able to consent to a procedure such as bloodwork but not to cardiac surgery (Nelson, 2002). In addition, consent is fluid. A person may be able to consent to a particular procedure at one time but not able to consent to the same procedure at another time.

Although each province and territory in Canada identifies a certain age at which an individual may be presumed capable of giving and refusing consent, age itself is not the governing criterion for determining if an individual has the capacity to consent (Morris, Ferguson, and Dykeman, 1999). Rather, when a minor is capable of understanding and appreciating the nature and consequences of a specified treatment or procedure, he or she may be capable of providing consent. For instance, studies on cognitive abilities and age suggest that 14 year olds understand as much as 18 year olds and 15 year olds are as competent as adults (Billick, 1986). Where a minor has the capacity to consent, the views of the minor should be given due consideration. The statement of the UN Convention on the Rights of the Child (1990) provides that 'parties shall assure to the child who is capable of forming his or her own views the right to express these views freely in all matters affecting the child, the views of the child being given due weight in accordance with the age and maturity of the child' (Article 12). However, the determination of when a child has the capacity to consent is complex. Therefore, capacity evaluations should be conducted when minors are faced with treatment decisions.

Two concepts are generally used to determine the capacity of a minor. The first concept is that of emancipation, where the minor is taking care of his or her own needs as evidenced by such factors as having a job or being married. In this situation, the minor is viewed as experienced in making decisions and thus capable of making medical decisions. This is known as the emancipated minor rule. The second concept is maturity, which focuses on the intellectual and emotional development of the person. When maturation sufficiently allows the young person to appreciate the risks and benefits of treatment, both immediate and long-term, the mature minor rule is applied (Downie, Caulfield, and Flood, 2002; Sneiderman, Irvine, and Osborne, 2003). The mature minor can consent to non-therapeutic treatments (that is, not medically necessary or elective), such as terminating a pregnancy, blood donation, cosmetic surgery, and contraceptives. Although a mature minor may have the capacity to consent, his or her consent or refusal to consent will not necessarily determine the treatment plan. For example, in the case of *B.H. v. Alberta* (2002), a 16 year old refused to consent to blood transfusions to treat her leukemia. The court found that although she was a mature minor and her opinions must be considered, they did not necessarily need to be followed, and therefore a treatment order was issued. Despite the legal rules and precedent-setting cases regarding a minor's capacity to consent, there is considerable variability in practice, with some health care facilities placing emphasis on the rights of the mature minor and others insisting on parental involvement (Rozovsky, 2003). Even where minors have the capacity to consent, there are often concerns that children's wishes are not respected. A British study of a child and adolescent mental health unit, for instance, revealed that in 4 of 42 consecutive cases children were unaware of their appointments and 14 of 42 came unwillingly (Paul, Foreman, and Kent, 2000).

Social work ethical guidelines in Canada and the United States until very recently have remained surprisingly silent regarding the issue of the capacity of children to consent, only addressing children in relation to the social worker's duty to protect vulnerable clients from harm (Antle and Regehr, 2003). However, because social workers are frequently in situations where they are working with both the child and the family, there is an obligation to ensure that children are informed about what is going to happen to them, that they have an opportunity to express their views, and that parents consider these views when making decisions regarding treatment and consent. The Canadian Association of Social Workers guidelines on informed consent and confidentiality (2007) states: 'Social workers who have children as clients must determine the child's capacity to consent and explain to the child (where appropriate), and to the child's parents/guardians (where appropriate), the nature of the social worker's relationship to the child and others involved in the child's care.' Where children do not have the legal capacity to provide consent, the practice of obtaining assent is becoming increasingly common, whereby children are asked to express their agreement with the treatment plan verbally or in writing. Although this is not legally binding, it does provide a formal way of ensuring that the child feels respected and that her or his views are clearly documented.

Whether an individual has the capacity to consent is to be evaluated by the practitioner who proposes the treatment. In some jurisdictions, persons may challenge capacity evaluations before consent and capacity boards (which will be discussed later in this chapter), in which case formal capacity assessments may be completed by specially trained professionals such as psychologists, psychiatrists, or social workers. Where an individual does not have the capacity to consent, substitutes to consent should be sought (discussed later in this chapter).

Consent Must Be Informed

Consent or refusal to consent must be offered by an individual based on information provided by the practitioner about the benefits and potential risks of the course of treatment. Clearly, in any treatment decision, there are a vast array of possible outcomes, some highly unlikely; disclosure of each and every one could result in information overload and impair the ability to make a decision. In *Reibl v. Hughes* (1980), the Supreme Court of Canada stated that practitioners have a duty to disclose 'all material risks'. In addition, the legislation in some jurisdictions defines specific information required to be disclosed, including the nature of the treatment, the expected benefits, the material risks, the material side effects, alternative courses of action, and the likely consequences of not having the treatment. Further, details of who will be participating in the procedure, including student interns, should also be provided (Dykeman, 2000).

However, in some situations an individual may be harmed by receiving the full scope and depth of disclosure as outlined above. In *Reibl v. Hughes*, 1980 the Supreme Court stated: '[I]t may be the case that a particular patient may, because of emotional factors, be unable to cope with facts relevant to recommended surgery or treatment and the doctor may, in such a case, be justified in withholding or generalizing information as to which he would otherwise be required to be more specific' (p. 13). Therefore, if a health care provider believes the person's mental health would be compromised or emotional state would be significantly affected, the professional may limit the information provided to the patient. Dickens (2002) cautions, however, that this does not imply that the obligation to provide information is erased. Health care professionals may need to consider alternative means to ensure that information is conveyed to the patient in a manner that is less distressing.

Consent Must Be Voluntary

An individual's decision to consent or refuse consent must be free of coercion or undue influence. Such influence may include financial incentives, unnecessary fear, or influence created by the therapeutic alliance between the patient and the health care provider (Regehr and Antle, 1997). Information must not be presented in a manner that induces unnecessary fear in the patient—for instance, 'You must do this or die.' In addition, it is important that practitioners be keenly aware that the power of the therapeutic alliance itself can in some circumstances induce a person to suspend critical judgment in an effort to please the practitioner. For instance, if a surgeon is seeking consent for a procedure, the patient may feel that refusing consent will displease their doctor and indicate that he or she does not trust the doctor's skill. If a social worker is seeking consent, the person may feel that refusal may result in a withdrawal of social support.

The question of whether consent is voluntary often arises in cases involving minors. Even if a minor is found to have the capacity to consent, he or she must also be free to decide voluntarily; this may not be the case if the child is heavily influenced by his or her parents. For example, T.D. was a 13-year-old Saskatchewan boy with cancer whose parents had refused treatment on his behalf. The court determined that T.D. was a child in need of protection and granted authority to consent to the minister for social services. A petition was then made to the courts to declare T.D. a mature minor so that he could refuse treatment on his own accord. The courts, however, determined that he was highly influenced by his family and did not allow him to consent as a mature minor (*Re: T.D.D.*, 1999—also known as *Re: Dueck*, 1999).

Some jurisdictions have mechanisms for appealing decisions dealing with capacity and consent of an individual through boards or panels, whereas in other jurisdictions recourse is only through the courts. One of the defining features of the consent and capacity legislation in Ontario, for instance, is the creation of the Consent and Capacity Board (Rozovsky, 2003). This board is an administrative tribunal created to adjudicate disputes surrounding issues of capacity and consent in relation to treatment, admission to care facilities, personal assistance services, management of property, as well as involuntary admission and community treatment orders (Hiltz and Szigeti, 2004). In Alberta, if two physicians complete a form (Form 11 under the Mental Health Act) indicating that a patient is incompetent to provide consent, treatment can be administered without consent. However, the patient does have the right to appeal this decision to a review board and treatment will be suspended until the appeal is heard (Alberta Mental Health Act, 2000). On the other side of the spectrum, British Columbia mental health legislation allows that the director of a psychiatric facility may authorize treatment for patients committed to hospital involuntarily without obtaining consent (Friday, 2005) (see Box 3.1).

Box 3.1 Elements of Consent

- A person must have the capacity to consent.
  - A person's ability to consent must not be impeded by mental health, health, or maturation.
- Consent must be informed.
  - Information must be available about all risks and benefits of treatment.
  - Information must also be available about the risks of no treatment.
- Consent must be voluntary.
  - Consent must be free of overt or implied consequences for consent or non-consent.

Advanced Directives

The prior wishes of a patient who is at this time deemed to be incapable of consent are central to the decision-making regarding involuntary treatment. In the case of *Sevels v. Cameron*, 1995 a patient suffering from schizophrenia expressed a wish, while competent, to not be treated with neuroleptic medication, a request with which the substitute decision-maker and treating health team was forced to comply. The judge stated: '[W]ishes are not a mere factor in best interests. They are the expression of the right of individuals to determine what will be done with their bodies.' One way in which clients can express this wish is through an advanced directive.

An advanced directive is written while a person is competent to specify what decisions should be made about treatment if she or he becomes incapable of delivering consent. At times, people with severe mental disorders may be incapable of fully appreciating and weighing the relative risks and benefits of treatment options versus no treatment. At other times, these same people may clearly understand these issues and after careful consideration, have a preferred course of action (Appelbaum, 1991). When patients remain in control of the content of advanced directives, they can increase their sense of autonomy and decrease the sense of coercion that is associated with emergency mental health treatment (Ritchie, Sklar, and

Steiner, 1998). A Ulysses Contract, named after the classical hero, is often included in a mental health advanced directive. Ulysses, who knew he would be unable to resist the call of the sirens that would lead to the destruction of his ship, ordered that he be tied to the mast and be disregarded when he begged to respond. Under this contract, a person may request detainment or restraint and may waive the right of appeal of involuntary admission and treatment (Bay et al., 1996).

Substitute Decision-Makers

If the individual does not have an advanced directive in respect of the treatment being considered, an alternative decision-maker will need to be identified for the individual. A person may designate a power of attorney (person granted authority to act on behalf of the grantor) for personal care prior to becoming incapable of consenting. If there is no power of attorney in place, then the decision-maker will be an individual or entity identified under the law. Substitute decision-makers are entitled to all information regarding the treatment of the person's care that may be relevant to the decision. In making decisions they must consider the patient's best interests as well as the wishes expressed by the patient when he or she was competent (Vayda and Satterfield, 1997).

Even if treatment is authorized for an incompetent patient, based on the necessary considerations and following the required procedures, certain treatments are still excluded; for instance, Saskatchewan and Ontario exclude psychosurgery. In addition, the Manitoba Vulnerable Persons Living with a Mental Disability Act of 1993 specifically excludes research and sterilization that is not medically necessary from the decision-making authority of a substitute decision-maker. Other interventions such as restraint and seclusion also remain controversial.

Community Treatment Orders

In response to legislative restrictions on involuntary admission to hospital and the move to deinstitutionalize those with serious mental health problems, there has been a recent movement to community-based treatment. In 1995, Brian Smith, a popular sportscaster in Ottawa, was shot and killed by a man who was suffering from paranoid schizophrenia but had refused treatment. A coroner's inquest was conducted and recommended changes to mental health legislation in Ontario that, when introduced in the legislature in December 2000, received the support of all parties (*Burlington Post*, 2001). Known as Brian's Law, this legislation made two major changes to the Ontario Mental Health Act and the Health Care Consent Act. First, it deleted the word *imminent* from the criteria of 'imminent and serious bodily harm', allowing for earlier intervention. Second, it created community treatment orders (CTOs) by which a person may choose to comply with treatment in the community instead of being involuntarily admitted to a hospital (Ministry of Health and Long-Term Care, 2000). These changes to Ontario legislation are an excellent example of the influence of high-profile cases and public pressure on public policy.

Orders for community mental health treatment (known as leash laws by opponents) represent one of the most controversial issues in mental health law. Under these laws, a person who suffers from a serious mental disorder may agree to a plan of community-based treatment. This action is less restrictive than being detained in a psychiatric facility, but once the patient agrees to the order he or she will be required to comply with its terms and may be returned to the issuing physician for examination if there are reasonable grounds to suspect non-compliance (Hiltz and Szigeti, 2004). In the United States, which has a longer history of outpatient commitment, various measures are used as leverage to encourage compliance—access to welfare funds and housing; avoidance of hospitalization and jail (Monahan et al., 2001). In Canada, community treatment orders were first introduced into Saskatchewan in 1995. Other provinces (Manitoba, British Columbia, PEI, and Alberta) adopted similar measures in the form of leave certificates (Trueman, 2003). In 2005, Nova Scotia enacted the Involuntary Psychiatric Treatment Act with the aim that 'treatment and related services are to be offered in the least-restrictive manner and environment with the goal of having the person continue to live in the community or return to the person's home surroundings at the earliest possible time'. This Act specifies:

> A psychiatrist may issue a community treatment order respecting a person where the criteria in clause (3)(a) exist.
>
> **(3)** A community treatment order must
>
> (a) state that the psychiatrist has examined the person named in the community treatment order within the immediately preceding seventy-two hours and that, on the basis of the examination and any other pertinent facts regarding the person or the person's condition that have been communicated to the psychiatrist, the psychiatrist is of the opinion that
>
> (i) the person has a mental disorder for which the person is in need of treatment or care and supervision in the community and the treatment and care can be provided in the community,
>
> (ii) the person, as a result of the mental disorder,
>
> (A) is threatening or attempting to cause serious harm to himself or herself or has recently done so, has recently caused serious harm to himself or herself, is seriously harming or is threatening serious harm towards another person or has recently done so, or
>
> (B) is likely to suffer serious physical impairment or serious mental deterioration, or both,
>
> (iii) as a result of the mental disorder, the person does not have the full capacity to make treatment decisions,
>
> (iv) during the immediately preceding two-year period, the person
>
> (A) has been detained in a psychiatric facility for a total of sixty days or longer,

(B) has been detained in a psychiatric facility on two or more separate occasions, or

(C) has previously been the subject of a community treatment order, and

(v) the services that the person requires in order to reside in the community

(A) exist in the community,

(B) are available to the person, and

(C) will be provided to the person.

What is the effect of legislation permitting community treatment orders? Toronto studies show that hospital days are reduced by 94 to 96 per cent after one year and that 80 per cent of clients receiving case management stay engaged in treatment following expiry of their CTO (CMHA, 2004, personal communication). Saskatchewan enacted CTOs in 1994, so has a longer history of using them. However, a study conducted there by O'Reilly and colleagues (2000) revealed findings similar to those in the United States (Torrey and Kaplan, 1995): although psychiatrists view the orders positively, they rarely use them. For example, in the 21 months from April 1996 to December 1997, only 96 orders (each valid for 3 months after which they must be renewed) were issued in a population of approximately 1 million people.

Ontario indicates that it enacted CTOs in 2000 as 'part of the government's plan to create a comprehensive, balanced, and effective system of mental health services that provides a continuum of community-based, outpatient and inpatient care' (Ministry of Health and Long-Term Care, 2000). The goal is to eliminate the revolving-door syndrome, where individuals improve while in the hospital only to relapse after discharge because they don't take their medication. However, for the subjects of CTOs some argue that the prospect of 'being forcibly taken to a physician for examination, which may lead to an involuntary admission, simply for failing to take medication as prescribed, is often very troubling' (Hiltz and Szigeti, 2004, p. 273). Therefore, the topic of CTOs continues to be emotionally charged.

Protection of Financial Security

Incapacity to manage finances is certainly not a ground for involuntary admission to hospital, regardless of whether mental health problems impair judgment, but it is often a concern of family members seeking to have someone admitted against their will. Each jurisdiction has a mechanism to declare persons incapable of managing their own funds and have them managed by another authorized individual. In 1927, Ontario's Hospitals for the Insane Act provided a role for the public trustee to act as 'committee of the estate' for a person confined in a psychiatric hospital who had no other person to act as trustee. Interestingly, under this Act the power to appoint a trustee for persons in Saskatchewan and Manitoba also resided with the lieutenant-governor in council of Ontario. A more recent example is the Incompetent

Person's Act (1989) of Nova Scotia. The Ontario Substitute Decisions Act provides a mechanism by which someone can grant an individual power of attorney for property when they are capable, in anticipation of the possibility that they may become incapable of managing their finances. This form is often completed when preparing a last will and testament. Someone who is paid to provide health, social, or housing care cannot be designated as a power of attorney. In Ontario, under the Mental Health Act, a physician must assess financial competence upon admission to a psychiatric facility. However, the Act does not cover certificates of financial incompetence for those who are not inpatients (Lieff and Fish, 1996). According to the Ontario Court of Appeal, the test for financial competence includes:

- the ability to understand the nature of the financial decision and the choices available;
- the ability to understand his or her relationship to the parties to and potential beneficiaries of the transactions; and
- the ability to appreciate the consequences of making the decision.

A person who is incapable of providing consent to medical treatment may be equally incapable to manage their financial affairs. A power of attorney for personal care does not encompass financial matters and is entirely distinct from a power of attorney for finances. Further, the substitute decision-maker for health care does not automatically become the decision-maker for financial issues.

Ideally, a person has, while they are competent, considered that there may be times when they are unable to manage their financial affairs because they are on vacation or ill and thus has assigned a financial power of attorney. As discussed earlier in this chapter, a power of attorney is the authority given by one person to another to act on his or her behalf. The authority can be comprehensive, or relate to certain specified acts or types of decisions (Fowler, 2004). If a power of attorney has not been signed while the person is competent, upon loss of capacity, an application can be made to the court designating someone known to the patient or the public trustee takes over the financial responsibilities of the individual. Note that when a family member or friend seeks authority to manage the finances for a person after the person is no longer capable of granting such authority on his or her own, the court process is lengthy and contains many steps that include: 1) a notice of application; 2) an affidavit of the applicant; 3) management plans that demonstrate the best interest of the incapable person; 4) medical affidavits (Schnurr, 2004). The public trustee may or may not be involved in this process, depending on the jurisdiction. In Saskatchewan, for instance, the public trustee is charged with investigating all applications with respect to property decision-making. The public trustee may inform all other relatives about the application. In addition, the property decision-maker must provide the public trustee with an annual accounting and inventory of the person's property (Government of Saskatchewan, 2002).

The public guardian and trustee in each jurisdiction is an independent and impartial public official and is an officer of the court. The public guardian and trustee of British Columbia, for instance, 'operates under provincial law to protect the legal rights and financial interests of children, to provide assistance to adults who need support for financial and personal decision making, and to administer the estates of deceased and missing persons where there is no one else able to do so' (www.trustee.bc.ca). Application for the public guardian and trustee to assume responsibility requires documentation and a procedure specified by each province, verifying the incapability of the individual to manage his or her own affairs. At times, less formal options are available; for example, Alberta offers informal trusteeship to incapable parties who only require assistance with the handling of monthly government cheques, through which trusteeship arrangements are made with the government departments issuing the cheques.

The Duty to Warn and Protect

The duty to warn and protect applies when a social worker has reason to believe that a client will cause serious harm to another person. This concept of duty to warn others has a long tradition in the United States, where it was highlighted and clarified by the famous *Tarasoff* decision (*Tarasoff v. Regents of University of California*, 1976) in California in 1976. In that case a patient told his treating psychologist that he intended to kill his former girlfriend Ms Tarasoff. The therapist, concluding that the patient was dangerous, contacted the campus police but did not warn the intended victim. Ms Tarasoff was subsequently killed and her family sued the therapist. Despite defence arguments that the duty to warn violated the accepted ethical obligation to maintain confidentiality, the courts ruled in the plaintiff's favour. The court concluded that the confidentiality obligation to a patient ends when public peril begins. While the *Tarasoff* decision, requiring a duty to warn and protect third parties, did not apply in Canadian jurisdictions, it was generally assumed that Canadian courts would offer a similar decision should the issue arise (CASW, 2005). Nevertheless, mental health practitioners continued to question their responsibilities because no provincial or federal statutes (except in Quebec) require or permit therapists to report clients who threaten to seriously harm a member of the public (Carlisle, 1996).

The Supreme Court of Canada clarified this issue in the 1999 case of *Smith v. Jones* (Chaimowitz, Glancy, and Blackburn, 2000). In the course of a forensic psychiatric examination of Mr Jones, Dr Smith became concerned that Mr Jones would carry out his fantasies to kidnap, rape, and kill prostitutes. Dr Smith notified defence counsel of his concerns, who requested that Dr Smith keep this confidential under solicitor–client privilege. Dr Smith began civil action to allow for disclosure. After a series of appeal processes through the BC courts, the Supreme Court of Canada ruled that danger of serious harm to the public overrules solicitor–client privilege, the highest privilege recognized by the courts. As such, the duty to protect now exists when the following three elements are in place: 1) in the event that risk to a clearly identified person or group of persons is determined; 2) when risk of harm includes bodily injury, death, or serious psychological harm; and 3) when there is an element of imminence, creating a sense of urgency (Chaimowitz and Glancy, 2002).

From a practice perspective, what must a social worker do when caught between the duty to warn and protect and the duty of confidentiality? Appelbaum (1985) recommends a three-part approach: 1) assessing dangerousness; 2) selecting a course of action; and 3) implementing and monitoring. First, during the clinical interview, the social worker assesses the risk that this person may present. This involves a thorough assessment, good note-taking, and possible consultation with other professionals, particularly if the social worker is not experienced or skilled in this area. Second, once a determination has been made that the person is dangerous, the social worker needs to determine if he or she suffers from a mental disorder that may qualify for certification under mental health legislation. If the social worker believes the person suffers from a mental disorder and has agreed to assessment, the social worker must ensure transport of the person to a hospital or physician for assessment regarding voluntary or involuntary hospitalization. If the social worker believes that the person does not suffer from a mental disorder or refuses assessment and there is an identifiable victim and a reasonable belief that imminent harm may be suffered by such a victim, the social worker must warn the intended victim and law enforcement agencies. The third part of the approach requires monitoring the situation on an ongoing basis and ensuring that the intervention is effective. That is, the duty to protect does not end once someone has taken that person to be assessed by a physician (Regehr and Kanani, 2006). As noted earlier in this chapter, however, there is no guarantee that the person will be admitted to hospital or will remain in hospital until the risk is eliminated. Therefore, ongoing monitoring is a duty.

Mental Health Records

Confidentiality is central to the provision of health and mental health services. It is imbedded in the right to privacy that is articulated in the *Universal Declaration of Human Rights* (United Nations, 1948) and the *International Covenant of Civil and Political Rights*. Although the *Canadian Association of Social Workers Code of Ethics* requires that 'social workers respect the importance of the trust and confidence placed in the professional relationship by clients and members of the public' (CASW, 2005, p. 7), the code does identify several exceptions to the rule of confidentiality. These include written authorization by the client, information required by a statute or order of a court of competent jurisdiction, or a threat of harm to self or others. (Duty to protect issues are discussed in greater detail in Chapters 5 and 11.) Although these standards for practice appear clear, their actual application creates a number of dilemmas for social workers. Recent legislative enactments and court decisions have muddied the waters further regarding what information is confidential and what information the social work practitioner ought to reveal (Glancy, Regehr, and Bryant, 1998; Regehr, Bryant, and Glancy, 1997).

In addition to the ethical confidentiality obligations, social workers will be subject to legislation specific to confidentiality and privacy that govern the collection, maintenance, use, and disclosure of information. Canada has two federal privacy laws, the Privacy Act and the Personal Information Protection and Electronic Documents Act. The Privacy Act, which took effect in 1983, imposes obligations on federal government departments and agencies to respect privacy rights by limiting the collection, use, and disclosure of personal information. The Personal Information Protection and Electronic Documents Act sets out ground rules for how private-sector organizations may collect, use, or disclose personal information in the course of commercial activities. The provinces and territories have also enacted legislation governing the collection, use, and disclosure of personal information. These Acts prescribe the circumstances under which practitioners may grant access to or disclose information to the individual from whom it was collected and/or other third parties. Further, social workers should be aware that they may also be subject to various provincial statutes governing confidentiality, access, use, and disclosure in their specific areas of practice, including provincial education acts, child and family services acts, hospitals acts, and mental health acts (Solomon and Visser, 2005).

For social workers working within organizations, specific policies regarding privacy of information should have been developed by the organization in compliance with the requirements of applicable legislation. Social workers not working in organizations, however, are required to develop their own privacy policies, practices, and procedures in accordance with the law. The Ontario College of Social Workers and Social Service Workers Privacy Toolkit (OCSWSSW, 2005) is recommended as an excellent resource for this purpose.

Client Access to Records

As stated above, privacy legislation allows client access to information by various stipulated means. This legislation reinforces an earlier judgment of the Supreme Court of Canada (*McInerney v. MacDonald*, 1992) that established the right of clients to have access to all mental health and medical records regarding their care. This includes not only records compiled in the treatment facility to which the request for access is directed, but also all records obtained from other facilities following the signed consent of the client. If a treating professional has reason to believe that access to the information contained in a clinical record may be harmful to the client or a third party (such as a family member who has provided information), she or he may, as defined by legislation, be able to deny the request for access or apply to the court to deny the request for access. For instance, under the Ontario Mental Health Act, if the record is compiled in a mental health facility, the attending physician may block access to all or part of the record if he or she states in writing that in his or her opinion disclosure will be harmful. However, if the potentially dangerous information is contained in records that have been forwarded to another facility subsequent to a signed release of information form, the worker who authored the records may not be informed that the information is to be released and therefore may not have the opportunity to make application to have the information kept private.

While initially viewed with alarm by practitioners, client access to records is now seen by some as having benefits. For instance, clients are given the opportunity to correct or amend erroneous records. Further, when aware that clients will access records, social workers tend to ensure that records are better organized, shorter, more factual, and more goal-oriented (Gelman, 1992). It has also been suggested that involving clients in the production of case records can be an effective tool in the treatment process (Badding, 1989).

Access to Records in Criminal and Civil Cases

Access to the treatment records of victims has been the centre of considerable controversy over the past few years (Regehr, Bryant, and Glancy, 1997). In criminal court proceedings, arguments have focused on balancing the legal rights of the defendant, particularly in sexual assault trials, with the privacy rights of the victim. As a result of the vocal concerns of therapists and other victim advocacy groups, changes to the *Criminal Code* have placed restrictions on access to victims' treatment records (Statutes of Canada, 1997). Although subsequent court decisions challenged the legislation on the basis that it violated the *Canadian Charter of Rights and Freedoms* (1982), these provisions were recently upheld by the Supreme Court of Canada (*R. v. Mills*, 1997). Nevertheless, if victim records are determined to be relevant to the case, they can become a part of the criminal trial.

In the case of civil litigation, individuals who initiate legal proceedings that put their treatment, medical condition, or health in issue are viewed as waiving the right to confidentiality and implicitly consenting to the disclosure of confidential information relevant to the action (*P. [L.M.] v. F. [D.]*, 1994). Thus, the defendant in a civil action has access to records of the complainant's care. This has significant implications in cases where victims choose to sue their abusers. In addition, access to records may also be granted in family law disputes. For example, during a custody dispute, a husband requested the psychiatric records of his wife be disclosed to support his claim that she could not care for children (*Gibbs v. Gibbs*, 1985). The court concluded that the potential harm to the children was the greater risk and thus ordered disclosure of records despite her doctor's conclusion that it would likely be harmful to her. The demand for clinical records generally comes in the form of a subpoena. The development of law in this area arose in the context of high-profile sexual assault cases (*R. v. O'Connor*, 1995; *R. v. Mills*, 1997) and subsequently resulted in changes to the *Criminal Code*.

Today, professionals whose records are subject to subpoena have standing in criminal proceedings and a right to object to the order to produce confidential files. For example, in criminal cases involving sexual assault or similar charges, the accused may apply to a judge trying the case for the production of clinical records and set out the grounds on which the records are relevant to an issue at trial or to the competence of a witness to testify. Seven days' notice of the application must be served on the prosecutor, the complainant, or witness, and the record-holder. An in-camera hearing is held at which the record-keeper may appear and make submissions. Following this, a judge may order production of the record if he or she deems it necessary in the interest of justice. In doing so, the judge is mandated to take into consideration a number of defined factors, including the salutary and deleterious effects on the accused's right to make full answer and defence, the right to privacy and personal dignity of the complainant or witness, society's interest in encouraging the reporting of sexual offences, society's interest in encouraging treatment for complainants of sexual offences, and the effect of the determination on the integrity of the trial process (Glancy, Regehr, and Bryant, 1998). If the judge orders production of the record, he or she has the discretion to impose conditions in order to ensure, to the greatest extent possible, the privacy of the complainant or witness. These conditions can include that the record be edited as directed by the judge, that a copy of the record rather than the original be produced, that the record be viewed only at the offices of the court and the contents not be disclosed, and that names and addresses regarding any person be severed from the record.

Despite the fact that subpoenas represent both significant risk to the privacy of the client and inconvenience to the social worker who is receiving it, serious sanctions can be imposed by the courts if a subpoena is ignored. However, a subpoena is not a licence to breach client confidentiality (College of Physicians and Surgeons of Nova Scotia, 2006) and it does not grant the social worker permission to speak to a lawyer, police officer, or anyone else about the content of the records or any aspect of the client's treatment.

Possible Social Work Interventions in the Case Example

Social work interventions in the situation of Michael and his family described in our case example at the beginning of the chapter fall into two broad categories, information and advocacy. At the present time, the family is approaching the social worker seeking assistance with hospitalization at a time when Michael is acutely ill. The social worker's role therefore is to provide information regarding Michael's rights to determine his own treatment direction, and the circumstances and mechanisms under mental health legislation in which the family may be able to obtain assistance with involuntary admission or treatment (assuming Michael does not have an advanced directive or has not designated a substitute decision-maker). In general, the grounds for involuntary admission will be limited to the issue of safety as defined by the specific provincial legislation. Given the recurrent nature of Michael's illness, there may also be an option for a community treatment order. The social worker can assist the family to link with the necessary resources such as the justice of the peace or medical practitioners who may be able to assess Michael in his home. Further, the social worker can discuss with the family means of ensuring their safety should they become concerned that Michael's anger may result in violence.

If the social worker establishes a longer-term relationship with this family, he or she may also have the opportunity to work with Michael when he is not acutely ill and when he is able to make competent decisions about his care. Michael can be assisted to consider which treatment options are consistent with his values and are in his opinion in his best interest. Michael can then be encouraged to write an advanced directive or designate a family member or friend who is respectful of his wishes and will make decisions regarding his care that are consistent with his values should he be incapable of providing consent. Should Michael be admitted to hospital on an involuntary basis or be ordered to receive treatment, the social worker should inform him of his rights and ensure that he has access to advocacy services.

Summary

Mental health legislation in Canada impacts social work practice in mental health in two key areas. First mental health legislation sets clear guidelines regarding issues of consent to treatment and in which circumstances individuals can be hospitalized and treated against their will. Social workers must be knowledgeable about these issues in order that they can advise both individuals with mental health problems and their families about their rights and options. Secondly, mental health legislation governs access to treatment records. Social workers must be aware of the limits of confidentiality of the records that they produce and the means of protecting the confidentiality of clients with whom they work.

Key Terms

Advanced directives
Affidavit
Civil liberties
Coercion
Consent and Capacity Board
Criminal Code of Canada
Detainment
Emancipation
Jurisdiction
Power of attorney
Public trustee
Recourse
Subpoena
Ulysses Contract

Discussion Questions

1. How is advising family members of means to obtain involuntary admission and treatment for an ill relative consistent with or contrary to social work values?
2. What is a social worker's role with regard to issues of consent to treatment?
3. What are the ethical issues involved in community treatment orders?
4. How can social workers balance obligations regarding confidentiality with mandated requirements regarding access to records?

Suggested Readings and Weblinks

Canadian Association of Social Workers (CASW) (2007), Informed Consent and Confidentiality: CASW Guidelines (Ottawa: Canadian Association of Social Workers).

Friday, S. (November 2005), 'Informed Consent and Mental Health Legislation: The Canadian Context', *Vancouver/Richmond Mental Health Network Society* (accessed at http://francais.ccamhr.ca/communications/Informed_Consent.pdf).

Ontario College of Social Workers and Social Service Workers (OCSWSSW) (2005), *Privacy Toolkit for Social Workers and Social Service Workers: Guide to the Personal Health Information Protection Act, 2004 (PHIPA)* (Toronto: OCSWSSW) (accessed at http://www.ocswssw.org/sections/pdf/PHIPA_Toolkit_Final_Web.pdf).

Chapter 4

Social Work Assessment in Mental Health

Objectives:

- To discuss the nature and importance of assessment in mental health social work practice
- To consider assessment within a cultural context
- To present a framework for social work assessment and formulation
- To present a framework for conducting mental status exams
- To consider issues related to classification and diagnosis of mental health problems

Assessment is key to social work practice regardless of the context. Before any type of intervention can be considered, a social worker must understand the multiple factors influencing the situation at hand, the stakeholders involved, the history leading to the current state of affairs, and the possible solutions that might be available (see Box 4.1). In the organizational context, this is often referred to as a SWOT analysis, which refers to consideration of strengths, weaknesses within the organizations, and the opportunities and threats in the environment in which the organization exists. In clinical contexts, the assessment considers the intersection between the person who is identified as needing assistance in some form and their environment. Although there are similarities in the assessment process within the various domains in which social work practices, such as child welfare, health care, and settlement services to immigrants and refugees, there are also differences. In mental health social work practice social workers are required to be skilled in standard psychosocial assessments, which will be familiar across all domains of practice. In addition, however, social workers in mental health must be capable of performing mental status examinations in order to assess the nature and severity of a mental health problem from which a person may be suffering. Social workers must also be familiar with the classification of mental health problems as specified by the *Diagnostic and Statistical Manual* (DSM) to communicate effectively with other members of the interdisciplinary team. This chapter outlines the standard

Box 4.1 Social Work Defined

The social work profession promotes social change, problem solving in human relationships, and the empowerment and liberation of people to enhance well-being. Utilising theories of human behaviour and social systems, social work intervenes at the points where people interact with their environments. . . . Social work bases its methodology on a systematic body of evidence-based knowledge derived from research and practice evaluation, including local and indigenous knowledge specific to its context. It recognises the complexity of interactions between human beings and their environment, and the capacity of people both to be affected by and to alter the multiple influences upon them including bio-psychosocial factors.

(International Federation of Social Work, 2009)

social work assessment, the mental status examination, and the classification of mental disorders standardized by the *DSM*.

A social work assessment in mental health brings a unique perspective to the multidisciplinary team. The social worker considers challenges, strengths, supports, and barriers at multiple levels that affect the experiences of a person suffering from a mental health problem and the choices available to him or her (see Figure 4.1). At the individual level, the person comes with biological, psychological, and interpersonal strengths and challenges that have been influenced both by their unique genetic endowments and environmental experiences. At the familial level, characteristics of individual family members, the structure of the family, and relationships between family members have a tremendous impact on challenges experienced by people suffering from mental health problems and on the resources available to them for coping with crisis and difficulty. The community context includes the availability of resources in terms of formal services and informal supports. It also includes the cultural context in which this person resides, such as the cohesion of the community and attitudes towards mental health concerns. Further, it is important to consider whether this person and/or their family members experience exclusion on the basis of any factors such as race, religion, sexual orientation, or social class. Finally, at the societal level, policies and practices are in place that limit or enhance opportunities. What is the immigration status of this person and does it influence access to services and entitlements? Are there affordable housing options for this person and their family? How do legislative frameworks influence their ability to obtain or refuse treatment?

Blackstock (2009) highlights how the multiple influences model (often referred to as the ecological model) while attempting to integrate a broader perspective into the assessment process continues to be focused on the individual. This focus can be a mismatch with the worldview of the client. When working with Aboriginal clients, for instance, the view focuses on the interconnection of experience and knowledge over the span of generations. Blackstock notes that within social work, ecological theory is generally believed to apply well to work with Aboriginal peoples because of the perspective that the individual is nestled within his or her

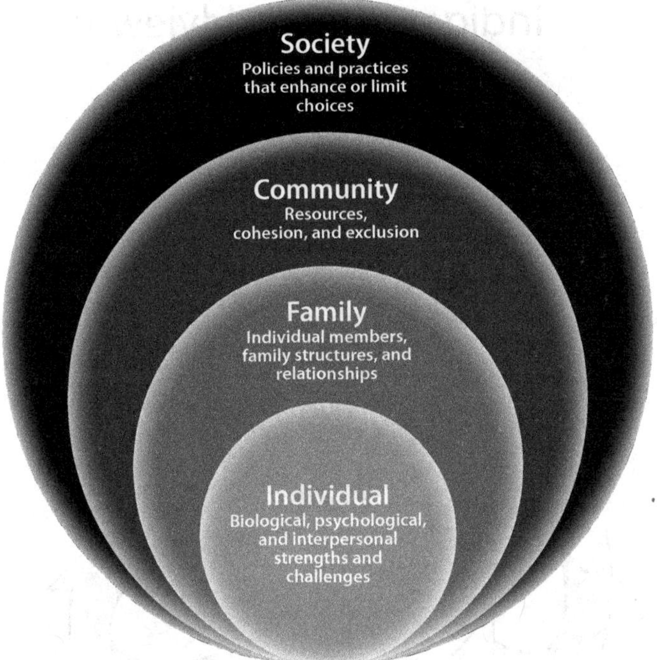

Figure 4.1 Multiple Levels of Influence in Social Work Assessments

community and societal context as shown in Figure 4.1. Yet, such an approach continues to ignore that within Aboriginal epistemology, or knowledge, 'the child, family, community, and world are wholly affected by four interconnected dimensions of knowledge—emotional, spiritual, cognitive, and physical—informed by ancestral knowledge, which is to be passed to future generations in perpetuity'. These four interconnected themes are demonstrated in Figure 4.2. From this perspective, the multiple levels of influence model in Figure 4.1 is transformed from a series of concentric circles demonstrating the manner in which the individual is embedded within their culture to a series of interconnected circles. The social work assessment must therefore consider the worldview of the client and his or her cultural group and ensure that the assessment takes into account this unique perspective.

Assessment within a Cultural Context

The mental health system and social work practice within it is without question heavily influenced by broader social, political, and economic structures in society (Bhugra and Bhui, 2001). Social work assessments in mental health must therefore be conducted in a manner that recognizes the social and cultural context in which the assessment occurs. The availability of services and access to health systems is dependent on political and economic structures that subtly or not so subtly exclude members of groups defined by ability, ethnicity, race, gender, social class,

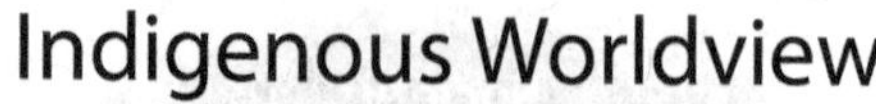

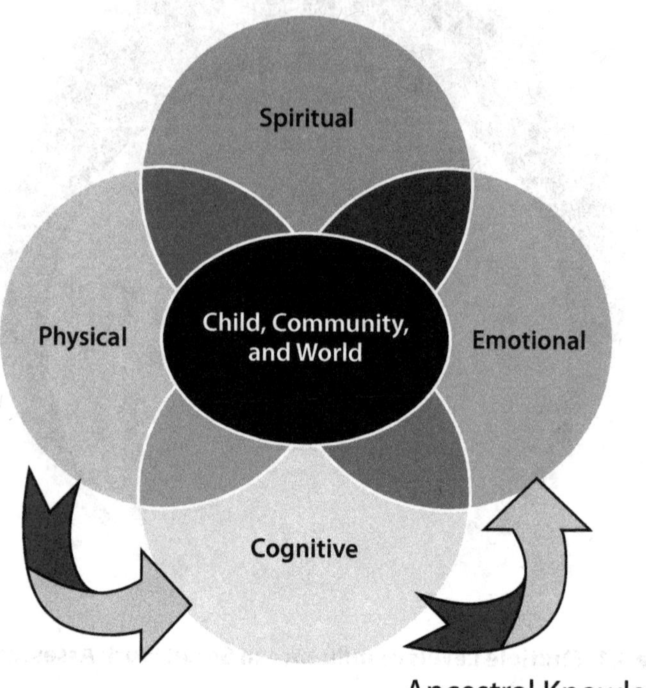

Ancestral Knowledge (intergenerational)

Source: *Ecological Theory from an Aboriginal Perspective*, Blackstock, 2009.

Figure 4.2 Applying an Aboriginal Framework to Social Work

and sexual orientation. Immigrants and ethnic minorities are repeatedly found to bare a disproportionate burden of illness and have unequal access to health care throughout the Western World (Department of Health, 2003; Lai, 2004; Hwang et al., 2008). After entering the mental health system, difference continues to influence assessment and treatment. The assessment process in mental health relies heavily on observation and assessment of behaviours and judgments regarding the perceptions and the means of expression of the client, all of which result in a final formulation of the challenges this person faces, including whether or not he or she suffers from a major mental illness.

Hwang and colleagues (2008) have proposed the Cultural Influences on Mental Health model (CIMH) to serve as a framework for understanding the complex intersection between culture and mental health. Within this model, it is proposed that culture contributes to differences in 1) the prevalence, etiology, and course of mental illness; 2) the expression of distress; 3) diagnosis and assessment; 4) coping styles and help-seeking behaviour; and ultimately, 5) appropriate treatment and intervention. Various aspects of their model are outlined below.

Cultural Influences in the Prevalence, Etiology, and Course of Mental Illness

Culture frequently influences life experiences, including such things as exposure to trauma and exposure to stress. For instance, refugees often enter Canada having experienced a variety of traumatic events, including war, genocide, violence, famine, and political persecution. Groups exposed to such violence have increased rates of post-traumatic stress and depression as evidenced by studies conducted with people from Southeast Asia, Africa, Bosnia, and Kurdistan (Hwang et al., 2008). In addition to the traumatic circumstances that contributed to a decision to leave the home country, the journey to Canada may similarly be life-threatening. People leaving Vietnam or other parts of Southeast Asia often travelled by boat in perilous conditions that included unseaworthy vessels, insufficient stocks of food and water, violent storms, and pirates (Gong-Guy, Cravens, and Patterson, 1991). Refugees may have spent time in camps throughout the world that were similarly characterized by overcrowding, scarce resources, inadequate housing and sanitation, rape, and violence. Undoubtedly, all these experiences contribute to increased risk of mental health issues and to the development of views of people in authority (such as mental health professionals) that will affect their willingness to access services. Regardless of immigration status, those entering a new country frequently experience acculturation stresses including adaptation to a new environment, loss of social supports, and barriers to employment, education, services, and housing.

Whether they are new to the country or whether their people pre-dated the arrival of the Europeans, as in the case of Aboriginal Canadians, racialized individuals and those with other forms of difference experience discrimination at both an interpersonal and systemic level. Such experiences influence the development of mental health and other problems. A history of state treatment of Aboriginal peoples provided by the Royal Commission on Aboriginal Peoples (1996a) provides an arresting account of the process of colonization, including the development of the residential school system as early as 1874, all of which has contributed to increased risk for Aboriginal peoples on many social indicators. In 2001, the reported average income of Aboriginal people in Canada was $19,132, fully 36 per cent below the national average of $29,769 (Statistics Canada, 2001a). Unemployment rates of Aboriginal peoples are considerably higher than those of the non-Aboriginal population (Statistics Canada, 2001b). The death rate for Aboriginal persons between 25 and 44 years of age is five times higher than the general rate and the life expectancy for both Aboriginal men and women is 6.7 years lower than for non-Aboriginals (Health Canada, 2004). Aboriginal women experience violence at disturbingly high rates (Goel, 2000; Bohn, 2003), the overall mortality rate resulting from violence being three times higher for Aboriginal women than women who are non-Aboriginal (NWAC, 2004). Aboriginal people comprise 3.3 per cent of the nation's population, yet they account for approximately 12 per cent of Canada's federal offender population (Royal Commission on Aboriginal Peoples, 1996b). This is more prevalent in some provinces; for instance, in Manitoba Aboriginal people constitute approximately 12 per cent of the population, yet account for over one-half of the 1,600 people incarcerated on any given day of the year in correctional institutions (Aboriginal Justice Implementation Commission, 2004). Clearly, these social factors intersect with the development of mental health concerns and must be taken into account in our assessment of risk and needs.

Cultural Differences in the Expression of Distress

Expressions of distress vary widely across cultures. Somatization, or the degree to which a person describes distress in physical terms, is one type of expression of distress that is highly influenced by cultural norms. Research suggests, for instance, that people from Asian cultures are more likely to describe symptoms of distress as physical, such as gastric distress, headaches, or body pain, whereas Western people from Western cultures are more likely to state that they are sad, depressed, or experiencing some other emotional disturbance (Hwang et al., 2008). Early studies reported by Hwang and colleagues found that 88 per cent of Chinese psychiatric patients versus 20 per cent of American-born psychiatric patients reported no typical psychiatric complaints, rather focusing solely on physical concerns, and that nearly 70 per cent of Taiwanese patients had predominantly physical complaints. A recent article (Ryder et al., 2008) confirms that people presenting with distress in China are more likely to report considerably higher rates of somatic symptoms than patients in Canada. However, this study suggests that this is due to an overemphasis in Western cultures on personal experiences and emotional distress rather than an Asian overemphasis on somatic distress. These authors concluded that *Western psychologization* may be more of a cultural phenomenon than *Asian somatization.*

Cultural differences occur not only in the expression of symptoms related to a particular mental health concern, but also result in conceptualizations of entirely different illnesses than are described in North America and Europe. The *Diagnostic and Statistical Manual* (*DSM*) described later in this chapter identifies culture-bound syndromes, which are defined as recurrent patterns of expressing troubling experiences that are generally limited to specific societies or cultural areas. The *DSM* lists 25 of these particular expressions of distress. Examples are provided in Table 4.1. Clients from cultures where such forms of expressing distress are accepted as commonplace will describe their experiences in very different terms and will have very different ideas about what treatments might be effective than will someone of European heritage raised in Canada.

Cultural Influences on Diagnosis and Assessment

Research identifies clear differences in rates of diagnosis of certain illnesses between various groups. For instance, research consistently finds that individuals of African and Afro-Caribbean backgrounds, particularly males, are more likely to be diagnosed with schizophrenia in Western countries than are individuals of other races (Fearon et al., 2006; Selten, Cantor-Graae, and Kahn, 2007). Many reasons

Table 4.1 Examples of Culture-Bound Syndromes

Name	Region	Description
Amok	Malaysia	• Outbursts of violent, aggressive, or homicidal behaviour
Cafard	Laos, Philippines, Polynesia	• Precipitated by slight or insult • Often accompanied by persecutory ideas, amnesia, exhaustion
Mal de pelea	Puerto Rico	• Return to previous state following episode
Ataque de nervios	Latin America	• Uncontrollable shouting, trembling, crying • Dissociative experiences, seizure-like or fainting episodes • Sense of being out of control • Generally a direct result of stressful event related to family (e.g. death, conflicts)
Shenjing shuairuo (neurasthenia)	China (included in the Chinese Classification of Mental Disorders)	• Physical and mental fatigue • Dizziness, headaches, pain, gastric problems, sexual dysfunction • Sleep disturbance, memory loss
Taijin kyofusho	Japan (Japanese Classification of Mental Disorders)	• Intense fear that one's body displeases or offends others due to appearance, odour, facial expression, or movement

Source: Adapted from APA, 2000

have been suggested for this, including the biases of mental health professionals and the effects of disadvantage and adversity related to systemic racism (Luhrmann, 2007). Other research has pointed to increased risk of psychotic illness as being related to migration and specifically the effects of parental separation in childhood (Morgan et al., 2007) caused by migration and social policies that make it difficult for families to immigrate together. The migration theory appears to be reinforced by research with other groups. For instance, high rates of psychotic illness and schizophrenia diagnosis in immigrant groups in the United States who originated in Western Europe have been associated with migration and neighbourhood density (Veling et al., 2008).

Disparities in diagnosis between groups, based on race, also occur in other diagnostic categories. Some studies point to higher rates of diagnoses of depression among people of Chinese origin in North America, while others suggest lower rates (Hwang et al., 2008). In a study of 406 children presenting with mental health problems, African-American children were 5.1 times less likely to receive a diagnosis of autism than white children (Mandell et al., 2007). African-American children were more likely to receive a diagnosis of conduct disorder than white children (15.7 per cent versus 6.7 per cent) and were far less likely to receive a diagnosis of adjustment disorder (2.5 per cent versus 12.8 per cent). In summary, there is an awareness that diagnosis and culture are linked, but research on incidence rates and causes of differential rates of diagnosis is far from conclusive.

Cultural Influences on Help-Seeking

Help-seeking behaviour is influenced by cultural beliefs and norms as well as by cultural understanding of mental illness and expressions of distress as discussed above. Individuals who believe their distress is physically based will more likely seek assistance from medical practitioners than from a professional who focuses on psychological or interpersonal factors. Further, stigma related to mental illness may cause many people to avoid mental health services. For example, Gong-Guy (1991) and colleagues report that refugees from Southeast Asia associate mental health treatment only with severe pathology requiring permanent institutionalization. Thus, they indicate that in these groups all interventions are highly stigmatized and treatments are to be shunned. Other beliefs include that mental illness in the family affects marriageability of other family members due to inheritability of illnesses or a belief that illness is related to past family transgressions. Cultural beliefs may therefore dissuade the use of mental health services and rather move people to informal supports, spiritual leaders, or indigenous healers (Hwang et al., 2008).

Social Work Assessment

According to Gold (2002) assessment is an essential part of social work practice at all levels of intervention including individuals, families, groups, organizations, or communities. In each case the assessment involves two components, data collection and data analysis. In a social work assessment, data is generally collected from a range of sources including what the individual presents, information from family or significant people in the person's life, other professionals involved with the person, records available from health care or social service organizations, and social policies and organizational practices that may create or hinder choices available to the person being assessed.

In mental health social work assessments, the worker begins with a standard model of social work assessment that considers key aspects of the person's current situation and history. The format of the assessment interview varies in its structure depending on the nature of the assessment situation. Assessment interviews conducted in an emergency situation will understandably be brief and focus quickly on key points. Assessments conducted with individuals with whom the social worker will have multiple contacts occur at a slower pace and are more comprehensive. Any assessment regardless of the nature, however, is dependent on the worker establishing some type of working alliance with the client in order that the client trusts that the information he or she is about to provide is going to be used in his or her best interest and will be kept in confidence. Thus, an assessment interview should begin with the worker introducing him- or herself, identifying his or her role in the organization, and identifying the purpose of the meeting. It is also necessary to identify the limits of confidentiality of information obtained in the interview. For instance, a social worker in a hospital will be sharing the information with other members of the interprofessional team, and this should be made explicit. A social worker in private practice is bound to confidentiality unless the client consents to release of information or unless information is revealed that suggests that the client is at risk of harming themselves or others.

The written format of a social work assessment follows an outline similar to that in Box 4.2. The manner and order in which this information is collected, however, will vary because clients generally tell their story in the way that makes the most sense to them. The social worker asks open-ended questions, directing the interview to areas that have not yet been covered. However, overly rigid adherence to an interview guideline will often result in missing important information. The assessment usually begins with the social worker asking why the client is here or, if he or she is not here voluntarily, why others might have thought assessment and/or treatment is needed. The corresponding written format begins with a description of the presenting problem from the perspective of the referral source, the perspective of the client, and the perspective of the client's family if they were involved in the assessment process or have provided information in advance. As indicated in Box 4.2, other information collected includes a description of the client's personal history, psychiatric history, family members and others important in the client's life, current life situation, treatment history, and other professionals or agencies that may currently be involved with the client.

Once the social worker has asked all the questions that seem pertinent, it is important to end the interview by asking the client whether there is any question or area that has been missed. The authors learned from experience how critical this question is. At the conclusion of a two-and-a-half-hour interview with the family of a young offender who required a mental health assessment, the mother and father were asked whether there was anything that had been missed. The mother responded that it was probably important to know that she and her husband were not really the young man's parents. He was actually the child of their daughter but because she was so young at the time of the birth, they took the baby as their own and referred to his birth mother as his sister. The client had never been told this information. The interview then took another half-hour while additional missed information regarding this story was obtained.

At the conclusion of an assessment interview, the social worker should summarize the information collected to ensure this is how the client understands the situation. Where possible, an agreement can be made with the client about next steps. Where an agreement is not possible, for instance, the social worker believes the person needs treatment but the person does not agree, or where a safety issue exists, the social worker should inform the client about what is to happen next. For instance, 'I am going to consult with (my colleagues, the Children's Aid Society, the psychiatrist) about this and will get back to you.'

Box 4.2 The Social Work Assessment

Identifying data

Presenting problem

- Information obtained from referral sources and other professionals
- A summary of the problem as viewed by the client and family

Brief personal history

- Developmental history: any critical health events in gestation or early years; pace of development and educational attainment
- Relationship history
- Educational and employment history

Mental health history

- Course of the present problem: what symptoms or problems have been experienced? when did they emerge? how long have they been a problem? are they constant or fluctuating?
- Previous treatment: other therapy, hospitalizations, medications, have there been any diagnoses shared with the client or family member?

Family constellation

- Brief description of members of the nuclear family: current relationship with the client; current social situation in terms of relationship status, occupation etc; any history of mental health, substance abuse or legal problems
- All other significant family members (biological or family of choice) involved in the client's life

Cultural/spiritual/social context

- Cultural identity: degree of identification with cultural group, cultural influences on problem identification/formation
- Religious affiliations
- Spiritual beliefs that influence the client's view of the issues and solutions
- Social inclusion/exclusion

Current situation

- Present concerns about health/mental health; current treatment including medications
- Living situation, income, employment, legal status, immigration status
- Current relationships

Mental status

- To be completed if there are any indicators of mental status issues during the interview

Suicide risk

- To be completed if there are any indicators of suicidal thought or self-harm during the interview

Formulation

- Predisposing factors: why this person? Vulnerabilities/history/stressors
- Precipitating factors: why now? Major stresses/critical events
- Perpetuating factors: what maintains the problem? Social-environmental factors/health/substance use/personality
- Protective factors: what are the strengths? Supports/successes/abilities
- Plan: where do we go from here? Client wishes/intervention/referral/advocacy

Most of the components of a written social work assessment can be understood in terms of stating the 'facts' of the case as presented by various sources. These facts should be presented without prejudice or opinion. For instance, in describing the family, the social worker may indicate that the client states that she has a dysfunctional relationship with her mother. However, the social worker should not conclude in this section that the client does have a dysfunctional relationship. Rather, the social worker could record that the mother seems to have negative views about her daughter and record examples of comments made that would reflect this statement. Statements should include comments like 'according to X' and 'Y believes that'.

The formulation is the place where the social worker synthesizes the data and draws conclusions about the case based on his or her expert opinion (see Box 4.2). In the formulation, the social worker considers the factors that predispose the client to experiencing the current problems including their vulnerabilities, their history, and the stressors that they have encountered. This may include, for example, a family history of mental illness, deprivation or abuse in childhood, or a history of convulsions in childhood. Next, the social worker identifies what precipitated the current crisis and caused the client to come for treatment at this time. The precipitants may be relational, environmental, maturational, physical, or psychological. For instance, a client with a history of sexual trauma may arrive at a social worker's office years after the event but her distress might have been triggered by entering into a relationship, having a daughter reach puberty, or being confronted with an assault on someone else. Often the problem that a client presents with is perpetuated by other factors such as substance abuse, being in a violent relationship, poverty, or being barred from critical life goals by public policies such as in the case of an internationally educated professional who is depressed because he or she is barred from obtaining work commensurate with his or her education and experience. Protective factors refer to the strengths and supports that a person has. A social worker could refer to the tremendous resilience this person has shown in the face of adversity and the manner in which they have creatively dealt with roadblocks. In addition, spiritual beliefs and the faith community may be strong protective factors. Finally, the plan emanates from the formulation and represents a combination of the social worker's recommendations and the client's views about what is acceptable and feasible.

Weerasekera (1993) provides an excellent overview of the multiperspective model of formulation (see Table 4.2). Within this model, both individual factors and systemic factors that contribute to the problem are considered. At the individual level, biological factors can include genetic predispositions, current health, neurological issues. Cognitive factors include both cognitive abilities and perceptions and beliefs that the individual holds about their situation(s). Dynamic factors include psychological distress; present-day relational issues and issues caused by previous life experiences such as trauma; and prior relationships, particularly with family, and ability to form current relationships. The spiritual domain includes the spiritual beliefs that the individual holds that offer comfort or cause distress. Systemic-level factors consider the opportunities and challenges provided by

Table 4.2 The Multiperspective Formulation

	Individual factors				Systemic factors			
	Biological	Cognitive	Dynamic	Spiritual	Familial	Cultural/ community	Opportunities (education, employment)	Social policy
Predisposing								
Precipitating								
Perpetuating								
Protective								
Plan								

Source: Adapted from Weekasekera, 1993.

people and systems that the client encounters. While the cultural and community context can address challenges and supports at the community level, the opportunity structure considers such factors as access to education, employment, affordable housing, and transportation. Finally, the policy domain considers laws that address safety for the client if she is a victim of violence, youth criminal justice policies and alternative justice models for troubled young people, and immigration, among others.

Mental Status Examinations

The basic social work assessment is conducted in almost all areas of social work practice. In mental health social work practice, however, an additional task is determining whether or not a person suffers from symptoms of a mental health problem or major mental illness and the degree to which these symptoms impinge on the individual's life. Mental state examinations are therefore conducted as a means for determining the presence or absence of signs and symptoms of mental health distress. A standard mental status examination consists of the following elements: appearance, attitude and behaviour, speech and thought content, speech and thought form, mood and affect, perception, and cognition (see Box 4.3) (Kendell and Zealley, 1983; Goldberg and Murray, 2006).

Appearance, Attitude, and Behaviour

The first window into the mental state of a client is the manner in which he or she looks and behaves. Obviously, dress and appearance in our society is highly individual and is influenced by cultural factors (such as garments or accessories worn for religious reasons), by the group with which one identifies (for instance, Goths), and by personal taste. Thus, consideration of appearance must not be directed by a social worker's expectation that an individual's appearance should

Box 4.3 Aspects of a Mental Status Examination

- Appearance, attitude, and behaviour
- Mood and affect
- Speech and thought form
- Speech and thought content
- Perception
- Cognition
- Insight and judgement

reflect his or her own. Aspects to note regarding appearance include whether the person is unkempt, has paid little attention to hygiene, is dressed in a manner that is inappropriate to the season (such as wearing several layers of heavy clothing in summer), is dressed in an idiosyncratic manner (such as wearing a negligee or evening gown during the day), or has an unusual style of makeup (such as having lipstick smeared on his or her face). Also included in appearance are the person's posture (huddled in a corner or lying across the floor) and the person's facial expressions.

Behaviour and attitude in an emergency room or office setting can often be observed from afar before the interview begins. Is the person able to sit in the waiting room and read a magazine or is he or she pacing back and forth in an agitated manner? How does the person behave towards other people in the surrounding area—does the person appear frightened, does the person speak to others in an engaging manner, does he or she appear hostile or suspicious of others? Are interactions with others appropriate to the current situation? Are there any unusual mannerisms or repetitive gestures? Are any actions speeded up or slowed down? Attitude continues to be assessed as the assessment progresses. How does the person engage with the social worker? Can he or she make eye contact? How does the person understand their illness and/or problem?

Mood and Affect

Mood refers to the pervasive emotional state that a person experiences whereas affect refers to the present emotions that are being expressed. It has been suggested that weather is to climate zone as affect is to mood. Mood is assessed by asking questions about the depth, duration, and intensity of a particular state and the degree to which this state fluctuates. Terms to describe mood can include: depressed, irritable, stable, dysphoric, expansive, or euphoric. Affect can be labile (fluctuating throughout the duration of the interview). It can be described as constricted or flattened when there is a limited range of emotion or no evidence of expressed emotion. Affect can either be appropriate or congruent with the situation or incongruent, for instance, when a person begins to laugh when telling the story of someone who has died.

Speech and Thought Form

This aspect of a mental status examination considers the physical characteristics of speech including the quantity, rate, and production of speech (Kaplan and Sadock, 1996). Descriptions of speech can include whether it is pressured or speeded up; whether it is slowed down and contains expected pauses; whether the speech is clear or slurred; loud or whispered; flows smoothly or is staccato. Does the person use strange words or syntax, rhymes, or puns? Is speech spontaneous, does the person only provide brief answers to direct questions, or does the person not respond at all?

Obviously in describing speech and thought form, the ability of the person to speak the language of the interviewer must be taken into consideration. Further, cultural and situational factors must be taken into account. If this person has been brought to hospital against his or her will, is not familiar with the surroundings, and does not have English as a first language, their speech will be considerably different than that of an English-speaking person who attended the interview voluntarily with the purpose of seeking assistance. Further, individuals who are very familiar with the mental health system and have had multiple periods of treatment and hospitalization will frequently know the interview format as well as or better than the interviewer and their speech and answers will be consequently affected.

Speech form provides a window into certain aspects of thought form. The following are some examples of disturbances in thought form (Kaplan and Sadock, 1996):

- *Neologism:* new word created by the person
- *Word salad:* incoherent list of words
- *Circumstantial thinking:* person reaches the final point after including many irrelevant details
- *Tangential thinking:* person never reaches final point and moves from one topic to another
- *Perseveration:* person is unable to move away from a particular point or phrase
- *Echolalia:* person repeats the words of others in a repetitive persistent manner
- *Loosening of associations:* ideas shift from one to another with no obvious link
- *Derailment:* sudden deviation from the original point mid-sentence
- *Flight of ideas:* constant shifting from one idea to another, although there is some vague association between the ideas
- *Blocking:* abrupt interruption in speech
- *Clang associations:* rhyming or putting words together that sound similar without an apparent point

Speech and Thought Content

Although thought content is the specific target of the mental status examination, thought content is only accessed through speech. Thought content can include worries or anxieties that the person is suffering from fears, ruminations, and suicidal ideas. It can also include delusions, preoccupations, compulsions, and phobias. Delusions are fixed false beliefs that are not consistent with the person's cultural or religious background. Such delusions may include content that is persecutory, grandiose, somatic, or erotic. Specific types of delusions are described in more detail in Chapter 7 in the discussion of schizophrenia and other psychotic illnesses; however, a list of examples follows (Kaplan and Sadock, 1996):

- *Somatic delusions:* false beliefs involving the functioning of the body
- *Persecutory delusions:* false beliefs that one is being harassed, cheated, or persecuted
- *Delusions of grandeur:* exaggerated ideas of one's importance
- *Ideas of reference:* beliefs that events refer to oneself, for instance, that the radio is speaking directly to the person
- *Thought withdrawal:* someone or something is stealing the person's thoughts
- *Thought insertion:* someone is putting thoughts in the person's head
- *Erotomania:* delusional belief that someone is in love with the person

Perception

Disturbances of perception include hallucinations, depersonalization, and dissociation. Questions that will allow a person to speak about their perceptual disturbances include: Do you ever hear voices when there is no one around? Do you ever see things that other people do not see? Do you ever have strange sensations in your body? Do you ever feel that you are not really here? Common perceptual disturbances include (Kaplan and Sadock, 1996):

- *Auditory hallucinations:* hearing voices or other sounds not heard by others (this is the most common delusion in psychotic disorders)
- *Visual hallucinations:* seeing things
- *Olfactory hallucinations:* smelling things (more common in medical disorders)
- *Tactile hallucinations:* often involving bugs crawling up the skin
- *Somatic hallucinations:* a false belief that something is happening to the body, such as something growing in the stomach
- *Hysterical anesthesia:* loss of feeling in some part of the body with no medical cause
- *Depersonalization:* sense that the self is unreal, unfamiliar
- *Derealization:* sense that the environment is strange or unreal

Cognition

Cognition in a mental state refers to the person's orientation, attention, concentration, and memory (Goldberg and Murray, 2006). Orientation refers to the person's ability to identify person, place, and time. It is assessed simply by asking the person if he or she knows where they are and how they got here, whether they know the current date or day of the week, and do they know who the interviewer is. Attention and concentration refer to the degree to which the person is able to concentrate on the interview. Simple tests for attention and concentration can be asking a person to say the months of the year in reverse order or asking people to subtract serial 7s from 100 (93, 86, 79, 72 . . .). Chapter 10, Delerium and Dementia, presents examples of simple tests for cognition.

Long-term memory is best assessed by comparing the person's account of their life with others. Individuals with certain cognitive difficulties will attempt to cover gaps in their memory by making up stories or facts. This is referred to as confabulation. It occurs because the person knows that they should be able to come up with the requested information, but as they are unable to, filling in missing data is a way of saving face.

Insight and Judgment

Insight is the degree to which the person's understanding of events fits with that of others. For instance, a person can be asked 'Why do you think the police arrested you and brought you to hospital?' It is important that pejorative opinions do not form the basis of this part of the examination. For instance, the person may understand that others believe that he or she suffers from schizophrenia and simply not agree with the diagnosis. This may not reflect poor insight but rather be a carefully considered determination, or it may simply be that the person holds out hope for a different outcome. Judgment refers to the degree to which the person is able to consider the consequences of his or her actions or assess a particular situation.

The *Diagnostic and Statistical Manual* (*DSM*)

The *Diagnostic and Statistical Manual* (*DSM*) has long been a lightning rod within the field of social work regarding how to conceptualize human behaviour (Newman, Clemmons, and Dannefelser, 2007). One frequent concern is the way in which the *DSM* counteracts the strengths-based perspective of social work, focusing solely on pathology and dysfunction. This pathology is individualized and ignores the larger social context that contributes to distress. Further concern focuses on the use of labelling that can result in stigma, discrimination, and, perhaps most concerning to some, an internalization of the stigmatized identity on people who are given labels of a mental illness (Kutchins and Kirk, 1997). Another concern is the degree to which the use of such an individualized model may absolve social workers of the duty to advocate for social and institutional change (Mitchell, 2003).

Further, critics point to the way in which the social construction of mental illness is reflected in the *DSM*. Mitchell exemplifies this point by recalling that homosexuality was identified as an illness in the *DSM* from 1968 to 1973.

On the other hand, social work educators have identified positive aspects to the use of the *DSM* by social workers, including assisting social workers to communicate effectively with others on the interdisciplinary team, organizing thinking, directing research efforts related to mental health, and linking treatment approaches to specific challenges (Newman, Clemmons, and Dannenfelser, 2007), thereby enhancing evidence-based social work practice (see Table 4.3). There is no definitive answer to whether the *DSM* should or should not be embraced by social work as a profession. Nevertheless, social workers in mental health must be aware of the *DSM* and familiar with its use. A social worker cannot communicate with the interprofessional team in mental health without knowing the language of the *DSM*, even if simply to dispute its use or to disagree with a particular diagnostic category in which a client has been placed. If using the *DSM* as a tool, social workers must not lose sight of the aspects of the recovery model described in Chapter 1 and ensure that diagnosis does not eliminate hope and that clients are centrally involved in the planning for their treatment and recovery.

History of Classification

Although classification of diseases began as early as 1742 in Europe, the first *International Classification of Diseases* (*ICD*) was established in 1855 for the purposes of developing a common language to describe the causes of death. After several revisions, the sixth revision (*ICD*-6) was adopted by the World Health Organization in 1948 as a means to standardize disease classifications across the world (Dilling, 2000). In the United States, a need was identified to develop a classification system specific to mental illness in the 1800s for the purposes of gathering statistical information. The first US census that attempted to identify the incidence of mental illness was in 1840 and contained one category, idiocy/insanity.

Table 4.3 Advantages and Disadvantages of the *DSM*

Advantages	Disadvantages
• Enhancing interprofessional communication	• Countering strengths-based perspectives of social work
• Organizing thinking	• Pathologizing
• Directing research efforts	• Individualizing, ignoring social contributors such as oppression, poverty
• Linking treatment to specific challenges	• Stigmatizing/labelling
• Enhancing evidence-based practice	• Socially constructed views of mental illness

Seven categories appeared later in the 1880 census, including mania (elated mood and excessive energy), melancholia (depression), monomania (holding a delusional belief), paresis (loss of movement), dementia (cognitive deterioration), dipsomania (craving for alcohol), and epilepsy (APA, 2000).

In 1952, the American Psychiatric Association published the first edition of the *Diagnostic and Statistical Manual for Mental Disorders* (*DSM*-I). This edition was developed by a committee of leading clinicians and researchers based on their experience and the current literature on mental illness. The draft was sent to 10 per cent of the membership of the American Psychiatric Association for review, although no results of the survey were reported (Widiger and Clarke, 2000). This was followed by *DSM*-II in 1968, which was similar in process of development and structure. *DSM*-III (1980) followed by *DSM*-III-R (1987), however, represented a new model for development. One aspect was an attempt to use research findings to support the diagnostic validity of all categories of diagnosis. However, this was hampered by the dearth of research literature within the field of psychiatry and other disciplines in mental health, resulting again in a system of categorizing that was reliant primarily on the clinical judgment of the developers. Further, *DSM*-III first introduced the concept of multiaxial diagnoses (Dilling, 2000), which will be discussed later in this section. Development of *DSM*-IV began in 1988 and led to publication in 1994. *DSM*-IV was based on 175 literature reviews, 36 studies of diagnostic criteria, and finally 12 field trials testing the reliability and validity of the classifications. Minor changes were made to *DSM*-IV resulting in the newest edition of the manual *DSM*-IV-TR in 2000 (TR refers to text revision).

The Multiaxial Assessment

A *DSM* assessment is conducted using five axes that categorize issues the client is facing (see Box 4.4). This classification system is intended to be a short-form summary of the issues discussed in the assessment. Axis I contains what are termed to be clinical disorders including but not limited to dementia, depression and anxiety, schizophrenia, eating disorders, and substance use. Axis II contains various forms of personality disturbance. Axis III contains medical conditions that are potentially relevant to the mental health problem of which the person is suffering. For example, the person may have a thyroid disorder that when overactive (hyper) can cause anxiety or mania or when underactive (hypo) can cause depression. Axis IV contains psychosocial and environmental problems including issues related to the family or significant others, occupational, educational, housing, legal, or economic problems. In conducting a multiaxial assessment, a person may have a diagnosis or problem on each of the first four axes, or may have no diagnoses or problems on any of these axes. Axis V is the assessment of global functioning (GAF). The GAF is a scale that is expressed as a number from 1 to100, 1 being the lowest level of functioning and 100 being the highest. It is often used on admission to hospital and on discharge in order to note changes in functioning as a result of treatment.

Box 4.4 *DSM* Multiaxial Assessment

Axis I Clinical problems	• Delirium and dementia • Substance abuse • Schizophrenia and other psychotic problems • Depression, mania, anxiety • Mental disorders due to a medical condition • Eating disorders • Adjustment problems
Axis II Personality disturbances Mental retardation	• Paranoid personality • Schizoid/schizotypal personality • Borderline personality • Antisocial personality • Histrionic/narcissistic/avoidant/dependent • Obsessive-compulsive personality
Axis III General medical conditions	• Neurological • Endocrine • Neonatal or antinatal complications • Respiratory/digestive/circulatory
Axis IV Psychosocial and environmental	• Primary support group • Social environment • Educational/occupational • Economic/housing • Access to health care • Legal
Axis V Global assessment of functioning	• Rate from 1 to100 • Charts progress or deterioration

Source: Adapted from APA, 2000.

Summary

The social work assessment is critical for informing work with a client or client system. It allows social workers to understand the context in which the individual lives including their community, their society, their family, and their physical and economic environment. The assessment allows the social worker to determine how the client interprets their environment and what influence this interpretation has on their well-being. Further, the assessment allows the social worker to view some of the strengths and challenges inherent in the individual related to their biological self, their cognition, their personality structure, and their ability to relate to the world.

Social work assessment in mental health practice is both similar and different to assessments in other areas of practice. As with other areas of practice, the social worker must be skilled in collecting data relevant to the psychosocial assessment and in analyzing the data for a comprehensive formulation. As with other areas of practice, culture and context are critical to understanding the nature of an individual's stressors and concerns. Beyond this, however, cultural expressions of distress in terms of specific symptoms and even in terms of culture-bound syndromes require additional knowledge on the part of the social worker in mental health. Finally, mental health practice requires the social worker to be skilled in performing mental status examinations and knowledgeable about the *DSM* as a form of classification for the purposes of communication. Clearly, social workers in mental health must have specialized knowledge and advanced skills in order to practice effectively.

Key Terms

Confabulation
Depersonalization
Dipsomania
Dissociation
Epistemology
GAF
Hallucination
Labile
Mania
Melancholia
Monomania
Paresis
Pathologizing
Pejorative
Psychologization
Somatization
Staccato
Stigma
SWOT analysis

Discussion Questions

1. How may cultural expressions of distress affect assessment of mental health issues and treatment planning?
2. How may the factors related to the social determinants of health affect an individual's mental health?
3. What unique perspectives may social work bring to mental health assessments that other members of the interdiscipinary team may not?
4. What are the risks of using the *DSM* as part of a social work assessment?

Suggested Readings and Weblinks

American Psychiatric Association (APA) (2000), *Diagnostic and Statistical Manual of Mental Disorders* (4th edition) (Washington, DC: APA Press).
Health Canada (2004), *First Nations and Inuit health: Improved Health of Aboriginal Peoples* (accessed at http://www.hc-sc.gc.ca/ahc-asc/index_e.html).

Chapter 5

Suicide and Self-Harm

Objectives:

- To describe the nature and incidence of suicide and self-harm behaviour in Canada
- To identify factors contributing to suicide risk and self-harm
- To present a model for risk assessment
- To discuss ethical and legal issues related to working with suicidal clients
- To discuss the impact of suicide on families and friends
- To identify evidenced-based interventions for social work practice with clients who are suicidal or exhibit self-harm behaviours

Case Example 1

Tuan is a 21-year-old international student taking a BSc in Chemistry in Canada. Tuan's family have saved much of their life to afford him this opportunity. The hope is that he will progress to medical school, get Canadian citizenship, and eventually be able to sponsor his family to join him in Canada. He came to Canada with English language skills that would allow him access to university, but he does not feel fluent in English and frequently misses the nuances of conversations; as a result, he feels socially awkward and does not feel a part of university life. He spends much of his time outside of classes alone in his residence room studying. Now in his second year of university, Tuan is finding the university work increasingly difficult; his concentration has been suffering and regardless of how much he studies, he does not seem to be able to grasp concepts or memorize facts. As a result grades have been dropping this year and he has been feeling increasingly panicky about getting high enough grades for admission to medical school. Today Tuan received news that he had failed the final examination in one course. He is devastated, cannot bear the thought of sharing this humiliating news with anyone, and fears that he has brought great shame on his family. Tuan can think of no option other than suicide to get him out of this situation.

Case Example 2

Sarah, age 26, was sexually abused as a child between the ages of 10 and 15 by her stepfather. At age 15 Sarah disclosed the abuse to her mother, who called her a whore and threw her out of the house. Sarah was fortunate to have an aunt who lived in the same city and welcomed her into her home. Sarah struggled to complete high school while living with her aunt but became involved with a rough crowd who drank, took drugs, and were sexually promiscuous. After high school, Sarah moved out of her aunt's home at her aunt's request and worked at a number of service jobs both in restaurants and retail sales. She continued to struggle with alcohol use and was frequently in and out of relationships with men, all of which at first seemed perfect but then ended in a crisis. Sarah has periods of intense despair where the memories of her abuse and her mother's rejection overwhelm her. At these times, she will take a razor and make cuts across her wrist, watching the blood drip into the sink. She is embarrassed about the resultant scars and thus always is seen in long-sleeved clothing. Sarah has seen many different mental health therapists about her abuse and is known in the emergency rooms of three local hospitals. On several occasions Sarah has felt such anger and despair that she has taken an overdose of pills prescribed by one physician or another to help calm her. At times her suicide attempts have led to hospitalization. Today Sarah received a phone call from her mother telling her that her sister was to be married, but that she was not to come to the wedding. Sarah is beside herself and has come to the emergency department having consumed a large amount of alcohol and is shouting that this is the last straw and she is unable to go on.

Case Example 3

Sue Rodriguez was a 42-year-old woman suffering from amyotrophic lateral sclerosis (ALS, also known as Lou Gehrig's Disease). The prognosis for her type of ALS was a steady loss of physical ability, followed by death. Near the end of her life, it was anticipated that she would be conscious and aware of her situation but completely dependent upon the care of others and the support of artificial respiration, hydration, and nutrition. She commenced a court action, asking that the *Criminal Code* provision prohibiting assisted suicide be declared contrary to the *Canadian Charter of Rights and Freedoms* (Regehr and Kanani, 2006). She requested that a qualified physician be allowed to set up technological means by which she might end her life by her own hand at the time of her choosing, when she was no longer able to enjoy life. This request was denied. It is uncertain whether her death in 1994 involved assisted suicide or voluntary euthanasia, however, no charges have been laid (Special Senate Committee on Euthanasia and Assisted Suicide, 1995).

Case Example 4

In 2007, local health care workers in Shamattawa First Nations, a community in Northern Manitoba, reported that 74 kids had attempted suicide, and another 82 had indicated they were going to do it. That accounted for more than one in four of the 600 youth living in Shamattawa. In the first five months of 2008, 37 children and 10 adults in the community attempted suicide, and 52 others told health care workers or family they planned to kill themselves (Reynolds, 2008). The problems in this community located 2000 kilometres north of

Winnipeg, first hit the national press in 2002 when three people committed suicide in the community in one month, bringing the total to 32 in one decade or 1 out of every 30 people in the 900-person community (CBC, 2002). In the aftermath of the 2002 crisis, government crisis teams were dispatched and federal and provincial governments joined forces to fast-track a $100,000 suicide prevention program in Shamattawa, establishing a new healing centre in the remote community. But in the end little was accomplished. There are lengthy waiting lists for substance-abuse treatment facilities in the North. There are no recreational facilities in Shamattawa except for a drop-in centre which, in 2006, was found to be contaminated by a fuel leak. A planned arena was never built because of an ongoing court dispute. There are very few employment opportunities. Sexual assaults are not uncommon. A doctor flies in once a month to provide medical care; a pediatrician and optometrist fly in once a year.

Suicide

'The term suicide is applied to all cases of death resulting directly or indirectly from a positive or negative act of the victim himself, which he knows will produce this result' (Durkheim, 1951, p. 44). Suicide is a behaviour or action, not a distinct psychiatric disorder. The act of suicide or attempted suicide results from the interaction of a variety of personal, interpersonal, historical, and contextual factors (Kirmayer et al., 2007). Suicidal ideation can emerge from extreme personal circumstances, which are either long-standing, such as in the case of chronic illness, or transient, such as in the case of interpersonal loss. Suicide can be culturally congruent and at least tacitly condoned by a community, or can be viewed as a criminal act or a cardinal sin. High suicide rates in a particular community can be the result of poverty, hopelessness, and despair related to historical and contextual factors, as in the case of suicide in Aboriginal communities.

When assessing and planning social work interventions with individuals who are suicidal, it is important to differentiate among acute suicide risk, chronic suicide risk, and risk-taking or self-injurious behaviour.

- ***Acute suicide risk:*** refers to a person who at a particular moment in time is experiencing intense wishes to be dead, often related to a particular life event that to the individual is of catastrophic proportions. In general, these feelings are transient and if the acute situation is managed, suicide risk diminishes. It is important to be aware that the perception of loss is entirely personal; thus, for one individual a break-up of a relationship, even one of short duration, may precipitate suicide risk but in another person would seem to be a more minor life setback. People who are at chronic risk of suicide may also have periods where they become a more acute risk due to a life event or the onset of a particular stage in a long-standing illness.
- ***Chronic suicide risk:*** occurs most commonly in individuals suffering from a long-term health or mental health problem that appears to have no possibility of relief. For these individuals, the future looks bleak and the contemplation of suicide is less an impulsive act but rather a more reasoned decision arrived at and sometimes sustained over a period of time in which the person has considered other options.

- ***Self-harm or self-injury:*** occurs in some individuals who harm themselves without lethal intent. For instance, a person who repeatedly cuts themselves may be attempting to relieve intense personal distress. The self-injurious behaviour results in some relief. However, these individuals remain at high risk of eventual suicide either because they have periods of acute risk related to specific situations or because they accidently kill themselves while inflicting self-harm.

Incidence and Prevalence

In the year 2000, approximately 1 million people died from suicide resulting in a worldwide mortality rate of 16 per 100,000, or one death every 40 seconds. Suicide is now among the three leading causes of death for those aged 15 to 44 (WHO, 2007). Within this average there is an enormous variation, ranging from a suicide rate of 70.1 per 100,000 for males in Lithuania, to a rate of 0.3 per 100,000 in Jamaica. In general, rates for males are higher than those for females with the exception of China where rates for females are higher. A comparison of suicide rates in selected countries can be found in Figure 5.1 (note that rates for Africa are unavailable).

In general, highest rates are found in Eastern Europe and the former USSR region, lowest rates are found in Central and South America and moderate rates are found in North America and Southern Europe. Canadian suicide rates are somewhat lower than the international average, at 11.6/100,000. Gender-specific rates are 18.3/100,000 for males and 5.0/100,000 for females. Mental disorders, particularly depression and substance abuse, are estimated to be associated with 90 per cent of all suicide-related deaths in the world.

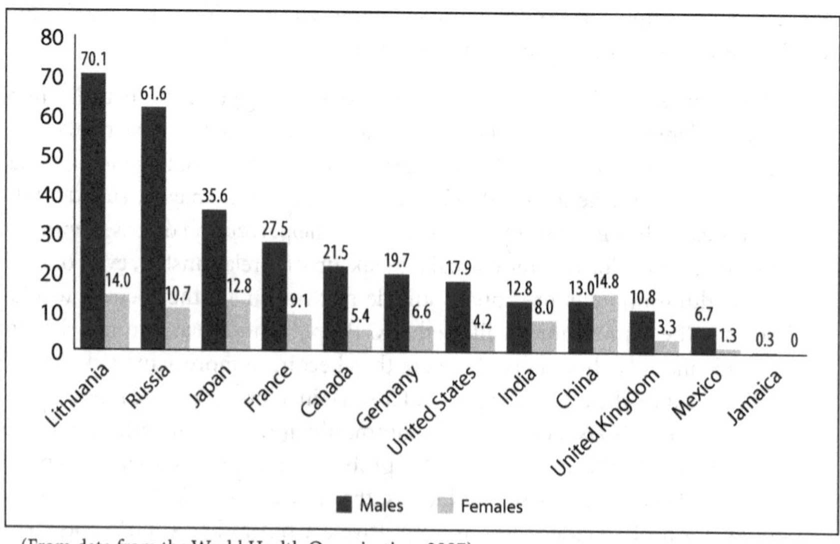

(From data from the World Health Organization, 2007)

Figure 5.1 Suicide Rates per 100,000 in Selected Countries

Suicide in Aboriginal Canadians

While the overall suicide rate in Canada has been declining, the rates in some Aboriginal communities have been rising for the past two decades (Kirmayer et al., 2007). The suicide rate among First Nations Communities is approximately twice the national average, and among the Inuit it is 6 to 7 times the national average. Female Aboriginal youth are 4 times higher than Canadian females as a whole and rates among male Aboriginal youth are 2.6 times higher than the national average (Health Canada, 2005). Aboriginal youth on reserves are 5 to 6 times more likely to die of suicide than youth in other parts of the country. The most common method of suicide is hanging, accounting for almost half of the suicide deaths in First Nations youth, followed by the use of firearms in males (35.3 per cent) and drug overdose in females (30 per cent). While overall increased rates are highly concerning, rates in specific communities are alarming. For instance, in British Columbia, Aboriginal males age 10 to 19 are 8 times and females are 20 times more likely to commit suicide than non-Aboriginal youth of the same age (MacNeil, 2008). In the Sioux Lookout area during the period of 1992 to 1995, the suicide rate in First Nations males 10 to 19 years of age was over 50 times higher than youth of the same age throughout the country (Health Canada, 2005).

Some factors that are associated with suicide in all youth populations include: mental health problems (depression, substance abuse, anxiety, or conduct problems associated with impulsive and aggressive behaviour); a history of physical or sexual abuse; a friend or family member who has attempted suicide; poor relationships with parents; and poor school attendance or performance. In Aboriginal youth, however, historical government policies that attempted to force acculturation through the residential school system, isolation of communities, inadequate resources, and resultant community anomie are additional factors (Kirmayer et al., 2007; MacNeil, 2008). It is suggested that the act of suicide among Aboriginal youth reflects an overwhelming sense of shame and hopelessness within a fractured cultural, economic, and political environment (Ferry, 2000). These youth live in environments that often have inadequate housing, contaminated water and soil, poverty, the presence of drugs and alcohol, and an absolute lack of opportunity. Families frequently have histories of substance use, mental health challenges, and suicide. In addition, fetal alcohol syndrome (FAS) is consistently higher than the national and international averages. In one Manitoba community the incidence of FAS was found to be 100 cases per 1,000 live births compared to a world frequency of 1 to 3 cases per 1,000 live births. In sum, these environments carry all the risk factors for suicide and the result is tragedy.

Factors Contributing to Suicide

Social-Environmental Factors

Emile Durkheim, a French sociologist, published his book *Suicide* in 1897 in which he explored the concept of suicide within a framework of social integration. In this book he divided suicide into three categories: 1) egotistic suicide, in which the individual is unconnected with any social group and his or her despair relates to lack of social integration; 2) altruistic suicide, in which the suicidal behaviour is associated with excessive integration into a group, such as in the case of a politically or religiously motivated suicide bomber; and 3) anomic suicide, where a person's connection with the larger society is disturbed, thereby resulting in a feeling of disconnect from the goals and aims of society. Anomie is thought to occur in the wake of some sort of dramatic change in social or economic circumstances, such as after the stock market crash in 1929 or in prolonged periods of cultural despair, such as in the case of Aboriginal communities. From the social-environmental perspective, suicide is understood to arise from a convergence of factors related to the presence or absence of social pressures and opportunities in the interpersonal environment.

Intrapsychic Factors

Freud described suicide as aggression turned inwards. That is, suicide was seen as the result of angry, murderous urges towards another as a result of some form of injury to the self. Indeed, researchers have found that hostility and aggression is linked to suicidal behaviour (Mann et al., 1999). This anger and aggression is often related to personal histories of abuse and neglect. For instance, impulsivity, self-harm behaviours, and suicide attempts are found more commonly in individuals who are survivors of childhood physical and sexual abuse (Carballo et al., 2008). It is hypothesized that growing up in an environment of fear, pain, and unpredictability can lead to disconnection from others and a profound sense of self-blame and self-hatred. These reactions may be turned against the self at times of high stress or distress (Herman, 1992). A further intrapsychic factor that has received considerable research support is hopelessness about the future and about one's own ability to change current and future circumstances (Reinecke, 2000). Clearly, this sense of individual hopelessness is often intricately linked to social-environmental factors that oppress individuals and groups, limit choices, and block opportunities. From an intrapsychic perspective, therefore, suicidality results from a complex and heterogeneous mix of intolerance of negative affect, low frustration tolerance, impulsivity, and intolerable psychic pain (Nierenberg et al., 2008).

Genetic and Neurochemistry Factors

Strong genetic links have been suggested in suicidal behaviour. Adoption studies for instance find a six- to fifteen-fold increase in suicide in biological relatives of adoptees when compared to rates in adoptive families (Brent and Mann, 2005). In twin studies, the concordance rate between dizygotic (fraternal) twins for suicidal behaviour is 0.7 per cent and suicide is 0.7 per cent. Among monozygotic (identical) twins the concordance rate between suicidal behaviour is 14.9

per cent and suicide is 23.0 per cent, a remarkably higher rate. Similarly, family proband studies show higher rates of suicide among those who are first degree relatives of suicide attempters (30.3 per cent) versus those in a control group (3.6 per cent).

While it is established that there are neurochemical components to some mental illnesses such as schizophrenia (see Chapter 7) and depression and mania (see Chapter 8), suicidality may have a neurochemical component that is independent of psychiatric illness. Suicidality is associated with distinct neurotransmitter and receptor profiles (Nierenberg et al., 2008). Specifically, those individuals lacking in one receptor (5-HT_{1b}) are likely to have higher levels of impulsivity, aggression, and substance abuse, all of which contribute to suicide risk (Mann et al., 1999). Further, serotonin deficiency (related to 5-H1AA) has been found in patients suffering from depression who attempted suicide.

Self-Harm Behaviour

Deliberate self-harm involves the destruction of body tissue without suicidal intent (Cumming, Covic, and Murrell, 2006). In general, this behaviour is divided into three categories:

1. ***Stereotypic self-harm:*** involves repeated acts such as head banging and the biting of oneself often associated with developmental delays, autism, and neurological disorders such as Tourette syndrome.
2. ***Moderate self-harm:*** is the most common form of self-harm and typically involves cutting (as seen in Case Example 2 of Sarah) and skin-burning. This type of behaviour is usually associated with borderline personality disorder, dissociative states, complex post-traumatic stress, and eating disorders. Moderate self-harm can be episodic or repetitive.
3. ***Major self-harm:*** is the rarest form of self-harm and is usually associated with psychosis. This results in severe injury such as self-castration or amputation. Often the specific form of mutilation is related to a particular delusion, for instance, that a particular body part is rotting or possessed.

Self-harm behaviours are generally related to impulse control, which, from a biological perspective, are related to lower pre-synaptic serotonin availability. In individuals who repeatedly self-harm, there is a reported reduction in anxiety and psychophysiological arousal. Individuals who self-harm will often refer to the act as self-soothing or as resulting in lower levels of psychic pain. It can also be an external representation of internal pain. Alternatively, self-harm can be a form of self-punishment for individuals who experience excessive self-blame. Self-harm behaviours frequently begin in adolescence and end in middle age. Individuals who self-harm are at 66 times the risk of suicide when compared to the general population.

Assessment of Suicide Risk

In assessing suicide risk, the social worker goes through a series of categories of information, attempting to collect data with which to gauge the current level of risk of a lethal attempt (see Box 5.1). One issue to be considered is whether this person is in a group with a higher risk of suicide than other groups. For instance, as noted earlier, males are at higher risk of actually committing suicide in almost every country in the world, although women are at higher risk of attempting suicide or self-harm. Young men and men over the age of 65 are at particular risk. Aboriginal youth are at higher risk than youth in other cultural groups, particularly if living in impoverished or isolated communities. Some occupational groups are at higher risk than others, for instance, doctors and nurses are in the highest risk occupations (primarily due to access to lethal drugs), followed by manual labourers in low-paid jobs. The lowest risk occupations are people in the armed forces, architects, and engineers (Agerbo et al., 2007).

A previous suicide attempt is the best predictor of a future suicide or suicide attempt (Mann et al., 1999). Among people with depression who die of suicide, for instance, 40 per cent have made previous attempts (Kaplan and Sadock, 1996). Individuals who engage in self-harm behaviours are at high risk of eventual suicide. This group of individuals frequently also make multiple suicide attempts that have a low level of possible lethality, often referred to as 'parasuicide'. However, those who engage in parasuicidal attempts have a 20 to 47 per cent chance of eventual death from suicide (Cumming, Covic, and Murrell, 2006) and therefore it is important not to dismiss their suicidal ideation as merely 'attention seeking'. Critical in the consideration of previous suicide attempts as risk factors for future or current suicide is the degree of impulsivity in the acts and the severity of previous attempts. People who are subject to impulsive behaviour are at higher risk of future attempts and eventual death by suicide. The difficulty for clinicians, however, is determining whether this particular period in time represents a high risk or not, because an impulsive person's risk of suicide can fluctuate very quickly. Despite these high numbers, overall only 20 to 30 per cent of people who eventually commit suicide have made previous attempts; thus, it is important to consider other factors.

Alcohol use acts as a disinhibitor with respect to suicide and is associated with depression. Up to 15 per cent of people with alcohol abuse commit suicide (270/100,000 population). About 80 per cent of alcohol-dependent suicides are male. Heroin abusers have a rate of suicide 20 times that of the general public (Kaplan and Sadock, 1996). The risk of suicide for individuals with histories of mental illness is 3 to 12 times that of the general population. Age-adjusted suicide rates for people suffering from depression is estimated to be 400 per 100,000 for males and 180 per 100,000 for females. Up to 10 per cent of people with schizophrenia die from suicide, most within the first few years of their diagnosis. Suicide accounts for 19 per cent of deaths in bipolar patients (Carballo et al., 2008). Associated with the presence of a mental health problem is current mental status. Those individuals who are severely depressed may focus entirely on suicide and annihilation and be at extremely high risk due to their inability to foresee a future

Box 5.1 Assessment of Suicide Risk

Demographic considerations	• Gender (males are at higher risk) • Age (highest risk for youth between 15 and 24, followed by men over 65) • Upper or lower socioeconomic group • Unemployment or retired • Single, widowed, or divorced • Social isolation
Other self-destructive behaviour	• Previous suicide attempts, how impulsive? • Other self-harm behaviours
Alcohol use	• Alcoholics have 15 per cent eventual mortality rate by suicide • Suicide attempts are preceded by alcohol intake in 50 per cent of men and 30 per cent of women
Past psychiatric history	• The person's and their family's – affective disorders have 15 per cent mortality by suicide – among suicides, 45 to 70 per cent have affective disorders
Present mental status	• See mental status exam in Chapter 4 • Severe depression • Command hallucinations
Precipitating events	• Recent loss or separation • Is there a clear precipitant? • Can there be some resolution to the problem?
Method or plan	• Abstractly considered suicide • Has given thought to method • Has prepared for suicide – saving pills, purchased gun • Level of intent to die • Lethality of method – drug overdose common in Canada (1/3 suicides, 2/3 attempts)
Resources	• Personal resources • Resources within the person's network • Community resources
Future plans	• Immediate plans – what will you do when you leave here today? • Longer-term plans

free of depression. Individuals who suffer from command hallucinations aimed at self-destruction, such as voices that tell them they are worthless and should kill themselves, are at very high risk, even in the absence of other risk factors.

Family history of suicide and mental disorder is another important risk factor. In general individuals with family histories of suicide are at higher risk of suicidal attempts and completed suicide. This is particularly true in individuals that have a history of childhood physical or sexual abuse (Carballo et al., 2008). It appears that there is a complex interaction between family history of suicide and current suicide risk. One aspect may be genetic, as perhaps evidenced by a tendency towards earlier onset of depression and mania in those who have had a family member suicide. Not surprisingly, however, individuals with family histories of suicide are found to be more pessimistic about the future (Nierenberg et al., 2008). A further possibility is that if someone in a person's family has committed suicide, the taboo against suicide is somehow lifted and suicide may become a viable option for dealing with intolerable situations and states. However, imitation alone does not explain the increased incidence of suicide in families because studies where close friends are exposed to teenage suicide do not demonstrate higher rates of suicide despite higher levels of depression and post-traumatic stress disorder (PTSD), suggesting that suicidality itself may be inherited (Brent and Mann, 2005).

In addition to these factors, social workers evaluating for suicide risk must determine whether there is an acute precipitant of the current suicidal ideation and whether this precipitant can in any way be diminished in intensity or resolved. Social workers should ask very directly about suicidal ideation and intent. This includes questions related to an exact plan for suicide. Possible questions are listed as follows:

- Are you feeling so badly about the current situation that you have been thinking about hurting yourself? (Easing into the conversation about suicide and self-harm. Clients will frequently ask if you mean would they kill themselves and will assure you that they will not.)
- How would you hurt yourself? (Determining whether this is self-harm behaviour or suicidal behaviour if they have answered the previous question in the affirmative.)
- Do you have access to pills/a gun? How many pills do you have? Where is the gun? (Exploring preparation for the specific method that they have considered. For instance, a person may state that they would shoot themselves but have no access to firearms. Alternatively, a person may have been saving pills for the occasion.)
- Have you made any other preparations? Or have you thought about what would happen to your kids if you were gone? (Exploring other types of preparation and planning. For instance, has the person recently written a will?)
- Have you ever hurt yourself before? What did you do to yourself? What happened? Did you get treatment? (Exploring the seriousness and impulsiveness of previous attempts or self-harm.)

- Do you know anyone who has committed suicide? What was that like for you? (Exploring family history and attitudes towards suicide.)
- What were you planning to do when you left here today? (Assessing whether the person has other plans for the day, expects to see someone, etc. When the person has no plan at all, this adds to risk.)

In the end, it is difficult to predict suicide as individual risk fluctuates dramatically particularly in individuals with high levels of impulsive behaviour. If there is any question in the mind of the social worker assessing the client, he or she should seek consultation and not feel obligated to make a decision about risk alone. Clients at high risk are often hospitalized, but, where risk can be managed, community-based treatment is usually preferred in order to support individual coping skills.

Suicide Scales for Assessment

Social workers may find it useful to use scales to assist with the assessment of suicide risk. Although there are many suicide scales in use, many have very little data supporting their use. A study conducted at the Centre for Addiction and Mental Health compared a variety of scales to clinical assessments. They determined that six scales identified high-risk patients: the SAD PERSONS Scale, the revised Beck Depression Inventory, the Beck Hopelessness Scale, the Beck Anxiety Inventory, the Beck Scale for Suicidal Ideation, and the High-Risk Construct Scale. Of these, the most accurate were the Beck Scale for Suicidal Ideation (BSS) and the High-Risk Construct Scale (Cochrane-Brink, Lofchy, and Sakinofsky, 2000). However, these researchers and others (Harriss and Hawton, 2005) have found that while these scales are important adjuncts to clinical assessment, no scale predicts whether clients will ultimately die of suicide. Further, these scales are not accurate enough to suggest that a particular cutoff point should result in hospitalization.

Ethical and Legal Duties in Working with Suicidal Clients

Probably more than any other clinical situation, a suicidal client forces the social worker to confront complex ethical questions while at the same time being faced with urgency, uncertainty, and risk. On one hand, it seems that protecting the lives of individuals is central to social work values; on the other hand, a person contemplating suicide who suffers from a chronic and life-threatening health condition, such as in the case of Sue Rodriguez, may be quite different from the person acutely suffering depression who expresses suicidal thoughts. What is a social worker expected to do in these circumstances? In general, there is consensus in the literature that the practitioner is obliged to do absolutely whatever he/she can to help the suicidal client find a way to live. While there may be circumstances where suicide is a reasoned decision, the prevailing opinion is that if it is unclear whether the person can make a rational and autonomous decision, the practitioner should err on the side of caution and intervene. The choice to intervene may provide an opportunity for a second chance and can always be reconsidered and reversed (Mishna, Antle, and Regehr, 2002).

While the literature on suicide may allow for the possibility of suicide as a rational decision, what about the legal and ethical obligations of social workers? Mishna, Regehr, and Antle (2003), in reviewing the legal obligations of social workers in Canada with respect to suicidal clients, consider two main factors: 1) the standard of care that the practitioner is required to provide; and 2) the duty to disclose confidential information that a client may be suicidal. Physicians have a well-defined duty under the law to try to prevent suicide. If physicians, particularly psychiatrists, do not take adequate measures to protect life or are negligent in meeting the standard of care, they may be held liable (Regehr and Kanani, 2006). Indeed, failing to prevent suicide is a leading reason for malpractice suits against mental health professionals and institutions in the United States (Corey, Corey, and Callanan, 1998). However, the potential liability of a social worker with regard to a client's suicide is uncharted territory in Canadian law. Although the fact that no social worker has been held civilly liable or criminally responsible for a client's suicide may offer some comfort, it certainly does not guarantee future immunity from liability. To ensure protection from this outcome, social workers must follow standards of care in working with suicidal clients, including performing thorough assessments, providing recommended treatments, and being informed of and following decisions related to breach of confidentiality when a client threatens self-harm (Mishna, Regehr, and Antle, 2003). In terms of social work ethics, whereas the *Code of Ethics* (2005) underlines confidentiality as a central ethical duty, the *Guidelines for Ethical Practice* of the CASW (2005) state:

> Social workers who have reason to believe that a client intends to harm him/herself are expected to exercise professional judgement regarding their need to take action consistent with their provincial/territorial legislation, standards of practice and workplace policies. Social workers may in this instance take action to prevent client self-harm without the informed consent of the client. In deciding whether to break confidentiality, social workers are guided by the imminence of self-harm, the presence of a mental health condition and prevailing professional standards and practices (CASW, 2005 Standard 1.6.3).

Social workers must therefore rely on practice guidelines, which call for careful evaluation, a good therapeutic alliance, and consultation.

The preceding discussion does not fully address the issue of a client with a chronic condition who has determined that suicide is the most reasonable choice given their current condition and the anticipated course of their illness. Mishna, Regehr, and Antle (2003) note that self-determination is central to social work ethics and values and a fundamental human right in Western society. However, there have always been limits to self-determination especially in situations where a person has diminished capacity for decision-making and consent. This is dealt with in detail in Chapter 3. Thus, a social worker must include consideration of capacity when determining suicide intervention in situations of chronic risk.

It is important to note that while suicide and attempted suicide are not illegal in Canada, assisting with a suicide is a criminal offence. Section 241 of the *Criminal Code* provides that everyone who: 1) counsels a person to commit suicide; or 2) aids or abets a person to commit suicide, whether suicide ensues or not, is guilty of an indictable offence and liable to imprisonment for a term not exceeding 14 years. Individuals with life-threatening illnesses and their doctors have gone before the courts attempting to establish a constitutional right to assisted suicide; however, despite the efforts of Sue Rodriguez (Case Example 3) to change Canadian law on this point, in 1993 the law was upheld by the Supreme Court of Canada (Regehr and Kanani, 2006).

The Impact of Suicide on Family and Friends

Death by suicide results in special issues and challenges for those who are left behind. Parents of those who have committed suicide are first dealing with general issues related to the loss of a child. The loss of a child is seen as a violation of the natural world order and interrupts the continuity of the family, and their anticipated future (Maple, 2005). Such a loss can lead to mental health and physical health issues, disrupted marital relations, and increased morbidity, including suicide risk. When the death is caused by suicide, additional factors emerge: 1) the survivor struggles to find meaning in the death; 2) there are high levels of guilt for not preventing the death; 3) survivors experience a sense of abandonment by the deceased; 4) stigma and absence of social supports; and 5) fear. Parents in particular feel guilt related to their perceived inadequacies as parents and often a sense of moral guilt related to past wrongdoings (Parrish and Tunkel, 2005). Related to this, they may feel fear for their remaining family members, particularly related to future possibilities of mental illness and suicide (Clark and Goldney, 1995). Family members feel isolated and stigmatized, and social supports are often not forthcoming. Some have suggested that family members feel shunned by the community). As a result, a conspiracy of silence may emerge and the deceased person is not spoken about, as if to suggest that he or she did not exist. This does not allow for the process of grieving in survivors. Friends and peers of the deceased are often in a state of shock, which in the case of youth is compounded by age-related inexperience and emotions.

Finally, one factor that is more frequent in suicide-related deaths is the horror of the death scene. Images of the death scene obviously occur when a family member or friend has discovered the deceased; however, they can also occur as a result of imagined scenes based on what has been learned about the death (Clark and Goldney, 1995).

Interventions

Psychosocial interventions for people who are at risk of suicide fall into two main categories: 1) crisis intervention to deal with acute risk; and 2) longer-term treatment such as dialectic behaviour therapy or interpersonal therapy to manage chronic risk and self-harm. The second category of interventions is discussed in Chapter 12 on personality disorders.

Crisis Intervention with Acute Suicide Risk

Crisis intervention is a brief treatment approach that is based on the premise that support, education, and guidance provided in a timely manner can assist individuals to mobilize their inherent strengths and resources for the purposes of moving towards a speedy resolution of the distress caused by a particular occurrence. Crisis intervention focuses on the resolution of an immediate problem. The goal is to prevent further deterioration and return to at least a pre-crisis level of functioning. In working with suicidal clients, crisis intervention focuses on reducing acute risk through diminishing affective arousal and assisting the client to develop some immediate plans. This model of intervention was originally proposed by Caplan in 1964 and later by Golan in 1978. Most recently, Roberts (2000) defined seven stages of crisis intervention as follows:

1. *Planning and conducting a thorough assessment*, including any acute risk of harm to self or others. The assessment process has been described in detail earlier in this chapter.
2. Rapidly *establishing rapport*, demonstrating respect, acceptance, and a nonjudgmental attitude. Rapport is established very quickly in a crisis situation through the demonstration of concern for the problems that are being experienced by the person in distress and a desire to assist with basic needs. Such assistance can include offering food or drink in the emergency room and ensuring the person is comfortable and protected from the chaos that may be characteristic of the environment.
3. *Identifying various dimensions of the current problem* including the 'last straw' of precipitating events. As discussed in Chapter 4 on assessment, the social worker attempts to quickly identify the biopsychosocial domains of the current problem. What are the underlying struggles that this person encounters? What has led up to the current crisis? In general, the social worker should be prepared for the fact that the client in crisis will present a wide range of problems, including those that have been continuing for sometime and those that are new. The social worker needs to be careful not to become overwhelmed and rather begin to organize the problems in his or her own mind as the assessment interview continues.
4. Active listening while *exploring* and describing previous *coping strategies* and *successes and resources* available. The social worker using a crisis intervention approach seeks to discover the strengths that the client has within themselves and within their social network. Who could help them if they needed help? How have they coped in the past? If the client describes positive coping, reinforce their abilities and celebrate their successes. For instance, while a client might not identify this as a particular success, the social worker may remark 'I see you as someone with tremendous strengths and resources based on the fact that you managed to complete high school despite all the challenges that were thrown your way.' Be prepared that even if the client is able to accept the positive reinforcement, he or she may

not be able to handle the stresses this particular day and may need further intervention.

5. Generating and exploring *alternative strategies* for managing the problem. Once the client has laid out the problems he or she is encountering, the social worker summarizes the issues for the client. For instance, 'I can see that you are managing many problems. Some of these have been going on for a long time, such as your relationship with your mom, your problems in school. . . . On top of all of that, in the last two days X has happened.' The social worker then suggests that some of the issues can't be dealt with right now, but that a referral for future counselling is certainly possible. Also, it is important for the social worker to emphasize that together the client and the social worker might be able to come up with some ideas to manage the most recent problems over the next couple of days. At this point the social worker searches for possible solutions by gently exploring alternatives with the client. At any point, the social worker has to be prepared to change tactics and move from a community-based approach to other measures such as hospitalization if the client does not appear to be able to engage in problem-solving and suicide risk remains high.
6. Developing and formulating an *action plan* with the client. Once alternatives have been explored, the social worker and the client move to an immediate action plan. Generally, both the client and the social worker have some responsibilities in the plan. For instance, the social worker may undertake to contact a parent, friend, or other support person who can assist the individual. The social worker may also undertake to do some advocacy work with a professor, landlord, or source of funding to reduce some systemic pressures on the client. The social worker may arrange a shelter bed and provide a taxi for the client to get there. The client also agrees to undertake some tasks such as discussing their concerns with a particular person or following through on a task that he or she has been avoiding. In formulating the action plan, the social worker will often provide notes to the client with necessary phone numbers or steps to be followed.
7. Establishing *follow-up* plans. Follow-up plans tend to be short-term in crisis intervention. For instance, a client can agree to visit or phone the social worker the next day. Follow-up plans can also be longer term in nature, although it is important to note that quite commonly clients who attend crisis services do not follow through with referrals to longer-term services. It is hypothesized that this may be due to the fact that he or she is a crisis-oriented person who does not engage in longer-term strategies, or that crisis intervention performed correctly and at the ideal time creates change in and of itself and no further assistance is needed. That is, a competent person might just need to sort through some difficulties with another person during a time of acute stress. All follow-up plans with people who are potential suicide risks must include strategies and options should the person feel that they are at acute risk of suicide and need immediate assistance. Such options include suicide hotlines and hospital emergency departments.

Some practitioners and treatment centres employ no-suicide contracts, whereby the client undertakes to promise the therapist, or even sign a document, that he or she will not attempt suicide. There is no empirical support for the effectiveness of such contracts in reducing suicidal behaviour (Reinecke, 2000). Some have suggested that this is simply an approach that reduces therapist anxiety and may in fact cause a breach in the therapeutic alliance if the client does not follow the contract and makes an attempt.

While limited research has considered the efficacy of this model, it is non-intrusive and focuses on client needs and wishes. Studies that do exist combine a number of types of interventions under the heading of crisis intervention, although one meta-analysis does provide some support for crisis models (Roberts and Everly, 2006).

Hospitalization for Acute Risk

Where suicide risk is particularly high and outpatient treatment is unable to ensure safety, hospitalization may be required. In general, hospitalization is viewed as a short-term measure to treat an acute psychiatric illness, such as depression, or to get someone who is a chronic risk through a particularly difficult time. This is discussed further in Chapter 12 on personality disorders.

Counselling Interventions for Self-Harm and Fluctuating Risk

Although crisis intervention is useful in times of acute suicidal risk, individuals who have long histories of abuse and neglect that later result in self-harm behaviours and chronic fluctuating suicide risk require longer-term counselling interventions. These interventions are discussed in more detail in the chapters on trauma and grief and on personality disturbance. In general however, the approach includes: providing support and validation; providing stability; containing distress; and working through and managing crises. In addition, two particular forms of longer-term intervention dialectic behaviour therapy (DBT) and interpersonal therapy (IP) have been shown to be effective. These are discussed in Chapter 12.

Pharmacological Intervention for Suicide Risk

The essential principle of treatment in this area of suicide risk is careful assessment and treatment of the underlying disorder. Most commonly this involves treatment of depression and mania, schizophrenia, borderline personality disorder, and substance abuse (see chapters later in this book for more information). Suicide and self-harm are common in all these mental health problems and should always be part of the initial and ongoing assessment. If an individual is assessed as having a high suicide risk, the general principles of treatment should be applied as described earlier in this chapter. Psychopharmacological treatment may or may not be a part of the action plan. For instance, treatment of depression through the use of medication decreases the risk of suicide. One study demonstrates a clear relationship between the number of prescriptions for Selective Serotonin Reuptake Inhibitors (SSRIs) and Serotonin Norepinephrine Reuptake Inhibitors (SNRIs) dispensed in a given area and time period and suicide rates (Gibbons et al., 2005). That is, as prescriptions increase, suicide rates decrease. A study looking at national suicide mortality files between 1990 and 2000 demonstrated a similar association in youth suicide rates (Olfson et al., 2003). Although this fact may be true on a population basis, in Chapter 6 we discuss how risk of suicide may increase on an individual basis in the initial stages of recovery. Therefore, careful monitoring and supervision with regular follow-up is essential.

A body of research has established that decreased serotonergic activity is associated with suicidal behaviour (Mann et al., 1999). Studies emanating from this work support the use of lithium carbonate in decreasing suicide rates (Bocchetta et al., 2007). This is especially effective in those suffering from mood disorders but also applies across the diagnostic spectrum.

Social Work Interventions with Families and Communities after Suicide

Family interventions following suicide can take several forms, including work with individuals who are most affected, work with couples struggling in the aftermath of losing a child, meetings with the family as a group, and support groups of suicide survivors. In general the intervention must include several elements (Kaslow and Aronson, 2004):

- demonstrating compassion, acceptance, and gaining trust;
- shifting flexibly between a supportive, educative, and counselling stance;
- assessment of each member of the family to determine their unique needs and risks; and
- addressing issues of blame, stigma, shame, guilt, and fear.

In order to do this, the social worker must examine his or her own reactions to suicide and be prepared for being exposed to painful emotions and distressing information.

Support groups for survivors of suicide can be of benefit to bereaved individuals to share experiences of stigma and isolation (Parrish and Tunkel, 2005). Hopmeyer and Werk (1994) conducted a study comparing five types of bereavement groups in Montreal. Aspects of group intervention that family survivors of suicide reported as most helpful included: 1) sharing similar experiences; 2) gaining comfort and reassurance; learning new skills for coping; 4) sharing with others what they had learned; and 5) gaining assistance for their depression.

Suicide does not occur in equal rates in all communities and as noted earlier in this chapter, when suicide rates are high in a particular community, the impact is felt well beyond the individual families. As a result, community-based interventions are necessary to fully address the after-effects of suicide and the ongoing risks. A community-based program for families following suicide was initiated in a high-risk neighbourhood in Galway, Ireland. This project emerged because of the realization that suicide was a common issue within the community resulting in many bereaved families and one that the community support programs felt ill-equipped to deal with. This family support program was embedded in the ecological perspective and focused on the impact of suicide on all aspects of the system and the possibilities of support from multiple levels. The program was planned through a community development process. The final program began with the distribution of cards that described issues related to suicide and supports available to all households in the community. An information night was held for all community members and a video was made to encourage discussion and impart information. The model emphasized the supports needed by the extended family, friends, neighbours, and the community in general and identified not only formal services but also informal mechanisms for assistance (Forde and Devaney, 2006).

There have been many diverse approaches to working with Aboriginal communities in Canada where the tragedy of suicide permeates (Leenaars, 2000). Such approaches are vital because the causes of suicide in these communities are related to mental health, health, and substance problems that stem from poverty, marginalization, and oppression (Kirmayer, Simpson and Cargo, 2003). One aspect of comprehensive community approach involves re-articulating tradition through reconciliation and renewal. The Aboriginal Healing Foundation, which was established in 1998, has focused on developing community-based services, workshops and gatherings, cultural activities, and training and educational programs. Another aspect has been focusing on youth identity and community empowerment. This has involved including youth in decision-making processes and the development of community services. Mental health programs are being directed towards youth mental health and cultural identity. At the larger level, self-governance models are being implemented to allow for local control over social services, education, and resources, with the aim of building community capacity and addressing issues of despair and hopelessness.

Possible Social Work Interventions in the Case Examples

Case Example 1: Tuan

Tuan is suffering from acute suicide risk as a result of situational factors. He is under a great deal of pressure and feels that he has failed and let his family down. Tuan has no social supports in the city and is quite isolated. The following could be aspects of a sound social work intervention:

- The first step with Tuan will be to conduct a thorough assessment to determine if there are other underlying factors affecting a suicidal ideation; for instance, does he suffer from depression, has he previously had suicidal thoughts, and/or has anyone in his family suffered from depression or attempted or committed suicide? If these are additional risk factors, a consultation for mental health problems may be in order.

- A further aspect of the assessment will be determining the degree of present risk. Does he have a plan and how serious are his intentions?
- Next, the social worker will move into crisis intervention strategies. What solutions might Tuan consider for the problem? Will Tuan allow the social worker to intervene within the university in order to get him assistance with tutoring and an opportunity to retake the exam because of impairments caused by stress?
- The social worker will then work to build social supports for Tuan. Will he agree to attend events at the international student centre? Is there someone at the university who can be helpful (residence don, registrar, etc.). Is there someone within the city (a distant relative or family friend, a classmate) with whom he can connect and spend time? Will Tuan allow the social worker to be in contact with his family and if so is the family likely to be supportive?
- Upon working out a strategy, the social worker will assess whether the suicide risk remains acute. If so, Tuan may need to be taken to hospital for assessment. If not, a follow-up interview and plan can be established should he become acutely distressed again.

Case Example 2: Sarah

Sarah has a tragic life history that has led to ongoing distress which is manifested in self-harm behaviours and recurrent suicidal risk. The social worker is likely seeing Sarah in the emergency room and will probably take some of the following steps to intervention:

- The social worker will begin by allowing Sarah to describe her story and the factors that led to this acute situation today. It is possible that as a result of the support and empathy of the social worker, Sarah will begin to feel better.
- The social worker will determine if Sarah is presently seeing a mental health professional and what the plan is for their work together. The social worker may, with Sarah's consent, call that therapist to discuss possible plans.
- The social worker will attempt to use problem-solving approaches with Sarah in order to see if the current crisis can be abated. For instance, are there social supports that can be drawn upon to assist at this time of crisis? Are there some self-care or self-soothing strategies that Sarah has used in the past that may work at this time?
- If Sarah's agitation and risk does not remit, it is possible that she may need a period of brief hospitalization to help her through the crisis period. The social worker will then have to seek consultation on this matter with someone who has admitting privileges (often a physician).

Case Example 3: Sue

The case of Sue is not one in which there has been a rash decision to commit suicide. Instead, Sue explored all options and determined that rather than die in a painful and debilitating manner, she would prefer to have control over her own death. The social worker must consider the following issues:

- A social worker cannot counsel suicide or assist with suicide regardless of his or her moral beliefs about the subject.

- A social worker must assess whether the client is competent to make decisions about his or her own future and whether he or she suffers from a mental health problem (such as depression) that is influencing their judgment.
- The social worker should continue to provide support and counselling to reduce stress and social isolation, assisting with any factors that are making life more difficult to. That is, any factors that may contribute to suicide risk should be diminished or eliminated if at all possible. The social worker must be careful not to give up.
- On the other hand, it has been suggested that in the case of chronic and unremitting mental or physical illness, a social worker's conviction that suicide can and must be prevented may reflect an avoidance of the ethical dilemma and responsibility (Mishna, Antle, and Regehr, 2002). That is, the continuation of enforced treatment may only intensify the unbearable pain and distress for the suicidal individual. Narveson (1986) writes that the intervention may be 'what the professional insists is "treatment," and what the subject regards as, simply, a refined variety of torture' (p. 107). Some writers suggest that if a practitioner is able to empathically hear the clients' unbearable suffering and death wishes, this may build trust in the relationship with the therapist. They speculate that paradoxically this may foster some hope in the clients (Nelson, 1984). Thus, listening to the client as he or she discusses their pain, may in fact diminish risk.

Case Example 4: Shamattawa First Nations

In the case of Shamattawa First Nations, while suicide unquestionably affects individuals and their families, the causes of suicide are not individual. Rather they reflect the results of systemic oppression, abuse, and neglect. Social work interventions therefore must be much broader than the individualized interventions described in the previous cases.

- All strategies for community interventions in the prevention of suicide and in the recovery of suicide must emanate from the community itself and not be imposed from the outside.
- Social services must be designed by the local community in collaboration with social workers in a way that meets the needs of their members.
- Social workers can work with communities around issues of reconciliation and self-governance in order to restore cultural identity and a common sense of purpose and future.

Summary

All social workers working in the area of mental health will be faced with clients who are at risk of suicide. The despair that individuals suffering from major mental disorders experience at various times in the course of their illnesses may lead to suicidal thoughts and attempts. The emotional dysregulation and recurring interpersonal crises that individuals with personality disorders encounter can lead to fluctuating or chronic risk of self-harm and suicidal behaviour. The average person encountering a life crisis or significant loss may uncharacteristicly consider suicide at a particularly bleak time. Further, individuals who are members of certain groups that are plagued with disadvantage and substance abuse may have learned that suicide is a viable alternative. It is essential that social workers develop skills in the assessment of suicide risk and in intervention with people who are experiencing acute risk. Work with suicidal clients is generally stressful and often fraught with ethical dilemmas. Everyone working with suicidal clients must ensure that they have a good team of colleagues within their own discipline and within the interdisciplinary team, to ensure that they have consultation available in order to make reasoned and competent judgments and to ensure that they can obtain professional support when the stresses of this work take its toll.

Key Terms

Anomie
Concordance
Disinhibition
Dizygotic twins
Euthanasia
Fetal alcohol syndrome (FAS)
Intrapsychic
Monozygotic twins
Parasuicide
Tourette syndrome

Discussion Questions

1. What is the obligation of social workers to intervene in cases of acute suicide risk?
2. Do social workers have the same obligations in cases of suicide decisions arising from chronic illness as they do in acute suicide risk?
3. What moral and religious values may influence the work of social workers with clients who are contemplating suicide? Do these values conflict with ethical and legal guidelines?
4. What reactions may social workers have to clients that engage in self-harm behaviours and how might these reactions affect the therapeutic relationship?

Suggested Readings and Weblinks

Kirmayer, L., Brass, G., Holton, T., Paul, K., Simpson, C., and Tait, C. (2007), *Suicide Among Aboriginal People in Canada* (Ottawa: Aboriginal Healing Foundation).

Social Workers: Help Starts Here. *Suicide Prevention* (accessed at http://www.helpstartshere.org/mind_and_spirit/suicide_prevention/default.html).

World Health Organization (2007), *Suicide Prevention* (accessed at http://www.who.int/mental_health/prevention/suicide/suicideprevent/en/).

Chapter 6

Trauma and Traumatic Grief

Objectives:

- To describe trauma response as a continuum of distress
- To describe factors that contribute to trauma response
- To discuss the intersections of trauma and grief reactions
- To identify evidence-based approaches to working with individuals suffering from trauma and grief

Case Example 1

Jasmine is a 23-year-old student living in residence at university. Jasmine had been a shy girl in high school and had never dated. While at university Jasmine was raped. She described her experience as follows

> It was January and I was finishing my last year. I lived in a co-op residence. And I had lots of wonderful friends there. And there was this one guy who lived three doors down from me. He was really screwed up, into drugs, alcohol. He was majorly mixed up. And I wanted to help him. And we became friends. We talked a lot. I remember he told me that I looked just like his ex-financée who had dumped him and that he would do anything to hurt her. I thought he meant just emotionally. Well that one night he kept calling me her name, the night he raped me. I don't think he knew it was me. But I'm not excusing him. He was drunk and on cocaine, may not even know what he did. He pounded on my door at two a.m. He needed someone to talk to. . . . No one else around . . . swearing . . . calling me a tease . . . calling every name in the book . . . pinned in a low chair . . . ripped nightgown . . . forced oral sex which I've never done, never wanted to do, and then he raped me. He didn't beat me or anything. The verbal abuse was a horrible violation. I should have screamed, but I didn't. In the past when drinking he got very aggressive with other people. So I thought I better watch it. . . . Afterwards, he left. I went to the

> shower and scrubbed myself for an hour. I just felt so dirty. I hoped someone would come in, but on the other hand I didn't want anyone to. I was convinced it was my fault. That maybe he was right, maybe I was giving off signals. But then I really didn't think I did. And I sort of thought that if I did, then that's his problem. I was really convinced that I should die. That I asked for it. . . . I didn't want to tell my parents because I was worried that they would take me out of there and I didn't want to leave. I was really worried that I was pregnant. What would I do? I was terrified that he would get me again. I saw him every day and he acted like nothing happened. I did tell his best friend, who was also my friend. But he just said I must be wrong. He asked, are you sure it was rape?

As a result of this experience, Jasmine began to have nightmares of being assaulted and became extremely fearful. In addition to locking her dorm room when she was in there, she would wedge a chair in front of the door. She did not like to go out at night and made excuses about her workload to explain why she did not attend parties. She tried to arrange to walk to all classes and the library with friends, which she realized they thought was odd because she had not shared the rape with them. Jasmine felt highly anxious, she had trouble concentrating on her work, and felt tearful and sad all the time. Somehow, however, she managed to complete the year and graduate but with much lower grades than she had achieved in the past.

Case Example 2

In every respect the Brown family appeared to be the perfect family. The two parents and four healthy children, aged 1 year to 8 years of age, engaged in many activities together, including yearly camping trips among the woods and lakes in the North. On one such trip, the family was busy organizing dinner, collecting firewood, and getting water. Each child had a task that they were going about performing. When the family all got back together, however, it was evident that three-year-old James was missing. After a few minutes of frantic searching, Ms Brown went down to the lake and discovered James floating in two feet of water. She screamed for her husband and began performing CPR. They radioed ahead to the Park Station to have an ambulance meet them from a local town and drove at high speed to the station with the other three children jammed into the back. From the onset, however, it was evident that James was not being revived. They met the ambulance who whisked James away to the local small hospital. But the ambulance drivers later admitted that they simply did not want to pronounce him dead on the scene. The Browns returned home to make funeral arrangements for their young child.

The Nature and Prevalence of Trauma Reactions

Trauma has become part of the common lexicon of our society and as a result many commonplace events are referred to as traumatizing and a wide variety of reactions are referred to as traumatic stress. As social workers in mental health, it is important to differentiate between traumatic stress as a clinical diagnosis and other types of stress or crisis reactions; this helps to predict the course of the distress and the interventions that are most likely to result in positive outcomes. In this chapter we are conceptualizing trauma response to fall on a continuum that includes crisis, acute stress, post-traumatic stress, complex post-traumatic stress, and personality disturbance, as shown in Figure 6.1. Personality disturbances are covered in extensive detail in Chapter 12.

Individual response to distressing events is highly varied. Several studies have demonstrated that rates of trauma exposure over the life course is between 60 and 80 per cent but nevertheless, rates of experiencing post-traumatic stress disorder (PTSD) are only 5 to 8 per cent (Ozer and Weiss, 2004; Koenen, 2006; Bonnano et al., 2007). The reported lifetime prevalence for PTSD in the general population of the United States is reported to be 5 per cent for men and 10 per cent for women (Kessler et al., 1995; Resick, 2000) but one study puts lifetime rates as low as 1 per cent (Gore-Felton et al., 1999). A nationally representative study of 512 Israelis who had been directly exposed to a terrorist attack and 191 who had family members exposed demonstrated that while 76.7 per cent had at least one symptom of traumatic stress, only 9.4 per cent met the criteria for PTSD (Bleich, Gelkopf, and Solomon, 2003). A study of Latino primary care patients in the United States revealed that of those who had experienced political violence in their homeland only 18 per cent met the criteria for PTSD (Eisenman et al., 2003). These findings provoked Shalev (2002) to suggest that 'traumatic events' may be more appropriately called 'potentially traumatizing events'. A number of sets of factors combine to help us understand the intensity, nature, and duration of symptoms and responses to stressful or traumatic events. These sets of factors include event factors, individual factors, and environmental support factors.

Event Factors

The first factor is the nature of the event itself. One aspect of this is the *dosage* or *level* of trauma exposure which in many studies has been found to correlate

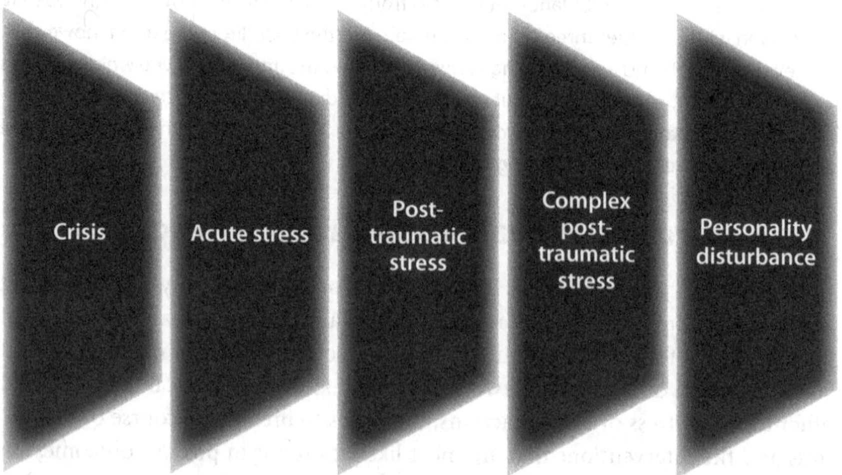

Figure 6.1 Continuum of Trauma Reactions

with the development of post-traumatic distress (Resnick et al., 1992; Mollica et al., 1998; Marmar et al., 1999). For instance, Orcutt, Erickson, and Wolfe (2002) found a relationship between Gulf War veterans who experienced higher levels of combat exposure and high rates of PTSD. Similarly, Mollica and colleagues (1998) found that there was a relationship between the degree of post-traumatic stress and the degree of violent exposure experienced by both Vietnamese and Cambodian survivors of mass violence and torture. Blanchard and colleagues (1995) demonstrated that survivors of motor vehicle accidents had higher levels of trauma symptoms if they had greater injuries or were at greater risk of death. Among emergency responders, Bryant and Harvey (1996) found that volunteer firefighters who were exposed to multiple traumatic events were more likely to report symptoms of traumatic stress. Other authors argue, however, that the dose-effect model is inadequate in explaining post-traumatic stress reactions and that other event-related factors are more important in differentiating the degree of suffering a person experiences after traumatic exposure (Yehuda and McFarlane, 1995; Bowman, 1999; Paris, 1999).

Therefore, it is important to consider other aspects of the event that may influence response, such as the degree to which it is *personalized* to the individual. That is, whether just one person was a victim rather than the event being shared by many others. Further, whether the event was *intentionally* directed at the individual or was a random accident can have an impact on traumatic stress reactions. There is an important difference in the development of trauma symptoms when the event is attributable to human rather than natural causes. Most people believe it is profoundly different to be hit by a rock that fell out of the sky than one that was thrown by another human being (Briere, 2000). An example of these two factors is demonstrated in reactions to sexual assault, which is both highly personalized and intentional. Post-traumatic reactions are common in women who have experienced sexual assault. In one study, 94 per cent of women were found to meet the criteria of PTSD at 1 week post-rape, 65 per cent at 4 weeks post-rape, and 47 per cent at 12 weeks post rape (Rothbaum et al., 1992). Another crucial event factor in trauma response is the *secondary losses* or *stressors* (Brewin, Andrews, and Valentine, 2000; Green et al., 2001; Hobfoll, 2001). For instance, someone encountering a tornado may have lost loved ones, their possessions, and their community, all of which will continue to influence their ability to recover.

Individual Factors

A second set of factors influencing trauma response relate to the person encountering the event. Researchers have highlighted the importance of individual differences in resilience and vulnerability in determining the intensity and duration of trauma-related symptoms (Bowman, 1999; Paris, 1999; Yehuda, 1999). Resilience, or the ability to manage stressful life events effectively, generally results from having previously encountered serious life challenges and having coped successfully (Rutter, 1993; Rutter et al., 1995). Individual vulnerability factors include biological predeterminants (True et al., 1993; Yehuda and McFarlane, 1995), cumulative life stressors (McFarlane, 1988; Mollica et al., 1998), previous mental health problems, and cognitive coping skills (Janik, 1992; Hart, Wearing, and Headley, 1995; Beaton et al., 1997). In addition, early life experiences have an influence on later trauma response. Regehr and colleagues (Regehr and Marziali, 1999; Regehr, Marziali, and Jansen, 1999) conducted research with women who had been raped. In this research, women with positive early life experiences were more able to mobilize adaptive coping mechanisms, thereby diminishing the impact of the sexual assault experience. In contrast, women with disruptive or traumatic early life experiences had negative views of themselves and others, which were reinforced by the rape and subsequently interfered with their ability to activate coping mechanisms. Although vulnerabilities and resilience capacity may not predict the occurrence of acute distress, they may be important in inhibiting its resolution or amelioration of symptoms (Kardiner, 1941). Thus, while the severity of the stressor (or dosage) may be the primary determinant of acute trauma symptoms, prior life experiences and pre-existing personality factors are presumed to be the primary contributors to the development of chronic trauma symptomatology (McFarlane and Yehuda, 1996).

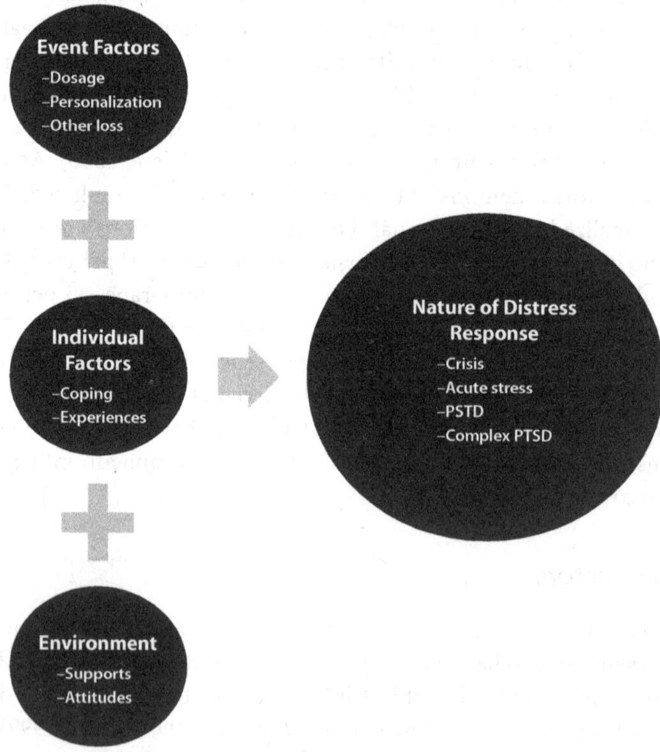

Figure 6.2 Factors Contributing to Distress Response

Environmental Support Factors

A final factor influencing trauma response is the degree of support in the environment. This support includes the individual's personal network, community resources, and the community response to the event. In the case of sexual violence, community attitudes to violence and victims of sexual assault and abuse, court and police response, and the availability of counselling and other supports can have a profound impact on response and recovery (Regehr et al., 2008).

In summary, although many studies have supported the view that the intensity of the trauma has a bearing on the severity and chronicity of trauma symptoms it is becoming increasingly clear that trauma exposure and distress do not have a simple cause and effect relationship. Rather, traumatic events may act as precipitants, the severity of the response to which is determined by individual differences and the environment in which the affected person finds himself or herself (Regehr and Bober, 2005).

Types of Trauma Response

Crisis

A crisis is 'a period of psychological disequilibrium, experienced as a result of a hazardous event or situation that constitutes a significant problem that cannot be remedied by using familiar coping strategies. A crisis occurs when a person faces an obstacle to important life goals that generally seems insurmountable through the use of customary habits and coping patterns' (Roberts, 2000, p. 7). As a result of exposure to crisis-producing events, people may feel a sense of disorganization, confusion, anxiety, shock, disbelief, or helplessness that may increase as usual ways of coping appear ineffective.

There are two primary types of events that can result in a crisis response: 1) situational and 2) developmental. *Situational crises* were first described and documented in 1944 with the early work of Lindemann following a 1942 fire in the Coconut Grove nightclub in Boston in which close to five hundred people died. Lindemann observed and documented the reactions of the survivors, which included somatic responses, behavioural changes, and emotional responses such as grief and guilt. Situational crises are now understood to span a wide range of events including diagnosis of a life-threatening or serious illness, job loss, or divorce and separation. Caplan (1964) built on the work of Lindemann and expanded crisis theory to include the concept of *developmental crises* such as the birth or adoption of a child, adolescence, marriage, and retirement. He suggested that the adaptation required by even expected events can tax an individual's coping resources and lead to crisis response. Crises are commonly viewed to have a number of characteristics that are listed in Box 6.1.

Box 6.1 Characteristics of Crisis

- *They are perceived as sudden.* Even if one anticipates a particular developmental event, when it arrives, the changes that accompany it are perceived as sudden. For instance, although one anticipates the birth of a baby, the changes in sleeping schedules, lifestyle, and relationships within the family feel sudden and unexpected.
- *The individual is not adequately prepared to handle the event and normal coping methods fail.* An event does not become a crisis if the individual has coping strategies that match the situation. The loss of a job can be a crisis for some and an opportunity for those who had been planning to start a small business for some time.
- *Crises are time-limited, lasting one day to four to six weeks.* In general, it is thought that people cannot function at a heightened level of arousal for prolonged periods of time. Thus, individuals work hard to adapt their coping strategies to match the situation and mobilize social supports to assist. Those who are unable to adapt may develop other more serious mental health or emotional problems.
- *Crises have the potential to produce dangerous, self-destructive, or socially unacceptable behaviour.* In times of disequilibrium, people may be so distressed that they feel suicidal. Some may express their distress by lashing out at others and undermining social support networks.
- *There is a feeling of psychological vulnerability that can potentially be an opportunity for growth.* Crises are said to offer both danger and opportunity. Frequently, people emerge from a crisis situation with a greater confidence in their own strengths and abilities and new strategies for life.

Crisis response is considered to occur in stages:

1. The *pre-crisis or equilibrium stage*, where a person is unaware that the crisis is about to occur and is functioning in their customary manner;
2. The *impact phase*, when the event actually occurs;
3. The *crisis phase*, when the person is aware of the event and perceives it as a threat in some way; this phase has two elements: a) confusion and disorganization during which functional level declines and the person experiences symptoms of anxiety, fear, and helplessness; and b) trial and error reorganization during which the person attempts various strategies to improve the situation and manage—some work and some do not;
4. The *resolution phase*, when the person regains control over their emotions and works towards a solution; and
5. The *post-crisis phase*, when the crisis situation has been successfully managed and the person resumes what is now to be their equilibrium.

This new equilibrium may be at the same level of functioning that the person had prior to the crisis. However, the crisis may also cause new learning and new insights to develop and result in a higher level of functioning, or the person may become depleted and now be at a lower level of functioning. This variable outcome has led to the common statement that the Chinese symbol for crisis is made up of two symbols representing challenge and opportunity, although linguists dispute this colloquial belief.

Acute Stress and Post-Traumatic Stress

The experience of psychological trauma in response to exposure to horrific events is a theme that can be found in the earliest of literature. Achilles in Homer's *The Iliad* and Hotspur in Shakespeare's *Henry IV* are frequently cited as excellent portrayals of what we now understand to be traumatic stress reactions following involvement in combat. Psychiatrist Pierre Janet wrote in 1919: 'All famous moralists of olden days drew attention to the ways in which certain happenings would leave indelible and distressing memories—memories to which the sufferer was continually returning, and by which he was tormented by day and by night' (quoted in van der Kolk and van der Hart, 1989, p. 1530). In the late 1800s and early 1900s many physicians began describing reactions to traumatic events in terms of physical responses such as an 'irritable heart' (DaCosta, 1871; Oppenheimer and Rothschild, 1918), post-traumatic spinal cord injuries due to nervous shock and without apparent legions (Page, 1885), and 'neuraesthenia', a physical disorder associated with fear (Mott, 1918); as well, reactions were seen to be psychological, such as 'war neurosis' (MacKenzie, 1920) and 'shell shock' (Southward, 1919).

Two main theories emerged out of this literature. The first was proposed by Freud who suggested the concept of 'anxiety neurosis' or 'hysteria' in which a horrific psychological event leads to physical consequences (Turnbull, 1998). The second suggested that the impact of physical forces on the central nervous system experienced during a traumatic event, such as a rail disaster or combat, resulted in a temporary neurological dysfunction that in turn led to symptoms. However, this interest in the effects of psychological trauma on individuals subsided after the end of the First World War and did not resurface again until the mid-1970s. At that time interest in the effects of war on Vietnam veterans emerged, resulting in the concept of 'post-traumatic stress' and interest in the effects of rape on victims also emerged, resulting in the concept of 'rape trauma syndrome' (Burgess and Holstrum, 1974). Together, the pressures arising from the needs of these two highly divergent groups of sufferers resulted in official recognition of PSTD in the *Diagnostic and Statistical Manual, Third Edition* (*DSM* III) of the American Psychiatric Association in 1980.

Acute stress and *post-traumatic stress* as defined in *DSM* IV TR (APA, 2000) have similar etiologies and symptom patterns. The major difference is that acute stress symptoms occur between two days and four weeks after a traumatic event, whereas in post-traumatic stress, symptoms must last for more than one month. For both acute stress and post-traumatic stress, an individual must be exposed to a traumatic event in which he or she: 1) experienced, witnessed, or was confronted with actual or threatened death or serious injury; and 2) the person's response involved intense fear, helplessness, or horror. Symptoms of both acute stress and post-traumatic stress fall into three clusters. *Re-experiencing symptoms* include intrusive thoughts, nightmares, and feelings as if the event were recurring, and intense psychological and/or physiological distress at exposure to cues that retrigger the event. *Avoidance symptoms* include efforts to avoid thoughts or stimuli that are reminiscent of the event, avoiding people and places that cause distress, inability to recall important aspects of the event, restricted affect, and feelings of detachment. *Arousal symptoms* include difficulty falling or staying asleep, emotional outbursts, difficulty concentrating, hypervigilance, and exaggerated startle response. Biological correlates of these reactions include increased heart rate, skin conductance, and blood pressure (Pole, 2007).

Recent work has focused on the neurobiological effects of trauma related to central nervous system reaction and hypothalamus, suggesting that trauma exposure can alter stress pathways in the brain (Ozer and Weiss, 2004; Galea et al., 2006). As a result of exposure to an experience of fear or danger, individuals undergo neurophysiological changes that enhance the capability for fight or flight (van der Kolk, 1997; Yehuda, 1999). These biological responses generally return to normal levels within a period of hours. In individuals suffering from post-traumatic stress, however, several biological alterations remain; these include an exaggerated startle response that does not diminish, increased activation of the amygdala, a part of the brain involved in processing fear (Antai-Otong, 2007), and reduced size of the hippocampus, a part of the brain involved in learning and memory (Morgan et al., 2001; Lindauer et al., 2006). The hippocampus has a close connection with the hypothalamus, which regulates hormonal activities through the hypothalamic pituitary axis (HPA). The hypothalamus, in turn, releases substances such as corticotropin releasing factor (CRF), which act on the pituitary gland and subsequently target organs such as the adrenal glands that secrete hormones regulating bodily mechanisms. One of the hormones released by the adrenal is called cortisol, the so-called stress hormone. Individuals suffering from post-traumatic stress have demonstrated increased cortisol levels (although not in all studies), which is consistent with the stress hormone hypothesis (Shea et al., 2004). This process is thought to contribute to the experience of arousal and re-experiencing symptoms (Yehuda, 2002). Studies have suggested that failure to modulate the neurobiological stress response in the early stages after traumatic exposure may contribute to the development of chronic post-traumatic stress symptoms.

Complex Post-Traumatic Stress

Judith Lewis Herman in her ground-breaking book *Trauma and Recovery* (1992) identified that the concept of post-traumatic stress was inadequate in describing the reactions of individuals who were survivors of prolonged and extreme trauma and abuse situations. Such situations include survivors of horrific childhood abuse, women in long-term abusive relationships, concentration camp survivors, and prisoners of war. Post-traumatic stress according to the criteria in the *DSM* is attributed to survivors of circumscribed traumatic events, that is, those that have a clear beginning and end. Herman argued that survivors of prolonged abuse develop characteristic personality changes that affect both their sense of identity and their ability to form and sustain interpersonal relationships. As a result, she proposed a new diagnosis called complex post-traumatic stress. Elements of complex post-traumatic stress are as follows:

- *A history of subjection to totalitarian control over a long period of time*;
- *alterations in affect regulation*, including dysphoria, chronic suicidal thoughts, self-injury, explosive anger, and compulsive or extremely inhibited sexuality;
- *Alterations in consciousness* such as dissociative episodes, depersonalization, reliving the experience;
- *Alterations in self-perception* including shame, guilt, self-blame, and a sense of being completely different from others;
- *Alterations in perceptions of the perpetrator*, such as ascribing unrealistic power to the perpetrator, idealizing the perpetrator, or rationalizing the abusive behaviour;
- *Alterations in relations with others*, including isolation and withdrawal, distrust or overtrusting behaviour, and disruption in relationships; and
- *Alterations in systems of meaning* such as loss of faith, hopelessness, and despair (Herman, 1992, p. 121).

Intersections between Grief and Trauma

Grief is an aspect of trauma that has been largely unrecognized in current-day research and training around the issue of trauma and recovery. Two parallel streams have emerged in the professional and academic literature regarding grief and trauma. The grief literature has focused on the process of mourning the loss of a loved one. The theory in this area has concentrated on relational dimensions and bereavement accompanying the experience of detaching from the deceased. Treatments recommended involve remembering the deceased, working through feelings, and attaining a new relationship with the missing loved one. The trauma literature has examined responses to exposure to horrifying and life-threatening events. Theory and research in trauma has long considered both the psychological and physiological dimensions of terror and its aftermath. Distressing memories and physiological reactions are viewed as symptoms of a disorder. Treatment is aimed primarily at symptom management and eradicating intrusive images of the traumatic event. Yet trauma and loss are often not mutually exclusive. People survive accidents that their loved ones do not. Family members are murdered. Children die suddenly. Depending on the suddenness and violence connected with the loss, the sense of justice associated with the loss, and the nature of the relationship between the deceased person and the survivor, people may suffer trauma and loss simultaneously (Regehr and Sussman, 2004).

Because virtually all humans can be expected to experience significant loss at some time in their lives, grief is viewed as a normal, albeit distressing, process. High levels of emotion are experienced, but are viewed as having a clearly defined goal, that is, helping the bereaved to abandon the commitment to the relationship to the deceased (Freud, 1917; 1957). Movement towards resolution is conceptualized to

Table 6.1 Types of Trauma Response

Type	Causes	Time frame	Reactions
Crisis	• Unexpected event that overwhelms the individual's coping ability	• 4 to 6 weeks	• Helpless/overwhelmed • Impaired decision-making • Heightened anxiety • Risk of uncharacteristic or self-destructive behaviour
Acute stress	• Exposure to event involving actual or threatened death or serious injury • Response to event involved intense fear, horror, and helplessness	• Within 2 days to 4 weeks of event	• Numbing/derealization/ depersonalization/amnesia • Intrusion /avoidance/arousal symptoms • Marked disturbance in functioning
Post-traumatic stress	• Exposure to event involving actual or threatened death or serious injury • Response to event involved intense fear, horror, and helplessness	• More than 1 month • Acute <3 months • Chronic >3 months	• Intrusion—nightmares, flashbacks • Avoidance—dissociation, restricted activities • Arousal symptoms—sleeplessness, hypervigilence
Complex post-traumatic stress	• History of prolonged, totalitarian control (POW, severe childhood abuse)	• Indefinite	• Alterations in affect regulation • Alterations in self-perception • Alterations in consciousness • Distorted view of perpetrator • Disturbed relationships • Alterations in systems of meaning
Personality disturbance (see Chapter 12)	• Childhood abuse • Parental neglect • Societal structures that cannot make up for parental pathology	• Indefinite	• Unstable self-image • Impulsivity/self-mutilation • Affective instability (intense anger) • Transient paranoid ideation • Brief psychotic episodes

occur in stages or phases during which individuals complete a series of mourning tasks. One of the inaugural writers in this area was Elisabeth Kübler-Ross who in her famous text *On Death and Dying* (1969) identified five stages of grief: denial, anger, bargaining, depression, and acceptance. Dr Kübler-Ross's conceptualization of loss arose out of her work in Switzerland with terminally ill patients who were anticipating death. It has since been expanded to apply to a wide variety of forms of loss. Central to this stages-of-death-and-grief model, however, is the understanding that grieving and the experience of loss are highly individualized and that not everyone will pass through each stage; that the order in which people experience these stages may vary; and that people can become stuck in any one stage.

- *Denial:* involves a conscious or unconscious process of refusing to accept that the loss has occurred or is about to occur.
- *Anger:* the externalization of grief. People may be angry at the lost loved one for abandoning them (i.e., if he would have taken better care of his health, he would not have died). The anger can also be directed at people who may have saved the person, such as the health care team, at the self for not doing more to help, or at random others who are not involved in the loss at all but are perceived as not fully appreciating the extent of the loss.
- *Bargaining:* typically thought to occur in the anticipation of death whereby a person bargains with God (i.e., I will become a better person if this death does not occur.).
- *Depression:* occurs when the extent of the loss is fully realized by the person.
- *Acceptance:* the time when the person is able to move forward with other life tasks despite the loss (Kübler-Ross, 1969).

Other subsequent authors have suggested other sets of stages related to the grieving process; in general, however, three stages are conceptualized (Regehr and Sussman, 2004). The first stage is described as acute grief and is characterized by numbness, frequent yearning for the deceased, and denial of the permanence or reality of the loss. Although bereavement theorists are hesitant to provide timelines for normal grief patterns, this stage is thought to typically last a number of weeks, generally six to eight (Worden, 1991; Humphrey and Zimpfer, 1996). Once the permanency of the loss becomes a reality, the bereaved is typically thought to experience an extended period of disorganization and despair that can last several months (Schuter and Zisook, 1993). Finally, as the intensity of loss-related emotion begins to subside the bereaved individual enters a phase of re-organization in which he or she must learn to function in an environment without the deceased and come to a new sense of the lost relationship (Bowlby, 1980; Worden, 1991). This stage is still accompanied by elevated emotions; however, the frequency of yearning and crying and the centrality of the loss in the bereaved individual's life begins to diminish. According to many grief theorists the process of normal grieving is expected to last between one to two years and varies depending upon the nature of the relationship between the deceased and the bereaved and the circumstances surrounding the death.

Although grief theory and trauma theory have differing perspectives on the etiology and outcome of tragic events, clearly bereavement and trauma are not mutually exclusive. Prigerson and colleagues (1999) have proposed a diagnosis of *Traumatic Grief*, based on post-traumatic stress criteria. Their model has two central elements: 1) the death of a significant other and that the response to the death involves intrusive, distressing preoccupation with the deceased person such as yearning, longing, or searching; 2) symptoms that include efforts to avoid reminders of the deceased, feelings of purposelessness and futility about the future, a sense of numbness or detachment resulting from the loss, feeling shocked, stunned, or dazed by the loss, difficulty acknowledging the death, feeling that life was empty and unfulfilling without the deceased, a fragmented sense of trust, security, and control, and anger over the death. Empirical evidence confirms that when trauma and loss occur together, subsequent reactions are more prolonged and distressing (Regehr and Sussman, 2004). Therefore, it is necessary to understand what may contribute to traumatic grief. One factor that may lead to traumatic grief is the *enormity* of the event (Stroebe, Schut, and Finkenauer, 2001). That is, how significant this loss was to the person. Green and colleagues, in studying the survivors of the Beverley Hills Supper Club Fire that killed 165 people (Green, Grace, and Gleser, 1985) and the survivors of a dam collapse at Buffalo Creek (Gleser, Green, and Winget, 1981), found that the *closeness of the relationship* with people lost in the disaster predicted similar or higher levels of distress as that of personal life threat. Others suggest that the quality of the bond, ambivalence related to the relationship, or unhealthy attachments are important predictors (Worden, 1991; Field et al., 1999). Similarly, when death is violent, such as due

Source: Regehr and Sussman, 2004, 'Intersections between Grief and Trauma: Towards an Empirically Based Model for Treating Traumatic Grief', *Brief Treatment and Crisis Intervention*, 4(3): 289–309.

Figure 6.3 Intersections between Grief and Trauma

to accident or homicide, bereavement has been found to be more complicated in terms of prolonged symptoms of PTSD and depression (Thompson, Norris, and Ruback, 1998; Kaltman and Bonanno, 2003). Factors that contribute to traumatic grief in individuals who have lost a loved one to murder include not only shock and disbelief, but also a sense of *injustice* regarding community and legal response to the event (Rock, 1998; Armour, 2002). In addition to the cause of death, factors related to perceptions of justice include the age of the deceased, whether or not the death was expected, and the co-occurrence of other losses or stressors. Death of a child, as illustrated in the case example of the Brown family, is uniformly associated with prolonged and complicated grief in parents. In the case of death during disaster, other concurrent losses and disruptions add to the experiences of loss and trauma (Najarian et al., 2001; Norris, Friedman, and Watson, 2002).

Interventions

In the area of trauma and traumatic grief, we must be cautious not to assume that all those who are confronted with a traumatic event or loss will require intervention. As noted earlier, although many people are confronted with potentially traumatizing events, most will not develop PTSD. Similarly, traumatic loss does not predict traumatic grief reactions that require intervention. For instance, in one study, only 16 per cent of those who lost a family member to homicide sought treatment (Freedy et al., 1994). While it may be tempting to attribute this absence of treatment-seeking to negative causes such as denial or avoidance, it may also demonstrate that individuals have a remarkable capacity to deal with the aftermath of tragedy. Thus, interventions following traumatic exposure or loss must be highly sensitive to the needs of clients and respectful of individual coping styles. For instance, denial and avoidance in the early stages after a horrifying or disturbing event may be highly adaptive because they can assist people to contain arousal and intrusion symptoms. In a review conducted by Regehr and Sussman (2004) it appeared that in the case of normal bereavement, denial was equally effective to intervention, suggesting that the reflex response of health care professionals to refer people to bereavement groups after a loss may not be useful to many people. This is not to suggest that social workers cannot be helpful to individuals who encounter loss and trauma, but rather that interventions must be carefully considered.

In considering the evidentiary base of interventions for post-traumatic responses, one of the challenges in conducting research in this area is the degree to which symptoms spontaneously remit. The *DSM* in fact differentiates between acute stress and post-traumatic stress due to the fact that symptoms do tend to diminish on their own after a traumatic event. For instance, as indicated earlier in this chapter, while 94 per cent of rape victims in the study by Rothbaum and colleagues (1992) met the criteria for PTSD at 1 week post-rape, this reduced to 65 per cent at 4 weeks post-rape and 47 per cent at 12 weeks post-rape. Thus, while there are hundreds of original reports describing the effectiveness of treatments for individuals who have been exposed to traumatic events, the vast majority are not empirically based studies (Solomon and Johnson, 2002). The natural diminishing

Table 6.2 Psychosocial Interventions for Trauma

Type of Trauma Response	Interventions
Crisis	*Crisis intervention* (Chapter 5) • Organize issues • Support coping • Reinforce strengths • Aid with decision-making • Assess risk
Acute stress	*Supportive counselling* • Reinforce strengths • Support coping *Psychoeducation* • Information • Normalization *Symptom management with CBT* • Distraction • Avoidance • Relaxation • Exercise
Post-traumatic stress	*Symptom management with CBT* • Relaxation • Thought stopping • Desensitization? *Psychotherapy* • Resuming lost activity/relationships • Meaning-making • Remembering?
Complex post-traumatic stress	*Symptom management with CBT* *interpersonal therapy* (Chapter 8) • Establishing safety • Remembrance and mourning • Reconnection
Personality disturbance	*Symptom management with CBT* *interpersonal therapy or dialectic behaviour therapy* (Chapter 12) • Do no harm (avoid iatrogenic effects) • Reduce chaos, be clear about limits • Avoid prolonged hospitalization • Shift focus away from suicidal or self-destructive behaviour • Focus on here and now—avoid explorations and interpretations of previous life events
Traumatic grief	*Symptom management with CBT* *psychotherapy* • Exploring relationship issues • Problem-solving • Enhancing ability to engage in social relations

of symptoms of PTSD requires that controlled studies be considered when discussing efficacy. While many excellent reviews and meta-analyses exist of the research related to treatment efficacy for traumatized individuals, it is generally acknowledged that only cognitive-behavioural and psychopharmacological methods have been subject to rigorous evaluation with controlled trials (Ehlers and Clark, 2003). Thus, while other models are discussed in this chapter, social workers must be cautious to ensure that clients are experiencing their assistance as helpful.

In the case of crisis or in the early phases following a traumatic event or traumatic loss, crisis intervention is the most common approach because it focuses on assisting people to mobilize their strengths, make decisions, and take action to move forward (see Chapter 5). As symptoms persist, cognitive-behavioural strategies for symptom management and regaining a sense of cognitive control have good empirical evidence to support their use. At later stages psychotherapy, dialectic behaviour therapy (see Chapter 12), or interpersonal therapy (see Chapter 8) can also assist in managing depression and anxiety, integrating the trauma into a sense of self and enhancing the ability to relate to others.

Cognitive-Behavioural Approaches to Symptom Management in Trauma Reponse

A number of reviews of the effectiveness of cognitive-behavioural (CBT) approaches for post-traumatic stress have been conducted which conclude that CBT is effective in reducing the severity of post-traumatic stress symptoms in individuals who have experienced a wide range of traumatic events and in individuals who suffer from both acute and chronic symptoms (Rothbaum and Foa, 1996; Follette, Ruzek, and Abueg, 1998; Harvey, Bryant, and Tarrier, 2003; Bradley et al., 2005; Bisson et al., 2007). Further, CBT has been demonstrated to have superior effects over supportive therapy in the treatment of post-traumatic stress in a number of controlled studies (Bryant et al., 1999).

Cognitive-behavioural therapies come in a variety of forms. Exposure Therapy is based on the notion that the common strategy of avoiding trauma-related memories and cues interferes with emotional processing of the event by reinforcing erroneous cognitions and fears. During imaginal and *in vivo* exposure and recounting the event, individuals are assisted to manage the resulting anxiety and allow distress to habituate. Stress Inoculation Training, based on social learning theory, teaches individuals to manage fear and anxiety through cognitive-behavioural techniques. Cognitive therapy assists individuals to identify trauma-related dysfunctional beliefs that influence response to stimuli and subsequent physiological and psychological distress. Some have provided evidence that exposure therapy in combination with stress inoculation training or cognitive therapy yields the most positive results (Hembree and Foa, 2003); others have provided evidence that inoculation does not necessarily enhance other cognitive methods and provided alone, they are equally effective (Tarrier et al., 1999; Harvey et al., 2003). It is important to note that exposure methods are more selective in the criteria for inclusion, that is, people with personality disturbances, current life crises and self-harm behaviours are often screened out. Thus, it is suggested that this model of treatment should be used only when a sound therapeutic alliance has been formed and a thorough assessment has been completed to ensure that clients have the capacity to manage the increased arousal that occurs during the treatment (Calhoun and Atkeson, 1991). Individuals in this type of treatment group should be assessed to have the capacity to tolerate high anxiety arousal, no active suicidal ideation, no comorbid substance abuse, and most importantly no current life crises (Foy et al., 2000). Thus, if they are equally effective, CBT methods without exposure may yield a lower risk of iatrogenic effects.

Group treatment methods are less clear-cut. One form of group treatment is the single session debriefing model that has been the subject of much controversy regarding efficacy. In general, however, findings suggest that when used with professionals exposed to trauma in the context of their jobs, people find them helpful and supportive, but they do not relieve trauma symptoms and may in fact exacerbate them (Regehr, 2001). When applied to victims of trauma, however, the results are more concerning. Mayou, Ehlers, and Hobbs (2000) randomly assigned road traffic accident victims to psychological debriefing or no treatment groups. At 4 months post-injury, they reported that the psychological debriefing was ineffective and at 3 years, the intervention group remained significantly more symptomatic. They concluded that patients who initially had high intrusion and avoidance symptoms remained symptomatic if they received intervention but recovered if they did not receive intervention. Bisson, Jenkins, Alexander, and Bannister (1997) reported that burn victims who received debriefings had significantly higher rates of anxiety, depression, and PTSD 13 months following their injury than of burn victims who did not. It has been suggested that the exposure elements of this group intervention are responsible for the iatrogenic effects in victims.

Longer-term group models using CBT have more promising results. Foy and colleagues (2000) reviewed six studies of CBT group treatment with trauma survivors (three wait-list control studies and three single-group pretest–post-test studies) and indicate that all showed positive outcomes on PTSD symptom measures. Reported effect sizes ranged from 0.33 to 1.09 with a mean of 0.68. Larger treatment effects were reported for avoidance symptoms than intrusion symptoms.

Therefore, although treatment approaches for resolving trauma that are described in the literature are diverse, there is evidence that cognitive-behavioural methods are effective in symptom reduction. Several different models of CBT exist, some that focus on cognitive restructuring, some that focus on symptom management, and some that focus on exposure to traumatic imagery followed by anxiety management. There is evidence to suggest that each method can be effective; however, there is concern that exposure therapy may increase distress and increase treatment dropout in high-risk groups. Pharmacological treatment for individuals with extremely high levels of distress should also be considered.

While most models of CBT involve a structured process, there are some single CBT-based strategies that can be of assistance to individuals who are attempting to manage symptoms of post-traumatic stress. Structured breathing exercises can be extremely helpful in assisting individuals in reducing autonomic arousal. Social workers can learn these techniques and become proficient enough to teach others through yoga classes or relaxation therapy tapes. Individuals with traumatic stress frequently awaken at night having had a nightmare. When they awaken, their heart is racing, they are sweating, and unable to fall back asleep. People who have this experience will then frequently lie awake for hours with recurrent thoughts of the event circling around in their minds. Social workers can discuss several options for people who experience this. One option is to get up and write down the repetitive thoughts, say them into a tape recorder, or speak to someone at a distress centre. Having expressed the intrusive thoughts or images, they are likely to diminish for the time being. Another option is distraction through watching TV, going for a walk (if it is safe and the person is comfortable), reading a book, or doing some low-impact activity. Once the high-anxiety symptoms are reduced and the thoughts diminished, the person is more likely to be able to return to sleep, although they may need to re-do their regular bedtime routine before going back to bed. A further technique is to assist the person to identify ways to reduce arousal and re-stimulating traumatic response through avoidance of certain places or stimuli (for instance, violent movies). While this may not be a long-term solution, it can assist people to regain a sense of control in the immediate situation. If the fears and thoughts persist beyond the time of acute stress disorder (4 weeks) then other longer-term CBT approaches may be in order.

Approaches to Traumatic Grief

Regehr and Sussman (2004) reviewed the research literature regarding treatments for traumatic loss. From their review, there is evidence that individuals who suffered a traumatic loss and had unresolved relationship issues, may benefit from relationship-oriented therapy; however, not in every case. Murphy and colleagues (1998) studied the effects on parents who had recently lost a child to homicide, suicide, or accident. Identified as a high-risk group, these parents were randomly assigned to a combined emotion-focused and problem-focused group or a no-treatment control. Of note was the trend that mothers starting the intervention with high amounts of grief symptomatology and high levels of distress improved more in the intervention group when compared to the control situation. Conversely, those experiencing low symptomatology were worse off in the intervention than those in the control group, suggesting again that for those with normal grieving, intervention may in fact be iatrogenic, that is, cause an adverse effect. Fathers did not show long-term improvements from the intervention. CBT aimed at cognitive restructuring and symptom management appears to be effective for individuals with traumatic loss (Sireling, Cohen, and Marks, 1988; Brom, Kleber, and Defares, 1989); however, if the treatment includes exposure therapy, some individuals suffering from traumatic loss may experience increased distress (Shear et al., 2001).

The following is a summary of findings related to treatment approaches to traumatic grief (Regehr and Sussman, 2004).

Not all people with traumatic loss require treatment.

- Those with unresolved relationship issues towards the deceased may benefit from relationally based therapy.
- Those with unresolved relationship issues towards others may benefit more from therapy aimed at providing immediate support and problem-solving rather than interpretation and conflict exploration.
- CBT aimed at cognitive restructuring and symptom management appears to be effective for those experiencing distressing intrusion and arousal symptoms.
- Those with traumatic loss may experience increased distress in exposure therapy.

Pharmacological Treatment for Trauma and Grief

Although psychosocial therapies are generally considered the treatment of choice, research demonstrating that traumatic exposure can affect neurotransmitters and hormones has led to the conclusion that medication may be helpful for some individuals (Cooper, Carty, and Creamer, 2005; Stein, Ipser, and Seedat, 2005). Certainly, medications are frequently prescribed for people suffering the after-effects of both trauma and grief. As a result, social workers should be aware of any medications that their clients may be taking. The social worker can discuss the impact these medications may have on the symptoms that the client is experiencing and on treatment with the physician (if they are part of a multidisciplinary team) and encourage the client to discuss this with their physician.

Antidepressants are the most studied and most used treatments for post-traumatic stress and grief (Antai-Otong, 2007). Selective Serotonin Reuptake Inhibitors (SSRIs) (see Chapters 7 and 8 for more discussion) are often used, based on findings of low serotonin metabolites (5HIAA) in cerebrospinal fluid in individuals with post-traumatic stress, particularly those people who have impulsivity problems and repeated episodes of self-harm as a result of complex post-traumatic stress (Schoenfeld, Marmar, and Neylan, 2004; Stein et al., 2005). Several studies have suggested that these medications alleviate intrusion, avoidance, and arousal symptoms. Older antidepressants, such as the tricyclic antidepressants, have been shown to have positive effects especially on symptoms of panic.

Biomedical research has established that post-traumatic stress is likely also associated with increased levels of norepinephrine (noradrenaline) in certain parts of the brain that deal with the emotional pathways (Schoenfeld et al., 2004). This can contribute to experiences of anxiety associated with re-experiencing, hyperarousal, and numbing symptoms. Benzodiazepines (e.g., Valium) are perhaps the most often used and most often requested medications in the treatment of post-traumatic stress as a result of the belief that they will decrease the symptoms of stress and anxiety. Paradoxically, little evidence supports the efficacy of these agents; they carry the risk of abuse and dependency, and have been found to interfere with psychosocial treatments. On the other hand, recent studies have established that beta-adrenergic blockers such as Propranolol can help alleviate the symptoms of hyperarousal, avoidance, and perhaps re-experiencing, in both adults and children. In fact, the administration of adrenergic blockers within hours of the trauma and over the next 10 days can significantly decrease the development of post-traumatic stress as measured after one month.

Possible Social Work Interventions in the Case Examples

Case Example 1: Jasmine

Jasmine is suffering from symptoms of either acute stress or post-traumatic stress (depending on the duration of the symptoms). Social work interventions with someone experiencing the aftermath of this type of horrifying event vary, based on the timing of the intervention.

- In the early stages, the social worker will provide crisis intervention. This will entail assisting to deal with the immediate aftermath and any issues she may have to face, for instance, reporting to police, if this is her choice. The social worker will reinforce her strengths and coping and help her to draw upon appropriate social supports.
- In the days and weeks that follow, the social worker will explore and normalize symptoms that Jasmine is experiencing and assist her to manage her distressing symptoms (intrusion, arousal, and avoidance) through techniques that will help her feel more in control.
- If Jasmine wishes to discuss the rape, the thoughts and images that intrude upon her, or the impact she feels this has had or may continue to have on her life, the social worker will be open to this. However, if Jasmine prefers to cope by avoiding memories and discussions related to the rape, the social worker should respect this.
- If the symptoms persist for longer periods of time, the social worker can discuss treatment alternatives with Jasmine, such as exposure therapy or psychotherapy and then engage in these treatments if the social worker is qualified to do so.

Case Example 2: The Brown Family

The loss of a child frequently leads to profound grief reactions, and witnessing the death of one's child will often lead to traumatic grief.

- Immediately after a death, family members have a great number of practical matters to deal with, at a time when they are often shocked, overwhelmed, and unable to focus. Thus, social work skills in crisis intervention and liaising with various organizations and agents can be an invaluable support. Families must make funeral arrangements, deal with autopsies, death certificates, insurance, and sometimes the police, at the same time as providing supports for surviving children.
- In addition to assisting with resources, managing various systems, and mobilizing social supports, social workers can provide supportive counselling and an opportunity for family members to discuss their horror. This discussion of horror and grief can go on for long periods of time—long after members of their social network are prepared to hear their thoughts. Thus, the social worker's role as a support can be invaluable.

Summary

While response to distressing and horrifying life events has increasingly been categorized as post-traumatic stress disorder by the public and practitioners alike, reactions to these events can take many forms, ranging from crisis response to acute stress disorder, to post-traumatic stress, to complex post-traumatic stress and personality disorder, to traumatic grief. The severity of the response is based on a combination of event factors, individual factors, and the nature of the recovery environment. Intervention approaches must be tailored to the specific needs of the client and their ability to tolerate distress. Although some methods of intervention can be highly effective for some, they can be iatrogenic to others.

Key Terms

Anxiety neurosis
Arousal symptoms
Avoidance symptoms
Cortisol
Crisis
Derealization
Dysphoria
Equilibrium
Iatrogenic
Irritable heart
Neuraesthenia
Post-traumatic stress
Re-experiencing symptoms
Resilience
Secondary losses
Shell shock

Discussion Questions

1. Why can it be important to differentiate between types of traumatic response?
2. How can interventions contribute to increased distress and symptoms in people experiencing trauma?
3. What types of systemic interventions may social workers consider when working with traumatized populations and how may this help ameliorate distress and symptoms?

Suggested Readings and Weblinks

Herman, J. (1992), *Trauma and Recovery* (New York: Basic Books).

Social Workers: Help Starts Here. *Grief and Loss* (accessed at http://www.helpstartshere.org/mind_and_spirit/grief_and_loss/default.html).

Solomon, S.D., and Johnson, D.M. (2002), 'Psychosocial Treatment of Posttraumatic Stress Disorder: A Practice Friendly Review of Outcome Research', *Journal of Clinical Psychology*, *58*(8): 947–59.

van der Kolk, B., McFarlane, A., and Weisaeth, L. (1996), *Traumatic Stress: The Effects of Overwhelming Experience on Mind, Body, and Society* (New York: Guildford Press).

Chapter 7

Schizophrenia and Related Psychotic Illnesses

Objectives:

- To present multiple factors contributing to the development of schizophrenia
- To introduce recent findings regarding the neurobiology of schizophrenia
- To discuss symptoms and challenges associated with schizophrenia
- To describe other forms of psychotic illness
- To present evidence-based psychosocial interventions that promote recovery
- To introduce the psychopharmacological interventions as a part of recovery

Case Example

Tom is a 19-year-old male admitted to the local general hospital psychiatric unit.

He is the third child born to middle-class, first-generation immigrant parents. He was born with the umbilical cord around his neck, although there were no apparent immediate adverse consequences to this. His developmental milestones were mostly age-appropriate and his parents reported that his childhood seemed uneventful, although, compared with his older sisters, he was always quiet and somewhat of an introvert. Tom did not do well at school and his parents, who owned a local car dealership, decided to send him to a private school so that he would get some extra attention. At the age of 15 his family became aware that he was hanging around with a group of local youths and skipping school. His sisters informed his parents that the people with whom he was spending time were 'losers and stoners' who took advantage of Tom and made fun of him. By this time Tom was smoking marijuana regularly and perhaps using other drugs.

When he was 17 Tom was found wandering around a nearby park at 5 o'clock in the morning and the police took him to the local hospital where he was admitted. He was diagnosed as suffering from a 'drug-induced psychosis'. Tom signed himself out of hospital after three days. He also decided to quit school. The following year Tom registered in a course in auto maintenance at the local community college. However, within six weeks he stopped attending class and spent all his time in his room. His parents reported that he became increasingly preoccupied with spaceships and aliens. Recently, his parents became concerned because he was burning pieces of paper in his room, which he said would keep the aliens away. He barricaded the door of his room; it took a local police officer to persuade him to go to the hospital where he was admitted for assessment on an involuntary basis. On admission his speech was difficult to understand because of the severity of his thought disorder. He reported that aliens had been taking thoughts out of his head and had been constantly occupying his room, whispering.

Tom was treated with medication during his admission to hospital and his psychotic symptoms diminished. On discharge, however, he remained highly anxious and was unable to return to school. He was not interested in any follow-up after this admission and stopped taking prescribed medication. He spent most of his time sleeping and lying on the couch at home, refusing social contact. Within a short period of time, his psychotic symptoms returned and Tom was diagnosed as suffering from schizophrenia.

The Nature of Schizophrenia

Schizophrenia is a major mental illness that affects millions of people worldwide. The illness is characterized by two types of symptoms: *positive* psychotic symptoms include thought disorder, hallucinations, delusions, and paranoia; *negative* functioning symptoms include impairment in emotional range, energy, and enjoyment of activities. In order for a diagnosis to be made, the positive symptoms must persist for at least one month and in general result in severe impairment in job and/or social functioning that persists for more than six months. Schizophrenia has a profound impact on those who suffer from it and on others who are close to them. The illness tends to affect many aspects of the individual's functioning, including their ability to relate to others and to integrate into society. Typically, the course of the illness has been viewed to be chronic and the prognosis relatively hopeless.

Indeed, it has been largely in response to characterizations of schizophrenia and its course that the recovery movement and the recovery model described in Chapter 1 have emerged. In support of the premises of the recovery approach and its focus on hope for the future of people with schizophrenia, recent longitudinal studies have suggested that many persons do improve or recover from the illness (Thara, 2004). Although biological factors associated with the illness significantly influence difficulties with functioning, it is the expectations of chronicity and social decline held by mental health professionals, the general public, and ultimately patients and their families that also contribute to the challenges faced by people with this illness (Williams and Collins, 2002). As a result, social workers have critical roles to play in assisting individuals with schizophrenia and others in their lives to overcome these challenges and attain the most positive outcomes possible.

Prevalence and Incidence of Schizophrenia

Epidemiological studies of any illness frequently result in a wide variety of estimates of prevalence and incidence of illnesses. In part this is because of differences in diagnostic practices related to both the variations in the illness and the lack of standardized methods for ensuring consistency. As well, it is partly due to different sampling methods and the degree to which the population selected is truly representative of the larger society. Prevalence is defined as the number of cases present in a thousand people in the general population at a given time or over a defined time period. Meta-analyses of studies conclude that the prevalence of schizophrenia in North America is between 1.4 and 7.2 per thousand. The incidence of schizophrenia, defined as the number of new cases in a population per thousand people arising in a given time period, is generally considered to be between 0.17 and 0.54 per thousand people per annum (Picchioni and Murray, 2007). The reason why the prevalence of schizophrenia is so much higher than the incidence is that this is an illness that generally starts in early adulthood and often becomes chronic. Schizophrenia is responsible for 1.1 per cent of 'total disability adjusted life years' worldwide and 2.8 per cent of the 'years lived with disability' worldwide (Jablensky, 2000). People diagnosed with schizophrenia are estimated to make up about half of all patients in psychiatric hospitals and may occupy as many as one-quarter of the world's hospital beds. In 1996, the total direct cost of schizophrenia in Canada (including health care costs, administrative costs of income assistance plans, value of lost productivity, and incarceration costs attributable to schizophrenia) was estimated to be $2.35 billion. The indirect costs of schizophrenia are estimated to account for another $2 billion yearly (Public Health Agency Canada, 2002).

Schizophrenia is more common in males than females, with a ratio of 1.4 to 1. It is also likely a more serious illness and harder to treat in males. Most experts in the field agree that the prevalence is higher in urban populations and is in fact rising in these populations, while it appears to be decreasing in other populations, such as in rural populations and small towns. Incidence and prevalence are approximately the same throughout the world's developed and developing countries. However, as discussed later in this chapter, the outcomes of the illness may be differential. There are certain exceptions to the universal incidence; for instance, the Hutterites and certain Pacific island populations are reported to have particularly low rates (Jablensky, 2000). These differences may be artificial, however, because it could be that in small homogeneous populations people who do not fit in leave or are driven out, and end up in larger centres, thereby increasing the prevalence in the urban population.

Factors Contributing to the Development of Schizophrenia

As with all mental health problems, the etiology of schizophrenia is far from definitively known. A variety of causes have been posited and investigated, which included genetic predispositions and neurobiology, substance abuse, and family/environmental influences.

Social and Family Influences

The prevalence of schizophrenia in urban centres has been the subject of considerable debate and research. Some researchers have suggested that this may be related to increased environmental stressors and decreased social cohesion. Others suggest that rates in cities are an artifact of the illness, not the cause. Faris and Dunham (1939) noted higher rates of people diagnosed with schizophrenia in urban areas, especially in low socioeconomic groups. They coined the term *social drift* to suggest that people with schizophrenia drift down the socioeconomic ladder to inner-city centres where transient and socially mobile populations exist. Hollingshead and Redlich (1954), in an early body of research that helped to delineate some social factors associated with schizophrenia, discovered that the fathers of those with schizophrenia were likely of a higher socioeconomic group than the clients themselves, suggesting that the clients had 'drifted' down the social scale, probably because of their illness.

In the 1950s it was the trend to look for family problems as the cause of all illnesses. Schizophrenia was no different in this regard and many authors focused on problems in communications within the family and family dynamics as a cause for schizophrenia. This led to the coining of the term *schizophrenigenic mother*, that is, a mother who caused schizophrenia in her offspring, generally by creating *double binds* (Bateson et al., 1956; Sluzki et al., 1967). The double bind is described as a situation where a person is faced with two conflicting demands by someone who has a close and powerful relationship with the individual. The power of the double bind is that the conflicting message is not overt and the consequence of either choice is likely the withdrawal of love. Eventually these concepts led to an entire form of therapy—strategic family therapy—which focused on changing the mother's behaviour and family interactions, thereby curing schizophrenia or at least reducing relapse (Haley, 1976). More recently, however, increased knowledge regarding the biological basis for the disease has discredited this theory as mother-blaming without justification.

Substance Use

A significant risk factor for the development of schizophrenia is early drug use. It has long been known that cocaine, amphetamines, and other hallucinogens may precipitate schizophrenia, especially in vulnerable individuals. There is an emerging literature on the use of cannabis and its effects on the risk of schizophrenia. Recent research suggests that at an individual level, cannabis use increases the risk of schizophrenia twofold. At the population level, it has been estimated that the elimination of cannabis use would reduce the incidence of schizophrenia by 8 per cent (Arseneault et al., 2004). Although this conclusion may not be widely accepted by laypersons who support the use of cannabis, these studies have been replicated and controlled for a number of confounding factors, including the possibility that those developing schizophrenia may use drugs to alleviate its symptoms. Drug use alone does not cause schizophrenia; rather, it interacts with genetic and other risk factors to increase the probability of schizophrenia developing. Co-morbid (or co-occuring) substance use also influences the course of the illness in that those who abuse substances have higher relapse rates, greater numbers of psychotic symptoms, increased violence, increased homelessness, and decreased compliance with treatment (Dixon, 1999).

Biological Factors

While all mental health problems have a complex set of biological, psychological, and social factors that contribute to their development and continuation, some have clearer evidence of a biological basis than others. Recent biological and neurological research has pointed to the important influence of these factors in schizophrenia. This is significant for social workers because it provides an alternative understanding of factors contributing to schizophrenia that moves away from a model that blames the illness either on families and the family environment or on personality traits or deficits in the individual. For example, some of the symptoms associated with schizophrenia can be viewed by others as laziness, lack of motivation, or obstreperousness. Providing families and individuals with information about biological contributors gives them information about potential challenges and allows them to develop a plan towards recovery.

Genetics

Genetic studies, including family studies, adoption studies, twin studies, and now more sophisticated gene-mapping, definitively demonstrate biological contributors to schizophrenia. One method for considering the contribution of genes is to compare the lifetime risk in the general population to that in first-degree relatives of people with schizophrenia. The lifetime risk for schizophrenia in the general population is just below 1 per cent; this risk is increased to 6.5 per cent in first-degree relatives of people with schizophrenia (Kendler et al., 1993). Monozygotic twins who share the same genetic structure have a concordance rate of schizophrenia of approximately 40 per cent (Cardno et al., 1999). It appears that there are multiple genes involved and that each has a small but additive effect. If a person inherits several risk genes, he or she is particularly susceptible to this illness (Owens and Johnstone, 2006). The fact that the concordance rate in monozygotic twins is 40 per cent, but not 100 per cent, suggests that an interaction with the environment is necessary in even the most strongly genetically disposed individuals.

Obstetrical Complications

Another risk factor that is significant in the development of schizophrenia is the presence of obstetrical complications. These complications include hypoxia (being deprived of oxygen), prematurity, and low birth weight. In addition, those born in the winter months are more likely to develop schizophrenia because prenatal maternal infections, often influenza, may cause subtle damage to the developing brain of the fetus (Murray and Castle, 2000). Prenatal rubella, for instance, has been found to be associated with later development of schizophrenia with a ten- to twentyfold increase in risk among those exposed (Brown, 2006). Similarly, prenatal exposure to influenza in the first trimester is associated with a sevenfold increase in risk and a threefold increase in risk in the second trimester.

Neurobiology

Increasingly, the attention regarding the etiology and progression of schizophrenia is focused on neurobiology and neurotransmission. A neuron is a nerve cell that sends and receives electrical signals over long distances within the body. Communication of information between neurons is accomplished by movement of chemicals across a small gap called the synapse. These chemicals, called neurotransmitters, are released from one neuron at the presynaptic nerve terminal. Neurotransmitters then cross the synapse where they may be accepted by the next neuron at a specialized site called a receptor. The action that follows activation of a receptor site may be either excitatory or inhibitory. Neurotransmitters are therefore the intracellular messengers in the body. The quantity of transmitters available may determine a given function of the brain. It is generally considered that some kind of change in the availability of neurotransmitters occurs in schizophrenia. It is not clear whether this change is a cause or a consequence of a structural brain abnormality.

Dopamine is one of the neurotransmitters that has been identified as critical in schizophrenia. The original theory, known as the 'Dopamine Hypothesis' was based on four empirical studies that supported a link between schizophrenia and dopamine activity (Owen and Simpson, 1995). The hypothesis states that the brain of people with schizophrenia produces more dopamine than is the norm. It is this increased dopamine that is believed to be responsible for the symptoms of the disease. The knowledge in this field has exploded, however, and it may be that the original theory is somewhat of an oversimplification. There is much debate in the scientific community as to the exact mechanism by which altered dopamine levels contribute to schizophrenia. Nowadays it is believed that other neurotransmitters, as well as a number of other complicated compounds, such as second messengers, transduction systems, and effector enzymes, all play a role.

Dopamine is secreted by only a small proportion of neurons. However, it seems to have an effect on a large number of neurons. Over the past 50 years it has been noted that drugs that increase dopamine (agonists) or decrease dopamine (antagonists) modulate psychotic symptoms. In particular, the antipsychotic medications block dopamine receptors and decrease psychotic symptoms. Amphetamine, which is a dopamine agonist and therefore increases available dopamine, can induce psychotic symptoms. Positron Emission Tomography (PET) is a nuclear medicine technique that provides a three-dimensional image of the chemical processes in the body. Studies using PET technology studies have generally supported the dopamine theory, demonstrating an increase in dopamine receptors and a decrease in other receptors, such as some serotonin receptors in people who have schizophrenia.

Another way of studying the brain is by measuring brain waves using electroencephalogram (EEG) technology. Sophisticated EEG studies have shown differences in brain-wave activity in people with schizophrenia. This may be related to the finding that people suffering from schizophrenia have an increased rate of eye-movement abnormalities, especially affecting what is known as *smooth pursuit tracking* or the ability to follow an object with one's eyes. Kraepelin (1904), in his careful observations of a number of people with schizophrenia in the late nineteenth century, described a type of attentional abnormality. In a recent trend to look at intellectual impairment in schizophrenia, his observations have been proven remarkably accurate and it is now established that many people with schizophrenia have differences in their ability to concentrate and process information and in their memory. In a fascinating study, Walker and colleagues (1994) looked at home movies of people who were later diagnosed as suffering from schizophrenia and had blind raters compare these persons with controls. The raters could reliably predict those who later developed schizophrenia by minor abnormalities in their movements and socialization, suggesting support for the neurobiological model for understanding the illness.

Recent use of Magnetic Resonance Imaging (MRI) scans, a magnetic imaging technique that produces a three-dimensional image of the structure of the body, has improved upon older evidence, which was based on Computerized Axial Tomography (CAT) scans, a process using a computer to take pictures of the body through 'slices' that can be then put together to gain an accurate picture of what is going on in the body three-dimensionally. MRI studies have demonstrated characteristic findings that may contribute to our understanding of the development of schizophrenia. In particular, there is evidence of increased ventricles or spaces in the brain of those suffering from schizophrenia. This is likely a result of the fact that there is a loss of tissue in the cortex of the brain, especially in certain areas such as medial temporal structures. Post-mortem studies have attempted to clarify these findings. Gliosis is an abnormality of brain neurons that is generally considered a sign of past inflammation caused by infection or other types of brain injury. This abnormality has been found to be common in certain types of cases of schizophrenia, where there are other neurodevelopmental abnormalities. It can also be tentatively concluded from these findings that the process begins in the first or second trimester of pregnancy.

Taking all these findings together, researchers generally consider that a 'neurodevelopmental model' of schizophrenia is the best model available. The theory begins with a number of genes that each exert a small but significant effect on making the individual vulnerable. In the early development of the individual, perhaps as early in some cases as the first trimester of pregnancy, there may be an environmental insult such as an infection, an immune disorder, or a metabolic disorder that affects the brain causing a susceptibility that remains hidden or dormant. In addition there may be brain abnormalities that also remain undiscovered. Later, however, in adolescence or early adulthood various environmental or biological factors may trigger the illness. As a result, people may develop schizophrenia, as in the case example of Tom earlier in this chapter, or may develop other similar mental health problems such as a schizophreniform disorder, which is discussed later on in the chapter.

Course of Illness

As noted earlier, until quite recently schizophrenia was considered fundamentally a chronic condition with progressive deterioration. The traditional view was that there are three phases of schizophrenia: it begins with an early deteriorating course that may last for 5 to 10 years; this is followed by 10 years of a middle phase where the client may be somewhat stabilized but suffers regular relapses, often requiring admission to hospital, and experiences marked impairment in social and occupational functioning; finally, the disease is described as gradually improving over the next 10 years, although with continuing functional deficits. Recent longitudinal research, however, has ameliorated this dire prognosis. Current reviews of longitudinal studies that cover the course of the illness over 5 to 30 years suggest that there is heterogeneity in the outcome of the schizophrenic disorders and that somewhere between 21 and 57 per cent of people with this illness show improvement or recovery (Jobe and Harrow, 2005).

A number of factors are associated with the more positive outcomes of the illness. The time between the first onset of psychotic symptoms and the initiation of treatment, for instance, is directly associated with the response to treatment and outcome. That is, earlier onset and a long duration of untreated psychosis in the initial stages predicts a poor response later on. Early detection and immediate treatment is therefore critical. A number of studies have suggested that intervention in high-risk populations even before the onset of psychotic symptoms could delay or prevent the onset of psychosis (Malla et al., 2005). Other factors associated with more positive outcomes include a previously well-adjusted personality, having close friends, having an acute onset versus a slow and progressive onset, abstaining from drug use, being married, and being female (Jablensky, Schwartz, and Tomov, 1980; Compton et al., 2005; Nordt et al., 2007). Finally, from a recovery perspective, hope and the active engagement of the client in the process of treatment planning, intervention, and recovery lead to more positive outcomes.

Symptoms and Challenges

Schizophrenia is an illness that most commonly presents in early adulthood, especially in first-year university. It is thought that the challenges of adolescence and possibly moving away from home to university represent significant environmental stresses that may precipitate the illness in those who are predisposed. In general, the onset of the first symptoms comes as a complete surprise to family members and it is only in later interviews that the characteristic changes that may have been present as early as childhood are retrospectively confirmed. This time of onset is highly troublesome for those diagnosed and for their families. It appears to all that the young person is on his or her way, having been accepted to university with the opportunity to seek new adventures and make new friends. Parents believe that they have successfully launched their offspring and dream about the future to which their child will aspire. Contact between the parents and child becomes more limited, which is socially appropriate for this life phase, but results in the young person becoming more isolated and in parents being unable to note early changes in behaviour or mood. Often, therefore, early symptoms of the illness are not detected by others. The young person who is beginning to suffer from symptoms is uncertain what is happening. He or she begins to feel highly anxious, which is attributed to the stresses of workload. Concentration is affected, and he or she begins to have sleep disturbances, which may be either the inability to sleep or excessive sleeping. The young person begins to avoid social contact in an effort to contain symptoms. As time progresses he or she begins to have active symptoms of schizophrenia including hallucinations and delusions. In others, the presentation is more insidious, evidencing a gradual change in personality. Sometimes, following an extended period of this insidious onset, the acute phase may suddenly appear, often precipitated by a stressful life event such as the breakup of a relationship, immigration, or moving away from home.

Symptoms of schizophrenia are divided into positive and negative symptoms. Positive symptoms are what has been imposed on the person and include hallucinations, delusions, disorganized thinking, and disorganized behaviour. Negative symptoms are what has been taken away from the person and include flattening of affect, poverty of speech, lack of motivation, lack of interest, and social isolation. (For full descriptions and definitions of these symptoms, see Chapter 4.) The most common presentation of schizophrenia is the onset of auditory hallucinations, often accompanied by bizarre delusions. As discussed in Chapter 4, a hallucination is defined as a sensory perception that has the compelling sense of reality of a true perception but that occurs without external stimulation of the relevant sensory organ. The auditory hallucinations experienced by people with schizophrenia often involve voices that comment on the actions of the person or read his or her thoughts out loud. These voices are experienced as a real perception to the individual and therefore can be quite distressing. The voices are distracting, drowning out other sounds in the world, such as the voices of other people. The voices are preoccupying and the client often searches for the meaning or cause of these troubling symptoms. Sometimes clients act on directives issued by voices, occasionally resulting in violence, especially towards those close to them. This is more of a risk if the hallucination is accompanied by a delusion supporting it.

A delusion is defined as a false belief based on incorrect inferences about external reality that is firmly sustained despite what almost everyone else believes and despite what constitutes incontrovertible and obvious proof or evidence to the contrary (APA, 2000). Characteristic delusions of schizophrenia may involve the belief that the client is being hypnotized or controlled by foreign influences. Another characteristic delusion in schizophrenia is the firmly held belief that someone is putting thoughts in one's head (thought insertion) or taking thoughts out of one's head (thought withdrawal) or broadcasting them out loud (thought broadcasting). Sometimes the delusions are bizarre, involving such things as aliens, space, or the CIA: for instance, the belief that a microchip has been implanted in a tooth and that this serves as a monitoring and controlling device.

In clinical assessment, the form or flow of speech and thought is distinguished from the content. The content of thought may reveal bizarre delusions as indicated above. The rate and flow of speech betrays the cognitive processing of the individual. In some clients with schizophrenia 'derailment' and 'tangentiality' of thought may be observed whereby a person begins with a preliminary idea and then goes off on a tangent. Sometimes sudden ideas or words are inappropriately inserted into a sentence. Sometimes words that are idiosyncratic to the client (neologisms) are used.

The so-called negative symptoms of the illness, which include lack of motivation, lack of volition or will, and a blunting of affective reactivity, are often observed in the longer-term course of the illness. Such symptoms are related to the significant impairment in social functioning that has been recognized as a cardinal problem of schizophrenia. The negative symptoms, with resultant interpersonal deficits, in addition to neurocognitive impairment, are together linked to the poor outcome of this disorder.

Williams and Collins (2002) do an outstanding job of identifying issues experienced by clients with schizophrenia through the use of a qualitative study. A central issue for clients was the manner in which the illness made them feel alienated from their friends and family. In part this stemmed from disagreements in defining the problems that the person was experiencing and, subsequently, disagreements about the need for assistance. This can be intensified if family members or others resort to the use of mental health legislation to force treatment. In part, this issue also stemmed from the inability to connect with others because of impairments caused by symptoms; subsequently, the reactions of others to their moods and behaviour caused clients to feel different. A second issue was the fear of being dependent throughout their lives, particularly on family members. Another was the sense that the person had lost everything that he or she once had, such as income, the ability to pursue education, a sense of competence, and previously held social roles. Finally, the social stigma associated with mental illness is acutely felt by those who suffer from schizophrenia. The view that others have of them further impedes the ability to develop and sustain social networks and supports and leads to discrimination in a wide variety of settings.

Family members also experience significant challenges in dealing with a loved one who suffers from schizophrenia. Muhlbauer (2002) uses a qualitative study to document the experiences of families who have a member with schizophrenia. She describes five phases for families (which are shown in Box 7.1) and uses the imagery of a storm at sea to describe their experiences of distress. Distress experienced by family members is related to a number of issues. For instance, the pessimism and stigma associated with schizophrenia have been found to add to family distress. Further, although the acute psychotic symptoms are without doubt upsetting for families to witness, it is the negative symptoms that are often described as the most difficult to manage for families (Magliano et al., 2005). Families often attribute these negative symptoms, such as lack of ambition or social isolation, as volitional on the part of the client. As a result, families may be highly critical of people with schizophrenia and may try to push them to be more active and engaged.

Although families are significantly affected by schizophrenia across cultures, cultural differences in family-related expectations and interaction patterns may also have an influence (Snowdon, 2007). That is, families from some collectivist cultures are less likely to seek the support of the formal mental health system and are more likely to have their family member with schizophrenia living with them. In addition, the stigma associated with schizophrenia that is pervasive in many societies can be more salient in some cultural contexts (Gong-Guy, Cravens, and Patterson, 1991; Hwang et al., 2008).

Box 7.1 Phases of Family Response to Schizophrenia

Phase	Characteristics
Phase 1 Development of awareness: Storm warnings	• Recognition of the problem • Increased concerns • Escalating but ineffective efforts to obtain assistance
Phase 2 Crisis: Confronting the storm	• Exacerbation of problems beyond the family's ability to control • Abrupt confrontation with the mental health system—problems communicating • Tremendous emotional distress
Phase 3 Cycle of instability and recurrent crises: Adrift on perilous seas	• Instability and recurrent crises • Anger, grief, loss • Searching for explanations and knowledge • Dissatisfaction with mental health system • Stigma
Phase 4 Movement toward stability: Realigning the internal compass	• Finding ways to regain control • Managing feelings of guilt and helplessness • Changing expectations • Struggling with limit setting • Developing symptom-management techniques
Phase 5 Continuum of stability: Mastering navigational skills	• Developing workable care patterns • Refining symptom management • Using support systems

(Muhlbauer, 2002)

Other Related Psychotic Disorders

There are several other psychotic disorders that are within the schizophrenia spectrum and may often be mistaken for schizophrenia. These include delusional disorder, schizophreniform disorder, schizoaffective disorder, and brief psychotic disorder. Each contains some elements associated with schizophrenia, but does not contain all the elements. It is not possible to diagnose schizophrenia definitively at the time a person first presents with symptoms because the diagnosis requires the persistence of positive symptoms for at least one month and continuous signs of the disturbance must persist for at least six months. Thus, usually people with schizophrenia may first be diagnosed as delusional or suffering from a brief psychotic episode and it is unclear whether the symptoms that they experience at that time are one-time-only problems, whether they will recur later, or whether they will develop into a more serious illness such as schizophrenia or a mood disorder.

A social worker's role at this point, therefore, is to educate and instill a sense of hope, but also to discuss the possibility of recurrence and make plans with the client and his or her family should symptoms recur.

The other forms of psychotic illnesses that are related to schizophrenia are as follows:

- *Schizophreniform disorder:* If a person is suffering from delusions accompanied by hallucinations, the initial diagnosis is likely of a schizophreniform disorder. If the total course of the illness continues over six months, then this leads to the diagnosis of schizophrenia.
- *Delusional disorder:* If delusional symptoms are confined to a single theme without other psychotic symptoms, this most likely suggests the diagnosis of a delusional disorder.
- *Schizoaffective disorder:* If the symptoms are occurring at the same time as a severe depression or mania and there is a period of delusions and hallucinations for at least two weeks in the absence of these affective symptoms, then a diagnosis of schizoaffective disorder may be made. Generally speaking, it is considered that this suggests a better prognosis than a diagnosis of schizophrenia.
- *Brief psychotic disorder:* This is defined as the sudden onset of at least one of the previously mentioned psychotic symptoms such as delusions, hallucinations, or disorganized speech or behaviour. In many cases the symptoms appear to be precipitated by a significant life event, such as the breakup of a relationship or the loss of a job. In some cases, however, there is no apparent precipitation. The psychosis is by definition short-lived, lasting at least one day and less than one month.

The Recovery Model and Schizophrenia

The development of the recovery model was precipitated largely by concerns regarding the negative beliefs about prognosis and chronicity that pervaded mental health services concerning schizophrenia—beliefs that spread to clients, families, and the general community. New treatment models led to recent research that refutes the belief that a diagnosis of schizophrenia means that there is no hope of recovery. As well, the recovery model was developed to counteract treatment decisions that were made by members of the interdisciplinary team without the input of the client; in this view, the client's role was to passively accept services rather than be active participants and decision-makers in their treatment and recovery process. The recovery model is a treatment concept where services are offered so that consumers (or clients) have primary control over decisions about their own care, building on their strengths and empowering themselves.

Social workers practising within the recovery model apply the principles of hope and self-determination at all levels of practice when working with people suffering from schizophrenia. At the direct-service level, they help individuals build positive relationships with others, develop meaningful daily activities, find a sense of purpose, and seek to attain personal growth (CMHA, 2008). Specifically, social workers provide individuals and families with information about the challenges associated with the illness and factors that are associated with recovery. They can then help them make informed decisions about their own treatment and recovery plan (Carpenter, 2002). Social workers assist clients to identify their inherent strengths and empower them to build on their capacities. They also connect clients with helpful community resources and support their use.

At the larger-system levels, social workers advocate for funding and develop community-based programs that support recovery. These include educational programs, employment assistance programs, supportive housing programs, and opportunities for social contacts. Social workers can also support the development of client-operated services that offer mutual aid and meaningful employment. The Raging Spoon in Toronto (Raging Spoon, 2008) is such a program. The Raging Spoon was initiated by a group of psychiatric consumer/survivors who came together with the notion of developing a business. The business started out primarily as a café and has now evolved into a large catering business. Over the years, the Raging Spoon has employed approximately 150 different consumer/survivors who might otherwise, without its assistance, have been unable to find steady employment. Finally, social workers can provide public education to address issues of stigma and to promote the concept of recovery.

Psychosocial Interventions That Promote Recovery

Social work interventions generally focus on assisting the individual to deal with the psychological sequelae of the illness, helping the individual create opportunities to improve social functioning and meet life goals, and working with families to optimize their functioning and their ability to provide social supports. The first task in working with clients towards recovery is to develop a trusting working relationship or therapeutic alliance. One of the inherent difficulties in working with individuals with schizophrenia, particularly those with paranoid delusions, is that they have difficulty trusting others or connecting with them. Therefore, development of collaborative relationships between social workers and clients may take extended periods of time and require persistence and flexibility. In addition to the effects of the illness that influence goal-directedness, clients with schizophrenia may be suspicious of the motives of the social worker or other members of the interdisciplinary team and may feel alienated from the treatment plan. As a consequence, they may frequently miss appointments or fail to 'follow through' on agreed-on goals or tasks (Coodin et al., 2004).

The recovery model offers some suggestions for developing a strong working relationship between the social worker and the client. First, the social worker must engage the client and his or her family in what Deegan (1996) refers to as the conspiracy of hope: although some aspects of the illness may seem overwhelming, there is always the opportunity for positive change and growth. Second, the social worker using the recovery model works in full partnership with clients and families developing individualized treatment plans where consumers choose what treatment will be provided, by whom, and when (Farkas et al., 2005). Finally, the recovery model is premised on the belief that a broad set of systems must work together to create opportunities for growth that include integrated services and a broad range of community supports to optimize social, educational, vocational, income, and housing opportunities (Sowers, 2005). Social workers, in their roles as brokers of services and advocates for clients and families, must ensure that services are coordinated. Social workers can engender trust in clients by working towards the success of these goals.

The rest of this section focuses on three evidence-based interventions commonly used by social workers in mental health that are consistent with a recovery model: 1) Assertive Community Treatment Approaches (ACT); 2) psychoeducational interventions with families; and 3) cognitive-behavioural treatment for schizophrenia.

Assertive Community Treatment (ACT)

For several years now there has been a shift away from traditional hospital-based care to community-based alternatives for severely mentally ill individuals. One of the most widely studied of these is Assertive Community Treatment (ACT). The key elements of this treatment approach include a multidisciplinary team that is on call 24 hours a day, *in vivo* treatment (in the person's own environment), and instruction and assistance with basic living skills (LaFave, de Sousa, and Gerber, 1996). This model then provides flexible, individually tailored treatments, linkages among agencies serving the client, and client involvement in service planning (Bachrach, 1993). The ACT approach is based on the belief that all citizens, including those challenged by the most severe and persistent mental illnesses, have a right to live a decent and satisfying life in the community (Test, 2002). Unique aspects of the ACT model are:

- All psychosocial services are provided directly by ACT team members rather than being provided by other organizations and brokered by the team.
- The ACT team is mobile and provides services in the community where the client actually is.
- Services are highly individualized to each client's concerns.
- Staff are available 24 hours per day, 7 days per week.
- Services are not time-limited and continue as long as the client needs and wants them.
- The ACT team works to adapt the environment to the client's needs, rather than requiring the client to adapt to the rules of the program.

The ACT team assists clients to get housing, financial resources, employment, and health and dental care. The ACT team provides supportive counselling, medications, treatment for substance use, education about symptom management, crisis support, and brief hospitalization as required.

Since the initial demonstration study by Stein and Test in 1980, outcome studies of individuals with schizophrenia and other related disorders have demonstrated reduced rates of hospitalization, increased medication compliance, better quality of life, and decreased legal problems (LaFave, de Sousa, and Gerber, 1996). According to a review by Salyers and Tsemberis (2007), despite some changes to the model over the past 30 years, ACT teams have remained effective in their mission of reducing inpatient stay and increasing the likelihood of remaining in the community despite failed economic, social, housing, and mental health policies that have resulted in people with psychiatric disabilities being in disproportionately high numbers in shelters, emergency rooms, jails, and living on the street. Further, they have been very effective in reducing homelessness among people with chronic illness (Nelson, Aubry, and Lafrance, 2007).

It is also important to note that the usefulness of ACT has been established with individuals of racialized groups who suffer from severe and persistent mental illness. A study conducted by Mount Sinai Hospital and Hong Fook Mental Health Association in Toronto identified that the functional impairment of minority clients suffering from schizophrenia is compounded by stressors related to migration and acculturation, language difficulties, socioeconomic disadvantages, inadequate housing, lack of access to services, and discrimination. An ACT team was therefore developed that targeted the Chinese (which represented 46 per cent of the client group), Tamil (20 per cent of the clients), Vietnamese (18 per cent of the clients), Afro-Caribbean (13 per cent of the clients), and other communities. At the one-year follow-up, significant reductions were found in hospitalization rates and severity of symptoms (Yang et al., 2005).

Psychoeducational Family Interventions

A second area of psychosocial treatment is aimed at members of the person with schizophrenia's social support system. As noted earlier, family members and others close to the client experience a wide range of emotions and frustrations as a result of being confronted with the symptoms of the illness, the course of recovery, and a mental health system that all too often does not meet expectations. The theoretical basis for this model of intervention is that families can provide a good buffer for the negative impact of schizophrenia and consequently those individuals with strong social supports tend to see more positive outcomes. In fact, despite common beliefs that mental health clients are isolated and alone, research indicates that more than 60 per cent of consumers of mental health services live with their families, 77 per cent have some ongoing contact with families, and families are often the first to recognize the warning signs of relapse (National Institute of Mental Health, 1991).

Yet, it has been observed that families are frequently managing highly distressing and disruptive behaviour in the ill person with little support or training. The most common approach to assisting others in the client's life is to provide psychoeducational individual and group interventions. These are aimed at educating families about aspects of the illness, teaching family members communication and problem-solving skills to deal with specific psychotic symptoms, and providing support and individual treatment for family members as required (Neill, 1994). Support groups, in particular, have been found to help family members overcome experiences of stigma, reduce feelings of isolation and burden, understand and accept the disease, and enhance problem-solving abilities in such divergent cultures as Croatia (Gruber et al., 2006), China (Chien, Chan, and Thompson, 2006), Sweden (Berglund, Vahlne, and Edman, 2003), and the United Kingdom (Kuipers, 2006).

Although all these resources are important for family members dealing with a person with schizophrenia, an additional issue is raised about the potential for physical risk should the individual become delusional about a family member. Thus, family members must also be taught to identify paranoid delusions, to take delusions seriously, and to develop a safety plan for themselves.

Cognitive-Behavioural Treatment

Contrary to earlier views, new research suggests that various modes of psychotherapy may be helpful in the treatment of schizophrenia and other psychotic disorders. Cognitive-behavioural treatment (CBT) is one model that has been more recently applied to schizophrenia. As discussed in more detail in Chapter 8, CBT is based on the premise that as a result of life experiences, individuals develop a series of complex cognitive structures that affect the processing of information about self and others. Called self-schemas, these cognitive structures are attempts by the individual to organize and summarize his or her own motivations, feelings, and behaviour as well as the motivations, feelings, and behaviour of others. Self-schemas govern how interpersonal information is attended to and perceived, which affects are experienced, and which memories are evoked (Horowitz, 1991). Self-schemas are also likely to be self-confirming in that judgments of others affect interpersonal responses. For instance, if an individual believes others will reject him, he will approach the interaction with anger and hostility, thereby increasing the chance of rejection by others.

This theory has recently been applied to the area of paranoid thinking. Kinderman and Bentall (1996) have suggested that paranoid individuals have discrepancies between their self-perceptions and how they believe their parents perceived them. In Kinderman and Bentall's model, which is substantiated by an emerging body of research, they suggest that persecutory beliefs are a product of cognitive processes that attribute meaning to events and interpersonal encounters in an attempt to maintain a positive view of self. For instance, the individual may believe 'I am not a failure; other people maliciously stop me from succeeding.'

In CBT, a client is taught to examine and then change the attributional processes that lead to emotional upset stemming from their delusions. Chadwick and Trower (1996) suggest a three-stage model of intervention. First, the therapist introduces the cognitive model and challenges the negative self-evaluative belief. Following this, the therapist teaches the client to challenge the negative self-evaluation himself. Finally, the client is taught to rationally challenge the delusion themselves. In an elegant experimental design, Chadwick and Trower demonstrate that delusions can be significantly ameliorated by cognitive intervention. Contrary to prevailing theories that the patient's self-esteem would be destroyed by the challenge to the delusions, because the delusions are seen to bolster self-esteem, in actual fact self-esteem and depression scores seemed to improve during the therapy. These authors caution that specific delusions require specific treatment and this model, although illustrative, cannot be used for all types of delusions.

Hogarty (1997) reports data to suggest that individual therapy combined with medication is beneficial for people with schizophrenia in preventing relapses, increasing adherence to treatment, and increasing social adjustment. Other studies have found that CBT is effective in reducing psychotic symptoms in people with schizophrenia (Dickerson, 2000; Bradshaw, 2003). Of particular interest is that CBT was found in one study to be effective in 50 per cent of medication-resistant psychotic patients (Kuipers et al., 1997). The authors concluded that CBT may well specifically target delusional thinking. From a recovery perspective, cognitive therapy is based on a partnership between the client and the therapist and on working together to empower clients to control self-defeating beliefs and behaviours.

Pharmacological Interventions as Part of Recovery

The biological basis of schizophrenia means that in almost all cases, medication is a primary form of intervention, augmented by psychosocial approaches. The goals of medication are to control acute symptoms of psychosis and to a lesser degree reduce negative symptoms in order to allow the client the opportunity to achieve life goals without constantly fighting the symptoms of the illness. The advent of antipsychotic or neuroleptic medications in the 1950s heralded a marked change to the course of schizophrenia by dramatically and significantly improving the outcome for patients. Whereas early medications were very broad in their span of influence, affecting many parts of the brain and resulting in many side effects, newer medications have benefited from neurological research and are more targeted. Clients in general report increased symptom control and decreased side effects when taking the newer medications compared to those they were prescribed years earlier. Nevertheless, side effects continue to result in discomfort. In addition, clients frequently experience the medication as an abdication of personal control, that is, complying with the demands of others and relying on pharmacology to control their emotions and behaviour (Cohen, 2002). Further, anyone who has tried to comply with a prescription for antibiotics is well aware that adherence to long-term medication regimes is very difficult, particularly for someone suffering from cognitive symptoms.

As indicated in Chapter 1, an important aspect of the recovery model is the realization that medications are only one tool among many used in the recovery process; people can move from *taking* medications to *using* them as part of their recovery process. Therefore, social workers need to be aware of both the benefits and the downsides in order to assist clients in making decisions about taking medication and to support them in maintaining a medication regime.

Acute Phase

competent or not.

In the acute phase of schizophrenia, the goal of medication is to facilitate a reduction in active psychotic symptoms and ensure that the client is not a danger to others or at risk of serious physical impairment to himself. In most cases, clients will be required to consent to medication in this phase; however, in certain circumstances where a client is not competent to consent, medication can be administered without consent (see Chapter 3).

Antipsychotic drugs are divided broadly into two classes, but individual drugs in each class vary considerably (Bezchlibnyk-Butler and Jeffries, 2005). The easiest terms to use in this classification are: 1) the conventional antipsychotics (see Table 7.1); and 2) the second-generation antipsychotics (see Table 7.2).

The conventional antipsychotic are sometimes referred to as neuroleptics. They were first found to have antipsychotic activities in the 1950s, and a number of different drugs have been added to this class since then. Their mode of action is likely related to the ability to block dopamine D2 receptors. It should be noted that it takes a few days or weeks to achieve this.

Table 7.1 Conventional Antipsychotic Medications

Generic name	Trade name	Daily dosage	Pros	Cons
Chlorpromazine	Largactil	75–100 mg	The standard conventional treatment	Risk of extrapyramidal side effects (EPS), tardif dyskinesia (TD)
Haloperidol	Haldol	2–100 mg	High potency	Drowsiness, weight gain
Trifluoperazine	Stelazine	5–40 mg	High potency	Drowsiness, weight gain
Perphenazine	Trilafon	12–65 mg	Medium potency	Drowsiness, weight gain
Pimozide	Orap	2–20 mg	May be specific for delusional disorders	Drowsiness, weight gain
Loxapine	Loxepac	60–100 mg	In-between the 1st and 2nd generation	Moderate side effect profile
Fluphenazine decanoate	Modecate	12.5–100 mg every 2–3 weeks	Injection every 2–4 weeks	Risk of EPS, TD, drowsiness, weight gain
Flupenthixol decanoate	Fluanxol (Inj.)	20–80 mg	Injection every 2–4 weeks	Risk of EPS, TD, less drowsiness, less weight gain

Table 7.2 Second-Generation Antipsychotic Medications

Generic name	Trade name	Daily dosage	Pros	Cons
Risperidone	Risperdal	1–10 mg	Low EPS, low weight gain, low drowsiness, available as long-acting injection	Sexual side effects
Clozapine	Clozaril	300–900 mg	Most effective agent ↓ aggression	Weight gain, seizures, agranulocytosis, drooling
Seroquel	Quetiapine	25–100 mg	↓ Anxiety, depression, well liked by clients	Weight gain, (moderate) drowsiness
Olanzapine	Zyprexa (Zydis)	5–20 mg	↓ Anxiety, depression, well liked by clients	Weight gain
Aripiprazole		10–30 mg	Less weight gain, less EPS/TD	Not yet available in Canada
Ziprasidone	Zeldex	20–160 mg	Less weight gain, less EPS/TD	Not for those with heart problems
Invega	Paliperidone	3–12 mg	Not metabolized in liver, does not interact with other drugs that go through the liver	New to Canada (2008)

One of the major problems of these agents is that dopamine receptors are also found in a pathway in the brain called the nigrostriatal pathway, which is related to neuromuscular control of a number of parts of the body (see Figure 9.1). Therefore, inadvertent effects on this brain pathway often cause troublesome side effects known as extrapyramidal side effects (EPS), which means that these bundles of neurons run outside of (extra) the pyramidal system in the brain. These side effects include acute dystonia, which occurs within hours or days of treatment in about 10 per cent of clients, most particularly young men. Characteristically, people with dystonia have muscle spasms, experienced as cramps in the muscles of the neck, tongue, eyes, or sometimes arms. These cramps are very uncomfortable, distressing, and sometimes frightening. A slightly longer-term effect is referred to as pseudo-Parkinsonism. The client presents with symptoms that mimic Parkinson's disease including a shuffling gait, drooling, tremors, and blank facial expression. Most at risk here are women over the age of 40.

Another troubling side effect is called akathisia. This is a subjective feeling of muscular agitation frequently accompanied by pacing. It is often distressing for the client who sometimes becomes angry and even violent as a result of the symptoms. A number of drugs have been used to treat these troubling side effects. There is no consensus in the field about whether these drugs should be given routinely to prevent side effects or only after the client develops the side effects. The most common anti-side-effect-medication is Benztropine (Cogentin), which may be given by injection in acute circumstances or in tablet form for longer-term use. Unfortunately, the anti-side-effect-medications themselves have significant side effects. Most commonly these include dry mouth, blurred vision, constipation, and sexual dysfunction.

Perhaps the side effect that is the most serious of the conventional antipsychotics is Tardive Dyskinesia (TD). This is a disorder of movement that may occur after chronic treatment with medications. The client presents with various repetitive non-goal-directed movements often involving the mouth and tongue, as well as grimacing. There are also odd movements of the fingers, toes, and limbs. Sometimes they can be so severe as to affect walking, breathing, eating, and talking. This disorder occurs in 20 per cent of clients treated with these medications for more than one year; thereafter, there may be another increase of up to 5 per cent each year. Clients receiving treatment for a long period of time should be continually monitored for the disorder. Sometimes the disorder emerges when medication is decreased or discontinued since the medication appears to mask the disorder to a certain extent. Tardive Dyskinesia tends to be chronic but may spontaneously improve in some clients. Recently, the outlook has improved because second-generation antipsychotics appear to suppress the disorder. There is no doubt that the second-generation antipsychotics are associated with a much lower risk of this serious and troublesome disorder.

Another major disorder that is a side effect of neuroleptic medication, which is uncommon but may lead to death, is called Neuroleptic Malignant Syndrome (NMS). If this syndrome develops it is a medical emergency and the client should be hospitalized. The features include hyperthermia, muscular rigidity, and an increase in pulse and blood pressure. A blood test of a particular enzyme called Creatrine Phosphokinase (CPK) can help diagnose the condition.

The second-generation or atypical antipsychotic medications (see Table 7.2) are characterized by the fact that they show a lesser propensity to cause extrapyramidal or neuromuscular side effects. It is thought that they show a higher ratio of serotonin (5-HT_{2A}) compared with dopamine (D2) blockade. This is referred to as the 5HT/DA ratio. It was originally thought that, as a class, they were more efficacious in treating psychotic symptoms, but recent evidence has questioned this (Lieberman et al., 2005). It has also been suggested that they improve the cognitive function that subsequently improves prognosis, and that they may improve negative symptoms, which are important for social and occupational functioning. Second-generation antipsychotics, and to a certain extent the conventional antipsychotics, also may have antidepressant, anxiolytic (anti-anxiety), and anti-aggressive actions. Clozapine (Clozaril) has been clearly proven to be the most effective antipsychotic and probably the most effective in treating negative symptoms. However, it has a number of troubling side effects. In particular, it causes agranulocytosis in 1 to 2 per cent of treated clients. In this condition, the client does not have white blood cells to resist infections and this can therefore result in death. Therefore, the client needs to have a white blood cell count every week for the first six months of treatment when this side effect is the most common. The use of this drug requires a commitment from the client and the therapist.

Both professional and lay media have recently devoted attention to one troublesome aspect of treatment with antipsychotics, that is, the development of Dysmetabolic Syndrome (Consensus Panel, 2004). This syndrome is characterized by weight gain, accompanied by elevated cholesterol, lipids, and triglycerides, as well as by insulin resistance that may lead to diabetes. Diabetes has been linked with schizophrenia for nearly one hundred years. However, numerous articles have also noted the link between both conventional antipsychotics and latterly with second-generation antipsychotics and diabetes. For this reason, clients should be reminded about diet and exercise and encouraged to follow a healthy lifestyle. The choice of medication should be determined by the risk of diabetes in each client.

Recovery Phase

The goals of treatment in this phase are to minimize the likelihood of relapse and rehabilitate the client into the community. At this stage medication should be reduced to the lowest effective dose to prevent relapse. Clearly, in reviewing the effects and side effects of medication in the preceding section, there are many factors that clients will need to take into account in their decision to remain on medication for a longer period of time. There is a significant body of research that demonstrates that relapse can be decreased from 72 to 23 per cent by remaining on antipsychotic medication. However, this requires a long-term commitment to medication that may be difficult for many clients to consider. For instance, if the client has had two or more acute episodes it is likely that he or she will need maintenance at the lowest effective dose for at least three years and perhaps a lifetime. Some clients who are committed to taking medication but do not wish to do so on a daily basis may consider changing to a long-acting injectable form of medication (see Table 7.2).

Clients who remain on medication for a longer period of time should be encouraged to monitor for weight gain and the possibility of diabetes. Those clients taking Clozapine may need blood tests on a regular basis. The client should be encouraged to go for regular assessments for neurological side effects such as Tardive Dyskinesia. Contingency plans should be made with the client and their family for early intervention in case there is an exacerbation of the illness. The goal would be to take action before an acute episode requiring hospitalization occurred.

Possible Social Work Interventions in the Case Example

Tom has very recently been diagnosed with schizophrenia and as a result he and his family are entering a new life phase that is probably overshadowed by questions and concerns about what this illness may mean for the future. The role of the social worker is critical in their recovery at this stage.

- At the individual level, the social worker will develop a relationship with Tom and explore his understanding of his experiences, his reaction to a diagnosis, his thoughts about medication, life goals prior to his first symptoms, and his current goals. The social worker can work with Tom to develop a treatment and recovery plan that fits with his goals and strengths.
- Similarly, the social worker can meet with Tom's parents to discuss their concerns, answer questions about the illness, and discuss possible treatment options. Tom's parents may need assistance setting realistic expectations. For instance, if Tom is living at home, what are the expectations for his behaviour and/or activities and are these reasonable? On the other hand, Tom's parents should be made aware of opportunities for recovery and growth and factors that can support this outcome.
- As a member of the interdisciplinary team, the social worker can inform the team of aspects of Tom's social environment that may affect his treatment and prognosis. The social worker can also assist Tom by expressing his choices for future treatment.
- At the community level, the social worker can refer and advocate for Tom to gain access to resources (such as disability insurance) and services (such as employment or housing programs). If Tom elects to return to his college program, the social worker can work with the school to ensure that adequate accommodations are made.
- The social worker may also identify that services in their particular community do not meet some of the needs for young people with serious mental illnesses and work to develop new programs for this population.

Summary

Schizophrenia is perhaps one of the most feared mental disorders in part due to its historical reputation as being chronic and untreatable, and in part due to the profound effect that it can have on individuals suffering from the illness and on their families. As indicated in the case example and throughout this chapter, symptoms can be frightening to those with the illness and their loved ones alike. People feel out of control and unable to manage the presentation and course of the illness. Nevertheless, advancing research and treatment methods show great promise and social workers have key roles to play assisting both clients and families to better understand the illness and to discover means for working towards the best possible outcomes. One of the most positive interventions that a social worker can provide is to instill a sense of hope and confidence that this disease can be managed and that improvement and recovery are possible.

Key Terms

Akathisia
Amphetamine
Anxiolytic
Benztropine
Co-morbid
Computerized Axial Tomography (CAT scan)
Concordance
Diathesis
Double bind
Dysmetabolic Syndrome
Dystonia
Gliosis
Insidious
Magnetic Resonance Imaging (MRI)
Meta-analyses
Monozygotic twins
Neurodevelopmental
Neuroleptic
Neuroleptic Malignant Syndrome (NMS)
Neuron
Neurotransmitter
Nigrostriatal pathway
Positron Emission Tomography (PET)
Prognosis
Tardive Dyskinesia

Discussion Questions

1. How may instituting a recovery model change the way in which current mental health treatment programs operate?
2. What impact may social work as a profession have on reducing the stigma related to serious mental illness?
3. How may social workers best help families living with schizophrenia?
4. What approaches could a social worker take to develop a collaborative working relationship with a person suffering from schizophrenia?

Suggested Readings and Weblinks

Canadian Mental Health Association (CMHA) (2008), *Back to Basics: Enhancing Our Capacity to Promote Consumer Participation and Inclusion: Discussion Guide on Recovery* (accessed at http://www.cmha.ca).

Public Health Agency of Canada (2002), *A Report on Mental Illnesses in Canada* (Ottawa: Health Canada) (accessed at http://www.phac-aspc.gc.ca/publicat/miic-mmac/chap_4_e.html).

Social Workers: Help Starts Here. *Schizophrenia: How Social Workers Help* (accessed at http://www.helpstartshere.org/Default.aspx?PageID=520).

Chapter 8

Depression and Mania

Objectives:

- To identify factors contributing to depression and mania
- To present symptoms and challenges associated with depression and mania
- To identify varying types of mood disturbance
- To present evidence-based psychosocial interventions that promote recovery
- To introduce psychopharmacological and other biological interventions as a possible part of recovery

Case Example 1

Jake is a 13-year-old boy who has had a lifelong interest in basketball. He has always enjoyed watching basketball with his father and playing with his father and brothers on their make-shift court on the front driveway. He was very excited to find that his middle school had a basketball team and eagerly anticipated the tryouts. Unfortunately despite his best efforts he did not make the team. On discovering this he felt sad and burst into tears. He could not concentrate on classes that afternoon and walked home so as to avoid having to talk to his schoolmates on public transport. When he got home, he went straight to his room and did not feel like eating. When his father returned from work he went to Jake's room and had a good talk. His father suggested they go out to a movie and for pizza with the family and Jake began to feel better.

Case Example 2

Shanti is a 30-year-old administrative assistant who has felt undervalued and understimulated in her job for some time. She was married for five years and has a two-year-old son. After the birth of their son, Shanti felt that her husband had lost interest in her and one month ago he left her for another woman. She attended her family practitioner's office complaining of general malaise and fatigue, accompanied by frequent indigestion. Her doctor could find no medical cause for her condition and suggested that she seek counselling. Since her husband left she is easily moved to tears and unable to make decisions about what to do next. She cannot envision her life as a single mother. She cannot concentrate at work and has been calling in sick two days a week since this happened.

Case Example 3

Stefan is a 38-year-old married accountant. His father had episodes of severe depression and, although Stefan is not sure of the details, he believes that his grandfather committed suicide. Stefan always felt a little down every winter. He felt that it had been a little bit worse every year. This year his depression was so severe that he could not go to work and reported that he woke up every morning at 4 a.m. and could not get back to sleep. He had no appetite, felt nauseous all the time, and had lost 10 pounds. He complained of feeling worthless and felt guilty about letting his father down and being a failure in life.

Case Example 4

Julie is a 28-year-old social worker who works with the provincial government. Recently she had taken on a lot of new projects but her work had become somewhat eccentric and idiosyncratic. Her colleagues noted her to be overtalkative, and she made off-colour jokes in the office that seemed unusual for her. When her supervisor suggested that her behaviour and general demeanour were out of order, she stormed out of the office and slammed the door. Gradually her behaviour bordered on the uncontrollable and it was suggested she take a leave of absence for a few days to sort herself out. Her supervisor also suggested that she seek psychiatric help. She attended a hospital outpatient department and had a preliminary interview and was asked to return three days later. However, in the meantime she decided to use the money in her RRSP to buy a Porsche Boxter and drive down to Graceland to pay homage to Elvis. A few days later a police officer in the United States contacted the clinic she attended on one occasion in Canada and reported that he had found Julie sleeping in her Porsche by the side of the road, having driven into a ditch. He reported that the interior of the car was a mess since she had bought approximately 250 CDs and many clothes and accessories at a warehouse outlet nearby. Julie suggested he call the mental health team. He reported that he would rather not take her into custody and would like to make arrangements for her to be returned to Canada and hospitalized.

The Nature of Depression and Mania

Perhaps more than any other symptoms in mental health, disturbances in mood are familiar to us all in one form or another. Mood disturbances span all age groups, all cultures, and extend as far back as recorded history. Hippocrates first described melancholia (now known as depression) as being related to the secretion of black bile because of the influence of the planet Saturn. Early English texts such as *The Anatomy of Melancholy* written by Richard Burton in 1621 contributed to European concepts of depression (Akiskal, 2004). In 1904, Kraepelin described manic-depressive illness, which he distinguished from both schizophrenia and depression, precipitated by situational misfortune. He believed that manic-depressive illness was hereditary and was caused by altered physiological functioning as opposed to situational depression, which was caused by a particular event or misfortune (Ingram, Scott, and Siegel, 1999). This is remarkably similar to current understanding.

Mood disturbances, and in particular a depressed mood, are on the surface, easily understood by everyone. However, in reality the spectrum of mood disorders is much more complex. The term *depression* is used widely by the general public and colloquially encompasses a range of experiences from the transient low mood that sometimes accompanies distressing events, such as in the case example of Jake, to an adjustment disorder with depressed mood that may follow events such as marital separation or bereavement, such as in the case of Shanti, to chronic depressive illness, such as in the case of Stefan. In addition, the spectrum of mood disturbances includes mania, as demonstrated by the case of Julie, which fluctuates with depression in some mental health problems such as bipolar disorder. Mental health researchers and writers have attempted to distinguish these different types of experiences. Although there are many ways to conceptualize mood disturbances, the *Diagnostic and Statistical Manual* (DSM) (APA, 2000) suggests the following typologies:

- *Major depression:* the presence of one or more major depressive episodes without a history of manic, mixed, or hypomanic episodes.
- *Adjustment disorder with depressed mood:* the presence of significant symptoms of depression that are reactive to identifiable psychosocial stressors; the symptoms develop within three months of exposure to the stressor.
- *Dysthymia:* a depressed mood that is not as severe as a major depressive episode but extends over a period of at least two years.
- *Bipolar I disorder:* the presence of one or more manic episodes usually accompanied by major depressive episodes. Mania can be described as excitement manifested by physical or mental hyperactivity, disorganized behaviour, and elevation of mood.
- *Bipolar II disorder:* characteristic major depressive episodes punctuated by at least one *hypo*manic episode. Hypomana is a less severe form of mania that does not cause significant distress or impair one's work, family, or social life.
- *Cyclothymia:* a disorder in which there is a period of at least two years with numerous periods of depressed mood alternating with periods of hypomanic symptoms.

Incidence and Prevalence

Canadian studies looking at lifetime incidence of major depression have found that 7.9 to 8.6 per cent of adults over 18 years of age and living in the community met the criteria for a diagnosis of major depression at some time in their lives, and between 3 and 6 per cent of adults will experience dysthymia during their lifetime (Public Health Agency Canada, 2002). Adolescents are a particularly high-risk group for depression, with one random community sample suggesting that 18.4 per cent of adolescents experienced at least one episode of recurrent depression (Fergusson, Boden, and Horwood, 2007). The quoted lifetime prevalence of bipolar disorder in Canada is 2.2 per cent, which is consistent with studies from other parts of the world that show an approximately 2.4 to 2.8 per cent lifetime prevalence (Rihmer and Angst, 2005; Eaton et al., 2007).

Epidemiological studies suggest that incidence rates of depression and bipolar disorder are relatively consistent throughout the world, although there is a tendency for Western nations to have higher rates than nations in East Asia. This is believed to be due to cultural/environmental differences including psychosocial stresses, consumption of alcohol and drugs, and perhaps family cohesion. Within the United States there are mixed findings related to racial differences in incidence rates for depression, with most large studies showing higher rates among Hispanic individuals than Black, Asian, and Caucasian people, although other research suggests that the highest rates are among Caucasians (Lara-Cinisomo and Griffin, 2007). There is a greater prevalence of mood disturbances in urban areas than in rural areas (Rihmer and Angst, 2005). Although the causes of regional differences are not clear, they may be related to stresses in the environment, availability of social supports, or as was postulated in Chapter 7 on schizophrenia, social drift. Women are consistently found to have higher rates of depression than men, whereas bipolar disorder occurs in approximately equal rates in men and women (Eaton et al., 2007; Fergusson, Boden, and Horwood, 2007). The age of onset for depressive disorders is at its peak between the ages of 30 and 35. The average age of onset for bipolar disorder is approximately 10 years earlier (between 20 and 25 years). The onset of both depression and mania are often associated with adverse life events or substance use. Of particular note is the period immediately following childbirth, which is a time of high risk for the onset of both depression and bipolar disorder.

Factors Contributing to Disturbances in Mood

As with other mental health problems, disturbances of mood occur as a result of a complex mix of social/environmental and biological factors. At times, the causation may appear to be primarily related to social/environmental events, perhaps in cases of adjustment disorder with depressed mood. At other times, biological factors may be predominant, such as in bipolar disorder. In most situations, however, the social/environmental and biological factors are intertwined. For instance, seasonal changes can have an influence on mood, yet some individuals are more susceptible than others.

Social and Environmental Factors

Social Stressors

Depression is highly influenced by the social determinants of health described in Chapter 2. One of these determinants is healthy child development. There is strong support in the research that adverse childhood experiences such as physical and sexual abuse predispose the person to later depression. It has also been noted that critical and disapproving parents may promote negative self-evaluations making an individual more vulnerable to depression in later life. In addition, research has demonstrated that the loss of a mother in childhood, especially for a female child, is a strong predictor of later depression (Brown and Harris, 1978). Other social determinants of health include social support, social environments, and employment and educational environments. Life challenges, particularly those that involve loss, such as interpersonal loss, job loss, or a marital separation, may precipitate depression in vulnerable individuals, but notably not all individuals (Ingram, Scott, and Siegel, 1999). There does appear to be a weak correlation between the rate of mood disturbances and social class, with the lower socioeconomic groups and those who are unemployed experiencing higher rates of depression. Being unemployed, being of lower socioeconomic status, and living alone are strong risk factors for depression (Fergusson, Boden, and Horwood, 2007). Lara-Cinisomo and Griffin (2007) demonstrated that in the United States, white, single mothers with no education were particularly at risk of depression especially if they had only adolescent children at home. The authors of this study suggested that this particular group of women had fewer protective factors, including larger extended families that could provide social support. A much earlier study also demonstrated risk more generally in women who were home with children. Brown and Harris demonstrated that women with three young children at home had increased rates of depression when compared with the general population. Thus, the social/environmental contributors to depression in particular are well documented and important for the consideration of social workers.

Seasonality

Seasonal influences on mood have been well established in the research literature. Epidemiological studies demonstrate that about 90 per cent of people report some seasonal influence on mood, social activity, appetite, weight gain, or energy level. About one-third of those reporting these alterations indicate that they experience seasonal changes as problematic (Oyane et al., 2007). For instance, rates of depression increase during the months of November through March. It is unclear whether a seasonal pattern is more common in depression or bipolar disorder; however, within bipolar disorder, seasonal variations appear to be more common in *Bipolar II* (depression alternating with hypomania) than *Bipolar I* (depression alternating with mania) (APA, 2000). The seasonal pattern of mood disorders was initially described and named *Seasonal Affective Disorder* by Rosenthal and colleagues in 1984. Subsequently, Kasper and colleagues (1989) identified symptoms that occurred at a lower level and termed this *Sub-Syndromal Seasonal Affective Disorder*.

The seasonal pattern of mood disturbance is so well established at this point that it has been included as one pattern of mood disturbance in the *DSM*. The incidence of a seasonal pattern seems to vary with latitude; that is, it is more common the further one gets from the equator. Depression is more common in northern latitudes in both the United States and Europe. There is also some evidence that there is a higher prevalence of mania the closer one lives to the equator. Women have a higher rate of seasonal patterns related to mood, and younger people appear to be at higher risk of winter depression than older people (APA, 2000).

Substance Abuse

Abuse of drugs and alcohol as well as a variety of medications may contribute to both depression and mania. Shaffer and colleagues (2006), for instance, noted an increase in the probability of depression of 2.04 in their observational work with substance abusers. Depression is commonly noted in individuals who seek treatment for cocaine with an estimated co-occurrence of 33 to 53 per cent. As many as 75 per cent of individuals who are dependent on opiates have co-occurring depression. Estimates of the co-occurrence of alcoholism and depression are less specific and range from 15 to 67 per cent (McDowell and Clodfelter, 2001). Among people with bipolar disorder, rates of alcohol abuse range from 21.4 to 54.5 per cent depending on the age of the sample (Oswald et al., 2007).

Biological Factors

Genetics

Studies that investigate the incidence of mental health problems within families have demonstrated an increased risk of major depression and bipolar disorder in relatives of those suffering from mood disturbances. For instance, first-degree relatives of those with bipolar disorder have a sevenfold increased risk of developing bipolar disorder than the general population. Family studies do not, however, differentiate between the contribution of genetics in the development of any mental health problem and the contribution of environmental factors, since family members share many environmental factors. One way of differentiating this is to compare the rate of an illness in monozygotic twins (who have identical genes) to the rates in dizygotic twins (who have only a proportion of their genes in common). In the case of depression and bipolar disorder, monozygotic twins demonstrate a 60 to 90 per cent concordance (Kelsoe, 2005). The comparable concordance rate in dizygotic twins is 12 to 35 per cent. While this indicates a significant genetic component to the development of the disease, it should be noted that there is not 100 per cent concordance even in monozygotic twins, suggesting that environmental and developmental factors have some part to play.

A more sophisticated way of looking at the influence of genetics on the development of any mental health problem is by attempting to isolate specific genes. One possibility is that the transmission is through an autosomal dominant gene. That is, in a chromosomal pair, one gene contains the illness and one gene does not, resulting in a 50 per cent chance of passing on the illness. A second possibility is that there are multiple genes that all exert an effect, suggesting a multifactorial effect. A number of studies have used the very sophisticated methods of genomewide scans in families that have at least one member with bipolar disorder (Detera-Wadleigh et al., 2007; Nwulia et al., 2007; Vonk et al., 2007). These studies support the hypothesis that a number of genes contribute to an inherited vulnerability to a bipolar disorder. Although it has no practical value as yet, this could be helpful information for the early detection of vulnerabilities to mood disturbances and thus lead to preventative interventions that focus on social and environmental influences in higher-risk individuals.

Neurobiology

As in the case of schizophrenia discussed in Chapter 7, neurotransmitters have been a focus of research related to depression and bipolar disorder. There is considerable evidence that drugs that decrease the monoamine neurotransmitters (specifically noradrenaline, serotonin, and dopamine), tend to cause depression and those that increase the monoamines tend to cause manic-like states. Magnetic Resonance Imaging (MRI) has allowed researchers to visually identify these processes. Specifically, MRIs have demonstrated that there is a decrease in the activity of monoamine neurotransmitters in people suffering from depression that remits when they are treated with antidepressant medications (Schaefer et al., 2006). Similarly, there is an increase in the activity of the monoamine neurotransmitters particularly in the orbitofrontal cortex in people with mania (Stahl, 2008)(see Figure 9.1). Position emission tomography (PET) studies have identified abnormalities in anterior and frontal brain structures in individuals with mood disorders, particularly those areas related to the regulation of emotion (Fitzgerald et al., 2006; Hajek et al., 2007). These studies are complemented by neuropsychological testing that has demonstrated disturbances in cognitive functioning and performance in bipolar sufferers (Mur et al., 2007). Some studies have suggested that obstetrical complications may have neurological implications that are subsequently related to depression and bipolar disorder. Although this view has been widely accepted, a recent systematic review has questioned the strength of the evidence (Scott et al., 2006).

Hormones

Hormones appear to have a significant impact on both mania and depression. For instance, a significant body of research has found increased concentrations of cortisol (known as the stress hormone) and the cortisol releasing factor (CRH) in the cerebrospinal fluid, the saliva, and the blood of depressed people (Belmaker and Agam, 2008). This then supports the association between depression and increased stress in the environment. Thyroid hormones are also implicated in depression. Hypothyroidism, or low levels of thyroid hormone (thyroxin), can cause a depressive-like syndrome and is also sometimes found in depression. On the other hand, hyperthyroidism, or high levels of thyroxin, can cause manic-like symptoms.

Combining Social/Environmental and Biological Factors

Consistent with the multiple influences model of assessment described in Figure 4.1, the development of mood disturbances does seem to be a complex interaction between biological vulnerabilities, social/environmental stressors, and personality (including coping styles). A person may inherit a biological vulnerability to either depression or bipolar disorder. Adverse childhood experiences, including neglect and abuse, may increase vulnerabilities. Environmental factors such as poverty, unemployment, or unsafe living conditions create stress and may tax coping skills. If substance abuse is used as a coping mechanism, the risk of mood disturbances increases dramatically. Finally, negative life events, particularly if there are multiple life events, especially including job loss, bereavement, and marital separation, can act as precipitants to depression or mania.

Post-Partum Depression

Post-partum depression is perhaps the best example of the interaction between biological and social factors in the development of depression. Although depression can affect any person at any time in their life, the post-partum period represents a time of particular risk. During the first two weeks after the birth of a child, between 50 and 80 per cent of women experience some degree of depressed mood often referred to as the 'baby blues' (Abrams and Curran, 2007). This is relatively short-lived, lasting three to five days and is characterized by crying, emotional mood swings, and feelings of anxiety and being overwhelmed. In approximately 10 to 13 per cent of women these blues develop into non-psychotic post-partum depression, although rates in low-income urban women can be as high as 26 per cent (Bledsoe and Grote, 2006). Most of these cases go undetected by health care providers and many go unidentified by the mothers themselves. However, post-partum depression has long-lasting harmful effects on infant and child well-being. In addition, depression occurring during pregnancy, which is reported in 13.5 per cent of women, is linked to dysregulation of hypothalamic–pituitary–adrenal functioning in the fetus, low birth weight, and prematurity. Post-partum psychosis, which is generally considered a major depressive episode with psychotic features or bipolar affective disorder, is rarer, affecting less than 1 per cent of women who give birth.

Risk factors for the development of post-partum depression are: 1) problems with spouse or partner; 2) other stressful negative life events, such as adverse housing conditions; 3) low levels of social support; 4) previous personal psychopathology; and 5) family history of bipolar disorder (Grote and Bledsoe, 2007). Hormonal shifts immediately post-partum involving estrogen, progesterone, and cortisol are likely also implicated.

Course and Symptoms of Depression and Mania

As we have noted throughout this chapter, mood disturbances cover a range of specific mental health problems, each with its own set of symptoms, course, and challenges. For the sake of simplicity, these can be divided into the depression (Unipolar) spectrum of disturbances and the bipolar spectrum of disturbances.

Depressive Spectrum Disturbances

Depressive spectrum disturbances are outlined in Table 8.1. In Case Example 1 earlier in this chapter, Jake experiences something that all of us encounter at one time or another. His experience could be described as a wave of depressive affect,

Table 8.1 Depressive Spectrum Disturbances

Type	Time frame	Symptoms
Dysthymia	Occurs more days than not for at least 2 years; no more than 2 months without symptoms	• Poor appetite • Insomnia • Low energy or fatigue • Low self-esteem • Poor concentration • Feelings of hopelessness • No major depression
Adjustment disorder with depressed mood	Occurs within 3 months of identifiable stressful event but does not last more than 6 months	• Marked distress beyond what others might experience if confronted with the same event • Significant impairment of social or occupational functioning • Some but not all criteria for major depressive disorder
Major depressive disorder • Can be single major depressive episode or recurrent • In severe cases may include psychotic features	At least 5 symptoms occurring for at least 2 weeks	• Depressed mood for most of the day, nearly every day • Markedly diminished interest in all activities • Significant weight loss or decrease in appetite • Insomnia or hypersomnia • Psychomotor retardation or agitation • Fatigue or loss of energy nearly every day • Feelings of worthlessness • Diminished ability to concentrate • Recurrent thoughts of death

generally defined as the prevailing mood in response to a specific situation. If the depressed mood related to a specific situation continues for more than two weeks and is associated with biological changes such as waking up early, loss of appetite and weight loss, and especially a slowing down of bodily functions, perhaps accompanied by uncharacteristic pessimism and a breakdown of usual coping strategies, then we could describe the experience as *adjustment disorder with depressed mood*. This is often accompanied by lowered self-esteem and self-criticism leading to helplessness (Parker, 2000). Adjustment disorder with depressed mood is illustrated in Case Example 2, the case of Shanti. Adjustment disorder with depressed mood represents a severe form of crisis response (described in Chapter 6) although similar events are likely to provoke the reaction. In adjustment disorder with depressed mood, individuals are more impaired and sadness and lack of ability to envision the future are characteristic features.

A more severe form of depression takes the guise of *melancholia*, a two-thousand-year-old term that many people believe is the core symptom of a *major depressive disorder*. This is illustrated in Case Example 3. The most significant characteristic is a distinct quality of mood, often described as a 'fog' or a feeling of 'being smothered' or as Winston Churchill described it, the 'black dog'. The person experiences pervasive hopelessness and an inability to see life beyond this fog. As a result, suicidal thoughts are common and suicide risk is high. Some serious depressive conditions are accompanied by the presence of psychotic features, characterized by delusions and, more rarely, hallucinations. Usually these are described as mood-congruent, that is, abnormal beliefs or perceptions related to a depressed mood; but occasionally they are mood-incongruent and often include delusions of guilt, delusions of being deserving of punishment, and somatic delusions.

Another type of depressive spectrum disorder is *dysthymic disorder*. It is characterized by mild depression, for more days than not, over a period of at least two years. Individuals have a number of additional symptoms such as appetite and sleep disturbance, low self-esteem, and hopelessness, suggesting that this is a chronic low-grade version of major depression. In this situation, the person feels generally sad and unmotivated for long periods of time. As might be imagined, this has a profound effect on personal relationships and achievement of life goals.

Bipolar Spectrum Disturbances

Bipolar mood disturbances include the presence of mania, hypomania, or mania with psychotic features in addition to periods of depression (see Table 8.2). Mania is perhaps the most characteristic of psychiatric disorders and is often easily diagnosed by a characteristic elevated or irritable mood, grandiosity, increased talkativeness, and disinhibition. If an individual suffers one or more manic episodes, usually accompanied by major depressive episodes, then the diagnosis of Bipolar I disorder is made. Bipolar II disorder is a more difficult diagnosis. It is often seen in an individual who suffered from recurrent major depressive episodes and only on careful history taking and observation is at least one hypomanic episode noted, leading to the diagnosis. A more moderate form of this disorder is cyclothymia. Cyclothymia is a chronic, fluctuating mood disturbance that involves numerous periods of depressive symptoms (which do not meet the criteria for major depressive episode) and hypomanic symptoms (which do not meet the criteria for mania).

Mania generally begins with elevated mood and increased energy. People entering a manic phase feel wonderful. They are happy, productive, more creative, their need for sleep is diminished, their self-esteem is raised, and their sexual interest is elevated. It is this phase that may explain the high incidence of reported bipolar disorder in famous creative people throughout history—Charles Dickens, Ernest Hemingway, Abby Hoffman, Edgar Allan Poe, Virginia Wolfe, and Vincent van Gogh. In Canada, Margaret Trudeau, wife of former Prime Minister Pierre Trudeau, has publicly stated that she has been diagnosed with bipolar disorder.

Table 8.2 Bipolar Spectrum Disturbances

Type	Time frame	Hypomanic/manic symptoms
Cyclothymia	At least 2 years of periods of numerous hypomanic symptoms and periods of numerous depressive symptoms; no more than 2 months without symptoms	• Elevated, expansive, or irritable mood • Inflated self-esteem • Decreased need for sleep • More talkative • Racing thoughts • Distractability • Increased activity • Excessive involvement in pleasurable activities
Bipolar I disorder	The occurrence of one or more manic episodes (lasting at least one week) often alternating with major depressive episodes	• Abnormally and persistently elevated, expansive, or irritable mood • Inflated self-esteem and grandiosity • Decreased need for sleep (less than 3 hours) • Racing thoughts • Distractability • Increased activity • Excessive involvement in pleasurable activities • Marked impairment in functioning • Psychotic features
Bipolar II disorder	One or more major depressive episode accompanied by at least one hypomanic episode	• See Cyclothymia

Unfortunately for people suffering from bipolar disorder, the initial stage of euphoria does not last and sufferers move into a manic stage. *Mania* is the Greek word for madness. It is derived from *mainomai*, which means 'to rage' or 'be furious'. In a manic phase people experience euphoria and indiscriminate enthusiasm. Their self-esteem is significantly elevated and often includes grandiose delusions about their power or even about who they are. For instance, people may believe that they are the monarchy or a deity. People in this phase do not sleep and often engage in excessive sexual activity with multiple partners. Their thoughts race, their speech is pressured, and their activity becomes increasingly erratic. It is not uncommon that as a result of the confidence and enthusiasm experienced in this state a person enters into business deals that later collapse, or spends all the money they've been saving for years. Family members can frequently identify early warning signs that a person is entering a manic phase. However, as a result of the wonderful way the affected person feels, he or she is unlikely to agree to mental health treatment. Commonly, it is only when the mania gets out of control that hospitalization and treatment occur. It is estimated that 75 per cent of individuals with bipolar disorder will relapse within 5 years of a manic episode. The risk of suicide is 15 times higher in people with bipolar disorder than in the general population (Rouget and Aubry, 2007).

The Recovery Model and Mood Disturbances

The recovery model has important relevance for individuals suffering from depression and bipolar illness due to the intersection of biological and social/environmental factors. Although a person may have a biological predisposition to develop a mood disturbance in response to stress, by managing the contributing social and environmental factors episodes of depression or mania can be avoided and the effects of the illness can be mitigated.

With a strong collaborative relationship and full knowledge of stressors, supports, and treatments, the client and social worker can develop a plan for treatment and recovery. Since the course of major depression and bipolar disorder is often long-term and intermittent, this collaborative relationship may continue for a prolonged period of time with breaks and changes along the way. There will be times when the client with depression appears to lack motivation or insight. At these times the social worker will need to draw on knowledge of the strengths and abilities that the client demonstrates when well and use this information to empower them and engender hope for the future. Similarly, as a client with bipolar disorder enters a new episode of mania, a strong collaborative alliance can help them make decisions in their best interest for the long term. Ongoing education regarding practices to promote stabilization, reduce stress, and avoid situations that may contribute to depression and mania is important. Education directed towards family members and others in the client's network may also be helpful at all phases of the illness. Further, the social worker is ideally suited to liaise with other members of the interdisciplinary team.

Treatment approaches for depression include psychosocial intervention alone, psychosocial intervention plus pharmacotherapy, or, in the case of severe depressive episodes, the adjunctive use of antipsychotic medication and possibly Electroconvulsive Therapy (ECT). In general, psychosocial approaches alone are recommended in the initial stages or for more mild forms of depression. Here the focus is on the client understanding the intrapsychic, social, and/or environmental issues that affect their mood and working to change these factors. Clients with more severe forms of depression may want to consider medication as a means of lifting mood and giving them the energy and ability to deal with psychosocial issues.

Suicide risk is a particularly important issue in the treatment of depression. As suicide risk fluctuates during the illness, frequent suicide risk assessment evaluations should be conducted. Indeed, suicide risk frequently increases during the initial stages of treatment. The exact causes for this are unclear but may be related to the fact that the client has a little more energy in the early stages of treatment than when they were severely depressed, and this energy may mobilize a suicidal attempt. There may also be biological factors that precipitate suicidal ideation and attempts in those who have just started antidepressant medications.

Special issues exist from a psychosocial perspective in assisting clients with bipolar disorder. At times when they are stable, clients should be encouraged to plan for the possibility of an acute episode. The most important initial factor is to ensure the safety of the client and others, during both the periods of depression and of mania. Unsafe sexual encounters, overspending, and grandiose themes may compromise the client's lifestyle to a substantial degree during periods of mania. Erratic driving and speeding and other lapses in judgment may threaten safety. In a very few cases, the person may become dangerous to others, generally when a person with mania is thwarted in their goals and switches to irritation and anger. Community-based interventions should include sufficient community supports and a contingency plan for emergencies. Most commonly in mania, admission to hospital is indicated when there is an acute episode; clients can also be involved in pre-planning what treatments they might wish to receive if this occurs. In situations where people suffer from periods of severe depression and/or mania, clients should be encouraged to examine the various treatment approaches that can be used during acute periods and prepare an advanced directive regarding their wishes should they be incapable of consent at some point.

Psychosocial Interventions That Promote Recovery

As noted earlier in this chapter, psychosocial approaches frequently involve identifying and addressing interpersonal, social, and environmental stressors that may be contributing to the mood disturbance. In addition, however, specific approaches such as cognitive-behavioural therapy, interpersonal therapy, and psychoeducation have been demonstrated to be effective in aiding the recovery process in mood disturbances.

Cognitive-Behavioural Therapy

Cognitive-behavioural therapy (CBT) has become one of the most commonly used models of treatment for social work practitioners and their colleagues in other mental health disciplines. For some time social workers have reported the use of this methodology with a wide range of client groups, including individuals with personality disturbances (Fisher, 1995; Heller and Northcut, 1996); people suffering from major mental illnesses (Albert, 1994; Jensen, 1994); and chronic pain sufferers (Subramanian, 1991). The techniques of CBT are frequently used with individuals or in group therapy but equally they can be applied to couples or families.

Cognitive-behavioural therapy incorporates cognitive, behavioural, and social learning theory components, to explain functioning as a product of reciprocal interactions between personal and environmental variables. Thus, the applicability of CBT to social work practice is immediately apparent. First, the focus on the individual/environmental interactions is highly consistent with social work theory. That is, individual responses shape the environment and the environment shapes the individual. Second, the emphasis on a collaborative relationship between the therapist and the client is consistent with social work values. In this model, the social worker and the client jointly identify goals for change, work together to understand cognitive structures that perpetuate maladaptive behaviours and emotional responses, and develop a joint strategy for altering both cognitions and behaviour. In addition, the clarity and brevity of this model make it appealing in view of the current push for cost-effective treatment modalities (Regehr, 2000). Finally, unlike many models of treatment, cognitive-behavioural treatment has been extensively researched, resulting in clear evidence of its efficacy in the treatment of depression (Bocking et al., 2005; Coelho, Canter, and Ernst, 2007; Fournier et al., 2008) and bipolar disorder through controlled trials and systematic reviews (Jones, 2004; Williams et al., 2008).

Beck's (1967) original work in cognitive therapy began with observations of people suffering from depressive illnesses. From these observations, Beck described a triad of depressive cognitions: 1) the self as inadequate; 2) the environment as not reinforcing; and 3) the future as devoid of hope. Clients holding negative cognitions are less likely to engage in behaviours that discount the beliefs. For instance, if one believes one is not intelligent and that others will not offer assistance, one is less likely to enroll in continuing education classes, thereby eliminating the possibility of success in that sphere. Further, if one believes that the future holds no promise, the effort required to attempt new behaviours appears useless. These behavioural responses to the negative beliefs reinforce feelings of worthlessness and intensify depressive feelings. The central tenets of cognitive therapy can thus be summarized as follows:

1. Individuals acquire beliefs or cognitive maps of the world from previous experiences. These beliefs become filters through which all information about subsequent interactions must pass.
2. Beliefs or assumptions that an individual holds about themselves, others, or the world in general, may accurately reflect their own skills and abilities and the environment in which they live. At times, however, these beliefs become distorted reflections of reality. Cognitive distortions can then lead to persistent intrusive thoughts of such things as low self-worth and negative views of others (see Box 8.1).
3. Cognitions influence how someone feels about him- or herself or a situation and how they will approach it. The manner in which a person deals with any situation affects the outcome and thereby confirms or modifies existing cognitive structures. As an example, a person who believes they will fail their driving test may approach the situation with significant anxiety that impedes their performance. Similarly, a person who believes that they will be abandoned in interpersonal relationships may approach a new relationship with hostility or overly clingy behaviour, thereby pushing a new partner away.

Box 8.1 Some Examples of Cognitive Distortions

Catastrophic thinking: small problems are always the beginning of a disaster
Filtering: attending only to negative information and ignoring positives
Overgeneralization: seeing one setback as a never-ending pattern of defeat
Polarization: viewing others as all good or all bad

(Adapted from Beck et al., 1979)

In CBT, individuals are taught to identify, evaluate, and challenge negative assumptions. These negative beliefs are then reframed in a positive or neutral light. Concurrently, individuals are encouraged to modify their behavioural responses in order to maximize the possibility of positive outcomes. These positive outcomes will modify cognitions and influence affect. A more recent adaptation of CBT, Mindfulness-Based Cognitive Therapy (MCBT) involves combining cognitive strategies with meditation. MCBT teaches people skills that allow them to become more aware of thoughts without judgment, viewing negative thoughts as passing events, not fact. This model has been subject to rigorous testing with good results of efficacy in both bipolar disorder (Yatham et al., 2005; 2006; Williams et al., 2008) and depression (Coelho et al., 2007). It has also demonstrated good effects in post-partum depression (Bledsoe and Grote, 2006).

Interpersonal Therapy

Interpersonal Therapy (IPT) is a treatment approach with well-established efficacy that was originally designed for use with people suffering from depression, but which has more recently been modified for use with bipolar disorder (Elkin et al., 1989; Jones, 2004; de Mello et al., 2005). The goals of IPT are to alleviate symptoms of mood disturbances by improving interpersonal functioning and working through the problems related to loss, change, isolation, or conflict in relationships that are associated with the onset or perpetuation of depressive symptoms. Therapeutic strategies include clarification of feelings, expectations, and social roles, education, and the development of social competence through problem-solving, role-playing, and communication analysis (Ravitz, Maunder, and McBride, 2008). Interpersonal therapy is short-term, typically less than 16 sessions. Its goals are rapid symptom reduction and improved social adjustment. IPT emphasizes the ways in which a person's current relationships and social context cause or maintain symptoms rather than exploring the deep-seated sources of the symptoms.

The theoretical roots of IPT are in attachment theory, which focuses on early interpersonal relationships in the development of adult interpersonal interactions. In people with depressive symptoms, improved interpersonal relationships can serve to increase social support and decrease negative experiences and cognitions. This can be particularly true in people with early life histories of abuse and neglect that contribute to later life depressed moods (Talbot and Gamble, 2007). For this group, IPT can address issues of chronic shame, social withdrawal, and attachment avoidance. In people with bipolar disorder, improved relations with others help to modulate social rhythms, in part through increased openness to feedback from supportive others, when a manic episode is on the horizon (Jones, 2004). IPT does not presume that psychopathology arises exclusively from problems within an interpersonal realm. It does emphasize, however, that these problems occur within an interpersonal context that is often interdependent with the illness process. IPT has demonstrated effectiveness in patients with depression, bipolar disorder, and post-partum depression (Yatham et al., 2005; 2006; Bledsoe and Grote, 2006).

Psychoeducational Approaches

The tremendously high rate of relapse among people with bipolar disorder (75 per cent in five years) and the influence of psychosocial factors for precipitants in relapse make psychoeducational approaches of particular value. The 'Canadian Network for Mood and Anxiety Treatments: Guidelines for Management of Patients with Bipolar Disorder' recommends psychoeducation as a first-line treatment approach in combination with medication (Yatham et al., 2005; 2006). Psychoeducation provides information on the disorder, its symptoms, and treatment, and the social and family consequences of this mental health problem. It assists clients to recognize prodromal, that is, early and non-specific, symptoms of relapse and assists clients to understand the nature of medication and reasons for compliance. Considerable evidence demonstrates that psychoeducation as an addition to medication significantly reduces the risk of relapse (Yatham et al., 2005; 2006; Rouget and Aubry, 2007).

Pharmacological and Medical Interventions as Part of Recovery in Depression

Although psychosocial interventions are effective in assisting with many aspects of depression and bipolar disorder, medication and other medical interventions are also frequently used, particularly for severe episodes but also to assist clients in maintaining mood stability. Clients and social workers should be knowledgeable about these various types of treatments to fully engage in discussions and decisions about treatment and recovery planning. Client decisions about treatment should be based on multiple sources of information regarding the benefits and drawbacks of each form of treatment.

Medication

Pharmacological interventions are frequently adjunctive to psychosocial interventions in the treatment of depression and are sometimes used alone, generally on the basis of client preference. The efficacy of interventions is important for both practitioners and clients to consider. One excellent source of evaluative data is *The Cochrane Library*, which publishes systematic reviews of the literature that appraise, select, and synthesize high-quality research evidence in a particular domain (see Chapter 1 regarding evidenced-based practice). A wide variety of research studies summarized by *Cochrane Reviews* support the notion that antidepressant medications are effective in the treatment of depression (Furukawa, McGuire, and Barbui, 2003; Lima, Moncrieff, and Soares, 2005; Deshauer et al., 2008). However, in a highly publicized article, Turner and colleagues (2008) argued that clinicians may be misled by the research on antidepressants because only positive trials of antidepressants are published and that negative trials submitted to the Food and Drug Administration are not. Blier (2008), by contrast, suggests that the Turner and colleagues approach is part of a trend that teaches the public to fear antidepressant medication when the major thrust in educating the public should be directed towards fearing depression and its stigma. He argues that antidepressants do work and the risk–benefit ratio of using antidepressants is in favour of their use. In the end, however, each client needs to make this judgment for him- or herself.

One of the most important points about the use of pharmacotherapy is that these medications should be used in adequate doses for an adequate period of time, before switching to another one. Many of these medications have to be started at lower doses in order to let the client adapt to the side effects. It is therefore necessary to build up the dose of medication for a period of time. This can be frustrating for the client who wants quick relief for their discomfort. However, changing medications too rapidly can be harmful and lead to a longer delay in achieving the right medication in the right dose. Clients on medication should be monitored; after four to eight weeks the situation should be reassessed to determine if there has been an adequate response to medication. If the client is clearly not responding to a given antidepressant despite the fact that he or she is taking the medication as prescribed and the medication has been given at a therapeutic dose for a reasonable length of time, then consideration should be given to switching to a different class of antidepressants.

There are three main eras in the treatment of antidepressants: 1) the Monoamine Oxidase Inhibitors and the Tricyclics; 2) the Selective Serotonin Reuptake Inhibitors; and 3) the Serotonin Norepinephrine Reuptake Inhibitors. The original antidepressants, the Monoamine Oxidase Inhibitors (MAOIs), were discovered serendipitously like many other medications. Iproniazid, which was widely used as an antibiotic for tuberculosis, was noted to have antidepressant properties. Interestingly, the older textbooks on tuberculosis still talk about the euphoria of tuberculosis, probably because sufferers were taking Iproniazid. Iproniazid then became used as the first MAOI antidepressant. The mechanism of action is to block the breakdown of the monoamine (called norepinephrine), which is believed to alleviate depression through increasing monoamines. The main problem with these medications, which are still used in certain cases today, is that if they are mixed with any food or a medication that releases norepinephrine, the client can have a dangerous elevation of blood pressure known as the tyramine reaction. As a result, clients on MAOIs must abide to strict diets, avoiding such common foods as aged cheeses, smoked meats or fish, soy, and certain wines and beers. More especially they have to avoid various drugs such as cold remedies and drugs used for anesthetics.

Shortly after the discovery of MAOIs, an artificially derived class of drugs was developed that mimicked the chemical structure of MAOIs in that they had three chemical rings. They were thus referred to as the Tricyclic antidepressants (TCAs). TCAs were found to be effective in the treatment of depression and to this day all new antidepressants are compared to the TCAs for efficacy. Despite their efficacy, however, they have a wide range of action in various parts of the body and thus produce a number of unwanted side effects.

Concern about the side effects of TCAs led to the development of the Selective Serotonin Reuptake Inhibitors (SSRIs) in the late 1980s. Fluoxetine (Prozac) was the first of this group. The advantage of this group of medications was that they *selectively* increased the role of serotonin in the neuroanatomical pathways of emotion. Thus the unwanted side effects of the TCAs were to a great extent avoided. Of course serotonergic action in and of itself has certain unwanted side effects. Thus, in the late 1990s in an effort to increase the efficacy of antidepressants there was a trend back to multiple monoamine blockage, with the hope that many of the unwanted side effects could be avoided. This led to the development of the Serotonin Norepinephrine Reuptake Inhibitors (SNRIs). The belief is that since they have two therapeutic mechanisms they may be more efficacious. It is not yet clear whether this is in fact the case although anecdotal experience and some data seem to confirm this hypothesis (Stahl, 2008). There are certain antidepressants such as Trazodone and Mirtazapine that are variations on these classifications but are useful in certain circumstances as outlined in Table 8.3.

Fifty to 85 per cent of clients with a single episode of major depressive disorder will relapse at some stage (APA, 2002). If the client has had two or more episodes, the risk of relapse is 70 to 90 per cent over the next five years (Shiloh, Nutt, and Wizeman, 2005). As a result, it is often necessary for a client to consider whether they will remain on medication for a prolonged period of time (Furukawa et al., 2007). Regardless of whether or not they continue on medication, clients will often need ongoing support. In addition, clients should be encouraged to develop a relapse prevention plan and education should focus on early signs of relapse and treatment resources that are available.

Electroconvulsive Therapy

Electroconvulsive Therapy (ECT) remains one of the most controversial treatments in psychiatry. Most of us have seen the horrific scenes of ECT being used as a punishment in Hollywood films such as *One Flew over the Cuckoo's Nest* or more recently *The Changeling*. In addition, psychiatric survivor groups have identified ECT as one of the ways in which psychiatry controls and abuses clients (Capponi, 2003). Nevertheless, treatment with ECT continues to be used in severe cases of depression that are not responsive to other forms of treatment. Meta-analyses of

Table 8.3 Medications for Depression

Name	Class	Dosage	Benefits	Side effects
MOAIs and Tricyclic Antidepressants				
Phenelzine (Nardil)	MAOI	45–90	Good for atypical depression	Dietary restrictions
Moclobemide (Manerix)	Reversible MAO–A inhibitor	300–600	Good for atypical depression	No dietary restrictions Not available in US
Amitriptyline (Elavil)	Tricyclic	75–300	Good when sleep required /inexpensive	• Troublesome • Anticholinergic side effects • Possible cardio toxicity • Cannot be used in glaucoma • Possibly more response in men • Lethal in overdose
Doxepin (Sinequan)	Tricyclic	75–300	Good when sleep required /inexpensive	
Imipramine (Tofranil)	Tricyclic	75–300	Good when sleep required /inexpensive	
Trimipramine (Surmontil)	Tricyclic	75–300	Good when sleep required /inexpensive	
Desipramine (Norpramin)	Tricyclic	40–200	Not widely used	
Nortriptyline (Aventyl)	Tricyclic		Not widely used	
Selective Seratonin Reducing Agents (SSRIs)				
Prozac (Fluoxetine)	SSRI	10–80	The original SSRI. No withdrawal symptoms	Long acting = slow onset and stays in system
Paxil (Paroxetine)	SSRI	10–60	Good for anxiety	Withdrawal symptoms
Luvox (Fluvoxamine)	SSRI	50–300	Good for anxiety	Gastric Problems
Zoloft (Sertraline)	SSRI	50–200	Good for anxiety	Gastric Problems
Celexa (Citalopram)	SSRI	10–60	Good for O-C symptoms	
Clomipramine (Anafranil)	SSRI	75–300	Good for anxiety	
Escitalopram (Cipralex)	SSRI	10–20		
Serotonin Norepinephrine Reuptake Inhibitors (SNRIs)				
Venflaxine (Effexor)	SNRI	75–375	Good for co-morbid anxiety	Gastric side effects
Duloxetine (Cymbalta)	SNRI	40–60	Possibly good for chronic pain	New to Canada (2008)
Mirtazapine (Remeron)	SNRI	15–60	Good when sleep required/dual action	Weight gain

Table 8.3 *Continued*

Other Antidepressants				
Name	**Class**	**Dosage**	**Benefits**	**Side effects**
Trazodone (Desyrel)	5HT Antagonist/ SSRI	150–600	Good for aggression Good when sleep required No sexual side effects	Rare but serious priapism
Buproprion (Wellbutrin/ Zyban)	NE–DA Reuptake inhibitor	100–450	Does not precipitate mania Good for co-morbid ADHD symptoms No sexual side effects	May precipitate seizures

ECT as a treatment form have demonstrated that it can be highly effective in treatment of depression (Janicak et al., 1985; Geddes and UK ECT Review Group, 2003; Kho, Zwinderman, and Blansjaar, 2005).

The history of ECT as a form of treatment dates back to Paracelsus who in the fourteenth century used camphor to induce seizures in an effort to relieve suffering caused by melancholia (Prudich, 2005). In 1934, Meduna, in Italy, used camphor and then insulin coma to treat a catatonic patient with success. By 1938, Bini and Cerletti had devised a method of placing electrodes on the head to induce seizures. ECT became very common in the 1940s as a first-line treatment for psychiatric disorder. It should be remembered that there were few if any pharmacological treatments available at this time. In the 1960s and 1970s the first randomized control trials proved its efficacy compared with antipsychotic medication and with sham ECT. Over the years newer techniques have developed, including the use of sophisticated brief anesthetic techniques with muscle relaxants.

The indications for ECT are generally considered to be treatment-resistant depression. When there is a high risk of suicide or dehydration or in the presence of depressive stupor, catatonia, or psychotic depression then it may be considered earlier in the course of treatment. ECT treatment takes about 10 to 15 minutes plus time for preparation and recovery. An IV is inserted into the arm to allow for the administration of anesthetic and muscle relaxant. Heart and blood pressure monitors are secured. A small electrode pad is placed on the person's head. An electric shock is administered that causes a seizure that lasts 30 to 60 seconds. The mechanism of action is likely due to an effect on the serotonergic system although this effect is somewhat different from that of antidepressants in that it seems that the electrical current increases the density of serotonin receptors. There is also some evidence that the pituitary may discharge more hormones as a result of the electrical current-induced seizure resulting in increased cortisol-releasing factors and therefore increased cortisol (Lisanby, 2007).

The side effects of ECT include the common risks of a general anesthetic, albeit the general anesthetic in ECT is an ultrabrief one. These include cardiovascular complications. Since the stimulus is applied very close to the jaw bone it used to be common for clients to break teeth but this can be prevented by using a bite block. The most serious and well-publicized sequelae are neurocognitive. It is common for the client to experience brief headaches and occasionally periods of confusion for some hours after the treatment. Many clients experience a brief period of amnesia for events immediately following the treatment. This is referred to as anterograde amnesia. This generally diminishes or is absent two or three weeks after the treatment ends. Some clients experience a memory gap of events prior to the ECT, referred to as retrograde amnesia. Generally speaking, these memories return although some clients are left with a spotty amnesia. It is known that bilateral electrode placement, a long anesthetic, and pre-existing cognitive problems increase the chances of neurocognitive sequelae. Researchers concur that cognitive side effects can be a problem and are seeking methods to reduce this risk through different types of wave forms and electrode placements (Eschweiler et al., 2007; Loo et al., 2007). Concurrent administration of lithium at the time of the ECT also increases the possibility of confusion and neurocognitive problems.

ECT is the most effective treatment for severe, unremitting depression. While there are active opponents of the treatment, there are also those who suffer from severe depression who believe that it is a life-saving treatment. As a result, clients who suffer from severe episodic depression should research this treatment when they are stable to make an informed choice about its use should they become severely incapacitated by depression.

Transcranial Magnetic Stimulation (rTMS)

A relatively new technology that holds promise for the treatment of depression is repetitive Transcranial Magnetic Stimulation (rTMS). The first use of electromagnetic brain stimulation was designed as a neurodiagnostic tool in England in 1985. The principle of the treatment is that an electromagnetic coil produces a short-lived electromagnetic field that easily passes through the skull and other tissues. It is believed to exert its action by increasing cortical excitability and therefore by an effect on neurotransmitters, including adrenergic and domapinergic systems. The treatment is generally administered daily over 10 days and some subjects have reported mild headaches but few other adverse effects.

Hasey (2001) reviews the clinical trials to date and concludes that rTMS has a positive effect in clients with major depressive disorder without psychosis. He noted, however, that the therapeutic benefits in double-blind, controlled trials using 'sham' treatments (equivalent to placebo in drug trials) are modest as yet. Newer studies support his conclusions (Martin et al., 2003; O'Reardon, 2007). It is noted that the side effects of this treatment are mild and there have been no longer-term adverse effects reported. In particular there does not seem to be any evidence at this stage of cognitive impairment and in fact some studies have suggested that rTMS may enhance cognitive function.

Light Therapy

Some clients experience major depressive episodes in late fall or early winter on a regular basis and are thus viewed as having seasonal affective disorder as discussed earlier in the chapter. This seems more common in northern climates where the days are significantly shorter in winter. Over the past 20 years bright-light therapy has been introduced and has been found to be helpful in at least the minor forms of this disorder. The therapy is characterized by regular daily exposure to ultraviolet filtered visible light. A special light box or visor administers the correct brightness of light for 30 minutes per day. Clients can be told to expose themselves to the light by having the box, for instance, in the kitchen while they have breakfast or by wearing a visor first thing in the morning. Side effects are minimal although some people report nausea, headache, and nervousness as well as eye irritation. There have been no reports of ocular damage. Initially the therapy should be given for 10 days although it is now thought that maintenance therapy can be continued all winter.

Psychopharmacological Treatment of Mania and Bipolar Disorder

In almost all cases, pharmacological treatment is the primary approach to the treatment of mania, augmented by psychosocial interventions. The goals of pharmacological treatment are 1) to control the symptoms in the acute phase and 2) to help the client remain in a stable state, free of acute episodes. During acute phases, clients are frequently treated with antipsychotic medication. These are discussed in detail in Chapter 7. As well as having mood-stabilizing properties in and of themselves, antipsychotics can be used to ensure that clients finally get some sleep and do not exhaust themselves.

The most common and effective treatment for maintenance of stability in mania and bipolar disorder is the use of lithium carbonate (Yatham et al., 2005; 2006). Lithium carbonate is a salt that was serendipitously found to be effective in the treatment of mania when it was used in some experiments on rats. The main side effects include nausea, diarrhea, thirst, and weight gain. While clients at times express fears of brain damage from this medication, recent research has demonstrated that it actually increases the growth of grey matter (Bearden et al., 2007). Following extensive research, lithium carbonate has been found to effectively prevent further manic episodes in 60 to 80 per cent of people, to minimize the risk of further depressive episodes, and to reduce death by suicide in clients with bipolar disorder (Smith et al., 2007). However, clients must be committed to reliably following the medication regime when using lithium, including not forgetting doses or taking extra medication, as there is a small 'therapeutic window'. The dosage is usually guided by reviewing the results of regular blood tests.

Possible Social Work Interventions in the Case Examples

Case Example 1: Jake

Jake is experiencing a mild mood fluctuation as a result of a life disappointment. This is a normal process. Jake has excellent social supports and many personal strengths and resources. He does not require social work intervention.

Case Example 2: Shanti

Shanti is experiencing depressed mood related to a life situation.

- A suicide risk assessment should be conducted to ensure that Shanti is not a risk to herself. Further, an assessment should be conducted to ensure that she is not a risk to her son. Appropriate measures should be taken if any concerns about risk exist (see Chapter 5).
- Social work intervention should focus on a problem-solving approach to assist Shanti to build on her own resources and supports. The social worker could also connect Shanti with additional community resources that might be appropriate to assist her (see Chapter 5).
- When her immediate crisis situation is resolved, the social worker and Shanti may decide to embark on more exploratory therapy that addresses her issues of loss and considers future goals.

Case Example 3: Stefan

Stefan is suffering from major depression.

- The social worker should conduct a complete assessment including suicide risk.
- Stefan should be advised that a consultation with a physician may be in order as, given the severity and length of his symptoms and his family history of depression and suicide, pharmacological or other interventions could be of assistance.
- Cognitive therapy or interpersonal therapy could be useful for Stefan, and the social worker should discuss psychosocial treatment options. If the social worker is not qualified to use these treatment approaches, appropriate referrals can be made.

Case Example 4: Julie

Julie is likely suffering from a manic episode. If this is the case, the symptoms may worsen before they improve, possibly rendering Julie a risk to herself or others and certainly causing distress. Julie should be assessed and this will likely occur in a hospital emergency room.

- If Julie is admitted to hospital, the social worker can work with Julie to plan her return to the community and her program of recovery. The social worker can also work with family and friends of Julie to assist them in understanding what has happened and make plans for future support.

- If Julie is not admitted to hospital, the social worker can work with Julie, if she agrees, to plan for treatment in the community. Alternatively, if Julie does not agree to intervention, the social worker may be approached by the family to discuss options to assist Julie. This may include education about the implications of mental health legislation (see Chapter 3).

Summary

Depression and mania fall on a continuum of mood disturbances that range from mild symptoms to debilitating illness. The causes of mood disturbances are multifactoral, incorporating a range of biological determinants, early life history factors, and current environmental and social factors. As a result, treatment approaches to mood disturbances are highly divergent. In some situations psychosocial interventions alone are the most effective means for dealing with the problem, at times a combination of biological and psychosocial interventions will be most effective, and in the case of acute manic episodes, medication is likely the first line of intervention. Social workers working with clients with depression or bipolar disorder require highly developed assessment skills in order to determine the nature of the issues the client is dealing with and subsequently to determine whether social work intervention alone is indicated or whether other members of the interdisciplinary team should be involved.

Key Terms

Autosomal dominant
Cerebrospinal fluid
Cyclothymia
Hypomania
Hypothyroidism
Mania
Orbitofrontal
Prodromal
Psychoeducation

Discussion Questions

1. How can psychosocial interventions ameliorate symptoms of depression?
2. How can social workers assist clients and families affected by bipolar disorder?
3. How can the recovery model be applied to work with clients affected by depression or bipolar disorder?
4. A number of controversial medical treatments exist for use with clients suffering from depression. What is the social worker's role with respect to clients using or considering these treatments?

Suggested Readings and Weblinks

Beck, A., Rush, J., Shaw, B., and Emery, G. (1979), *Cognitive Therapy of Depression* (New York: Guilford Press).

Post-Partum Depression. *The Mayo Clinic* (accessed at http://www.mayoclinic.com/health/postpartum-depression/DS00546).

Social Workers: Help Starts Here. *Depression: How Social Workers Help* (accessed at http://www.helpstartshere.org/mind_and_spirit/depression/how_social_workers_help/depression_--_how_social_workers_help.html).

Chapter 9

Anxiety

Objectives:

- To identify factors contributing to the development of anxiety
- To identify symptoms and challenges associated with anxiety
- To identify different types of anxiety disorders
- To present evidence-based interventions that promote recovery

Case Example 1

John is a 25-year-old computer programmer who works for a large Internet technology firm. He has a fear of germs and as a result takes extreme precautions to ensure that he is not contaminated. John cleans his work station area with antibacterial wash twice a day, once when he arrives in the morning at 8:45 and once when he finishes lunch at 12:40. He carefully lifts all items on his desk and cleans underneath them and he sprays his keyboard and telephone with a special product that he purchases on the Internet. John cannot tolerate others coming into his workspace and makes every attempt to limit communication to email and telephone. He will go into the offices of others, but does not touch anything. When he does interact with others, John must wash his hands and cleanse with Purell, an antibacterial hand lotion. Each hand washing must be performed in a particular way and takes several minutes to complete. When he is finished he takes out a special cloth from his pocket to turn off the taps and open the washroom door. John washes his hands so frequently and thoroughly that his hands are red and raw-looking. John cannot take public transit or elevators because of the concentration of germs in these public environments. At home John has similar rituals, but because he lives with his parents they have adapted to his behaviour and are careful to leave certain areas of the house for his exclusive use in order that his anxiety does not get out of control.

Case Example 2

Josi is a 33-year-old mother of two children who in the past enjoyed walks in the neighbourhood with her kids, volunteering at their school, and taking the children to programs at the library and community centre. One day two years ago, Josi was shopping at the local mall with a friend when suddenly she experienced a rush of immobilizing anxiety. Her heart started to race, she at first began sweating profusely and then felt as though the blood had drained from her body and began to feel chilled and shaky. She feared that she may be having a heart attack or a stroke. Her friend became extremely concerned and wondered about calling for assistance. Within a few minutes, however, it had passed and Josi was just left feeling frightened and exhausted. Upon returning home, Josi made an appointment with her family doctor who after a series of medical investigations reported that there was nothing physically wrong with her. Josi resumed all normal activities but continued to be a bit concerned about the event. Two months later, again in a shopping mall, Josi had a similar experience. This time, her doctor informed her that she was having panic attacks. Josi decided that she would only go to shopping malls with her husband or mother from this time forward because she feared if she were alone or with her children she would not be able to cope. After three additional panic attacks, two of which occurred in the grocery store, Josi decided that she could no longer shop and began finding alternative ways of getting groceries and clothing for her children. As time progressed Josi's panic attacks began to occur in other places and as a result, she has been further limiting her activities. She now arranges for her children to have play dates in her own home so that she will not have to go into public places and no longer volunteers in the classroom for fear she will humiliate herself and her children due to a panic attack.

The Nature of Anxiety

Anxiety states are experiences that are common to all humans. These states are characterized by two components: 1) a diffuse, unpleasant, and vague experience of apprehension; and 2) physical symptoms such as headache, perspiration, heart palpitations, general restlessness, difficulty sleeping, and gastric discomfort. Anxiety can have an adaptive function, warning the person of impending risk and allowing the person to take remedial action. For instance, in early days, anxiety that the family may starve during a long cold winter could have motivated people to harvest and store extra food. Similarly, now a person who is anxious about a test or upcoming interview may prepare for it and thus both decrease anxiety and increase chances of success. Anxiety becomes problematic when the symptoms are experienced to the extent that they no longer motivate adaptive behaviour but rather impede efforts to rectify the situation. Further, anxiety may not be easily tied to specific events and may instead be a more general sense of unease, discomfort, and foreboding making it difficult for a person to be able to take actions that will reduce distress.

Incidence and Prevalence

Anxiety states represent the most common of all mental health problems, affecting approximately 12 per cent of Canadians, about 9 per cent of men and 16 per cent of women, during a one-year period. The one-year prevalence in Canada for individual anxiety disorders is as follows: generalized anxiety disorder, 1.1 per cent; specific phobia, 6.2 to 8.0 per cent; social phobia, 6.7 per cent; obsessive compulsive disorder, 1.8 per cent; and panic disorder, 0.7 per cent (Public Health Agency Canada, 2002). In 1999, women were hospitalized for anxiety at higher rates than men in every age category. Women and men over the age of 65 had the highest rates of hospitalization. This was followed by young women aged between 15 and 19 years. The average length of stay is approximately 10 days.

In the United States, the lifetime prevalence of having an anxiety disorder is 28.8 per cent, most often involving social phobia (12.1 per cent) or specific phobias (12.5 per cent). The age of onset for anxiety disorders is lower than any other disorder with a median age of 11 years, indicating that anxiety disorders in childhood are a significant issue. This is compared to a median age of 30 years for mood disorders (Kessler et al., 2005). The direct and indirect costs of anxiety disorders in the United States are reported to exceed $40 billion annually (Smoller and Faraone, 2008). For example, in a review conducted by Hoffman and colleagues (2008), generalized anxiety disorder was associated with an average of between 1.5 and 5.4 impairment days in the past month, after adjusting for the presence of other mental health problems and sociodemographic characteristics. In a large general population survey in New York, anxiety disturbances were more common amongst people who are divorced and unemployed, and were significantly less common in people over the age of 65 than those who are younger. Further, there was a significant overlap between anxiety and major depression—that is, a large number of people suffer from both (Gwynn et al., 2008).

Causes of Anxiety

As with depression, which is closely linked with anxiety, the causes of anxiety are generally thought to be a complex interaction between biological predispositions and social/environmental factors.

Intrapsychic Factors

Rollo May in his classic book *The Meaning of Anxiety* (1950) traces descriptions of the intrapsychic experience of anxiety through such writers as Descartes, Kierkegaard, Nietzsche, and Kafka. These writers focus on societal influences that result in a sense of existential anxiety in which a person becomes aware of the profound meaninglessness of life and existence. From this perspective, existential anxiety is a fundamental, ontological experience, resulting from the recognition of the inherent uncertainty of the human condition. Kierkegaard suggests that the goal is not to remove anxiety but rather to confront the existential anxiety and move ahead despite it.

Early psychoanalytic theory focused on anxiety related to psychosexual developmental phases. Indeed Freud's use of the word *angst* (or *fear* in German) is the origin of the current term *anxiety*. Separation anxiety, in which a child fears separation from their main attachment figure (traditionally the mother) is central to this theoretical understanding and forms the underpinnings of adult anxiety. The threat in anxiety is differentiated from fear because it is vague and non-specific. It is a threat on a deeper level and attacks the core or essence of personality (May, 1950).

Social-Environmental Factors

High-stress environments can contribute to the development of anxiety. For instance, a child living in a violent household can be in a heightened state of arousal attempting to anticipate when violence might erupt. The chaotic nature of these types of environments often means that the child cannot reliably predict when the violent parent might erupt or when he or she might be kind and nurturing. The child then begins to live life on 'pins and needles' carefully attempting to avoid situations that might in their view cause the anger and violence. Similarly, a person living in economic distress, attempting against all odds to make ends meet, or a person in a high-stress job may begin to feel increasingly anxious as a result of their inability to satisfy the demands made of them.

Behavioural theories suggest that anxiety is a learned response to experiences in the environment. According to this theory a person becomes conditioned to respond in a particular way to certain situations. Cognitive theorists add that the anxiety experienced by a person is their interpretation of the situation, which may or may not be faulty. Thus, a person may have experienced negative interactions with certain people, subsequently generalizing this to all others and therefore responding to situations with anxiety that is not objectively rational. For instance, an individual may have been bullied in high school and as a result developed a rational fear of some people within the school environment. However, that fear may generalize and later they may perceive other social situations as dangerous and view themselves as socially incompetent. As a result, an invitation to a work-related cocktail party might cause significant anxiety and avoidance behaviours.

The pattern of behaviour described above is reflected in the notion of self-efficacy or competence as described by social learning theorists. Bandura (1977) suggests that expectations of competence or personal self-efficacy triggered by the contextual factors in any situation arise from diverse sources of information including judgments of past performance and previous responses from others. These judgments of efficacy in turn affect the outcomes of situations and thereby confirm or modify existing cognitive structures. For example, people who judge themselves to be inefficacious in managing potential threats approach such situations anxiously and experience disruptive arousal. This arousal, in turn, negatively impacts their performance and confirms feelings of inadequacy. Individuals who repeatedly perceive their efforts to be ineffective can develop 'learned helplessness' (Seligman and Garber, 1980).

The learned helplessness model has been used (somewhat controversially) to explain the behaviour of women in long-term abusive relationships. According to this model, women who have learned to expect battering as a way of life subsequently believe that they cannot influence its occurrence. As a result, their anxiety increases and their adaptive and self-protective behaviours diminish (Walker, 1979). Clearly, the problem with this formulation is it attributes the helplessness to the individual and does not take into account other barriers to self-protection, such as justice systems that do not properly protect victims, and economic and other social polices that do not create options for victims.

Biological Factors

Biological theories related to anxiety also have a long history. Selye (1936), for instance, focused on biological responses to stress and noted that when acute threats were encountered, biological adaptations served as protective mechanisms. Respiration and blood pressure increased, oxygen and energy shifted from the immune, digestive, and reproductive systems that were less essential for immediate survival, to the large muscles. This led to the development of his theory of General Adaption Syndrome, a three-stage model for stress adaptation involving: 1) alarm and mobilization, when the body prepared for action; 2) resistance, in which the body's stress response diminished and returned to normal functioning; and 3) exhaustion, which occurred if stress was unrelenting or repetitive. Anxiety responses, for instance, panic attacks, occur when there is a disruption in this process and there is significant autonomic arousal to relatively minor threats.

More recent biological research has determined that the primary region of the brain responsible for processing fearful material is the amygdala, which coordinates the autonomic response to fear (see Figure 9.1). Sensory information reaches the amygdala which in turn initiates autonomic nervous system responses and behavioural responses. The hypothalamic–pituitary–adrenal (HPA) axis is an interactive system of hormones released in response to stress. The hypothalamus releases corticotrophin-releasing factor (CRF), prompting the pituitary to release adrenocorticotropin-releasing hormone (ACTH), which in turn stimulates the adrenal cortex to release cortisol. This produces the 'flight or fight' response in which the autonomic nervous system regulates such things as heart rate, breathing, dilatation of blood vessels, and the emptying of the bowel and bladder. These responses are modulated by the prefrontal cortex of the brain, which assesses the threat cues and determines the actual degree of threat (Mathew, Price, and Charney, 2008). For instance, a loud noise that resembles a gunshot may cause an instant startle reflex and a sudden rise in heart rate. However, when the person then assesses that the noise was caused by a car backfiring, they work to calm themselves down, rather than run away. Anxiety disorders occur in individuals where this modulating function is impaired by one factor or another, resulting in a more chronic and pervasive fear response (Spiegel and Barlow, 2000; Stahl, 2000; Mojtabai, 2005).

Family and twin studies of panic disorder and phobias have provided consistent evidence that these mental health problems are familial trends. People with relatives with panic disorder for instance have a 5 to16 per cent increased risk of this particular illness. If a first-degree relative has a panic disorder, the risk of developing one is increased by seven times. Similarly, there is a six to nine times increased risk of developing phobias if one has a first-degree relative with a phobic disorder.

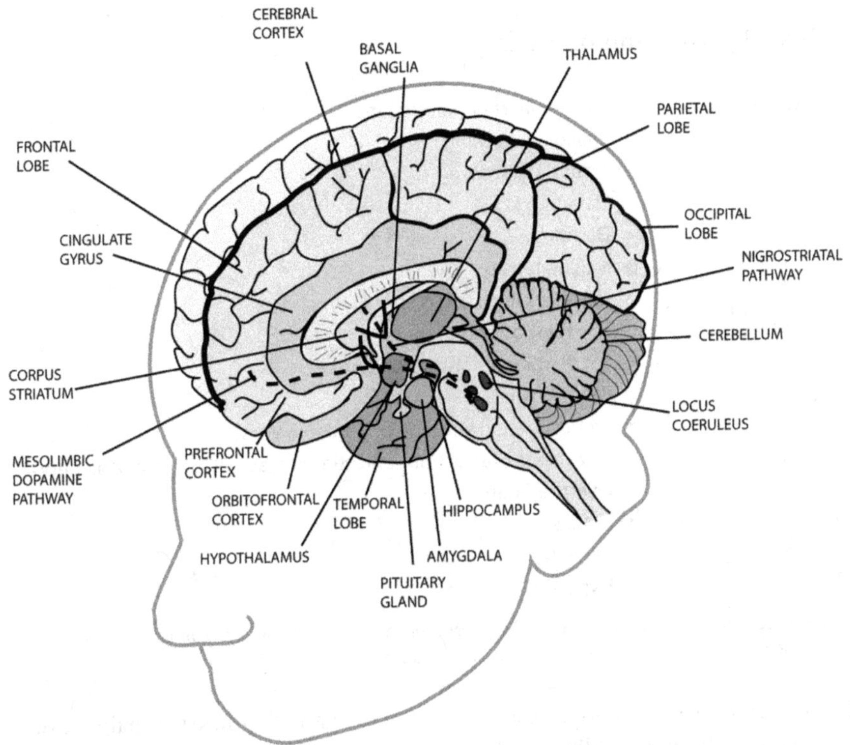

Figure 9.1 The Brain

Twin studies have reported heritabilities of 0.28 for panic disorders, 0.36 for agoraphobia, 0.10 for social anxiety disorder, and 0.24 for specific phobias.

Compared to other mental health problems such as schizophrenia and bipolar disorder, this rate of heritability in anxiety-related mental health problems is relatively low. Thus, while there is undoubtedly a genetic component, environment and other factors also appear to have a significant influence. Indeed, a large twin study that considered both diagnosis of panic and phobic disorders and personality factors found that genetic determinants of personality traits accounted for all the genetic influences on social phobia and agoraphobia (Smoller, Gardner-Schuster, and Covino, 2008). That is, inherited personality characteristics, such as the need for control over situations or being shy, were the genetic factors that predicted social phobia and agoraphobia. Similar results have been found for generalized anxiety disorder suggesting that it may be the personality traits that are inherited that predispose a person to an anxiety disturbance, but that the disturbance itself may not be inherited (Hettema, Prescott, and Kendler, 2004).

Symptoms and Types of Anxiety Disorders

Anxiety disorders have many common features (see Box 9.1). That is, anxiety disorders generally have three groups of symptoms—physiological, cognitive, and

Box 9.1 Symptoms of Anxiety

Physical	• Racing heart or palpitations • Shallow breathing • Trembling, shaking • Sweating • Dizziness • Muscle tension • Nausea and gastric distress
Cognitive	• Fearful thoughts • Fearful predictions • Fearful beliefs • Preoccupation with the potential threats
Behavioural	• Avoidance of situations and stimuli that will trigger the anxiety • Overpreparation • Rituals • Repeated checking • Hypervigilance

Reprinted with permission from *The Diagnostic and Statistical Manual of Mental Disorders*, Text Revision, 4th edn., (Copyright 2000). American Psychiatric Association.

behavioural. The physiological symptoms include a racing heart or palpitations, shallow breathing, trembling, shaking, sweating, dizziness, muscle tension, nausea, and gastric distress. The cognitive symptoms include fearful thoughts, fearful predictions, fearful beliefs, and preoccupation with potential threats. Behavioural symptoms include both avoidance of situations and stimuli that will trigger the anxiety as well as safety behaviours such as overpreparation, hiding, rituals, checking, and hypervigilance. As readers will recall from Chapter 6, these symptoms also occur in people with post-traumatic stress disorder. Although acute stress disorder and post-traumatic stress disorder are forms of anxiety, because of the prevalence and unique nature of the stressors that lead to these mental health problems, they have been covered separately in Chapter 6. Further, while this chapter identifies several types of anxiety, there is considerable overlap between each of the types of anxiety and controversy exists in the literature about whether they indeed constitute distinct entities. Nevertheless, it is useful for social workers in mental health to know how variations on anxiety are defined.

Anxiety symptoms are difficult for family and friends to understand and this adds to the distress experienced by sufferers. For instance, other people may become annoyed that the person with social anxiety will not attend a particular event or that a person with panic attacks cannot enter a shopping mall. To others these choices seem ludicrous and they may believe that just a little willpower will allow the person to overcome the fear or resistance. In addition, anxiety behaviours may be open to ridicule. For instance a person with obsessional traits can be made fun of for his or her constant attention to detail or focus on cleanliness. To the outsider, the person with an anxiety disorder can appear weak, ineffectual, or rigid and not ill. Family members may also feel the burden of stigma. For instance, if an anxious child refuses to go to school, the parents may be criticized by others for not exercising appropriate discipline because that they do not just make the child go.

Panic Disorder

Panic disorder is often a severe and disabling form of anxiety that is characterized by panic attacks. Panic attacks are defined as sudden, discrete episodes of very intense anxiety accompanied by feelings of impending doom. These attacks develop in a spontaneous manner, which the person initially feels 'came out of nowhere' (Cox and Taylor, 1999). They are accompanied by a number of physical symptoms such as intense sweating, palpitations, and dizziness in which the person fears that they may faint or have a heart attack. The person feels totally out of control and fears that he or she might either go crazy or die. While the first or second panic attack is totally unexpected, with the repeated experience of panic attacks the person begins to fear them and seeks to find ways to control both the onset and consequence of the attacks; this then results in maladaptive safety behaviours such as those that occur in agoraphobia. Indeed, the majority of people report that their first panic attack occurred in a public place and almost 40 per cent of people with panic attacks resulting in agoraphobia report that their first panic attack happened on a bus, plane, or subway.

Box 9.2 Characteristics of a Panic Attack

- Palpitations
- Sweating
- Trembling or shaking
- Sensations of shortness of breath or smothering
- Feeling of choking
- Chest pain or discomfort
- Nausea or abdominal distress
- Dizziness, lightheadedness, feeling faint
- Derealization (feelings of unreality) or depersonalization (feeling detached from self)
- Fear of losing control or going crazy
- Fear of dying
- Paraesthesias
- Chills or hot flashes

Specific Phobia

Fears commonly develop and then diminish throughout childhood. Typically, fear of separation from the caregiver develops between 6 and 22 months and goes away by 30 months. Fear of unfamiliar adults begins between 6 to 9 months and subsides between 20 and 24 months. Fears of animals, darkness, and monsters appear between 2 and 6 years. Fear of school occurs at the beginning of school and often reappears when a child transitions from elementary school to high school. Children between the ages of 8 and 16 often fear physical harm to either themselves or their parents (Cox and Taylor, 1999). Most adults can also identify some things that cause them fear such as balloons popping or fireworks (loud noises), standing on a chair or ladder (heights), being in a tunnel or elevator (small spaces), or spiders or mice. To others these fears are ridiculous and may seem funny. To those who experience the fears, they may also seem crazy, but they are nevertheless very real. In people with phobias these fears are felt with such intensity that they result in compensatory behaviours in order to avoid them. For instance, a well-known academic who refuses to travel by airplane when attending conferences or giving talks must factor in several days on either side in order to drive thousands of miles.

Agoraphobia

There are two types of agoraphobia, one which is accompanied by panic attacks and one which is not. Agoraphobia is defined by the *DSM* as anxiety related to being in places or situations where escape might be difficult or help might not be available in the event of a panic attack (APA, 2000). As a result of these fears, people with agoraphobia may be unable to leave the house alone, be unable to be in crowded places, or be unable to travel in a car or airplane. Consequently, people with this disorder tend to severely restrict their activities. This has a tremendous impact on the lives of the person suffering from this type of phobia and on the lives of others in their family. Compensations often must be made to deal with the fact that this person cannot go out of doors or cannot travel by certain modes of transportation.

Social Phobia (Social Anxiety Disorder)

While most people experience some anxiety in novel situations where they will be evaluated by others, such as job interviews, public speaking, or meeting the parents of a significant other, individuals with social phobia experience incapacitating anxiety in these situations. In order to reduce the symptoms the person may suddenly leave the social situation or in order to avoid the symptoms, the person may simply refuse to attend. However, these approaches serve to reinforce the person's beliefs that he or she is socially incompetent and as a result, avoidance symptoms increase. Social phobia is one of the most common anxiety disorders, particularly in women. At any time about 2 per cent of the population suffer from social anxiety disorder, an additional 3 per cent have subclinical threshold symptoms (that is, where several symptoms exist but not at a level to warrant a diagnosis), and 7.5 per cent have some symptoms of the disorder (Fehm et al., 2008). Social phobia is generally understood to begin during adolescence or early adulthood, although there is some indication that the symptoms may subside with age, making this less a chronic anxiety disorder than some others. Nevertheless, the nature of the problem has a significant impact on the quality of life of those who suffer.

Generalized Anxiety Disorder

Generalized anxiety disorder is characterized by persistent anxiety and worry that is out of proportion with actual events or circumstances. This anxiety is often related to minor, everyday occurrences such as work, finances, relationships, and the health and safety of loved ones. This pervasive worry is accompanied by a variety of somatic symptoms that cause significant impairment in social or occupational functioning and marked distress in the sufferer. People with generalized anxiety disorder often experience significantly reduced quality of life in the areas of general health, physical health, bodily pain, vitality, mental health, role functioning due to physical and emotional difficulties, and social functioning compared with those without the disorder (Hoffman, Dukes, and Wittchen, 2008). Primary symptoms include trembling, feeling shaky, tension headaches, exaggerated startle reflexes, difficulty sleeping, sweating, diarrhoea, and nausea. As a result of the physical symptoms, it is not uncommon that the person will visit his or her family doctor seeking relief for what feels like a biological illness. Paradoxically the concern over these physical symptoms becomes another cause of stress and worry. For instance, the person may become concerned that the diarrhoea is a symptom of colon cancer. Nevertheless a full medical work-up can be in order because the symptoms may in fact be secondary to such factors as excessive caffeine use, alcohol withdrawal, cardiac problems, or a hormonal imbalance. By definition this is a chronic condition that may become lifelong and as it develops as many as 25 per cent of people who suffer from it may also develop panic attacks (Kaplan and Sadock, 1996).

Obsessive-Compulsive Disorder

Obsessive-compulsive disorder (OCD) is a relatively common (affecting 2 per cent of the population), chronic, and disabling disorder that causes significant distress in sufferers and their families. As the name implies, it is characterized by two factors: 1) cognitive obsessions that increase the person's level of anxiety and thus lead to 2) compulsive behaviours aimed at reducing the anxiety. Obsessions are intrusive and persistent thoughts, ideas, impulses, or images that to others appear inappropriate. Common obsessions include fear of dirt or germs, concerns that the oven or other appliance has been left on and the house will burn down, or concerns that the house or apartment has not been properly secured and someone will break in. These obsessive thoughts cause considerable distress and consequently, individuals with obsessions usually attempt to ignore, resist, or suppress the thoughts or impulses or to counteract them by other thoughts or actions resulting in compulsions. Compulsions are repeated behaviours that occur in response to an obsession, usually in a ritualistic way. Compulsions can include behaviours such as hand washing, or repeated checking (such as of the oven or the locks) or mental acts such as praying, counting, or repeating words. The person often knows that the compulsion is not rational and thus will attempt to refrain from the behaviour; however, the anxiety then becomes unbearable and he or she must capitulate. In order to qualify for a diagnosis of OCD, these activities must take more than one hour per day to complete. In addition to the ritualistic behaviours, individuals with OCD will engage in avoidance behaviours, such as not shaking hands, so they do not have to engage in the rituals. As indicated in Case Example 1, the compulsions can begin to interfere with normal functioning and affect all aspects of the individual's life.

The average age of onset for OCD is 20 and among young people it is more common in boys than in girls. Further, it is more likely to be found in people who are single, perhaps because of the disruptive nature of the disorder on interpersonal relationships. People who have OCD often have other mental disorders as well. For instance, the lifetime prevalence of depression in people with OCD is approximately 67 per cent. In younger people the rate of concurrent tic disorders is in the range of 40 per cent (Kaplan and Sadock, 1996).

The Recovery Model and Anxiety

A key aspect of anxiety is that while there is a biological component, several models for understanding and treating anxiety are based on the premise that individuals can learn to control both physiological and emotional responses. Thus, most treatment approaches are highly consistent with the recovery model.

One aspect of this, however, is determining the cause of the anxiety. It is possible that what the person is attributing to a mental health problem (anxiety) is actually a general medical condition that may aggravate or mimic anxiety symptoms. These general medical conditions can include thyroid disorders, respiratory conditions, blood conditions such as anaemia, and cardiovascular conditions. Further, as noted earlier in this chapter, it is not unusual for someone with panic disorder to believe that they are having a heart attack or suffering from severe asthma. This may indeed be the case and thus the social worker should inquire whether a physician has been consulted. Even if the anxiety is exacerbated by or the manifestation of a medical condition, treatments that help the person assume some mastery over the symptoms can be very helpful. Thus, the recovery process can involve both treatment of the medical condition and the development of strategies to manage or deal with anxiety.

Psychosocial Interventions That Promote Recovery from Anxiety

Psychosocial interventions are a primary method of managing anxiety symptoms. These interventions require full explanation to clients prior to embarking on them because they can be difficult and increase anxiety for a period of time before they decrease anxiety. Clients thus must decide if this is a reasonable approach to their recovery.

Systematic Desensitization and Exposure Therapy

Cognitive-behavioural models that have been developed to manage symptoms of anxiety are exposure therapy and systematic desensitization. In this model of treatment, clients are exposed to anxiety-provoking stimuli in an attempt to develop a habituation response so that the stimuli no longer has power over the individual. As avoidance is prevented, it can no longer be rewarded by negative reinforcement, and anxiety is reduced. The client learns that fear goes away without having to resort to escape (Calhoun and Atkeson, 1991).

The first step in this approach is to develop an anxiety hierarchy in which the person creates a list of things that make him or her anxious in order of intensity. For instance, 1) a picture of a spider web, 2) a picture of a spider, 3) viewing a real spider web, 4) having a real spider web touch my hand, 5) running into a spider web that touches my face, 6) seeing a small spider, 7) having a small spider crawl on my arm . . . etc. In general, the person is then exposed to the lowest level of the hierarchy until the anxiety decreases. The person is then exposed to the next level. In some models of the treatment, however, the person is exposed to the highest level at the outset. This is referred to as flooding (Rothbaum et al., 2000). Exposure can be implemented in a number of different ways. For instance, exposure can be imaginal, in which case the therapist assists the client, who is in a relaxed state, to imagine in vivid detail the feared stimuli. A scenario is constructed for each level of exposure in order that the person can become fully immersed in the image. Exposure can also be *in vivo*, which literally means 'in life' or 'within a living cell or organism', but in this case means 'within the natural environment'. Thus, *in vivo* exposure involves the client being exposed to the actual stimuli. For instance, a person who is fearful of flying may first be encouraged to take the following steps: 1) drive by the airport; 2) go into the airport and look at airplanes; 3) walk down the ramp to the aircraft gate; 4) enter the aircraft while it is on the ground and the door is open; 5) sit in a seat and put the seatbelt on; and 6) take a flight. More recently, virtual reality tools have been used for exposure stimuli. Virtual reality integrates real-time computer graphics, body-tracking devices, visual displays, and other sensory input devices to immerse patients in a computer-generated virtual environment (Powers and Emmelkamp, 2008). Using the airplane example, flight simulators that are made to resemble working aircraft and are used to train airline crews are at times used to assist people who have fears of flying.

Systematic desensitization combines exposure to a feared stimulus with progressive relaxation techniques. In this model, short exposures to the feared stimuli are interrupted and interspersed with relaxation periods. Clients become skilled in the relaxation techniques and learn to use them whenever in a situation where their anxiety is beginning to be triggered by aversive stimuli. Over time, clients can approach the stimuli with no anxiety response at all. A further variation of this is stress inoculation training which involves psychoeducation, relaxation training, guided self-dialogue, covert modelling, role playing, and thought-stopping techniques. In covert modelling the client is taught to visualize the fear-invoking situation and imagine him- or herself confronting it successfully. This is then followed up with role plays where the person acts out successful coping in an anxiety-provoking situation (Calhoun and Atkeson, 1991; Rothbaum et al., 2000).

Exposure-based treatments for anxiety have some of the largest effect sizes reported in the literature (Powers and Emmelkamp, 2008) although various methods of CBT have also proven to be effective in dealing with anxiety (Norton and Price, 2007; Evans et al., 2008). It should be noted, however, that client anxiety will be activated by exposure to treatment and people need to be aware that the treatment will be acutely uncomfortable in order that they are consenting with full information. Virtual reality methods of exposure have been found in meta-analyses to be equally effective to *in vivo* exposure. As this model may provide the client with increased control, it may be that this should be the preferred method.

Family Cognitive-Behavioural Therapy

When anxiety problems occur in children, there is often a reciprocal relationship between the parent and the child. That is, children with anxiety disorders are more likely to have parents with anxiety problems (as discussed above this may be due to both genetic and environmental factors). Parents may facilitate anxiety by reinforcing or modelling avoidance or safety behaviours (Kendall et al., 2008). In adults as well, the family adjusts to the affected person's behaviour and may similarly begin inadvertently to contribute to the problem. Thus, involving the family in CBT treatment has the potential to improve success rates. Family CBT provides education to parents on anxiety and cognitive-behavioural strategies for addressing it. This model aims to modify maladaptive parental beliefs and expectations, teach parents constructive responses to their child's anxious distress, encourage parents to support the child's mastery, and teach parents and children effective communication skills. Further, parents are taught to use the skills themselves when they are feeling acutely anxious or distressed. This model has been found to be highly effective in working with children with anxiety disorders (Ishikawa et al., 2007).

Pharmacological Interventions That Promote Recovery from Anxiety

Due to the distressing nature of anxiety symptoms it is very common for medications and psychosocial interventions to be used in conjunction with one another with favourable results (APA, 2000; Antai-Otong, 2007). Medications can reduce acute symptoms while other methods such as CBT can assist the person to control the onset of symptoms and reduce the intensity of symptoms. A risk-benefit analysis of the use of medication should be performed in conjunction with the wishes and preferences of the client.

Anxiety disturbances tend to last for prolonged periods of time and often clients can have a relapse of symptoms. When medication is stopped, the relapse rate is somewhere between 30 and 50 per cent (APA, 2000). Generally, medication is initiated at low dosages and increased at weekly intervals until symptom relief is experienced. After 12 to 18 months a slow and careful withdrawal with frequent consultation is often attempted. Medications used for anxiety disorders are generally the same as used for depression; a more complete description can be found in Chapter 6.

Generally speaking, the first-line medications in anxiety are the Selective Serotonin Reuptake Inhibitors (SSRIs). This is supported by a significant body of

RCT research that demonstrates their efficacy (APA, 2000; Antai-Otong, 2007). The older tricyclic antidepressants (TCAs) have also been shown to be effective in the treatment of anxiety, although they tend to have more side effects and are more lethal in overdose (Stahl, 2000; Abramowitz, 2006). It is thought that clients with anxiety, particularly OCD, have more tolerance to the side effects of TCAs than those with depression, thus they are often prescribed higher doses. The monoamine oxydase inhibitors (MAOIs) have also been proven to be effective in the treatment of panic disorder and social phobia, especially. As discussed in the treatment of depression, however, they have significant drawbacks regarding the possibility of the serious hypertensive crisis.

The benzodiazapines, which include such drugs as Diazepam (Valium), Lorazapam (Ativan), and Alprazalam (Xanax), are perhaps the most commonly used medications for all types of anxiety disorders. This is not necessarily because they are the best treatments; in fact, many experts in the field warn against their use, particularly in panic disorders (National Institute for Health and Clinical Excellence, 2007). Extreme care should be taken when using these medications because of the risk of dependency and abuse. Even after only eight weeks of treatment 35 per cent of clients demonstrate symptoms of dependency and withdrawal. For this reason, many authors suggest that they are absolutely contraindicated in the presence of substance abuse. In addition, sedation and cognitive impairment including memory loss, particularly in the elderly, are common. Clients should not operate motor vehicles or heavy machinery when starting these agents. If they are used at all, they are best used as adjunctive therapy for the first two to four weeks in clients who do not have substance abuse problems or a family history of substance abuse, and only until longer-term treatments such as SSRI medications or CBT can take effect. In those who have used these agents for a period of time it has been demonstrated that CBT is helpful for withdrawing from these medications.

Possible Social Work Interventions in the Case Examples

Case Example 1: John

John suffers from an obsessive compulsive disorder (OCD) that significantly impacts his activities and his social functioning. However, whether or not John obtains treatment is entirely dependent on his wishes and the degree to which he feels impacted by the problem and its manifestations.

- Should John wish to develop a recovery plan, he should be informed of treatment options, including the various types of cognitive-behavioural therapies available and perhaps a consultation for medication. If John wishes to engage in CBT, the social worker will need to determine whether he or she is qualified to conduct the treatment or whether a referral is necessary.
- John's parents are also affected by his OCD. If John seeks assistance, they may also wish to be involved. Alternatively, they may seek social work advice independently.

Psychoeducational approaches can be very useful in helping families understand the nature of OCD and possible helpful approaches that they may take. If John is seeking treatment, family CBT may be of assistance in reinforcing and supporting positive changes.

Case Example 2: Josi

Josi suffers from a panic disorder that has increasingly restricted her activities and has now led to agoraphobia. This form of anxiety is generally highly disruptive and very concerning for those who suffer from it and their families.

- Josi may seek assistance in dealing with her anxiety and panic. Depending on the severity of her problems, she may need considerable assistance in attending appointments with a social worker and may need to begin with home visits if such an option exists.
- The social worker should begin by trying to understand if there are factors in Josi's environment, such as interpersonal stresses, that are contributing to her anxiety and then work with Josi to resolve some of these issues.
- Josi should be provided with information about various forms of intervention that may be of assistance to her in managing symptoms, including cognitive-behavioural approaches and possibly medication to control severe symptoms while she is attempting to increase her range of activities. She can then decide whether she wishes to participate in any of these interventions in her process of recovery.
- If her family members are significantly affected by her anxiety problems, psychoeducational approaches may be of use in order to ensure that their approaches are helpful and do not increase anxiety.

Summary

At times, all people are exposed to situations that cause some degree of anxiety and fear. To an extent, anxiety and fear are adaptive. Individuals can prepare for challenging situations as a result of anticipatory anxiety, arousal caused by anxiety can heighten senses and assist people to manage in emergency situations, and fear can provoke people to avoid danger. For many people, however, anxiety can move from being an adaptive response to being a maladaptive response that impairs ability and restricts activities and options. In these situations, a variety of intervention approaches can be employed that assist people to move from the state where they feel out of control and hence anxious, to regaining control over their emotions, their physical reactions, and ultimately their lives.

Key Terms

Covert modelling
Existential anxiety
Hypertensive
Inefficacious
Intrapsychic
Panic attacks
Paraesthesias
Separation anxiety

Discussion Questions

1. How may a social worker assist a student who is feeling significant anxiety related to tests and feels that this anxiety is severely affecting their performance?
2. How may family members assist someone with anxiety problems or exacerbate anxiety problems?
3. In what ways may the structure of mental health services impede work with individuals suffering from anxiety?

Suggested Readings and Weblinks

AnxietyBC. *Resources, Results, Relief. Complete Home Tool Kit* (accessed at http://www.anxietybc.com/resources/selfhelp_home_toolkit.php).

Public Health Agency of Canada (2002), *A Report on Mental Illnesses in Canada: Chapter 4 Anxiety* (Ottawa: Health Canada) (accessed at http://www.phac-aspc.gc.ca/publicat/miic-mmac/chap_4_e.html).

Social Workers: Help Starts Here. *Anxiety: How Social Workers Help* (accessed at http://www.helpstartshere.org/mind_and_spirit/anxiety/default.html).

Chapter 10

Delirium and Dementia

Objectives:

- To identify the causes of delirium and dementia
- To identify symptoms and challenges associated with delirium and dementia
- To present models for assessing memory loss
- To discuss special issues for family members
- To discuss elder abuse in the context of dementia
- To present evidence-based approaches to recovery

Case Example 1

Bill and Jean worked together for 28 years at a printing press producing cards for Valentine's Day, Mother's Day, and other events. They were known as the perfect couple, living across the road from their business in a humble abode where they frequently entertained co-workers for tea. As Bill approached his seventies he had increasing difficulty remembering names and phone numbers; gradually this forgetfulness extended to his long-term memory. Bill began to have difficulty finding words that he would previously have used in everyday conversations, and eventually he forgot how to use familiar objects such as the kettle. At times he would become confused, especially in the evening, becoming agitated and fearful. Their son and their family practitioner suggested that Bill should consider a long-term care facility, but Jean felt it her duty to look after him, for better or for worse. On one evening Bill thought he heard a stranger come into the house and when Jean tried to calm him, he wanted to escape out the front door. Bill became increasingly upset and pushed Jean out of the way, hitting her with his cane.

Case Example 2

John is a 53-year-old man who underwent major cardiac surgery secondary to complications caused by Graves' disease, a disorder of the thyroid gland that can result in cardiac, mood, and ocular problems. In the intensive care unit (ICU), John had various tubes and monitors attached to his body, including an IV feeding and medication tube, a catheter, and heart rate and respiration monitors. During the first few days in ICU, John spent most of his time sleeping, coming into consciousness for only brief periods of time. When conscious, he was not sure where he was or why he was there. He recognized his family members but was unable to recall others, such as his doctor. He seemed confused by others and repeatedly asked questions about where he was and why he was being held against his will. Within a few days, John returned to his normal cognitive functioning. Sometime later, however, he revealed to a family member that when in the ICU he believed that he was being held against his will by terrorists. Further, he believed that helicopters were hovering outside his window and armed men in black suits were hanging from these helicopters and attempting to enter his room by breaking through the window. He subsequently realized that as the hospital was a regional trauma centre, the helicopters were going to the hospital's heli-pad, carrying critically ill patients.

The Nature of Dementia and Delirium

Cognition, or thinking, encompasses all the domains for which our brains are responsible, including memory, language, judgment, problem-solving, and praxis (doing things). Dementia and delirium are conditions where there is a significant deficit in cognitive functioning that is considerably different from a previous level of functioning. Dementia is characterized by multiple deficits including impairment in memory. This is generally a progressive, deteriorating condition associated with advancing age, but it also might be associated with substance abuse.

One hundred years ago, Alois Alzheimer first described dementia and the characteristic changes that we now associate with Alzheimer's disease. While in earlier times dementia associated with old age was observed relatively infrequently, advances in medicine and public health have resulted in longer life expectancies and thus increased rates of illness associated with aging. The costs of dementia are considerable. The primary cost, of course, is a human one; that is, the inestimable anguish caused by seeing a loved and respected family member gradually declining before our eyes. In addition to this there are considerable costs to both health care and social services. The annual societal cost of care per patient with dementia is estimated to be $36,794 for those who suffer from the severe disease (Hux et al., 1998). This cost rises exponentially when there are behavioural symptoms requiring increased care (Murman et al., 2002). There are also indirect economic costs related to loss of productivity and increased financial burden on the families of those suffering from this illness (Barcia, 2000).

Delirium is a disturbance in consciousness and a change in cognition that develops over a short period of time, often secondary to a medical condition or substance abuse. The case of John earlier in this chapter is an example of such a condition. The defining characteristic of delirium is a fluctuating capacity to focus and sustain attention, in addition to impaired memory. Clients are often disorientated, not knowing who they are or where they are, or, more commonly, they are unaware of the date or the passage of time. Their mood may change suddenly, often resulting in states of anxiety or fear. At other times they may be euphoric, intrusive, or inappropriate. Characteristically in delirium tremens they are frightened and this is often accompanied by visual hallucinations and delusions. Sometimes they act out upon these delusions and attempt to leave the room or escape from a situation that they see as threatening. Some people with delirium are hyperactive, but some are quite the opposite. Notably those who are loud and boisterous come to the attention of the staff, while those who are withdrawn and quiet may be underdiagnosed.

Prevalence and Incidence

By the year 2031 it's estimated that at least three-quarters of a million Canadians will suffer from some form of dementia. Approximately two-thirds of these will have Alzheimer's disease (AD). The prevalence of dementia in people over 55 doubles every five years in the developed countries (Alzheimer's Disease International, 1999). It is estimated that in those over 71, 13.9 per cent of the population suffer from dementia; in the over-85 group this goes up to 19.6 per cent; and in the over-90 age group, 37.4 per cent of the population have this devastating disease (Plassman et al., 2007).

While dementia is universal, there are some differences based on demographic characteristics. Most studies suggest that females are overrepresented in the population of those suffering from dementia. There is an inverse relationship between years of education and the risk of dementia; that is, those with higher levels of education are more likely to develop the disease (Ott et al., 1995; Plassman et al., 2007). There are suggestions that urban populations have higher rates of prevalence than rural populations. Notable anomalies in the literature suggest that the Cree nation has a lower prevalence than other groups in North America and there is a lower prevalence in Nigeria than in other parts of the world (Alzheimer's Disease International, 1999). While the reasons for this are not fully understood, one possibility is that different forms of classification result in differences in reported prevalence (Riedel-Heller et al., 2001).

Delirium is a constellation of signs and symptoms caused by an assault on the brain, often secondary to another medical issue. Therefore, delirium is most commonly found in hospital inpatient wards and emergency departments. The incidence in emergency departments is approaching 10 per cent when strict operational criteria for diagnosis are used, but the incidence may be as high as 50 per cent using the criteria of the 'presence of altered mental state' alone (Davis, 2005). The incidence in general medical patients may be as high as 40 per cent. Delirium is often referred to as 'confusion' or a 'confusional state' in this setting. Most notably, following complicated surgery such as cardiac surgery, the incidence may be as high as 75 per cent and perhaps even higher in those undergoing hip surgery who may have a variety of risk factors.

Factors Contributing to Dementia

While dementia can be caused by a number of different conditions, such as hypothyroidism or vitamin B12 deficiency (Davis, 2005), it is generally related to one of two forms of deterioration: 1) that affecting the cerebral cortex and 2) that affecting subcortical areas. The cortical dementias include Alzheimer's disease and Pick's disease. Subcortical dementias include Huntington's dementia, Parkinson's dementia, and Lewy body dementia (see Figure 9.1).

Alois Alzheimer's groundbreaking work in 1906 described two types of microscopic findings in the brains of people suffering from Alzheimer's, namely, amyloid plaque and characteristic tangles in the filaments of the brain, known as neurofibrillary tangles. Later research has determined that the development of amyloid plaque contributes to the formation of the neurofibrillary tangles which in turn leads to damage of nerve cells, and subsequently their loss or atrophy. It has been established that the pathology associated with Alzheimer's results in significant neuronal loss such that the brain is lighter when weighed on post-mortem examination than those of people without this disease (Barcia, 2000; Stahl, 2000). More recently, studies of Alzheimer's have shown that the disease is inherited through autosomal dominant transmission, and one particular mutated gene has been identified.

Alzheimer's Dementia

Alzheimer's is the most common form of cognitive disorder and thus the area where we will focus much of the attention for the remainder of this chapter. In general, Alzheimer's is diagnosed by ruling out all other causes of cognitive impairment or dementia. Alzheimer's disease can be divided into early onset (before the age of 65) and late onset (after the age of 65). It can also be differentiated based on whether or not there are significant clinical behavioural issues that cause difficulties for family members and caregivers.

Vascular Dementia

This form of dementia develops secondarily to vascular disease such as strokes or multiple infarcts. It can occur with or without delirium, delusions, and/or depressed mood. Generally, symptoms include aphasia (language disturbances), apraxia (motor disturbances), agnosia (failure to recognize objects), and disturbances in executive functioning (planning, organizing, etc.).

Specific Medical Dementias

There are a number of dementias caused by specific medical conditions. These include: dementia due to head trauma; dementia due to Parkinson's disease; dementia due to HIV disease; dementia due to Huntington's disease; dementia due to Pick's disease; and dementia due to Creutzfeldt-Jakob disease (also known as mad cow's disease).

Substance-Induced Dementia

This type of dementia is the result of chronic substance use. Korsakoff's syndrome, which is often equated with substance-induced dementia, is a specific condition stemming from a vitamin deficiency caused by chronic alcoholism, or severe malnutrition.

Alcoholism often results in poor nutrition, which in addition to inflammation of the stomach lining, causes thiamine deficiency. Other causes can include dietary deficiencies, prolonged vomiting, eating disorders, or the effects of chemotherapy.

Factors Contributing to Delirium

While there are many causes of delirium as shown in Box 10.1, substance abuse and intoxication are the most common. Alcohol withdrawal is often associated with delirium tremens. Benzodiazepine (e.g., Valium) withdrawal can also cause delirium. Delirium is common following surgery, particularly cardiac surgery. Clients who have pre-existing risk factors, including high blood pressure, smoking, or a history of pre-existing cognitive impairment, are likely to have a higher prevalence, as are older people. Clients with a history of alcohol and drug abuse are particularly at risk.

Delirium Due to a General Medical Condition

A delirium caused by a medical condition is a disturbance in consciousness that develops over a short period of time (usually hours or days) and tends to fluctuate during the day. It can be associated with central nervous system assaults

Box 10.1 Causes of Delirium

Infections	Pneumonia Brain abscess
Traumatic	Head trauma Subdural haematoma
Metabolic	Endocrine (adrenal, thyroid, diabetes) Electrolyte abnormalities Drug abuse/withdrawal Toxins/medications Cardiac failure Liver failure Kidney failure
Carcinogenic	Brain tumour
Vascular	CVA (stroke) Transient ischaemic attack
Miscellaneous	Burns Post-op Seizure-related

such as head trauma, vascular disease (for instance, stroke), infection, or a brain tumour; metabolic disorders such as renal failure, dehydration, or hypoglycaemia; cardiopulmonary disorders, such as heart failure or respiratory failure; systemic illnesses or infections such as pneumonia; and systemic assaults such as trauma or sensory deprivation.

Substance-Induced Delirium

This type of delirium may be caused by intoxication or withdrawal. Substance intoxication delirium can occur within minutes or hours of taking a particular substance such as cannabis, cocaine, or hallucinogens, among others. However, it can occur over time with repeated use of some substances such as diazepam (Valium). Usually this resolves within a few hours or days as the substance leaves the body. Substance withdrawal delirium can last for a few hours or up to two to four weeks depending on the nature of the drug.

The Course of Dementia

The course of Alzheimer's dementia is typically characterized by a gradual and subtle onset that progresses slowly. The initial symptoms, only diagnosable by psychological testing, are referred to as mild cognitive impairment (MCI). MCI progresses to dementia at the rate of approximately 3 to 15 per cent per year, and within 10 years, 70 to 80 per cent of cases with MCI will have developed Alzheimer's (Backman, 2008; Craik, 2008). A person with mild clinical impairment generally experiences isolated memory impairment that gradually progresses to dementia over a period of 2 to 5 years. After a further 2 to 3 years, assisted living is often necessary due to significant deterioration in functioning. As the disease progresses there are a number of physical changes that include appetite disturbance and weight loss, difficulty walking, tremors, and incontinence. Later in the disease, clients have difficulty eating and swallowing and become bedridden, leading to further complications such as bedsores and bronchial infections. Eventually patients tend to die from pneumonia or blood poisoning, often 9 to 10 years after the initial diagnosis is made.

Vascular dementia, which is the second most common cause of dementia, is differentiated by a stepwise intellectual deterioration. This is thought to be caused by small progressive cerebral vascular accidents (CVA) or strokes. These mini- or micro-strokes gradually cause deterioration. Generally there is evidence of at least one significant stroke although this is not always the case. In vascular dementia the clinical history, neurological examination, and brain imaging studies can be used to confirm the diagnosis. There is generally a family history of vascular disease and the client may have other risk factors such as hypertension, smoking, or obesity. There is a wide variation in the symptomotology due to the fact that different areas of the brain may be targeted. Neuroimaging may demonstrate the exact lesions.

In Lewy body dementia there is progressive dementia with features of Parkinson's disease. It is not uncommon to have delusions in this disorder as well as visual hallucinations. The differential diagnosis is complicated by the fact that Lewy body dementia may appear in clients with AD. In the frontotemporal dementias such as Pick's disease there is marked change in personality and language. This is also characterized by gradual onset and a progressively deteriorating course. In some cases this occurs in a younger group than AD. There is often a family history of frontotemporal dementia.

Symptoms

Memory Loss

All people experience some cognitive differences as they age, and sometimes this leads to dementia. Those who go on to develop dementia have been found to demonstrate memory impairments many years before the clinical diagnosis is made in both Alzheimer's disease and vascular dementia (Backman, 2008). The earliest changes tend to be in recent or working memory where encoding and retrieval of information is required (Craik, 2008; Luo and Craik, 2008). Very often this presents itself as a difficulty noting and remembering names and finding simple objects such as car keys. Memory for specific events such as appointments or dinner dates may also be impaired. Other types of memory, for instance, general knowledge and biographical information, are generally only affected much later. Preclinical dementia or moderate cognitive impairment (MCI) can be diagnosable by specific cognitive testing. It is thought that 3 to 15 per cent of people with this convert to Alzheimer's disease each year and in 10 years 70 to 80 per cent of them will have Alzheimer's (Backman, 2008).

Personality Change

It is not unusual to find personality changes in those suffering from dementia often causing great distress to the family members and friends (Neugroschl et al., 2005). Characteristically there is apathy and listlessness with a narrowing of emotions, especially the loss of warmth and humour. The client seems to lose interest in everything and may sit all day apparently doing very little. Some display embarrassing and disinhibited behaviours, although this is most common in the frontotemporal dementias. Aggression is not uncommon and may be related to psychotic symptoms, such as delusions and hallucinations, as well as the perplexity of not knowing where they are or of not recognizing caregivers.

Functional Impairment

The first signs of functional impairment may be related to financial transactions or use of transportation. Later the client may become easily lost and be unable to discern the function of commonly used appliances such as a VCR or, as things progress, a kettle or a toaster. These initial changes may at first be subtle but as the illness progresses they become more marked. Activities of daily living, including dressing and attention to hygiene, may be impaired, leading to the necessity of providing increased support services.

Language

Generally speaking, the first facet of language to deteriorate is word finding. This may lead to unusual or idiosyncratic speech such as frequent repetition or use of malapropisms. Later, comprehension and all aspects of language may be affected.

Agnosis

This may initially present itself as a difficulty in recognizing and naming objects. Later there may be significant impairment and recognition of peoples' faces, even of close friends and family, a symptom which is particularly distressing. A sign that is perhaps the only pathognomonic sign of AD is the inability to recognize one's own face in the mirror (Lovestone, 2000), which can be very frightening. Pathognomonic refers to a sign or symptom that is so characteristic of a disease that it makes the diagnosis.

Psychosis

It is not uncommon for there to be psychotic symptoms in those suffering from AD. In fact, 10 to 50 per cent of people suffer from delusions. These are characteristically persecutory delusions but may also include delusions of misidentification (CAPGRAS syndrome) or delusions of jealousy. Hallucinations are not quite as common but may include the more usual visual hallucinations as well as auditory hallucinations.

Assessment of Dementia

Dementia is usually identified through a careful assessment, sometimes over a period of time in repeated visits. Home visits are often helpful in order to see the client in the context of their daily lives and to perform functional assessments. These can be surprising. In some cases clients who seemed quite impaired in the unfamiliar surroundings of a hospital can cope quite well at home. In other cases a client who appeared quite coherent at a single interview may appear dysfunctional in the complex atmosphere of home. Since the client is often unable to give a history, collateral information is absolutely vital. Thus, the role of social work can be of great assistance to the team in determining the extent of the illness and the consequences for the client and family.

Other members of the interdisciplinary team should be paying attention to possibly treatable causes of dementia such as diabetes, thyroid abnormalities, or vitamin B12 deficiency. Routine laboratory tests such as a full blood count, thyroid test, calcium test, and fasting glucose should be performed in all cases. A CT scan in order to seek other causes such as subdural haematoma (a brain injury in which there is bleeding into the lining of the brain) or hydrocephalus (abnormal accumulation of bodily fluid in the brain) is helpful and may reveal the typical atrophy (neuronal loss) found in Alzheimer's (Greenberg and Muraca, 2007).

Brief cognitive screening can be very helpful in identifying dementia and these are tests that social workers can perform in any setting (Feldman et al., 2008).

The results of these tests can assist social workers in determining whether a referral for additional assessment should be made and what types of social work interventions might be most useful—in that they are targeted towards the client's needs and abilities. The mini-mental state examination (MMSE) can be performed in 10 minutes and requires little training (see Table 10.1). A maximum score is 30; a score of between 18 and 26 demonstrates mild dementia; a score of 10 to 18 indicates moderate dementia; and less than 10 indicates severe dementia.

The clock-drawing test is a quick and simple test that again requires only a few minutes and little training. The individual is simply asked to draw a clock and write in the numbers and show the time at 10 minutes past 11. The test is surprisingly sensitive and specific.

Table 10.1 The Mini-Mental Status Exam

Maximum score	Score	
		ORIENTATION
5	( )	What is the: (year) (season) (date) (day) (month)
5	( )	Where are we: (state) (county) (town) (facility) (floor)
		REGISTRATION
3	( )	Name three objects and have person repeat them back. Give one point for each correct answer on the first trial. 1.______ 2.______ 3.______ Then repeat them (up to 6x) until all three are learned. [Number of trials ____]
		ATTENTION AND CALCULATION
5	( )	Serial 7's. Count backwards from 100 by serial 7's. One point for each correct answer. Stop after 5 answers. [93 86 79 72 65] Alternatively spell 'world' backwards. [D - L - R - O - W]
		RECALL
3	( )	Ask for the names of the three objects learned above. Give one point for each correct answer.
		LANGUAGE
9	( )	Name: a pen (1 point) and a watch (1 point) Repeat the following: 'No ifs, ands, or buts' (1 point) Follow a three-stage command: 'Take this paper in your [non-dominant] hand, fold it in half, and put it on the floor.' (3 points) [1 point for each part correctly performed] Read to self and then do: 'Close your eyes' (1 point) Write a sentence [subject, verb, and makes sense] (1 point) Copy design [5-sided geometric figure; 2 points must intersect] (1 point)

Score: ___ /30 Alert Overtly Anxious Concentration Difficulty Drowsy

Special Issues for Family Members Caring for Relatives with Dementia

Caregiver burden is defined as the negative impact on one's social, occupational, and personal well-being as a result of caring for an infirmed person, usually a relative. The burden experienced by caregivers of those with Alzheimer's or other forms of dementia results from functional deficits of the ill person, the degree to which he or she depends on family members for personal care, for instance with hygiene, disorientation of the ill person, and disruptive behaviours such as wandering and aggression (Sussman, 2006). As a result of this burden, family members often experience depression and a variety of physical health problems related to stress (Gonzalez-Salvador et al., 1999). In one study of family caregivers for individuals with Alzheimer's disease, 65 per cent exhibited symptoms of depression (Papastavrou et al., 2007). Clearly, this is an issue of great concern to social workers as the well-being of the client with dementia is highly contingent on the well-being of those family members who participate in their care.

Caregiver burden can be experienced by anyone caring for a person with dementia and is most commonly associated with care provided by offspring, primarily adult daughters who become caught between the needs of their impaired parents and the needs of their own spouses and adolescent children. However, it has recently been suggested that spousal caregivers often experience the highest burden of care. First, spousal caregivers are grieving the loss of their partner, as a result of a long and devastating illness. Although the person with dementia is physically alive, his or her psychological presence in the relationship dissipates as the disease progresses. In addition to facing the loss of their lifelong partners, spousal caregivers of persons with dementia are more likely to struggle with their own health problems, spend

Box 10.2 The Clock-Drawing Test

Method:

The person undergoing testing is asked to:

- Draw a clock
- Put in all the numbers
- Set the hands at 10 past 11

Scoring:

There are a number of scoring systems for this test.

The Alzheimer's disease cooperative scoring system is based on a score of five points.

- 1 point for the clock circle
- 1 point for all the numbers being in the correct order
- 1 point for the numbers being in the proper special order
- 1 point for the two hands of the clock
- 1 point for the correct time

A normal score is four or five points.

more hours per week caregiving, and care for relatives with more severe behavioural problems than other familial caregivers (Sussman and Regehr, 2009).

A significant degree of caregiver stress has emerged from the results of government policies that focus on deinstitutionalization, or the movement of care of elderly and infirmed individuals from institutional care to the community. Part of this move has been ideological; that is, it is better for individuals to be in the community. However, part of this move has also been financial, in that community-based care is far less expensive than institutional care. The lower cost is in large part due to limited resources flowing to community care and a reliance on family members to take over care responsibilities that might otherwise be provided by members of the health care team (Sussman and Regehr, 2009). For instance, family members may become responsible for medication management, for ensuring the person gets to medical appointments, for assisting with activities of daily living such as showering and dressing, and even for some medical treatments, such as the dressing of wounds. Social workers need to become familiar with the nature of tasks required of any family member and advocate for community-based services as required.

Abuse of Older People with Dementia

In 2002, the World Health Organization (WHO) published the *Toronto Declaration on the Global Prevention of Elder Abuse* that included the following definition: 'Elder abuse is a single or repeated act, or lack of appropriate action, occurring within any relationship where there is an expectation of trust, which causes harm or distress to an older person. It can be of various forms: physical, psychological/emotional, sexual, financial, or simply reflect intentional or unintentional neglect.' Further, the declaration states: 'Elder abuse is the violation of human rights and a significant cause of injury, illness, lost productivity, isolation, and despair. Confronting and reducing elder abuse requires a multi-disciplinary approach.' This statement by the WHO underlines that elder abuse is a universal issue and not limited to any one culture or country. Indeed, a special issue of *Educational Gerontology* in 2006 contained articles highlighting the problem of elder abuse in Israel (Rabi, 2006), Japan (Arai, 2006), Germany (Konig and Leembruggen-Kallberg, 2006), Brazil (Bezerra-Flanders and Clark, 2006), as well as with African-Americans (Tauriac and Scruggs, 2006).

The WHO estimates that the rate of elder abuse across Canada, the Netherlands, the United States, Finland, and Great Britain is between 4 and 6 per cent. According to estimates of the National Research Panel in 2003, between 1 and 2 million Americans age 65 and older have been injured, exploited, or maltreated by someone on whom they depended for care and protection. Further, it is estimated that for every one case that is reported, five or more go unreported. In Canada, approximately 7 per cent of four thousand adults aged 65 and older who responded to the 1999 *General Social Survey on Victimization* (GSS) reported that they had experienced some form of emotional abuse by an adult child, spouse, or caregiver in the past five years, 1 per cent reported physical abuse, and 1 per cent reported financial abuse (Statistics Canada, 2002). One-quarter of older adults who are victims of homicide are killed by family members, most commonly a spouse (39 per cent), adult child (37 per cent), or extended family member (24 per cent). More than half of older women who are murdered are killed by their spouses, versus 25 per cent of older male murder victims. Older men are twice as likely to be killed by their adult sons.

Why is elder abuse a growing issue? The population of older adults in the Western World is growing rapidly with improved health care, nutrition, and living conditions. In 2006 in Canada, the proportion of older adults was 13.7 per cent and it is expected to reach 20 per cent by 2024. The fastest-growing group are those adults over the age of 80—a group that is expected to rise 43 per cent between 2001 and 2011. In the United States, the proportion of older people hit 13 per cent in 1990 (11 years earlier than Canada) with 31 million Americans being at least 65 years of age. By the year 2030, it is expected that 85 million people will be 65 or older and 8 million will be over the age of 85. Other countries already have much higher proportions of persons aged 65 or over than Canada and the United States. In Japan, Germany, and Italy, roughly one person in five is 65 years or older. Increasingly, older adults are living in the community with family members and spouses. As people become more medically fragile or cognitively impaired, they place an increased burden on family members physically, emotionally, and financially. Increased family frustration combined with increased vulnerability of the elderly person can create a dangerous environment.

Assessment of Elder Abuse

While health care practitioners are most likely to be in a position to identify abuse in an elderly person, everyone has an obligation to ensure that vulnerable individuals in our society are safe from harm. Several tools exist for screening for abuse; some require training and others are simple to administer without training. One of the most user-friendly tools can be distilled into six short screening questions as shown in Box 10.3 (Fulmer et al., 2004; Bomba, 2006). The use of these questions not only identifies abuse but also demonstrates an openness to discussing issues of abuse and the desire to offer assistance.

Box 10.3 Elder Abuse: Screening Questions

1. Are you afraid of anyone in your family?
2. Has anyone close to you tried to hurt or harm you recently?
3. Has anyone close to you called you names or put you down or made you feel bad recently?
4. Does someone in your family make you stay in bed or tell you you're sick when you aren't?
5. Has anyone forced you to do things you did not want to do?
6. Has anyone taken things that belong to you without your OK?

If elder abuse is suspected, there are three issues to consider (Bomba, 2006): 1) Is the person safe? 2) Will the person accept intervention? and 3) Does the person have the capacity to refuse intervention? Not all abuse situations constitute an emergency and, thus, if the person is safe, it is possible to develop a longer-term relationship and move towards a plan to end the abuse if the person agrees to intervention. If the person does not agree to allow assistance, intervention can only be forced upon them if they do not have the capacity to consent to or refuse intervention. That is, people are allowed the self-determination to remain in abusive situations if they fully understand the nature and consequences of their decision. If they are not competent to consent or refuse, other options such as Adult Protective Services can be called in to assist.

When an elderly person is assessed as abused and he or she agrees to the intervention, safety plans and alternative living arrangements can be initiated. The problem arises when the person is unwilling to agree to the intervention. In such a case a determination must be made whether the individual is competent to consent. In order for a person to have the capacity to consent he or she must be able to understand information that is provided to them and how that information applies to their specific situation. The Ontario Health Care Consent Act (1996), for instance, states that a person is capable of consenting to treatment if 'the person is able to understand the information that is relevant to making a decision about the treatment . . . and able to appreciate the reasonably foreseeable consequences of a decision or lack of decision' (section 4[1]). Capacity is not viewed as a blanket status—it is specific to a particular procedure and a particular time frame. Thus, a person may be incapable of consenting to some treatments yet capable of consenting to others. For example, a person may be able to consent to such procedures as blood work, but not to major procedures such as cardiac surgery. In addition, consent is fluid. A person may be capable of consenting to a particular procedure at one time but incapable of consenting to the same procedure at another time (Regehr and Kanani, 2006). As a result of the complexities around the issue of consent and the risk of undermining the civil rights and self-determination of elderly individuals, Adult Protective Services as an approach to elder abuse remains highly controversial (Anderson and Mangels, 2006).

Recovery-Oriented Psychosocial Interventions for Dementia

The recovery model may not immediately seem applicable to working with people with dementia as a result of the progress deterioration associated with the illness. Indeed a search of various databases of scholarly articles only resulted in one article that addressed the use of the recovery model in cases of dementia. However, it is important to return to a definition of recovery when considering its application in this situation. Within the recovery model, recovery is not understood to be synonymous with sustained remission or cure. Rather, recovery can be defined as living a satisfying, hopeful, and contributing life even with the limitations caused by the illness (Anthony, 1993). From this perspective, social workers must have an optimistic and hope-inducing view of the ability of people to find meaning in their experiences and generate a narrative about themselves that does not include the disease and subsequent disability (Slade and Hayward, 2007).

In cases of dementia, early identification and treatment is essential. Various research studies have demonstrated that interventions focused on increased cognitive activity appear to be preventative of dementia and perhaps slow this conversion, although this is yet to be well-established (Herrmann and Lanctot, 2007; Seow and Gauthier, 2007; Stahl, 2000). These cognitive activities include discussions and any type of intellectual stimulation, such as regular crosswords. It has also been suggested that regular exercise and physical activity also play a preventative role. These activities can produce meaning, involve enjoyment, and engender hope.

Caregiver Support and Relief

One form of prevention attempts to address family stress caused by caregiving. In this approach, increased services are offered in the community, such as community nursing and day treatment programs for elderly individuals with physical disabilities (for instance, caused by stroke) or dementia. The notion is that increased services will result in reduced stress and burden; this in turn will reduce abuse caused by caregiver stress. A recent study of the spousal caregivers of people with dementia, however, suggests that services alone do not provide a simple solution to caregiver stress. Using interviews and surveys, the study found that in-home services such as homemakers, nurses, occupational therapists, and case managers, did little to reduce the burden on spouses caring for their partners with dementia. In fact, the stress of dealing with multiple service delivery people in the home created additional stress for some. Rather, the only effective service in reducing caregiver stress in this study was the provision of adult day treatment programs (sometimes referred to as daycare) that provided not only respite for the spousal caregiver, but also opportunities for social interaction for their partners with dementia (Sussman and Regehr, 2009). Thus, investment in day treatment would seem to be an effective means for reducing elder abuse caused by stress.

Reminiscence Therapy

Reminiscence therapy involves the recall of life events or the telling of one's life story either to an individual or within a group context. The main objectives of reminiscence therapy are to facilitate the recall of past experiences, strengthen the sense of personal identity, and promote interpersonal functioning, thus improving well-being. In addition, however, reminiscence therapy, particularly in a group context, provides cognitively impaired individuals with opportunities for social interaction and enjoyment. Controlled studies have demonstrated that this type of intervention both improves cognitive abilities and reduces depression in individuals suffering from dementia (Woods et al., 2005; Moos and Bjorn, 2006; Wang, 2007). In addition, caregiver strain showed a significant decrease for caregivers participating in groups with their relative with dementia in reminiscence therapy, and staff knowledge of group members' backgrounds improved significantly, thereby enhancing interactions between clients and staff. No harmful effects were identified on the outcome measures reported.

Reminiscence therapy is sometimes combined with other forms of treatment such as art therapy or music therapy. In these cases, the clients with dementia engage in some activity and then engage in discussions about topics that emerge from previous life experiences (Moos and Bjorn, 2006). The topics discussed are often of emotional significance and provide opportunities for clients to share their prior successes and achievements. It may also provide some opportunities for working through painful issues. Clients can work on their skills of listening to others and asking appropriate questions, which in turn enhances their ability to engage with friends and family outside of the group setting.

Reality Orientation

Reality orientation (RO) is a model of therapy intended to address the disorientation caused by lack of sensory stimuli in people with dementia. It is based on the belief that continually and repeatedly telling or showing certain reminders to people with mild to moderate memory loss will result in an increase in interaction with others and improved orientation. This in turn can improve self-esteem and reduce problem behaviours (Larkin, 1994). RO often involves using all the senses. Windows can be opened or walks taken out of doors to experience weather changes. Familiar smells or tastes can be introduced to remind people of experiences outside of institutional care. In people in early stages of dementia, RO can involve looking at newspapers and reviewing important issues (Spector et al., 2000). During the process, the person is reminded of the date, and of upcoming important events such as elections. Depending on the progress of the illness, flashcards, games, or puzzles can be used to stimulate mental activity. In very confused individuals, the focus may be on the person's name, family members identified in pictures, or familiar objects. The intervention can be administered individually or in groups; it can be delivered by caregivers and family members and in institutional settings can be engaged in by all members of the treatment team. A *Cochrane Review* (Spector et al., 2000) and other meta-analyses (Bates, Boote, and Beverley, 2004) conclude that RO has a significant short-term effect on cognition and behaviour.

Pharmacology as Part of a Recovery-Oriented Approach to Dementia

Medications Targeting Cognitive Functioning

The primary theory that relates to psychopharmacological therapy in dementia is the acetylcholine theory. According to this theory, a substance called acetyl COA combines with choline to produce acetylcholine. This is facilitated by an enzyme called choline acetyl transferase. Acetylcholine in its turn is broken down into two substances, acetylcholinesterase (AChE) and butyryl cholinesterase (BuChE). It has been established that a deficit of acetylcholine in certain parts of the brain leads to a decrease in memory. Conversely, restoring this deficit by increasing acetylcholine enhances memory. The medications most commonly used are called cholinesterase inhibitors. They work by delaying the breakdown of acetylcholine released into the synaptic cleft, thereby leaving more acetylcholine available.

As a result of these findings substances that boost acetylcholine levels have been devised and tested experimentally and clinically on clients suffering from dementia. However, despite early excitement about this approach, the results have been somewhat disappointing. While the response to these medications tends to be detectable with psychological testing and perhaps on rating scales done by caregivers, unfortunately the response is not detectable by the client. Generally speaking, the effects last for six months and for reasons that are unclear the client then reverts to her previous level of functioning. This may mean that the deterioration is delayed for six months, meaning in some cases six precious months at home, as opposed to the nursing home (Birks, 2006; Seow and Gauthier, 2007).

It is postulated that amyloid plaque formation causes inflammation in the brain that may be partly responsible for the symptoms of dementia. For this reason Aspirin and other inflammatory drugs have been used in the treatment of dementia. At this stage there is little evidence to support their use. As well, future research has been embarked upon that will look at the possibility of vaccines to prevent beta amyloid formation. This is very exciting research although it is not anticipated that these will be available in the near future.

There is a growing body of evidence from observational and anecdotal sources that omega-3 fatty acid supplements may have a protective effect against dementia. However, the few clinical trials available have shown that at best there was an arrested decline only in patients with mild forms of Alzheimer's. Various other agents have been used in the dementia, with varying degrees of success. Folic acid is one of the vitamins that has shown some promise in general use. It is known that decreased folic acid can be one of the reversible causes of dementia and it is thought that this deficit may play a more general role in cognitive disorders. However, the use of folic acid routinely has not been proven to have a positive effect. Ginko biloba demonstrated some early promise but the more exacting *Cochrane Review* demonstrated that although early trials showed some promise, these were small and unsatisfactory. Later, larger more rigorous trials found no difference between using a placebo and using ginko biloba. It is postulated that circadian rhythms are disturbed in dementia and this may result in some of the symptoms. Therefore, if the timing systems are synchronized by bright-light therapy (see Chapter 8) and melatonin this moderately improves sleep, attenuates cognitive function, and decreases aggression (Riemersma-van der Lek et al., 2008).

Medications Targeting Neuropsychiatric Symptoms

Apart from the core memory problems, other symptoms occur in 50 to 90 per cent of clients with dementia and are important factors resulting in the loss of functional abilities and, often, institutionalization. Institutionalization is a drastic step that results in separation from family and friends as well as loss of autonomy. It also increases the cost of caring for somebody with this serious disorder. The prevalence of agitation and aggression is alarmingly high in dementia and results in substantial anguish to clients and their caregivers. The first line of treatment is thought to be the SSRI antidepressants, which are discussed in Chapter 8. Generally speaking, doses are significantly lower than those used in younger clients with mood disorders. As well, a number of other agents have proved to be successful, including some of the anticonvulsant mood stabilizers, such as Carbamazepine as well as Trazodone and Buspirone (Glancy and Knott, 2003). Often agitation and aggression are secondary to delusions and hallucinations and therefore antipsychotics have been widely used for these disorders. Although conventional antipsychotics were used for many years, recently the second-generation agents have been used (Ballard, Waite, and Birks, 2006). The effects have been modestly successful with a response rate of over 60 per cent. A recent comprehensive study, the CATIE-AD, however, has demonstrated disappointing results in the use of antipsychotics in dementia (Herrmann and Lanctot, 2007). This comprehensive trial found an increased chance of death due to cardiovascular events or pneumonia at a rate of 2.4 times in those who were treated with second-generation antipsychotics. It should be noted that the outcome measure used in this trial was the time to the point where the medication was discontinued. This is an unusual outcome measure since most studies on most medications have measured clinical response. The study has been significantly criticized on these grounds. In practice these medications are widely used despite this recent warning. It is generally concluded that should the client be harmful to themselves or others, then these medications are still indicated. However, their use should generally be as short term as possible and consideration should be given to weaning the client off these medications if at all possible.

Recovery-Oriented Approaches to the Treatment of Delirium

The treatment of delirium can be effectively divided into three separate phases, although inevitably there is a lot of overlap among these phases: investigation of the underlying causes, instituting management of the acute phase, and stabilization and recovery.

Investigation of the Underlying Cause

The first stage of intervention is a thorough evaluation and risk assessment in order to establish a diagnosis in the context of any underlying conditions that may have predisposed the individual to this diagnosis (Foreman et al., 2003). This will often include collateral information obtained from relatives and caregivers. Since the client will be unlikely to give a coherent history, this may be vital in certain circumstances. For instance the client's medical history and a list of their medications are of paramount importance. It is also important to obtain a picture of the pre-morbid cognitive functioning of the client. Most commonly the client would be in a hospital setting allowing for a thorough physical examination and work-up. Following this a review of all results, including toxicology, is done, in order to identify the potential etiological factors. The next stage would be to attempt to treat or correct the underlying cause. For example, if the cause is a lack of oxygen (hypoxia), this could indicate that the administration of oxygen may prove to cure the problem.

Management of the Acute Situation

It is sometimes necessary to administer medications to treat psychotic symptoms and to prevent the client from harming themselves or others in an emergency situation (Barcia, 2000). Generally speaking, the use of antipsychotic medication remains the standard and recent reviews have supported this. The conventional antipsychotics have been used for many years and in low doses are still considered acceptable (see Table 7.1). In higher doses they themselves have side effects that may be troublesome. More recently the second-generation antipsychotics have been increasingly used and are at least as effective, with fewer side effects (see Table 7.2). In an acutely agitated client a small dose of a short-acting benzodiazepine (Lorazepam) is commonly used, often in conjunction with an antipsychotic.

Stablization and Recovery

It is essential to provide a therapeutic environment, monitoring the right amount of stimulation, along with calm and consistent reassurance. Both patients and family members should be provided with information about the disorder and the course of recovery. Exposure to familiar people and belongings can help restore calm in somebody who is perplexed about their situation. Family members can assist by talking about familiar people and events and by reminding the person where they are and what date, time, and season it is. Early mobilization is essential and as the client progresses, cognitively stimulating activities, such as providing conversation, games, and reading matter, as well as constant reality orientation, may be helpful (Foreman et al., 2003). Delirium can be a particularly upsetting experience for clients and their families, and mental health workers should provide follow-up discussions and possibly debriefing or brief therapy if this is considered likely.

Possible Social Work Interventions in the Case Examples

Case Example 1: Jean and Bill

Bill is suffering from dementia, characterized by progressive deterioration in cognitive functioning, personality change, and violence that results from frustration with his limitations and a lack of cognitive capacity to cope with the frustration. This is a disturbing and frightening situation for both Bill (although he may not overtly display his awareness of this) and for Jean as she watches her life partner change.

- The first task of the social worker is a risk assessment. Is there any reason to believe that the safety of either Bill or Jean is in jeopardy? A safety plan should be established to deal with any possible future violent episodes.
- Social work interventions with Bill will depend on his level of cognitive functioning. It may be that he is aware of his deficits and is able to discuss the meaning that they hold for him. In addition, techniques aimed at preserving memory such as reminiscence therapy and reality orientation can be very useful. These techniques can involve family members and can, in the end, be satisfying for all parties.
- The social worker should assess the stresses that Jean is experiencing and the supports available to her. Supportive counselling and advocacy for appropriate resources can be useful in reducing her stress and burden and assisting her to continue to care for Bill at home. However, the possibility of long-term care should be approached. Jean should be made aware of options available and the processes and timelines required to move to institutional care.
- If institutional care is being considered, Bill must be involved in the discussions to the degree that he is able to understand.

Case Example 2: John

John was suffering from delirium subsequent to major cardiac surgery. This delirium was relatively short-lived and cleared before he was discharged from hospital. A social worker involved in this case is most likely a medical social worker who regularly works in an ICU or on a surgical unit.

- Social work interventions in this case would focus on the family. In large part this will involve psychoeducation about the nature of post-operative delirium and reassurance that this is a normal and transient reaction. In addition, the social worker may discuss plans for John's return home and any adjustments that will have to be made based on his medical condition.

Summary

Two types of illnesses are generally grouped together as cognitive disorders. The first, delirium, is usually a transient state of confusion secondary to either substance abuse or a major medical problem, often one that results in surgery. The second type is dementia, which is an illness characterized by progressive deterioration in cognitive functioning that increasingly affects social interactions, emotional responses, and behaviour, and is eventually related to physical decline. In both dementia and delirium, work with family focuses on support, psychoeducation, and advocacy for resources. In dementia, work with clients can involve collaborating to restore and preserve memory and cognitive functioning through active use of cognitive strategies (such as reality orientation and reminiscence) and active engagement in satisfying activities.

Key Terms

Atrophy
Circadian rhythm
Delirium
Delirium tremens
Endocrine
Hydrocephalus
Hypoglycaemia
Malapropism
Pathognomonic
Renal failure
Subdural haematoma

Discussion Questions

1. What differentiates dementia from delirium?
2. How may social work interventions differ when working with clients and families suffering from delirium as opposed to dementia?
3. How may the recovery model be applied to work with clients with dementia?
4. In what ways can social workers use advocacy skills in respect to their work with clients with dementia?

Suggested Readings and Weblinks

Alzheimer's Society (see http://www.alzheimer.ca/english/index.php).

Social Workers: Help Starts Here. *Alzheimer's Disease/Dementia* (accessed at http://www.helpstartshere.org/seniors_and_aging/alzheimers_disease/dementia/default.html).

World Health Organization (2002), *Toronto Declaration on the Global Prevention of Elder Abuse* (accessed 12 August 2008 at http://www.who.int/ageing/projects/elder_abuse/alc_toronto_declaration_en.pdf).

Chapter 11

Substance Abuse

Objectives:

- To identify factors contributing to substance abuse
- To identify substances of abuse
- To present models for assessing substance abuse
- To present a spectrum of interventions for substance use

Case Example 1

Pearl is a happily married, 34-year-old woman who stays at home caring for her 6-year-old son. She was an accomplished ice dancer and met her husband, a stockbroker who works long hours, while travelling in international competitions. Pearl's father was an alcoholic and her parents separated when she was in her teens. Pearl suffers from repetitive migraines. She worked with her family practitioner to find a suitable medication, but the only one that worked well was oxycontin, an opiate that is subject to abuse. The doctor prescribed 30 tablets at a time, to be taken up to three times a day when the need arose for migraines. As time went by, Pearl began using more and more medication and frequently phoned her family practitioner's office for a repeat prescription. Her doctor tried to limit the prescriptions as best she could. However, Pearl then went to see another doctor and began obtaining repeat prescriptions for the same medication. In time, even this became insufficient and on one occasion she slipped the doctor's prescription pad into her pocket and wrote a prescription for herself (for 30 tablets). The pharmacist became suspicious and called the police to investigate, who charged Pearl with fraud.

Case Example 2

David is a 70-year-old male who was admitted to hospital after a minor accident that resulted in a complicated fracture of his leg. The reparative surgery was uneventful, but two to three days after surgery David became disoriented, somewhat frightened, and appeared to be reacting to visual hallucinations. He was diagnosed as having delirium tremens and was treated by the hospital staff. The abnormalities in his mental state resolved within 24 hours. Further history revealed that David had been in the habit of consuming a bottle of whisky a day for the past 20 years. Although his wife frequently suggested he cut down on his drinking and seek help, he had never admitted to having a problem. David is a retired family practitioner who has been married for 40 years. He has three sons, all of whom are accomplished professionals. He is somewhat shy and retiring, eschewing crowds, parties, and social events. However, when the family has a barbecue or other event he is often the life and soul of the party.

Case Example 3

Mark is a 20-year-old male who began smoking marijuana at the age of 13. He left school in grade 10 and moved into a friend's apartment downtown. He supports himself with part-time jobs. He frequents raves and dance clubs, where he uses a variety of club drugs including 'Special K' and 'crystal meth'. At times he gets extra cash by being a male prostitute. He also has begun to use 'crack' on a regular basis and he sometimes uses heroin to bring himself down. In order to support his habit, he and his associates committed a series of break-and-enters and he was eventually caught and arrested. Mark was born to a teenaged mother who could not control him and, subsequently, he was placed in a number of foster homes and group homes. In one of the foster homes he was sexually abused by an older brother. His father was a biker who at one time was diagnosed as having antisocial personality disorder and substance abuse.

The Nature of Substance Abuse

It is impossible to avoid issues of substance abuse in any branch of mental health work. Given the extraordinarily high prevalence of substance abuse and its pernicious effect on other disorders, its impact upon clients, their families, and society is staggering. Substance abuse is central to social work practice with one estimate suggesting that 61 per cent of social workers see substance abusers in some capacity, including assessment and referral; 19 per cent are involved in the treatment of substance abusers (Rapp, Siegal, and DeLiberty, 2003). Substance abuse is related to a number of psychosocial and physical problems (Minozzi et al., 2008). These problems are diverse and multiple and include the fact that 50 per cent of traffic deaths are attributed to alcohol. They also include the significant contribution of substances to interpersonal aggression (such as intimate partner violence and child abuse), crime, and homicide. Mood and anxiety disorders and suicide are also related to substance abuse. Social-economic correlates include unemployment and subsequent death and homelessness.

The World Health Organization (WHO) published a report entitled the *Global Status Report on Alcohol* (2004) in which it is suggested that 76.3 million people worldwide have a diagnosable alcohol disorder. It further states that 1 to 5 per cent of the gross domestic product of individual countries is spent on alcohol-related costs, including treatment, prevention, law enforcement, and lost productivity. In the United States, the cost of substance abuse is estimated to be 200 billion dollars per year (Nathan, Skinstad, and Langenbucher, 1999). In England alcohol misuse alone results in 17 million working days lost per year, alcohol-related crime and disorder cost the country 7.3 billon pounds annually, and lost productivity due to alcohol costs 6.4 billion pounds (Luty and Carnwath, 2008). The WHO estimates that 9.2 per cent of disease worldwide can be attributed to alcohol use. Such alcohol-related diseases include cancer, hypertension, cardiovascular disease, liver cirrhosis, fetal alcohol syndrome, and psychiatric disorders. In addition to this, alcohol contributes to motor vehicle accidents, interpersonal violence, and suicide (Witkiewitz and Marlatt, 2006). Drug abuse is associated with rebelliousness, antisocial behaviour, poor school performance, and affiliation with drug-using peers (Hall and Degenhardt, 2007).

A place to begin our analysis of substance abuse is by considering what constitutes abuse and substance dependence. This is important because terms such as *alcohol abuse* and *dependence* are somewhat socially derived. What constitutes abuse in one environment may be viewed as culturally appropriate behaviour in another. The *Diagnostic and Statistical Manual* defines *abuse* as a maladaptive pattern of substance use causing clinically significant impairment or distress (APA, 2000). *Dependence*, on the other hand, is defined as a maladaptive pattern of substance use leading to clinically significant impairment or distress, which further includes withdrawal, tolerance, ingestion of larger amounts than intended, unsuccessful efforts to cut down, excessive time spent in activities related to substances, narrowing of interests, and continued use despite knowledge of physical or psychological problems likely attributable to the substance. Dependence can be psychological and/or physiological in nature.

Substance abuse and dependence can involve prescription medications that were originally intended to treat another medical issue, they can involve street or illegal drugs, and they can involve alcohol use. Each type of abuse has its own complexities. For instance, alcohol use is pervasive in our society and falls on a continuum that ranges from social drinking leading to alcohol problems, leading to alcohol abuse, leading to alcohol dependence (Marshall, 2000). Therefore, specifying when the problem is abuse is more problematic than perhaps it is for the use of opiates such as heroin. In all aspects of drug abuse, the course of the problem is heterogeneous, that is, it differs by individual, and is likely related to individual psychopathology, social support, and psychosocial context. This suggests that an array of treatments are required, ranging from brief intervention to long-term therapeutic communities.

Incidence and Prevalence

According to Statistics Canada, in 2002 more than 600,000 Canadians were dependent on alcohol and nearly 200,000 were dependent on illicit drugs (Tjepkema, 2004). The 2004 *Canadian Addiction Survey* found that 6.2 per cent of respondents reported heavy drinking (five or more drinks on a single occasion for men and four or more drinks on a single occasion for women) at least once per week. Almost 9 per cent of people who drank alcohol in the past year indicated that personal alcohol use had caused them harm. Harm to self included physical health; relationship disturbances; financial problems; and employment, educational, or legal problems. Harm to the respondent caused by others due to alcohol use was 32.7 per cent in the past year and included verbal and physical abuse, humiliation, and relationship problems.

Overall, 44.5 per cent of Canadians reported using cannabis at least once in their life and 14.1 per cent reported using in the past year. Almost 1 in 20 Canadians indicated a cannabis use concern including failing to control use, cravings, and concern of others about the respondent's use. Excluding cannabis, the illicit drugs most commonly reported during the lifetime were hallucinogens (11.4 per cent), cocaine (10.6 per cent), speed, (6.4 per cent), and ecstasy (4.1 per cent). About 3 per cent of Canadians reported using at least one drug besides cannabis in the past year (Health Canada, 2005). Forty-five per cent of Canadians reported a lifetime use of illicit drugs. Of these, 17 to 35 per cent reported one or more harmful sequelae from drug use. The number of Canadians reporting the use of an injectable drug at some point in their life increased from 1.7 million in 1994 to a staggering 4.1 million in 2004 (Hall and Degenhardt, 2007).

It is reported that 14 to 16 per cent of Americans suffer from alcohol abuse or dependence (Eaton et al., 1984). About one hundred thousand people in the United States die annually from the various sequelae of drug and alcohol abuse and dependence. This is in addition to the estimated 50 per cent of highway fatalities caused by substance abuse, the high rates of domestic violence, and the propagation of certain infections such as AIDS and hepatitis (Nathan et al., 1999). In 1997, there were 40,000 'notified' opiate addicts in the United States. Since then there has been a 20 per cent increase annually. It is noteworthy that 70 to 90 per cent of opiate addicts also suffer from hepatitis C (Winstock and Strang, 2000).

Factors Contributing to Substance Abuse

When discussing the causes of substance abuse it should always be borne in mind that there are a multiplicity of factors at play, one or more of which may have salience in a particular individual. Substance abuse and dependence therefore involve a complex interaction of the particular drug on a particular host. Factors that are inherent to the drug itself are both social/environmental (for instance, availability, legal status, and social norms) and biochemical. The drug must have the ability to easily cross the blood-brain barrier and drugs with a short half-life (that is, those metabolized by the body more quickly) tend to be more addictive than those with a long half-life. Related to this, drugs with a rapid onset, such as crack, are likely more addictive than those with a slower mode of onset, such as MDMA (methylenedioxymethamphetamin). From a social/environmental perspective, longitudinal analysis has revealed that during adolescence and early adulthood factors such as availability and acceptability of substance use within a particular social group are primary determinants, but with increased age, genetic predeterminants begin to take precedence (Gillespie et al., 2007).

The literature is not clear whether the drug of choice is determined by a fit between the individual and his or her intrapsychic needs and the actions of the particular drug. If this is indeed the case then it supports the hypothesis that at least a proportion of drug abuse relates to self-medication, such as is illustrated in Case Example 1. For instance, women with anxiety disorders may be prescribed benzodiazepines (e.g., Valium), and because of the inherent addictive potential, become abusers of this drug. Similarly, some individuals with attention deficit hyperactivity disorder (ADHD) may find that illegal psychostimulants are helpful in treating their symptoms.

Psychosocial and Mental Health Factors

Alcohol and cannabis use have been demonstrated to begin in adolescence. Those who use cannabis heavily in both adolescence and young adulthood tend to continue on to daily cannabis use and graduate to greater overall illicit substance use. They also demonstrate poorer social outcomes (Patton et al., 2007). In early adulthood there is generally experimentation with a number of different substances. Some people appear to settle into a drug of choice. These choices are seemingly determined by current trends, availability, peer groups, and gender (Pihl, 1999). Other psychosocial factors that are important include a psychiatric history, especially a history of anxiety, depression, post-traumatic stress, or ADHD. The presence of behavioural problems with impulsivity in adolescence, and the adult equivalent, antisocial personality, is a powerful determinant of substance abuse (Wall and Kohl, 2007). A childhood history of neglect and/or physical and sexual abuse is another risk factor (Min et al., 2007).

Biological Factors

As with other mental health challenges, biological factors play a central role in the development of substance abuse. For instance, daily alcohol consumption during pregnancy is strongly associated with neurobehavioural disinhibition in offspring during childhood and adolescence, followed by substance abuse that continues into adulthood (Chapman et al., 2007). Further, it is likely that at least a part of the vulnerability to develop substance abuse problems is genetically mediated. Family, twin, and adoption studies have all pointed to a strong genetic contribution to substance abuse that is likely as high as 50 to 60 per cent of the predictability (True et al., 1999; Kendler et al., 2003). To date, research has not revealed a single gene for substance abuse, but rather it appears that a number of genes acting through a variety of mechanisms make an individual particularly vulnerable to abuse (Vanyuko et al., 2007).

One hypothesis suggests there is a neurochemical pathway for drug-seeking behaviour. This is supported by a number of diverse findings. For instance, abnormalities in dopamine transmission have been found to be associated with substance abuse (Haberstick et al., 2007). Recently the role of norepinephrine has been explored as a second neurotransmitter that interacts with dopamine in this reward system (Weinshenker and Schroeder, 2007). Another finding is that the speed at which alcohol is metabolized by the liver enzymes has been found to be directly proportional to the risk of dependency. In other words, those who quickly develop tolerance to alcohol because it is metabolized more quickly, and therefore presumably do not experience negative effects so quickly early on, tend to develop abuse and dependency. From a neuroanatomical perspective, the mesolimbic dopamine pathway is hypothesized to be the part of the brain that appreciates thrills or pleasure (see Figure 9.1). These thrills can be natural highs mediated by the body's own equivalent of drugs (endorphins) or synthetic highs derived from a variety of drugs. The process promotes the motivation and behavioural drive to seek rewards. When drugs are used repeatedly, this system is conditioned to trigger drug-seeking behaviour from stimuli that we know as craving or withdrawal, or even from cues such as associating with people in places where drugs are normally used.

The Association Between Substance Abuse and Other Mental Health Problems

As noted earlier in this chapter, the presence of a major mental health problem is a risk factor for substance abuse of all kinds. The presence of any mental health problem increases the probability of having an addictive disorder by 2.7 times (Goldstein et al., 2007). In one study of inhalant users, 70 per cent met the criteria for at least one lifetime mood, anxiety, or personality disorder (Wu and Howard, 2006). Van Laar and others (2007) noted any use of cannabis predicated an increase in the risk of depression and bipolar disorder and this was particularly so in more frequent users. They concluded that the association of cannabis use and the first incidence of these disorders is significant but the underlying mechanism has yet to be delineated. The odds ratio of having a substance abuse problem in an individual diagnosed with schizophrenia is 4.5 as compared with the general population (Regier et al., 1990). Amongst those with drug abuse problems the prevalence of antisocial personality disorder is 18 per cent (Nathan, Skinstad, and Langenbucher, 1999). This is generally considered to be associated with a poor outcome and greater severity of the disorder.

Anxiety disturbances are highly associated with alcohol and drug use problems (Brady, Tolliver, and Verduin, 2007; Levander, 2007). This relationship has led to the 'tension-reduction hypothesis' of alcohol use and abuse; that is, the view that people use substances in order to obtain relief from their anxiety. However, similar to many drugs, the ability of alcohol to reduce anxiety is inconsistent. Alcohol withdrawal is most clearly associated with increased anxiety and, of course, in this situation the ingestion of alcohol decreases anxiety, promoting the addiction cycle. In this way, the interactions of alcohol and anxiety tend to become a vicious cycle, increasing difficulties in the assessment and treatment of both problems.

In studies on individuals who have been diagnosed as having adult ADHD, rates of substance abuse disorder have been reported to be as high as 52 per cent. It would appear that cocaine or crack is the substance of choice in those suffering from ADHD. The relationship is not unidirectional, in that it could well be mediated by a family history of antisocial behaviour, sensation-seeking, and impulsivity, as well as abuse and neglect. It has also been postulated that there is a common genetic risk factor for ADHD and substance abuse, perhaps mediated through impulsivity and risk-taking. It is also possible that some people with ADHD choose psychostimulants in an attempt to self-medicate. However, the effects of cocaine and its derivatives are generally unpredictable on these individuals.

Drugs of Abuse

Opiates

Opium is derived from opium poppies and has been used for some six thousand years (Winstock and Strang, 2000). Over the years opium has been used by many cultures, most famously epitomized by the Opium Wars of the 1700s, occasioned when the British, having colonized India and its almost inexhaustible supply of opium, was able to trade this for tea in China, resulting in widespread abuses of opium. In 1805, morphine was synthesized and its use by the medical establishment was cemented. Any medication with such a powerful action was likely to be abused, but it was not until the mid-nineteenth century that Britain enacted legislation controlling its use. It was 50 years later before the United States enacted legislation.

Heroin (diamorphine) has long been considered the most commonly abused opiate. It can be injected, smoked, or taken intranasally. Recently a variety of opiates have been commonly abused, including oxycontin and oxycoset. These are prescribed for pain management and their use has dramatically increased recently with the medical profession's acceptance that they can be used for non-cancer pain management. As a result, large amounts are diverted to the streets and sold illegally on the black market, becoming widely abused by polydrug abusers (Ahmadi et al., 2007).

The brain has endogenous opiate receptors that affect the norepinephrine neurons located in the *locus coeruleus* (see Figure 9.1). There is a fairly rapid onset of dependency and tolerance. The effects of opiates include pain reduction, drowsiness, and euphoria. Withdrawal symptoms are characterized by a massive surge in norepinephrine activity. The classic withdrawal symptom involves a severe flulike illness with rapid pulse and high blood pressure and goosebumps, hence the term *going cold turkey*.

One of the more modern sequelae of opiate use has been the risk of transmission of viruses among injecting drug users, including HIV, and hepatitis B and C. This has been at the heart of harm-reduction strategies, utilizing such services as needle exchanges and methadone substitution, which have decreased some of the harmful sequelae.

Psychostimulants

The first use of psychostimulants is believed to be among South American Indians who used coca leaves in religious rituals. Later these leaves were reduced to powdered cocaine that was used for medicinal purposes. A small amount of cocaine was included in the original recipe for Coca-Cola, perhaps leading to its success. Early in the twentieth century, abuse of cocaine began to be noticed. In the 1970s, cocaine became very popular, then, after a short dip, there has been a recent increase in its use (Seivewright, 2000). In the 1990s it was discovered that a more potent type of cocaine could be produced by simply converting it to its hydrochloride form, which could either be smoked or used intravenously, leading to a very rapid onset of action. This form is known as crack and some have suggested that it can produce tolerance or withdrawal after its first ingestion, making it a prime drug of dependency.

Amphetamines were used as early antidepressants and also as appetite suppressants (Seivewright, 2000). However, since the 1970s they have been the subject of increasing recreational drug use. More recently, amphetamines have been converted to a more potent preparation known as methylamphetamine, which can be injected orally, intranasally, or intravenously.

The characteristic effects of stimulants include increased energy, euphoria, and decreased appetite. This is sometimes accompanied by insomnia and in some cases a paranoid psychosis and confusion. Not infrequently, other drugs such as alcohol, benzodiazepines, cannabis, or even heroin are used to counter the stimulant effects at the end of a long session of use. The deleterious effects are legion, including weight loss, dental problems, and infections resulting from injection. In addition to this, stimulants can adversely affect the heart, causing heart attacks or strokes. When taken in pregnancy they can cause premature labour and placental abruption. They are associated with anxiety, depression, and psychosis that can be indistinguishable from schizophrenia. They are also particularly associated with interpersonal aggression.

Hallucinogens

Drugs that alter the sense of perception and mood without causing confusion or disorientation are referred to as the hallucinogens. These too have been used for thousands of years, often in the form of various types of mushrooms. In 1938 Albert Hoffman synthesized *lysergic acid diethylamide* (LSD) in an effort to find a synthetic medication to induce childbirth. It is recorded that he ingested a small amount on his fingertips and experienced the first LSD trip. He returned to the lab and ingested a small amount for experimental purposes and recorded his experiences. However, he was able to record little and was accompanied home on his bicycle by a student soon thereafter (Abraham, 2000). LSD was later used experimentally in psychiatry and did provide the basis for a theory of the neuropharmacology of schizophrenia. However, by the 1960s the abuse of LSD became increasingly common. LSD is active in minute quantities that can be placed on sugar cubes or blotting paper. LSD users tend to start in adolescence and since the drug is not known to produce physical dependency most users abstain by their mid-twenties.

Various plants and fungi have hallucinogenic properties including psilocybin mushrooms that are common in many parts of Europe and North America and are also used recreationally (Hyde et al., 1978). As has been suggested, the primary effects of ingesting these plants are changes in sensory imagery, resulting in visual illusions and sometimes hallucinations. The loss of control sometimes leads to panic, known as a bad trip. In vulnerable individuals a psychosis may be generated similar to that seen in schizophrenia.

PCP (phencyclidine) also known as 'angel dust' was originally used as an anesthetic. It is often mixed with a variety of drugs and sold on the street under idiosyncratic names such as 'dust' or 'mist' (Abraham, 2000). It can be taken orally or smoked, the latter route causing an almost immediate effect. It has a complicated neuropharmacological profile mediated by a number of different types of receptors. The resultant high or intoxication includes agitation, impaired judgment, and a particular type of eye movement (*nystagmus*). It is said to be particularly conducive to violence. Delirium and a psychotic disorder can be produced. There is some evidence that it can produce physiological dependence.

Club Drugs

A number of drugs have more recently been popularized in raves and dance clubs, both in North America and Europe. The mode of action of these drugs is heterogeneous; the only characteristics that they share are the popular venues for their use.

Ketamine has similar actions to PCP, acting at the glutamate synapses. Like PCP, it was originally developed sometime ago as an anesthetic and was used for some early psychiatric experiments. Sometimes called 'K' or 'Special K', its actions include analgesia and amnesia, with some stimulant as well as depressant effects. Ketamine has a somewhat less hallucinogenic action than PCP. Higher degrees of intoxication can cause hallucinations, delusions, paranoia, and in very high doses it can cause coma, extremely high body temperatures, and muscle breakdown.

Gamma hydroxybutyrite (GHB) was originally developed as an agent for the treatment of various sleep disorders but quickly became a drug of abuse. It has been associated along with rohypnol as a 'date rape drug' because of its ability to cause disorientating and sedating effects as well as some retrograde amnesia.

Ecstasy is one of the substituted amphetamines, whose action is very similar to the other amphetamines although it may be weaker in its effects (Jacobs and Fehr, 1987). This was first synthesized in the 1980s as one of the new designer drugs. It is said to elevate mood, increase self-confidence, and increase libido. In higher doses, it may cause increased blood pressure and pulse with profuse sweating. Some people have paradoxical effects of increased anxiety and panic, and hallucinations and delusions have been reported. Cases of dependence have been reported. Chronic users appear to have altered serotonin transport mechanisms resulting in mood disorders and contributing to dependency.

Another amphetamine on the market is crystal meth. Although relatively new to the drug scene, it is estimated to have been used by 25 million people worldwide in the past 12 months. This makes it the most widely used illicit drug after cannabis. It can be ingested in tablet form, but if smoked or injected it causes an immediate 'rush'. It has a longer duration of action than cocaine and users often stay awake for more than 10 days. The short-term feelings of increased confidence, energy, and sexual performance often wear off to a period of anxiety, depression, and fatigue. Long-term consequences include a characteristic dental decay, weight loss, psychosis and paranoia, picking at skin, and irritability (Bramness and Kornor, 2007; Schreiber, Peles, and Adelson, 2008). Animal studies suggest that high-dose methylamphetamine damages dopamine nerve terminals in the corpus striatum, the same area that is damaged in Parkinson's disease (Buxton and Dove, 2008; Kish, 2008)(see Figure 9.1). Preliminary data suggest that chronic use may cause brain damage in humans. Crystal meth is highly addictive and the social, physical, and occupational sequelae can be devastating.

Screening for Substance Use

A first issue in the treatment of substances is identifying whether the person is dependent on a particular substance. While a large number of screening tools exist and can be found both in the literature and from helpful sources such as the Centre for Addiction and Mental Health, some very simple tools are available for routine screening. One example of such a tool that is widely used is the CAGE (Mayfield, McLeod, and Hall, 1974). The CAGE consists of 4 simple questions as shown in Table 11.1.

Harm-Reduction Interventions to Assist with Recovery

The recovery model originated in the area of substance abuse and then moved to other areas of mental health. From this perspective, clients must take ownership over their problem of substance use and work to manage or eliminate its consequences. Part of using this model is to acknowledge that many people with substance abuse problems will not choose to move towards total abstinence. Therefore, although the social worker, members of the health care team, and others in the client's life may believe that total abstinence is the best option, they must recognize that the client has control over his or her recovery process.

Table 11.1 The CAGE Screening Tool

C	Cut down	Have you ever felt you should cut down on your drinking?
A	Annoyed	Have people annoyed you by criticizing your drinking?
G	Guilty	Have you felt guilty about your drinking?
E	Eye-opener	Have you ever had a drink first thing in the morning to steady your nerves or get rid of a hangover?

Scoring
Each yes response equals a score of 1. A total score of 1 may indicate the need for further discussion. A total score of 2 or greater is clinically significant, suggesting a current or past alcohol problem and, therefore, warranting a more in-depth assessment.

Harm reduction is a policy framework and model of intervention that seeks to eliminate the negative consequences of substance use for those who choose not to engage in abstinence. Harm reduction is based on five assumptions:

1. Substance use is a reality of our world and thus it is more realistic to focus on reducing harm than eliminating substance use.
2. Although abstinence is the most effective means for reducing harm, it is not necessarily an objective of substance users.
3. Substance use inherently causes harm; however, some of the most serious harms (HIV/AIDS, hepatitis C, overdoses, etc.) can be eliminated without complete abstinence.
4. Services to the client must be user-friendly and relevant if they are to be effective.
5. Substance use must be understood from a broader societal perspective and not just at an individual level (MacMaster, 2004).

MacMaster argues that such an approach is highly consistent with social work values because it is based on client self-determination and engages the client as a partner in determining goals and strategies for change.

Canada began a concerted effort to address substance abuse beginning in 1987 with the original publication of *Canada's Drug Strategy* (CDS), which has since been updated on a five-year basis (Health Canada, 1996). The overall stated aim is to reduce the harm associated with alcohol and other drugs to individuals, families, and communities. The strategy had four pillars: prevention, treatment, harm reduction, and enforcement. In this regard, CDS endorses needle exchange, methadone maintenance, abstinence-oriented treatments, and the enforcement of laws related to illegal drugs. British Columbia has been a leader in responding to injection drug use at a provincial level, and the program in the City of Vancouver is cited as an example for the rest of the country.

Needle Exchange

Needle exchange in large part stems from the desire to reduce risk of transmission of HIV, hepatitis C, and other diseases that are spread through needle-sharing. Canada has had needle exchange programs since 1987; however, the first official exchange did not open until 1989 in Vancouver. By 1993 the federal government was cost-sharing outreach programs in four provinces. Kits including needles, bleach, and condoms were originally distributed from fixed sites and through street outreach; this program has now been expanded to mobile vans to increase the geographical area in which outreach can occur. In addition, some pharmacies now provide syringe exchange services. Although there are obvious concerns about needle-exchange programs in prisons, related in part to security issues, estimates of HIV prevalence among male inmates range from 1 to 4 per cent and among female inmates range from 1 to 10 per cent primarily because of histories of drug use. Further, prisoners have high rates of hepatitis C, with estimates ranging from 28 to 40 per cent (Public Health Agency Canada, 2001). As a result, there is support for needle-exchange programs at the policy level, although there is administrative resistance. Research using Centre for Disease Control data and comparing cities with and without needle-exchange programs suggests that such programs are in fact effective in reducing HIV rates (Hurley, Jolley, and Kaldor, 1997).

Needle exchange is rarely provided in isolation in any program. Other components include education regarding safer methods of drug ingestion, provision of safe space where staff can monitor client's health status, behaviour therapy with goals of reduction, and medication treatments (Rosenberg and Phillips, 2003).

Methadone Maintenance Programs

Methadone maintenance treatment is a long-term opioid replacement therapy that is used to manage dependence, reduce elicit opioid use, and increase treatment adherence. Methadone is a liquid medication, taken orally, that removes the euphoric effects of heroin and reduces withdrawal symptoms. Effects last for 24 to 36 hours. The aim is to allow the individual to return to normal functioning at work or school. Methadone maintenance programs have been supported by the federal government for several years. In fact, the sale and control of methadone is controlled by the Office of Controlled Substances within Health Canada. In order to prescribe methadone, physicians must be licensed through the Controlled Drugs and Substances Act and 699 physicians in Canada had these prescribing privileges in 2001 (Public Health Agency Canada, 2001). Methadone maintenance programs are also available in federal and some provincial correctional facilities where inmates were enrolled in programs prior to incarceration.

A *Cochrane Review* of methadone maintenance programs suggests that at higher doses, methadone can be effective in reducing use of heroin and cocaine. However, the reviewers do note the important fact that methadone itself causes dependence and higher doses are more likely to promote this (Faggiano et al., 2003).

Controlled Drinking

Controlled drinking as a form of harm reduction has a much longer history than other approaches. In the 1970s a great international debate occurred in the research literature and popular press about the viability of controlled drinking that focused on the work of Mark Sobell and Linda Sobell at the Addiction Research Foundation (ARF) in Toronto. The debate centred on a treatment method for severely dependent alcoholics and the nature and validity of research outcomes from studies conducted at ARF. The results from these studies suggested that moderate drinking may be a viable and preferred treatment goal for some individuals dealing with excessive drinking (Marlatt and Witkiewitz, 2002). Although some considered the findings to be exaggerated claims of success, the researchers suggested the debate occurred solely because the findings undermined the philosophy and beliefs of Alcoholic Anonymous (Sobell and Sobell, 1995). More recent reviews of many programs on controlled drinking suggest that moderate drinking is an achievable goal for some people with alcoholism problems (Carey et al., 2007).

Controlled drinking models come in a number of different forms that have been reviewed by Witkiewitz and Marlatt (2006). *Behavioural self-control training* (BSCT) is one that exists in a multicomponent therapy that includes self-monitoring of quantity, frequency, and urges to drink; establishment of goals and rewards; and drink refusal skills. This model has been found in meta-analyses to be effective in reducing drinking and superior to both abstinence approaches and other controlled-drinking approaches. *Moderation-oriented cue exposure* (MOCE) is based on classical conditioning and the extinguishing of the relationship between drink-related cues and drinking. Again, this model has established effectiveness. *Guided self-change* (GSC), the original model developed by the Sobells, is a strengths-based psychoeducational model that has empirical support. *Behavioural couples therapy* (BCT) is a more recent model that engages both the person who has the substance abuse problem and their partner, and has been shown to reduce drinking and improve the couple's relationship. Finally, *mindfulness-based relapse prevention* (MBRP) incorporates both cognitive-behavioural therapy strategies and meditation. Although this model has not been extensively tested, early studies are suggesting that it may be effective in reducing substance use in former inmates.

A self-help group using this particular model is *Moderation Management* (MM) and has the aim of reducing drinking to non-harmful levels. The program is offered in both traditional face-to-face groups and over the Internet. When compared to AA programs, MM attracts a higher percentage of women (66 per cent versuss 33 per cent) with higher levels of education (94 per cent had at least one year of college versus an average 11 years of school for AA). MM emphasizes balance in all areas of life and encourages discussions about other life problems and emotional issues. Although this self-help program does target a different population in need, evidence of efficacy is not yet available (Kosok, 2006).

Other Recovery-Oriented Psychosocial Interventions

Abstinence Programs

Alcoholics Anonymous (AA) is the most widely used self-help intervention in the world, with more than 2 million members. It is described as 'a fellowship of men and women who share their experience, strength, and hope with each other that they may solve their common problem and help others to recover from alcoholism' (Alcoholics Anonymous, 1972). AA views alcoholism as a disease that controls the minds and bodies of those who suffer from it. From this perspective, abstinence from alcohol use is necessary for healing and control. AA is founded on the Twelve Step Model of Recovery (see Box 11.1).

AA as a self-help model is highly attractive to some people suffering from substance abuse issues and provides a great deal of support and comfort. As a result, the Twelve Step Model has been expanded to other forms of addiction such as narcotics. For other people this model is not consistent with their worldview or their means of

Box 11.1 The Twelve Step Model of Recovery

1. We admitted we were powerless over alcohol—that our lives had become unmanageable.
2. Came to believe that a Power greater than ourselves could restore us to sanity.
3. Made a decision to turn our will and our lives over to the care of God *as we understood Him.*
4. Made a searching and fearless moral inventory of ourselves.
5. Admitted to God, to ourselves, and to another human being the exact nature of our wrongs.
6. Were entirely ready to have God remove all these defects of character.
7. Humbly asked Him to remove our shortcomings.
8. Made a list of all persons we had harmed, and became willing to make amends to them all.
9. Made direct amends to such people wherever possible, except when to do so would injure them or others.
10. Continued to take personal inventory and when we were wrong promptly admitted it.
11. Sought through prayer and meditation to improve our conscious contact with God, *as we understood Him,* praying only for knowledge of His will for us and the power to carry that out.
12. Having had a spiritual awakening as the result of these steps, we tried to carry this message to alcoholics, and to practice these principles in all our affairs.

seeking support. Social workers should be well aware of this model of intervention and assist clients to make their own decisions about its usefulness for them.

Motivational Interviewing

Motivation has characteristically been seen as a central issue in the treatment of substance abuse, leading to the belief that it is not until the client 'hits rock bottom' and the consequences of substance use are too severe, that he or she will be motivated to change. Studies of motivation for treatment do suggest that there is some truth to this old belief. Rapp, Siegal, and DeLiberty (2003), in a study on motivation in substance abusers, determined that motivation was associated with severity of substance abuse, whereas, surprisingly perhaps, legal coercion or self-referral for treatment was not. This is an important finding as practitioners are frequently suspicious of the motivation of those individuals who are forced to attend treatment by the courts. Also of note, motivation on entry into the program was not related to severity of substance use at the six-month follow-up. Thus, those who do not appear to be motivated at the outset have a more or less equal chance of recovery at the point of six months post-treatment. How then do social workers enhance and sustain motivation in clients for whom substance abuse is causing deleterious effects on their lives?

Motivational interviewing is derived from the Stages of Change Model (also referred to as the transtheoretical model of change) proposed by Prochaska and DiClemente (1982) and shown in Table 11.2. The model asserts that people will pass through five stages on their way to resolving a problem behaviour: pre-contemplation, contemplation, preparation, action, and maintenance. It is acknowledged, however, that people will not go through the stages in an orderly or linear fashion; rather, people may cycle through stages many times before change is maintained. An additional stage has been suggested, namely, relapse. The Stages of Change Model implies that change is rarely sudden. Each stage requires a certain task in order to facilitate the change.

Table 11.2 Stages of Change

Stage	Person's experience	Social worker's task
Pre-contemplation	The person is not aware of or does not acknowledge the problem that others identify.	• To heighten doubt or ambivalence about the problem behaviour
Contemplation	The person begins to be ambivalent about the possibility of making a change but has not made any plans to effect change as yet. There may be some discomfort or self-doubt as the person begins to weigh the pros and cons of making a change.	• To support resolution of the ambivalence in the direction in a healthy behavioural change • Reviewing the consequences of changing and not changing
Preparation	The person expresses the intention to make a change and begins to consider steps that would lead to change. Change is imminent.	• To help the person consider the available change options and their relative advantages and to ultimately select an appropriate course of action
Action	Deliberate strategies are used by the person to change or modify behaviour or the environment to achieve the goal.	• To provide support carrying out the change plans
Maintenance	Change is maintained by the person for at least six months; the challenge is to hold on to the gains that have been made.	• To provide positive feedback about the change and continuously develop strategies to overcome obstacles in maintaining the change.
Relapse	The person returns to the former pattern of problem behaviour. He or she may again deny it is a problem or feel remorse for having relapsed.	• To accept setbacks and encourage return to an earlier stage of change

(Adapted from Prochaska and DiClemente, 1982)

Motivational interviewing is a cognitive-behavioural technique first proposed by Miller and Rollnick in 1991 (see Box 11.2). The key in this approach is to not tell people that they may have a problem or what steps they should take. The approach underlines the importance of people describing or discussing their own perceptions of their own problems. Motivational interviewing has five basic principles: 1) express empathy; 2) avoid argument; 3) develop discrepancy; 4) roll with resistance; and 5) support self-efficacy (Miller and Rollnick, 2002). The process begins, however, as do all forms of treatment with establishing rapport, setting an agenda, and assessing readiness for change. In large part, the success of this model is dependent on the social worker's willingness to follow the client at his or her own pace and not impose change from the outside.

Motivational interviewing is a brief, low-cost approach to intervention that has established effectiveness with a variety of populations who are suffering substance abuse (Burke, Arkowitz, and Menchola, 2003; Vasilaki, Hosier, and Cox, 2006;

Box 11.2 Motivational Interviewing

Express empathy	• Convey acceptance for a person as they are; historical factors led to the current state of affairs • Listen, reflect, and seek to understand the history of this person or place; few people can move to change unless they believe that the person encouraging change understands how they got here in the first place and the ongoing challenges that they face (Regehr and Bober, 2005)
Avoid argument	• Active challenging of a person's position or beliefs will result in a defensive position and arguments for not changing • Question, ask for clarification, encourage the client to hear themselves
Develop discrepancy	• Assist the person to see how the current behaviour places them on a trajectory away from important goals or values • Provide information and, when appropriate, brief advice
Roll with resistance	• Reframe resistance as ambivalence (a less judgmental or pejorative term); change implies unpredictability and uncertainty in one's life • Understand that there's a difference between people who may not want to change and those who may not know how to change
Support self-efficacy	• Identify strengths • Celebrate successes

(Adapted from Miller and Rollnick, 1991)

Carey et al., 2007). It has not been shown to be more effective than other models of intervention for smoking or HIV risk-taking. Further, a *Cochrane Review* indicates that there is no evidence that motivational interviewing is any more effective than any other psychosocial intervention in treating individuals who suffer from both severe mental illness and substance use (Cleary et al., 2008). Thus, social workers should be cautious not to assume that it will be helpful in addressing all presenting problems.

Pharmacological and Medical Approaches to Support Recovery from Substance Abuse

From the perspective of health care professionals, the goals of treatment of substance abuse and dependence are first of all to successfully withdraw the person from the substance to reduce the acute harms they are suffering. The second goal is to decrease use and possibly achieve abstinence of the substance. Because substance use generally involves relapse, a third goal is increasing the time between relapses and decreasing the number of relapses (Pihl, 1999). Finally, a goal that has been adopted recently is to reduce the psychological and physical harm that is secondary to substance abuse and dependence.

The primary thrust of treatment of these disorders has been in the realm of psychosocial therapies. Psychopharmacologists have only sparingly contributed to the field of substance abuse. It is unclear whether this is because they have not been hopeful about any possible success of pharmacological approaches or if they feared that they would never be accepted. There are, however, some new treatments that may be of significant value (Vocci and Appel, 2007).

Management of Withdrawal

Withdrawal from substances is a complex process that often requires medical intervention. For example, if withdrawal from alcohol has previously been complicated by seizures, delirium tremens, or the individual has severe cardiac disease, then a hospital setting may be the appropriate place to attempt withdrawal. This may also be the case where people are suffering from other mental health problems that can be exacerbated during the process of withdrawal.

The pharmacological management of withdrawal from a particular substance is generally achieved by taking advantage of cross-tolerance with other agents (Pihl, 1999; Budney et al., 2007; Lanier et al., 2007; Nava et al., 2007). Therefore, a drug in the same or similar class is usually given for withdrawal. Usually, for instance, long-acting benzodiazepines are given for alcohol withdrawal because they have similar actions. B vitamins or multivitamins are often also given adjunctively for prevention of neurological complications. Some experts suggest reducing the amount of benzodiazepines 20 per cent each day and finally stopping it after three to five days. Other medications include beta-adrenergic blockers such as propanolol, or alpha-adrenergic receptor agonists such as clonidine, as well as gabapentin (an anticonvulsant).

For opiate withdrawal, a number of agents have been used, including clonidine, methadone, and bupenorphine. They are often accompanied by medications for nausea and vomiting (Amato et al., 2004). Cocaine and amphetamine withdrawal can generally be managed without any acute treatment other than supportive and symptomatic care. Contrary to popular opinion, withdrawal symptoms from cannabis dependence are more severe than many people are aware of. Common symptoms include irritability, anxiety, decreased appetite, weight loss, restlessness, and sleep difficulty (Budney et al., 2007). Usually these symptoms can be managed without medication, although one trial effectively used oral THC (the chemical found in cannabis) to suppress withdrawal symptoms.

Longer-Term Psychopharmacology for Alcohol Abuse

Several medications are used to help people break the cycle of long-term alcohol abuse. These medications can reduce cravings for alcohol. For instance, the medication Naltrexone has been used with some success (Ciraulo, Alpert, and Franko, 1997). The problem with this type of treatment is that it demands sustained motivation, so that if the client does not take it one day he or she may experience craving and relapse. Consequently, an extended-release, injectable form of Naltrexone increases success in some clients (Ciraulo et al., 2008).

The most commonly known medication to control alcohol abuse, however, is disulfiram or Antabuse. Alcohol is converted to acetaldehyde in the body and then broken down for elimination. Antabuse blocks the elimination of acetaldehyde in the body, which causes unpleasant adverse effects. It is taken on a daily basis usually in the morning; should the client drink in the day he would experience the unpleasant effects of flushing, choking, nausea, vomiting, and high blood pressure. Although Antabuse was widely used in the eighties, it is used less frequently nowadays. One of the major problems is that it requires the patient to take the drug on a regular basis.

Pharmacology for Opiate Dependence

As noted earlier in the chapter, the combination of psychosocial treatment and pharmacological treatment can reduce some of the harms of drug abuse, including the risk of infectious diseases, criminal activity, suicide, and accidental overdoses. Methadone is a synthetic oral opiate with a long half-life that can be given orally on a daily basis. The evidence over a period of 40 years has established that it is helpful in decreasing harm when used for maintenance therapy in association with psychosocial therapies. A number of studies suggest that it decreases criminal behaviour and promotes employment in certain groups of patients. A Cochrane meta-analysis suggested that higher doses are more successful than lower doses in preventing the client from supplementing with illegally obtained opiates. Many clinics administer methadone on a daily basis either by a nurse in the clinic or a pharmacist. Eventually clients may earn the privilege of 'carry-outs' that they can take home and self-administer (Amato et al., 2004).

Benzodiazepines should be avoided in the treatment of opioids, despite the wishes of the client. As discussed previously, these drugs are associated with disinhibition that may lead to relapse and appear to worsen depression (Schreiber et al., 2008). They are associated with negative outcomes such as risk of overdose and death, and also contribute to poorer retention in substitution programs. Surprisingly, despite these contraindications, in one study it was noted that 40 per cent of patients in one substitution program received at least one benzodiazepine drug (Bramness and Kornor, 2007).

Pharmacological Treatment of Cocaine Dependence

The most researched medications for use in the pharmacological treatment of cocaine dependence are antidepressants (Silva de Lima et al., 2003). The use of SSRIs has become widespread to alleviate the dysphoria with associated cravings (Moeller et al., 2007). A second group of medications used with some success are anticonvulsants; however, a *Cochrane Review* suggested that there was no evidence to support their use at this time (Minozzi et al., 2008). Other drugs have been tried in the long-term treatment of cocaine abuse including disulfiram (also known as Antabuse). Antabuse is used on the basis of two supportive theories. First of all, 60 to 90 per cent of cocaine-dependent individuals abuse or are dependent on alcohol. As well, Antabuse diminishes the pleasurable experiences of cocaine. Regular administration, therefore, may reduce the reward effects of cocaine and thereby prevent relapse.

Possible Social Work Interventions in the Case Examples

Case Example 1: Pearl

Pearl began to use and then abuse prescription medication as an attempt to eliminate the pain caused by her migraine headaches. As she became increasingly dependent, she eluded the attempts of her family doctor to limit her use by first double-doctoring and then by forging prescriptions. This has now resulted in criminal charges.

- Pearl's motivation for recovery will need to be assessed. Presumably she will now have external factors that contribute to motivation related to legal charges and family pressure.
- Motivational interviewing may be useful as a means for supporting Pearl to attain whatever goals she has set for herself.
- Groups and treatment programs focused on the specific needs of women or on the needs of professionals with substance use problems may also be useful for Pearl because she may distance herself from programs that serve a population with a wider range of social issues related to substance use.
- The social worker should seek Pearl's permission to work directly with her family physician to develop a coordinated plan for managing her pain while dealing with her substance abuse.

Case Example 2: David

David has a long-standing history of alcohol abuse that for the most part he has managed to hide from others. However, as his health status becomes compromised, the effects of alcohol use become more pronounced.

- The social worker should engage David and his wife in a discussion about the substance use and the effects. At this time the social worker can determine which stage of change David may be in.
- The health-related issues associated with David's drinking will require collaboration of the health care team.
- If David agrees, motivational interviewing, perhaps combined with controlled drinking or abstinence, may be appropriate.

Case Example 3: Mark

Mark has a long-standing history of polydrug abuse that at this time is sustained by a lifestyle that supports his abuse.

- The social worker will need to determine Mark's motivation for recovery.
- Harm-reduction strategies at this point are perhaps the most reasonable approach. However, it is possible that Mark is at a point where he wishes to move towards more aggressive approaches to recovery.

Summary

Substance abuse is a pervasive problem in most societies and certainly in Western society. Although it affects people from all walks of life, these problems are commonly experienced by individuals who may also seek social work assistance for other problems such as mental health concerns, impulse control issues, or histories of abuse and neglect. Therefore, social workers need to develop the skills to assess and intervene appropriately in these cases.

Key Terms

Analgesia
Antabuse
Anticonvulsant
Deleterious
Delirium tremens
Dependence
Endogenous
Euphoria
Insomnia
Mesolimbic dopamine pathway
Nystagmus

Discussion Questions

1. What legal, moral, and ethical issues could a social worker confront when working with clients with substance abuse problems?
2. How may harm-reduction programs coincide or conflict with social work values and ethics?

3. How may self-help groups, such as AA, intersect with social work interventions?
4. How can social workers assist family members of individuals with substance abuse problems?

Suggested Readings and Weblinks

Health Canada (1996), *Canada's Drug Strategy* (Ottawa: Health Canada) (accessed at http://www.caw.ca/whatwedo/substanceabuse/pdf/CanadasDrugStrategy.pdf).

Prochaska, J., and DiClemente, C. (1982), 'Transtheoretical Therapy: Towards a More Integrated Model of Change', *Psychotherapy Research and Practice*, 19(3): 276–88.

Social Workers: Help Starts Here. *Addictions* (accessed at http://www.helpstartshere.org/mind_and_spirit/addictions/default.htm).

Chapter 12

Personality Disturbance

Objectives:

- To identify factors contributing to the development of personality disturbance
- To identify types of personality disturbance
- To present evidence-based psychosocial interventions that promote recovery

Case Example 1

Mario is a 25-year-old man who has been charged with assault against his employer. He explains: 'Those b . . . s at work are always overlooking me for a promotion. This kind of s . . t is always happening to me.' He goes on to describe a pattern of interpersonal relationships in which others consistently overlook or undermine his special talents in order to further their own gains. He provides numerous examples where others have enlisted the assistance of superiors, colleagues, or the security services of the employer to ensure that he will not attain success. Mario indicates that he has amassed a huge collection of 'evidence' to support his claims, which he keeps locked in his home. As a result, Mario is unable to sustain relationships with significant others or friends, who he believes are just out to 'take' him. His job history reveals a variety of jobs, each of which ends with an angry outburst because of a perceived injustice against him.

Case Example 2

When the ambulance pulled up in front of the house neighbours gathered to try to determine who was injured or ill. It turned out to be the tenant in the basement apartment of some well-known people in the neighbourhood. Terry Barnes died of a cardiac arrest at the age of 58. Very few people recalled even seeing him on the street. No one had spoken to him. The landlords commented that he had lived there for more than 10 years, since before they had even purchased the house. He was pleasant when they spoke to him, but not forthcoming with personal information. He was clean, quiet, and always dropped his rent cheque in the door. They believed that he worked for a large insurance company, doing something in the area of data processing. The landlords did not know his next of kin and were not sure who to notify that he had died. A few days later the police indicated that they had contacted a sister who lived in the same city. When she came to pick up the possessions of her brother, she said that Terry had always been quiet and had few friends even in high school. He completed a college course in computer technology. He did attend family gatherings at holiday times and was always pleasant to be around, but they were not close and she did not know much about his life as he was 'a very private guy'.

The Nature of Personality Disturbance

Personality is comprised of emotional and behavioural traits that characterize an individual's interactions with the daily world. Personality traits result in patterns of perceiving and relating to the environment and others. These traits are relatively stable and are evident in a wide range of interpersonal and social contexts. When personality traits become inflexible and maladaptive and cause significant functional impairment or subjective distress, they may be considered personality disorders (Kaplan and Sadock, 1996). Personality disorders are perhaps the most controversial of diagnostic categories because they are highly subjective. In addition, the use of the term *personality disorder* often has pejorative overtones, suggesting that the person is just unlikeable. Everyone has some maladaptive personality traits, perhaps a bit of narcissism, hysteria, or obsessive behaviour. These traits fall on a continuum from being mildly annoying or amusing to highly problematic. So at what point does a person move from having traits that sometimes interfere with relationships with others to having a personality disorder? This is a question that has been hotly debated in the literature and one in which there will be no quick resolution. For the purposes of this chapter, *personality disturbance* will be a term used to describe individuals who come into contact with social workers and other mental health professionals and who, by the nature of their personality traits, are blocked from achieving certain life goals (see Box 12.1). For instance, they are unable to sustain meaningful relationships with significant others, family, or friends; they are unable to sustain employment or complete a desired course of education as a result of maladaptive patterns; or they are frequently in contact with the law because of antisocial behaviour towards others. In order to be considered a personality disorder or disturbance, these traits are not transient but rather endure for many years and can be traced back to adolescence and early adulthood.

Incidence and Prevalence

The prevalence of personality disturbance has been reported to be 6 to14 per cent in general population studies conducted in Canada, the United States, and Scandinavia (Ekselius et al., 2001), and 10 to 30 per cent in inpatient psychiatric facilities. Older individuals are less likely to be diagnosed with personality distrubances than younger persons. This may be because the intensity of problematic personality

Box 12.1 Characteristics of a Personality Disturbance

- An enduring pattern of perception, emotional response, interpersonal functioning, and/or impulse control that deviates markedly from the expectations of an individual's culture.
- The enduring pattern is inflexible and pervasive across a broad range of situations.
- The enduring pattern leads to significant distress or impairment in social, occupational, and other domains.
- The enduring pattern is stable and can be traced back to adolescence or early adulthood.
- The enduring pattern is not due to a mental disorder, substance abuse, or a medical condition.

(Adapted from APA, 2000)

traits tends to diminish over the life course, in part perhaps because neurochemistry changes as people age, resulting in diminshed impulsive and aggressive behaviour. It may also be in part due to the high suicide rate of individuals with certain types of personality disturbances. Community sample studies have demonstrated that individuals with personality disturbances have much higher rates of mental health treatment than the general population (18 to 33 per cent versus 6 per cent). Prevalence rates vary according to type of personality disturbance; the most common personality problem in the general population is antisocial (4.1 per cent of the general population), followed by avoidant (1.9 per cent), schizoid and obsessive-compulsive (each at 0.9 per cent), paranoid (0.7 per cent), schizotypal (0.6 per cent), borderline (0.5 per cent), histrionic (0.2 per cent), dependent (0.1 per cent), and narcissistic (0.03 per cent) (Samuels et al., 2002).

Factors Contributing to Personality Disturbance

The causes of personality disturbance vary to some degree with the specific type of personality problem. In general, however, as with all other mental health challenges, the etiology is best understood as the combined effect of biology, individual intrapsychic factors, and environment. Paris (1994), for instance, suggests that biological factors may be reflected in underlying temperament, which in turn is a major influence on the development of personality traits and ultimately personality disturbances. In discussing causation, it is important to note that not all personality disturbances have received equal attention in terms of research and the clinical and academic literature; consequently, more is known about some types of personality disturbance, such as antisocial personality and borderline personality, and less about others, such as narcissistic and histrionic. This is no doubt in part due to general population incidence and in part due to the relative burden on society and the mental health system of the various types of personality disturbance.

Social Environmental Factors

Various psychosocial theories address the development of personality disturbances. For instance antisocial behaviour in children has been described as the direct outcome of a breakdown in parental family management. Antisocial children often come from disadvantaged families characterized by financial difficulties, inadequate parenting, absent parents, parental substance abuse, and sexual abuse. These families may further be living in dangerous and disorganized neighbourhoods (Martens, 2000). This type of history can lead to the development of antisocial personality in adulthood.

In borderline personality, risk factors are related to a variety of childhood experiences and fall into three categories: trauma, early separation or loss, and abnormal parenting (Paris, 1994). Of these, trauma has received the greatest focus and has been repeatedly proposed as an explanation for the development of borderline personality (Herman and van der Kolk, 1987). That is, intense trauma, particularly if it is repressed, can produce a chronic form of post-traumatic disorder that affects the personality (see Chapter 6). Supporting this hypothesis are studies that point to long-term effects of childhood sexual abuse—including depression, suicidality, substance abuse, problems in intimate relationships, and revictimization, all of which resemble borderline pathology.

Intrapsychic Factors

One formulation is that personality disturbances emanate from disrupted or disordered attachments. As described earlier, these can be of a highly destructive form such as is seen in abusive childhood experiences. Even in less extreme situations, however, early attachment patterns are seen to be reflected in adult attachment behaviour (Bowlby, 1979). Attachment experiences, especially in childhood, become incorporated into perceptions of self and other. When early relationships with caregivers are marked with hostility, victimization, and blaming, later relationships are bound to be seen through the filter of these past experiences. That is, individuals who have experienced negative relationships with others are more likely to be suspicious of the motives of others and are less likely to trust that others are truly interested in their welfare. Individuals who have had abusive or neglectful parents, are likely to have developed self-protective mechanisms to reduce the possibility that they will be hurt. These same individuals will find it more difficult to open themselves up to warm and loving relationships with others for fear they will again be emotionally harmed. The nature of individual expectations and relationship skills play a large part in determining both the types of people with whom one will associate and how they will be accepted.

Attachment patterns are seen to fall into four categories:

1. *Secure attachment* is the most common and is found in 55 to 65 per cent of adults and children. People with secure attachment are likely to have had warm and responsive caregivers who met their needs. As a result, they have

the ability to form and sustain relationships with others, have a positive view of self and others, and are able to cope with life crises.

2. *Avoidant and dismissive attachment* is found in 15 to 23 per cent of people. Caregivers for people in this category were likely to be punishing and dismissive. In adulthood these individuals downplay affect, are suspicious of close relationships, and are overly self-reliant. In the extreme, this may result in avoidant personality disorder or obsessive-compulsive personality disorder.
3. *Ambivalent, dependent, and preoccupied attachment* occurs in 8 to 12 per cent of children and adults. Caregivers were likely to be emotionally erratic and intermittently available. This results in people who are preoccupied with relationships and a need for security, who are very concerned with the opinions of others, who develop coercive strategies to maintain relationships, and who exhaust others and drive them away. This may result in histrionic or dependent personality disorders.
4. *Disorganized, controlling, and unresolved attachment* occurs in approximately 15 per cent of people, resulting from caregivers who were unpredictable and scary. As a result, individuals can have unresolved losses and traumas, and relationships that are difficult and hazardous, even volatile and violent. This may result in antisocial or borderline personality disorder.

Self-schema theory builds on the concepts of attachment and suggests that as a result of early-life experiences, people develop cognitive structures or schemas regarding themselves and others. From this perspective, each person has a personality that is characterized in part by elements of his or her schematic repertoire. Schemas are cognitive maps of the world that organize information in a given sphere. Each person has schemas related to him- or herself, such as: I am lovable or unlovable, I am competent or incompetent, or I am worthy or unworthy. Each person also has schemas related to others, such as: people are essentially trustworthy or untrustworthy, or people are likely to help or not help me. These schemas help a person to predict the likely outcome of any given interaction or relationship. Schemas can be viewed as pervasive in that they influence the present, colour memories of the past, and promise to extend to the future. Schemas are also tenacious and do not easily adapt to new information (Horowitz, 1991). Personality disturbances can be understood to be constellations of maladaptive beliefs or schemas that influence perceptions, emotions, and behaviours. Schemas determine the understanding of a given situation, the emotional response, and consequently the behaviour of the person. As a result, although schemas are formed through early-life experiences, they are self-reinforcing through subsequent encounters with the world and other people. Thus, a person with a dependent personality may believe that he or she is helpless, that he or she must rely on others in order to manage in life, and that others may abandon him or her and therefore must be held very close. In the end, this behaviour may drive others away.

Neurobiological Factors

Researchers are increasingly finding neurobiological underpinnings of certain personality disturbances. In antisocial personality, for instance, brain injuries and cerebrovascular disorders have been found to cause antisocial and psychopathic personality changes. Some brain lesions, such as frontal lobe lesions, are related to specific core features of antisocial personality and borderline personality such as impulsivity and disinhibition (Martens, 2000). Magnetic Resonance Imaging (MRI) studies of people with borderline personality have also demonstrated reduced volume in the frontal lobe, hippocampus, and amygdala (Lis et al., 2007). In addition, there is evidence of a link between monoamine oxidase (MAO) activity and sensation-seeking and impulsivity. Specifically, associations have been found between low serotonin function and aggressive behaviour and higher levels of 5-hydroxy indoleacetic acid and impulsivity, irritability, hostility, and aggression (Martens, 2000). Abnormal electroencephalographs (EEGs) are also reported in people with impulse disorders and aggression.

Perhaps the most persuasive evidence of the role of neurobiology in the development of personality disturbances is that of antisocial personality. A number of studies have demonstrated EEG abnormalities and brain-imaging abnormalities suggesting low perfusion, that is, blood flow, in the frontal lobes of the brain. The frontal lobes are involved in executive decision-making and functioning as well as inhibition of inappropriate behaviours. These findings therefore are consistent with the idea that minor abnormalities in this region could produce callous, poorly planned, and disinhibited behaviour, which are characteristically seen in the antisocial personality (Carrasco and Lecic-Tosevski, 2000). There have even been some studies that suggest a neurobiological basis for moral behaviour (Moll et al., 2002). This finding is a topic of great discussion in the field of forensic mental health where the focus is on the nature of the cause of the crime, the rationality of the perpetrator, and his or her responsibility (Arturo, in press).

Genetic Factors

Twin studies suggest high genetic weighting with respect to some types of personality disturbances. For instance, studies with respect to antisocial personality in adults have found concordance rates of 51.5 per cent for male monozygotic twins versus 23.1 per cent concordance with male-male dizygotic twins. Interestingly, however, twin studies with juveniles find delinquency concordance rates at 87 per cent for monozygotic twins versus 72 per cent for dizygotic, perhaps suggesting stronger environmental influences at a younger age. Lyons and colleagues (1995) in teasing this out with a cohort of 3,226 pairs of male twins, discovered that 5 of 10 symptoms of juvenile delinquency could be attributed to genetics and the other 5 to environmental factors, whereas 8 of 9 symptoms of adult antisocial personality disorder could be attributed to genetics. Similarly, family proband studies, that is, studies that examine the development of traits or illnesses across generations of a family, demonstrate inheritance factors related to impulsivity and aggression in borderline personality (Paris, 1994). Other researchers have looked at the heritability of traits that contribute to overall personality. It is estimated that the heritability of traits is between 34 and 56 per cent. Specific traits are emotional dysregulation (38 per cent), novelty seeking (34 per cent), harm avoidance (41 per cent), reward dependence (44 per cent), persistence (37 per cent), self-directedness (49 per cent), and cooperativeness (47 per cent) (Livesley, 2005a).

Types of Personality Disturbance

Personality disturbances are viewed as falling into three clusters: 1) disturbances that are characterized by odd or unusual behaviour (schizoid); 2) disturbances that are characterized by externalizing behaviours such as aggression towards others and dramatic, erratic behaviour; and 3) disturbances that are characterized by internalizing behaviours such as fear and anxiety. Within each of these clusters are three or four specific patterns of maladaptive personality traits (see Table 12.1).

Table 12.1 Types of Personality Disturbances

Schizoid cluster (Odd/eccentric/unusual)	**Externalizing cluster** (Dramatic/aggressive/erratic)	**Internalizing cluster** (Anxious/fearful)
• Paranoid	• Antisocial	• Avoidant
• Schizoid	• Borderline	• Dependent
• Schizotypal	• Histrionic	• Obsessive-compulsive
	• Narcissistic	

Paranoid

Paranoid personality occurs in people who display a pervasive distrust and suspiciousness of others such that their motives are interpreted as malevolent. This begins by early adulthood and is present in a variety of contexts. These people tend to suspect that others are exploiting, harming, or deceiving them, perceiving attacks on their character or reputation that are not apparent to others. Remarks of others or events are interpreted as having demeaning or threatening messages. Individuals are preoccupied with doubts about loyalty or trustworthiness and are reluctant to confide in others. This frequently presents as recurrent suspicions (without justification) regarding the fidelity of a spouse or partner. This diagnosis is differentiated from paranoid schizophrenia and delusional disorder by the absence of psychotic features.

Paranoid symptoms can also occur as a result of a variety of medical conditions. For instance, paranoid ideation is associated with illicit drug use and solvent abuse. Diseases of aging such as Alzheimer's disease may also produce paranoid thinking. Evidence also reveals that paranoid symptoms may be related to sensory deprivation caused by such disabilities as deafness or blindness.

Finally, environmental factors may produce paranoid thinking such as social factors related to immigration and threatening social situations that result in experiences of powerlessness. These possibilities should be ruled out before entering into a treatment plan with a person experiencing paranoia (Regehr and Glancy, 1999).

Schizoid

Schizoid personality most resembles a person suffering from the negative symptoms of schizophrenia but without the acute psychotic symptoms. Schizoid individuals neither desire nor enjoy close relationships and rather are detached, solitary loners. These individuals will seek out activities and employment that do not require them to interact with others, such as computer programming. Affect is restricted and the person does not appear to react to criticism or positive life experiences. Facial expression is often hard to read and interactions are often bland. These behaviours appear to begin early in life and those later diagnosed as schizoid personality disorder are frequently described as solitary and underachieving in childhood (Wolff et al., 1991).

Schizoid personality may have unique etiological factors. One study looking at the after-effects of famine in Holland from 1944 to 1946 noted that those individuals who were *in utero* during the famine had higher levels of schizoid personality disorder, particularly if they were male (Hoek et al., 1996). Further, schizoid personality disorder is associated with low body weight in male children and adolescents (Hebebrand et al., 1997).

Schizotypal

Schizotypal individuals are usually described by others as odd, eccentric, or peculiar. They frequently have unusual beliefs that are not held with the same delusional conviction of individuals who suffer from schizophrenia but are rather characterized as superstitious. People with schizotypal personality may believe that they have supernatural powers or extraordinary perceptual abilities that are not understood in their cultural context. This is sometimes described as magical thinking. Their behaviour is considered unusual by others and their dress tends to be idiosyncratic. Similar to schizoid personality, individuals with schizotypal personality have impaired ability to relate to others and acute discomfort in interpersonal relationships, but their affect is not bland in the same manner as is seen in schizoid.

There is considerable overlap between both schizotypal and schizoid personality and Asperger's syndrome, which is on the autism spectrum in childhood (Wolff et al., 1991; Hurst et al., 2007). Asperger's is characterized by social difficulties, communication impairments, and repetitive-restricted activities. Schizotypal personality is associated with cognitive-perceptual difficulties, deficits in emotional awareness, and difficulties with emotional processing, all of which result in difficulties in reading social cues and differentiating between idiosyncratic beliefs and the beliefs of others in their environment (Berenbaum et al., 2006).

Antisocial

Antisocial personality (which is sometimes referred to as sociopathic, psychopathic, or ASPD) is perhaps the disturbance that has the largest impact on others in society. Indeed, for this reason it has been suggested that it was the first personality disturbance identified in the field of mental health. In 1809 Pinel described *Manie sans Delire* (mania without delirium) which involved emotional instability and social drift and was seen to be caused by inadequate education or a perverse, unreserved constitution (Sass, 2007). Sometime later, American psychiatrist Cleckley in his 1941 classic *The Mask of Sanity* described the psychopath as a person with antisocial behaviour that could not be derived from 'psychosis, neurosis, or mental handicap'. Elements of psychopathic personality in this description included superficial charm, unreliability and insincerity, inability to accept blame or shame, failure to learn from experience, incapacity for love, lacking emotion, poor interpersonal relationships, and inability to follow one's aim in life (Ogloff, 2006). This description is remarkably similar to present-day descriptions of antisocial personality, which is characterized by criminal, aggressive, and impulsive behaviour, conscience impairment, and substance abuse.

Although almost impossible to evaluate, it has been estimated that approximately 3 to 5 per cent of people in the general population would meet the criteria for antisocial personality or using a stricter criteria of psychopathy, 1 per cent of people. By contrast, 15 per cent of male prisoners, 10 per cent of forensic patients, and 7 per cent of female prisoners meet the criteria of psychopathy (Ogloff, 2006). Common biological, genetic, and environmental bases have been suggested for substance abuse and antisocial personality. For instance, disturbances in prefrontal functioning may be a common biological ground that links antisocial personality and substance abuse (Martens, 2000). Individuals with antisocial personality have a prevalence rate of substance abuse of 39.3 per cent. Men with antisocial personality are 3 times more likely to abuse alcohol and 5 times more likely to abuse drugs than the general population. Among women with antisocial personality the rate is considerably higher, and they are approximately 12 times more likely to abuse either drugs or alcohol.

Borderline

While antisocial personality may provide the biggest challenges to society, borderline personality perhaps provides the biggest challenges to the mental health system. Borderline personality is defined as a pervasive pattern of instability in interpersonal relationships, self-image, and affect, and marked impulsivity that frequently results in episodes of self-harm and suicide attempts (see Chapter 5). This disturbance is characterized by the frantic efforts of an individual to avoid real or imagined abandonment. Relationships are initially viewed in an idealized form but the needs of the individual with borderline personality often overwhelm others, and in the end they leave or fail to live up to expectations and are rejected. Personal identity tends to be unstable and there are frequent and dramatic shifts including changes in goals, values, friends, and sexual identity. Affective instability, ranging from elation to despair and fury are commonly experienced. Underlying this is a chronic sense of emptiness. People with borderline personality frequently present at mental health services desperate for assistance; however, they often drop out of treatment when a crisis is averted or because therapists are unable to meet their expectations and needs.

As noted earlier, one of the central formulations regarding the development of borderline personality is childhood abuse, particularly sexual abuse (Herman and van der Kolk, 1987). This formulation was first proposed by Stern in 1938 in his groundbreaking paper on borderline pathology where he noted that cruelty, neglect, and brutality of parents of many years' duration are factors found in these patients. This is seen to affect identity formation, that is, views of self, and regulation, that is, the ability to modulate emotion and manage stress. More recently, Herman (1992) has described the manner in which chronic childhood abuse creates a climate of terror that results in profoundly disrupted relationships, pathological attachments, constant alertness, distrust of others, self-hatred and self-blame, and disassociation. Herman suggests that this leads to a complex form of post-traumatic stress disorder (see Chapter 6) and in extreme cases, personality disturbance in the form of borderline personality.

Histrionic

An individual with a histrionic personality is uncomfortable with situations where he or she is not the centre of attention. He or she can be described as seductive, provocative, and dramatic. Emotions are close to the surface and readily shared with all others. Histrionic personality disturbance is characterized by: 1) discomfort in situations wherein he or she is not the centre of attention; 2) sexually seductive or provocative behaviour; 3) rapidly shifting and shallow expression of emotions; 4) use of physical appearance to draw attention to him- or herself; 5) an overly impressionistic style of speech; 6) self-dramatization, theatricality, and exaggerated emotional expression; 7) suggestibility; and 8) perception of greater intimacy in relationships than actually exists (APA, 2000). If personality is viewed on a continuum, these characteristics can be found in many people, famous and not famous; however, the prevalence of the disturbance at a clinical level is said to be 2 to 3 per cent and it is equally diagnosed in men and women (Nestadt et al., 1990). Among those with histrionic personality disorder, males are more likely to have co-existing antisocial personality and women are more likely to have co-existing somatization disorder (Lilenfield et al., 1986).

Narcissistic

Narcissistic personality disturbance is characterized by a grandiose sense of self-importance, superficiality, shallowness, and a lack of empathy for others. Specifically, narcissistic personality is indicated by: 1) a grandiose sense of importance,

2) preoccupation with fantasies of success, 3) a belief in one's special or unique status, 4) a need for excessive admiration, 5) a sense of entitlement, 6) exploitation of others, 7) a lack of empathy, 8) envy of others, and 9) arrogance (APA, 2000). Narcissistic personality is of particular interest because it provokes less distress in those suffering from it than in those in interpersonal relationships with narcissistic individuals. For instance, in a study that measured countertransference in psychiatrists and psychologists working with narcissistic individuals, clinicians reported feeling anger, resentment, and dread in working with these patients; devalued and criticized by the client; and avoidant to the point of wanting to discontinue treatment (Miller, Campbell, and Pilkonis, 2007). Similarly, these characteristics are likely to cause failures in intimate and other social relationships. As a result, treatment approaches to narcissistic personality often focus on the individual's partner, the one who suffers in the relationship, not the affected person him- or herself.

Avoidant

An individual with avoidant personality avoids social contact for fear of criticism, disapproval, and rejection. He or she experiences feelings of inadequacy and longs for closeness but is thwarted by an intense fear of intimacy. An area of considerable controversy in the literature is the overlap between social phobia (an anxiety disturbance—see Chapter 9) and avoidant personality disorder and whether the resulting anxiety and behaviour is the result of a mental health problem or a constellation of personality traits.

Avoidant personality is characterized by social inhibition that is manifested by: 1) avoiding occupational activities that involve significant social contact; 2) an unwillingness to become involved with people for fear of not being liked; 3) restraint in intimate relationships for fear of being shamed; 4) preoccupation with criticism and rejection in social situations; 5) inhibition in new social situations; 6) a self-view as being socially inept, unappealing, and inferior; and 7) an unusual reluctance to engage in new activities or take risks (APA, 2000). Social phobia by contrast is described as intense fear and anxiety in social or performance situations, which frequently has an onset in the mid-teens. Such situations can include parties where one is expected to meet new people, public speaking, and presentations in class if the person is a student. The distinction therefore is the pervasive nature of the pattern of behaviour and beliefs that span a wide range of contexts. Regardless of the theoretical distinction, however, researchers have found a moderate overlap of about 30 per cent between these two types of social distress. Twin studies have suggested that the genetic factors in social phobia and avoidant personality are identical (Reichborn-Kjennerud et al., 2007). These authors suggest that different life events may determine whether a person develops a personality disturbance that also impacts intimate personal relationships or whether their anxiety is more limited to social and performance situations. Regardless of the distinction, however, these individuals find themselves significantly impacted by their fears and often lead quite isolated lives as a result.

Dependent

An individual with dependent personality has a pervasive and excessive need for others to assume responsibility for most areas of life. This frequently leads to passivity, submission, and clinging behaviour resulting from a fear of separation or abandonment. In considering this formulation, however, environmental factors must be considered. For instance, elderly persons who suddenly find themselves in nursing homes or other institutional settings that thwart customary habits and activities and undermine their sense of competence may appear to be dependent and unable to make decisions; however, this may not be part of a lifetime pattern of behaviour but may merely be reactive to the current situation. Although concerns have been raised that diagnosis of dependent personality disorder may be gender-biased, at least one study found no gender differences in diagnosis (Reich, 1990).

Obsessive-Compulsive

Obsessive-compulsive personality falls on the continuum with obsessive-compulsive disorder (see Chapter 9). In this disturbance, perfectionism interferes with task completion. The personality is characterized by rigidity, perfectionism, isolation of affect, interpersonal control, and harsh conscience. The individual is: 1) pre-occupied with details, rules, and lists; 2) perfectionistic to the point that it interferes with task completion; 3) excessively devoted to work; 4) overconscientious; 5) unable to discard worthless objects; 6) reluctant to delegate tasks; 7) miserly in their spending style; and 8) rigid and stubborn (APA, 2000). From a developmental perspective, obsessive-compulsive personality can be seen to be overconforming and overidentifying with rigid parental expectations.

Recovery-Oriented Psychosocial Approaches to Intervention

The personality disturbances are highly divergent and thus a wide range of interventions can be considered. Some approaches can be understood to be more general and address common features. For instance, cognitive therapy is frequently recommended for addressing dysfunctional beliefs that result in problematic behaviours and attitudes (Beck and Freeman, 1990). Various forms of psychotherapy are also frequently used to address underlying causes and consequences of personality disruption. This discussion of psychosocial interventions begins with considering common challenges and helpful approaches to addressing personality disturbance. Other approaches are more specific to particular types of problems. Borderline personality in particular has received a great deal of attention both in the development of treatment models and in the testing of these models. In this chapter we will focus on two specific forms of treatment that have been empirically tested, Dialectical behaviour therapy and interpersonal therapy. We will also focus our discussion on interventions with individuals with impulse control problems because these individuals are at greatest risk of harm to both self and others and consume the most mental health resources when compared to other forms of personality disturbance.

General Issues and Approaches

People with personality disturbances present with a range of issues that make intervention challenging for mental health practitioners and change difficult for those who suffer the consequences of their own personality challenges. One issue is the pervasive nature of personality problems that begin early in life and affect all aspects of the person's interpersonal world. Personality and the ingrained behaviours and beliefs associated with it are slow to change regardless of the negative consequences to a person's life. A second issue is the degree to which we all defend our own personality structures, even if we know they are at times problematic. These structures evolved for a reason and are integral to who we know we are as a person. Thus, the suggestion that certain aspects of our own personality should change is highly threatening. This then leads to an additional challenge, individuals with personality disturbances who present to mental health practitioners and programs have a great deal of difficulty committing to a change process and thus frequently drop out of treatment. If they do not drop out of treatment, the personality traits that cause problems in other interpersonal relationships also cause problems in the treatment relationship. Therapeutic alliance can be difficult to establish and sustain. Mental health practitioners must also work hard to manage their own reactions to the individual's personality style, such as the example provided earlier in this chapter where the therapists reacted with anger to feelings of being belittled by narcissistic clients. As a result of these challenges, some common principles can be useful in working with individuals with personality problems (Livesley, 2005b; 2007):

- *Provide multiple interventions delivered in an integrated and coordinated manner.* Individuals with personality disturbances who present to treatment are frequently dealing with a range of issues that affect many aspects of their lives. Thus treatment approaches must address these varied issues. For instance, couple or family intervention may be required to address problems in close relationships, cognitive-behavioural approaches may be useful in targeting particular problematic patterns and behaviours, crisis intervention approaches may be needed during periods of acute risk and stress, and medication may be needed to target certain issues such as obsessive behaviours or impulsivity and aggression. Frequently these varied interventions will be offered by different members of the interdisciplinary team. As a result, communication and integration of approaches is vital to ensure that professionals are not working at cross purposes.
- *Provide support, empathy, and validation.* Because individuals with personality problems often encounter conflicts with others in their lives and simultaneously experience a great deal of anxiety about their own worthiness, empathy, support, and reinforcement for positive gains is important. Acknowledgment of the challenges and difficulties associated with change is also helpful.

- *Provide stability and set limits.* Individuals with personality challenges that include impulse control frequently have chaotic lives and chaotic relationships. Individuals with other types of personality challenges seek to control their own environments through limiting new contacts or repetitive behaviours. Although the social worker should be available for support and empathy, it is also important to set reasonable limits on access (such as specified meeting times and an appropriate number of telephone contact) and to set expectations for behaviour (for instance, threatening the receptionist does not mean that you receive additional time with the social worker).
- *Work to contain distress.* While the social worker must validate experiences of distress experienced by the client, encouragement of the expression of feelings of distress often lead to the escalation of emotion and a decreased ability of the client to manage. The focus should remain on the here and now and not become an exploration of previous life issues that will lead to emotional and behavioural disorganization. Work with the client to identify triggering situations and find ways to avoid these triggers, reframe the understanding of the situation, or deal with issues before emotional dysregulation occurs.
- *Be prepared for crises.* Individuals with impulse control issues related to their personality disturbance will have periods of crisis that may need changes in treatment approaches for a period of time. The task of the social worker is to ensure safety and assist the person to return to the previous level of functioning as soon as possible. Hospitalization may be required at times of acute crisis when there is no other way to ensure safety, but in general, there is little evidence that hospitalization is of lasting assistance. A general rule, therefore, is to avoid hospitalization whenever possible by mobilizing community-based supports.
- *Understand that change is slow.* As noted earlier, the nature of personality disturbance is pervasive and enduring and any change will occur slowly. If short-term treatment is all that is available, goals should be very modest and it should be understood that the person is likely to need other forms of intervention at other times.
- *Understand that motivation to change behaviour and attitude regardless of the consequences to the person's life will fluctuate.* Consider the Stages of Change Model and the techniques of motivational interviewing described in Chapter 11 as possible approaches for understanding and encouraging willingness to change.
- *Maintain a recovery model orientation.* Regardless of the views of either the social worker or others in the client's life about the need to change behaviours or attitudes, the client must be in control of their treatment and recovery process. Reviewing the consequences of the current problems and identifying possible courses of action will empower the client to make decisions.

Dialectical Behaviour Therapy

Dialectical behaviour therapy (DBT) is a comprehensive treatment that blends cognitive-behavioural approaches with acceptance-based practices adopted from Zen Buddhism. This model was first proposed by Marsha Linehan and colleagues (1991) as a result of the shortcomings of traditional CBT, which focused on changing client thoughts and behaviours but did not simultaneously attend to issues of acceptance and validation, resulting in treatment dropout. A dialectical philosophy blends and balances acceptance and motivation for change. From this perspective, mindfulness is incorporated into CBT in order to: 1) increase clients' control over their attentional processes; 2) assist clients to integrate emotional and rational thinking; and 3) help clients experience a sense of unity with themselves, others, and the universe (Lynch et al., 2006). The manualized treatment approach includes four basic modes of intervention, including individual therapy (one hour per week for one year), a skills-training group (2.5 hours per week), telephone consultation with clients, and weekly consultative team meetings to support therapists. The approach focuses on reducing life-threatening and suicidal behaviours. Specific aspects of DBT can be found in Box 12.2.

DBT has a considerable base of evidence to support its use in the treatment of borderline personality disorder. This evidence includes seven randomized controlled studies involving 262 people, over five separate comparisons. According to a *Cochrane Review*, DBT proved to be helpful on a wide range of outcomes, such

Box 12.2 Aspects of Dialectical Behaviour Therapy

Mindfulness	• Focusing on the moment, becoming one with the current experience • Awareness of own emotions without judgment
Distress tolerance	• Crisis survival strategies • Acceptance of reality
Emotional regulation	• Observe and identify emotional states • Reduce automatic responses to situations • Decrease vulnerability to negative emotions (reducing arousal) • Increase experience of positive emotions (focus on positives)
Interpersonal effectiveness	• Assertiveness training • Cognitive restructuring • Balancing personal objectives with retaining relationships and maintaining self-esteem

as admission to hospital or incarceration in prison, but the small size of included studies limits confidence in their results (Binks et al., 2006). In addition, DBT has demonstrated efficacy in randomized controlled trials (RCTs) with chronically depressed older adults, and with patients with eating disorders. Across studies, DBT results in reductions of self-injurious behaviour, suicide attempts and ideation, and hopelessness and depression (Robins and Chapman, 2004). Nevertheless, one of the major problems with DBT is that it is resource-intensive and expensive and thus it has not been instituted in many areas. Because the initial treatment phase lasts one year, there are often long waiting lists for treatment in places where the treatment is available (Paris, 2005).

Interpersonal Therapy

Interpersonal therapy (IPT) is based on the premise that distress occurs within an interpersonal context. Originally based on attachment theory, the model assumes that upsetting events trigger negative moods and these moods in turn impair interpersonal functioning thereby leading to further negative events (Markowitz et al., 2007; Ravitz, Maunder, and McBride, 2008). Initially the model was developed in the early 1970s for the treatment of depression and more recently it has been adapted for use with individuals with personality disorders, specifically borderline personality. Interpersonal therapy in the area of personality disturbance is based on a definition of personality that emphasizes understanding the meaning of interpersonal relationships in explaining maladaptive behaviour. The model focuses on the development of cognitive schemas based on early-life experiences with important attachment figures (Marziali and Munroe-Blum, 1994). IPT sessions are structured to focus on the individual's interpersonal successes and setbacks. Interpersonal successes are reinforced by the therapist. Interpersonal setbacks are met first with empathy for the client, followed by strategies for dealing with such situations in the future.

A common model of delivery of the IPT model is through group intervention. The IPT model of group therapy was designed to create a therapeutic context in which the person suffering from a personality disorder is able to replicate problematic interpersonal behaviours without having to resort to fight or flight strategies. The group therapists avoid 'fighting' by affirming the client's worldview and helping them expand their choices of behaviour and response. In particular, the therapists value the client's past attempts to manage life stresses (Marziali and Munroe-Blum, 1994). The group therapy model offers multiple and varied opportunities to interact with others and observe the consequences of both the client's own responses to situations and the consequences of other people's responses. In addition, the intensity of the relationship with the therapist is reduced in the group setting and more responsibility and control is experienced by the client.

Interpersonal therapy has a broad base of empirical support. Randomized controlled trials have demonstrated efficacy with depression, eating disorders, substance abuse disorders, anxiety disorders, and personality disorder (Markowitz et al., 2007; Ravitz, Maunder, and McBride, 2008). An RCT that compared IPT groups to individual psychotherapy demonstrated significant improvements in both types of treatment in areas of psychosocial adjustment and self-reported depression (Marziali and Munroe-Blum, 1994). Group treatment has the benefit of being more cost-effective than individual work.

Pharmacological Interventions

As noted earlier in this chapter, personality disturbances tend to be very difficult to treat because of their pervasive and ingrained nature. As we have discussed, the very problems such as splitting (viewing people as all good or all bad and often pitting people against one another) or distrust, characteristic of some individuals with personality challenges, render it quite difficult to form a good therapeutic alliance and to sustain this alliance over the long period of time necessary for change. Pharmacotherapy in personality disturbances is generally used to modify certain neurotransmitter systems that are responsible for specific symptoms inherent in personality variables (Soloff, 2005). In administering pharmacotherapy, all the general principles of treatment noted earlier apply. Most particularly, the goals of treatment should be agreed upon jointly with the client. Communication between members of the treatment team is essential (Schlesinger and Silk, 2005). Pharmacotherapy administered alone can never be considered the singular effective treatment in the complex problems associated with personality disturbance.

Pharmacological treatments with people suffering from personality challenges tend to focus on specific symptoms or manifestations of the disturbance. For instance, one of the most commonly used types of medication in borderline personality and antisocial personality is the antipsychotic group of drugs. Generally speaking, the antipsychotics are given to decrease the impulsivity that is characteristic of these disturbances. They also appear to decrease anxiety and produce a calming effect. Most particularly in borderline personality they reduce psychotic symptoms such as delusions of persecution, delusions of reference (beliefs that communications, such as on the radio, are about you—see Chapter 4), and hallucinations characteristic of the micropsychotic episodes that are sometimes observed. These medications are also used in schizotypal personality and paranoid personality disturbances because of the similarity of some of the symptoms to schizophrenia.

Antidepressants are also commonly used in clients suffering from personality disturbances, especially where there are prominent depressive symptoms as well as anger and impulsivity (Glancy and Knott, 2002). Another group of medications that have been used with some success are the mood stabilizers. Instability of mood is one of the cardinal core features of borderline personality, so theoretically it makes sense to use these medications. Nevetheless, while lithium has been used, its efficacy is uncertain and caution should be taken because it is lethal in overdose (Links et al., 1990).

Perhaps the most commonly used medication in personality disturbances are the benzodiazepines, such as Valium. Gutheil talks about the 'Catch-22' of treating borderline personality, in that these clients request and crave benzodiazepines but these medications tend to worsen their conditions (Peteet and Gutheil, 1979).

These medications tend to produce disinhibition, increased anger, and increased deliberate self-harm, and should be considered as contraindicated in borderline personality disorder (Carrasco and Lecic-Tosevski, 2000).

Possible Social Work Interventions in the Case Examples

Case Example 1: Mario

Mario has characteristics of what may be viewed as a paranoid personality. This leads to conflicts in many areas of his life.

- Given the interpersonal nature of his problems, interpersonal therapy may be useful for Mario to consider how he might modify his interactions with others.
- CBT could also be used to examine his assumptions about people and situations.
- Both these treatments, however, will require that Mario has a belief that he should engage in some sort of change. If he is distressed but uncertain about change, motivational interviewing may be of assistance.

Case Example 2: Terry

Terry has characteristics of schizoid personality. People like Terry will rarely come to the attention of social workers or other members of the health care team. They function relatively independently and have few contacts with others.

- If Terry had approached a social worker as a result of his distress, interpersonal therapy to address his concerns about social interactions may have been useful.

Summary

In summary, personality disturbance represent a wide range of problems in interpersonal functioning that can cause considerable distress to the individual suffering from the disorder and those in their family and social circle. Personality disturbance are insidious in their etiology, are often caused by many factors, and begin early in life. As a result of the pervasive and persistent nature of these disorders, treatment is challenging and there are no clear approaches that have high rates of success in a short time frame. Change relies on long-term approaches to alter interactional patterns and self-perceptions. While this is occurring, crisis intervention at the time when life stresses interfere with functioning is frequently necessary.

Key Terms

Algorithm
Cerebrovascular disease
Contraindicated
Dysmetabolic syndrome
Dysregulation
Electroencephalograph (EEG)
Idiosyncratic
Lesions
Transient

Discussion Questions

1. How may social workers engage in discussions about personality disturbances without assigning blame or becoming pejorative?
2. How may social workers intervene in the interdisciplinary team if other members are stigmatizing or rejecting clients with personality disturbances?
3. What challenges could a social worker encounter in their individual work with a client who has a personality disturbance?

Suggested Readings and Weblinks

Beck, A., and Freeman, A. (1990), *Cognitive Therapy of Personality Disorders* (New York: Guilford).
Bowlby, J. (1979), *The Making and Breaking of Affectional Bonds* (London: Tavistock Publications).
Mayo Clinic, *Personality Disorders* (accessed at *http://www.mayoclinic.com/health/personality-disorders/DS00562*).

Glossary

Advanced directives Instructions about health or mental health treatment made by a competent person in anticipation of future medical, cognitive, or mental health incapacitation.

Affidavit A written statement where the writer/signer swears to the truth of the document before a notary or other judicial officer.

Akathisia A syndrome characterized by extreme restlessness and inability to remain still; a subjective feeling of muscular agitation often accompanied by pacing.

Algorithm A set of specific instructions for calculations or data processing, now also used in describing a procedure for clinical decision-making.

Amphetamine A type of stimulant drug that increases levels of norepinephrine, serotonin, and dopamine in the brain.

Analgesia The inability to feel pain while still conscious.

Anomie Defined by Emile Durkheim as a state of normlessness or social disintegration.

Antabuse A drug used in the treatment of alcoholism to limit the metabolism of alcohol, thereby making the client extremely nauseous if he or she consumes alcohol.

Anticonvulsant A drug to help with seizures that prevents the rapid firing of neurons that precipitate a seizure.

Anxiety neurosis A term coined by Freud referring to excessive anxiety and worry caused by intrapsychic issues.

Anxiolytic A drug prescribed for the treatment of anxiety.

Arousal symptoms One of the three clusters of acute stress and post-traumatic stress symptoms, which include difficulty falling or staying asleep, emotional outbursts, difficulty concentrating, hypervigilance, and exaggerated startle response.

Atrophy The partial or complete wasting away of a part of the body or organ.

Autosomal dominant A pattern of trait transmission (or inheritance) in which an individual has one gene containing the illness and one gene not containing the illness on a pair of chromosomes; as a result, the person has a 50-50 chance of passing on the mutant gene, and therefore the disorder, to each of his or her children.

Avoidance symptoms One of the three clusters of acute stress and post-traumatic stress symptoms, which include efforts to avoid thoughts or stimuli that are reminiscent of the event.

Benztropine A drug used to treat Parkinson's disease, akathisia, and dystonia.

Cerebrospinal fluid A bodily fluid that collects in and around the brain.

Cerebrovascular disease A dysfunction in the brain related to the blood vessels that supply blood to the brain.

Chronicity A persistent and lasting medical or mental health condition.

Circadian rhythm The 24-hour cycle of the day for all living beings on earth.

Civil liberties Limits set by the government of its power, meant to protect people from the government and its potential misuses of power.

Coersion The practice of manipulating a person to behave in an involuntary way, sometimes by use of fear, threats, or intimidation.

Co-morbid The presence of more than one disease or disorder occurring at the same time.

Computerized Axial Tomography (CAT) scan A process using a computer to take pictures of the body through 'slices' that can be then put together to gain an accurate three-dimensional picture of what is going on in the body.

Concordance The presence of the same trait in two individuals.

Confabulation The filling in of memory gaps with false descriptions of events, often linked with suggestibility in severe amnestic syndromes.

Consent and Capacity Board An independent board legislated by the government that conducts hearings by its members, including lawyers, psychiatrists, and other members of the public, to review the application of restrictions under mental health legislation.

Contraindicated A situation where certain drugs, procedures, or activities would be deemed inadvisable.

Cortisol The primary stress hormone.

Covert modelling A cognitive behavioural technique in which a client identifies negative behaviour and ways to change this behaviour by rehearsing it.

Criminal Code of Canada The full listing and explanation of criminal offences and procedures in Canada.

Crisis A period of psychological disequilibrium experienced as a result of a hazardous event or situation that constitutes a significant problem that cannot be remedied by using familiar coping strategies.

Cyclothymia A chronic, fluctuating mood disturbance that involves numerous periods of depressive symptoms and some periods of manic symptoms.

Deleterious Harmful in an unexpected or subtle way.

Delirium A sudden state of severe confusion and rapid changes in brain function, sometimes associated with hallucinations and hyperactivity.

Delirium tremens An acute, sometimes fatal, episode of delirium usually caused by withdrawal or abstinence from alcohol following habitual use.

Dementia A progressive disease of the brain that results in declining cognitive function beyond that of normal aging.

Dependence A maladaptive pattern of substance use leading to clinically significant impairment or distress that further includes withdrawal, tolerance, ingestion of larger amounts than intended, unsuccessful efforts to cut down, excessive time spent in activities related to substances, narrowing of interests, and continued use despite knowledge of physical or psychological problems likely attributable to the substance.

Depersonalization An alteration in the perception of the self in which someone feels detached from their self and sees themselves as if from outside their body.

Derealization The change of perception of the external world in which events appear unreal or strange.

Detainment A procedure whereby a person is detained in hospital pursuant to the applicable Mental Health Act or other legal means.

Diathesis One's predisposition or tendency toward an affliction or condition.

Dipsomania An old term for a description of an uncontrollable craving for alcohol.

Disinhibition The reduction or loss of inhibition.

Dissociation An altered state in which thoughts, emotions, perceptions, and/or memories are disrupted and split off from the reality of what is happening in the present.

Dizygotic twins Non-identical twins, also known as fraternal.

Double bind A situation where a person is faced with two conflicting demands by someone who has a close and powerful relationship with the individual.

Dysmetabolic syndrome A condition characterized by weight gain, accompanied by elevated cholesterol, lipids, and triglycerides, as well as by insulin resistance, which may lead to diabetes.

Dysphoria An uncomfortable, unpleasant mood characterized by sadness, anxiety, irritability, and/or restlessness.

Dysregulation An emotional response that is not found under the normal accepted range of emotional reactions to a specific situation.

Dystonia A neurological disorder that induces muscle contractions in the body that can result in abnormal postures.

Electroencephalograph (EEG) Measurement of electric activity in the brain.

Emancipation Where a minor has been granted the legal authority of an adult by proving he or she is already an 'adult in practice', meaning the minor would be free of the decision-making powers or authority of his or her parents.

Endocrine A system of organs that release hormones and help regulate metabolism, growth, development, and mood.

Endogenous Something that arises from an organism, tissue, or cell.

Epistemology The theory of knowledge; a philosophy concerned with the conceptions of knowledge.

Equilibrium A stable or balanced state.

Etiology The study of causation, most often used in describing the origins of disease.

Euphoria A state of intense happiness or well-being.

Euthanasia Originally meaning 'good death', it has now come to mean the active acceleration of death by someone (often a health care professional) in situations where people are suffering from a painful illness that will result in imminent death.

Evidence-based practice The use of interventions for which there is sufficiently persuasive evidence to support their effectiveness in attaining the desired outcomes.

Existential anxiety Anxiety caused by a belief in the meaninglessness of life.

Fetal alcohol syndrome (FAS) A disorder first manifest at birth associated with females who drink alcohol during pregnancy; the offspring have certain characteristic features.

G8 An international forum of governments including Canada, France, Germany, Italy, Japan, Russia, the United Kingdom, and the United States.

GAF Global Assessment of Functioning: a numeric scale from 0 to 100 used by mental health professionals to rate the social, occupational, and psychological functioning of adult patients.

Gliosis An abnormality of brain neurons that is generally considered a sign of past inflammation caused by infection or other types of brain injury.

Hallucination An abnormal perception without a real stimulus.

Holistic The ideology that a system cannot be understood by looking at its parts, only by looking at it as a whole.

Hydrocephalus Abnormal accumulation of bodily fluid in the brain.

Hypertensive A condition of chronic high blood pressure.

Hypoglycaemia A disorder characterized by low blood sugar.

Hypomania A less severe form of mania; although the symptoms are similar to mania, hypomanic episodes differ in that they do not cause significant distress or impair one's work, family relationships, or social life.

Hypothyroidism A condition in which the body has low levels of the thyroid hormone thyroxin.

Iatrogenic An adverse effect or complication caused by medical treatment or advice.

Idiosyncratic Unusual temperament or personality traits.

Idiot A historical term that referred to the condition now called developmental delay.

Inefficacious Not producing a desired objective.

Informed consent A legal term in which a person can be said to have given consent to treatment based upon a reasonable understanding and appreciation of the risks, benefits, and alternatives to that treatment.

Insidious A condition appearing so slowly that it seems harmless at first, even though it is potentially very harmful.

Insomnia A condition in which a person either cannot sleep or has extreme difficulty in falling or staying asleep.

Insulin shock therapy A treatment of some mental illnesses that involved injecting a patient with large amounts of insulin thereby inducing a coma in which doctors believed the brain metabolism would slow and return to normal healthy levels

Interprofessional A working environment in which there are several professions that collaborate.

Intrapsychic Internal psychological processes.

Irritable heart The reactions of soldiers, at first in the US Civil War and continuing to the first world war, which are now understood to be the arousal symptoms of post-traumatic stress.

Jurisdiction The authority granted to a legal body or political leader to make decisions on legal matters and to hold responsibility.

Labile Instability, for example, of moods, wherein laughing, smiling, or crying uncontrollably is suddenly expressed and may last for several minutes.

Lesions Abnormal tissues found on the body usually from either disease or trauma.

Lunatic Historically a common term for a person who was mentally ill, a condition formerly called lunacy.

Magnetic Resonance Imaging (MRI) A magnetic imaging technique that produces a three-dimensional image of the structure of the body.

Malapropism A substitution of an incorrect word with a sound, usually with a comedic effect.

Mania Excitement manifested by physical or mental hyperactivity, disorganized behaviour, and elevation of mood.

Melancholia A type of severe depression characterized by biological symptoms such as a lack of energy, poor appetite and sleep habits, and a slowing down of bodily processes.

Mesolimbic dopamine pathway A neural pathway in the brain and a part of the limbic system.

Meta-analyses A combination of results from several studies, added together and subject to statistical analysis.

Monomania An obsolete term for a delusional disorder in which the client focuses on only one false belief.

Monozygotic twins Also known as identical twins, this refers to twins who share the same genetic structure.

Neuraesthenia A psychological disorder characterized by chronic fatigue and weakness, loss of memory, and generalized aches and pains, formerly thought to result from exhaustion of the nervous system.

Neurodevelopmental The development of the brain and nervous system.

Neuroleptic A form of antipsychotic medication.

Neuroleptic Malignant Syndrome (NMS) A serious neurological and metabolic disorder caused by a reaction to neuroleptic or antipsychotic drugs.

Neuron A nerve cell that sends and receives electrical signals over long distances within the body.

Neurotransmitters Chemicals that relay information between neurons or between a neuron and another cell.

Nigrostriatal pathway One of the four main dopamine pathways in the brain.

Nystagmus A type of eye movement in which movement in one direction is smooth and fast and movement in the other direction is jerky.

Orbitofrontal The area of the brain associated with decision-making.

Out of the Shadows at Last A report produced by a standing senate committee focusing on issues of mental health and mental illness.

Panic attacks Sudden, discrete episodes of very intense anxiety accompanied by feelings of impending doom and the bodily manifestations of anxiety.

Parasuicide An action in which someone mimics the act of suicide but does not intend suicide (usually involving self-harm, such as cutting).

Paresis A condition of loss of or the impaired movement of body parts.

Paraesthesias Tingling, numbness, or prickling of a person's skin.

Pathognomonic A symptom that is so indicative of a disease that it virtually diagnoses the disease by its presence.

Pathologizing To view as abnormal, either medically, psychologically, or otherwise.

Pejorative Aimed at discrediting or downplaying the merit of something.

Phenothiazines A group of antipsychotic drugs.

Pluralistic society The idea that many different beliefs, values, and ideas operate in society, which may all be correct and also in conflict with each other.

Positron Emission Tomography (PET) A nuclear medicine technique that provides a three-dimensional image of the chemical processes in the body.

Post-traumatic stress A set of avoidance, arousal, and intrusion symptoms that follow exposure to a life-threatening event.

Power of attorney A system of authorizing someone to make decisions on another person's behalf regarding legal or medical matters.

Prefrontal lobotomies A surgical procedure used to treat mental illnesses which involves cutting the connections to and from the prefrontal cortex.

Prodromal An early non-specific symptom (or set of symptoms) indicating the start of an illness before specific symptoms occur.

Prognosis A prediction to how a disease will progress and the severity of the effects of a condition on a patient.

Psychoanalysis A theoretical orientation developed by Sigmund Freud that studies and treats psychological functioning and behaviour.

Psychoeducation Educating clients about their own medical illnesses or psychological disturbances.

Psychologization The focus on psychological causes for a person's feeling of distress.

Psychotropic medications Any medication capable of affecting the mind, emotions, and behaviour; they act primarily on the central nervous system where they alter brain function resulting in temporary changes in perception, mood, consciousness, and behaviour.

Public trustee An office that operates under national legislation and works on behalf of a charitable or public group or individual to guide or make financial decisions.

Readmission Being readmitted to hospital after successfully concluding treatment but later relapsing.

Recidivism To relapse or fall back.

Recourse The action of turning to someone for help or assistance.

Recovery model An approach to mental disorder or substance dependence that emphasizes and supports an individual's potential for recovery.

Re-experiencing symptoms One of the three clusters of acute stress and post-traumatic stress symptoms that include intrusive thoughts, nightmares, and feelings that the event were recurring, and intense psychological and/or physiological distress at exposure to cues that retrigger the event.

Relapse Occurs when a person is affected by a condition with which they were previously affected and thought to have under control (for example, depression).

Renal failure A condition in which the kidneys don't function properly and decompensate.

Resilience The innate ability to withstand stress and adverse events.

Schizophrenogenic The belief that certain factors, for example, parental behaviour, can have a negative impact on a child's mental health, specifically causing schizophrenia.

Secondary losses Occur as a result of a traumatic loss, for example, losing a job after a hurricane levels your home and town.

Separation anxiety Where a child fears or experiences separation from his or her main attachment figure.

Shell shock A term commonly used during and after the first world war to refer to what is now known as post-traumatic stress.

Social determinants of health The economic and social conditions that can determine an individual's health.

Somatization The focus on physical symptoms when a person is feeling distress.

Staccato A term borrowed from music, describing an abrupt, changeable rhythm.

Stigma Social disapproval of actions or beliefs that are against cultural norms.

Subdural haematoma A brain injury in which there is bleeding into the lining of the brain.

Subpoena A written demand for someone to appear before the court or face punishment if they refuse.

Substitute decision-making In the case where a person is found incapable or unable to make their own decisions there are specific legal criteria to be satisfied for another person to make decisions about their treatment and on their behalf.

SWOT analysis A strategic plan that evaluates the Strengths, Weaknesses, Opportunities, and Threats involved in a project or intervention.

Tardive dyskinesia A neurological condition that may be a late side effect of drugs, resulting in involuntary and repetitive actions.

Tourette syndrome A neurological disorder characterized by tics (a sudden and repetitive motor movement or vocalization).

Transient Passing through quickly.

Ulysses Contract A freely made decision about one's own future that sets out the person's preference in case of medical or other incapacitation.

WHO World Health Organization: an agency of the United Nations that monitors outbreaks of infectious diseases such as SARS, malaria, and AIDS, and sponsors international efforts to prevent and treat diseases.

References

Aboriginal Justice Implementation Commission (2004). *The Justice System and Aboriginal People* (accessed at http://www.ajic.mb.ca).

Abraham, H.D. (2000). 'Disorders Relating to the use of Phencyclidine and Hallucinogens', in M.G. Gelder, J.J. Lopez-Ibor Jr, and N.C. Andreasen (eds), *New Oxford Textbook of Psychiatry* (Oxford: Oxford University Press).

Abramowitz, J.S. (2006). 'The Psychological Treatment of Obsessive-Compulsive Disorder', *Canadian Journal of Psychiatry*, 51(7): 407–30.

Abrams, L. and Curran, L. (2007). 'Not Just a Middle Class Affliction: Crafting a Social Work Research Agenda on Postpartum Depression', *Health and Social Work*, 32(4): 289–96.

Agerbo, E., Gunnell, D., Bonde, J.P., Mortensen, P.B., and Nordentoft, M. (2007). 'Suicide and Occupation: The Impact of Socio-economic, Demographic and Psychiatric Differences', *Psychological Medicine*, 37(8): 1131–40.

Ahmadi, J., Pridmore, S., Alimi, A., Cheraghi, A., Arad, A., Parsaeyan, H., et al. (2007). 'Epidemiology of Opium Use in the General Population', *American Journal of Drug and Alcohol Abuse*, 33(3): 483–91.

Akiskal, H. (2004). 'Mood Disorders: Historical Introduction and Conceptual Overview', in B.J. Sadock and V.A. Sadock (eds), *Comprehensive Text Book of Psychiatry* (8th edn) (Philadelphia: Lippincott Williams & Wilkins).

Albert, J. (1994). 'Rethinking Difference: A Cognitive Therapy Group for Chronic Mental Patients', *Social Work with Groups*, 17(1/2): 105–21.

Alberta Mental Health Act, S.A. 2000, c. M-13.1 (accessed at http://www.canlii.org).

Alcoholics Anonymous (1972). *A Brief Guide to Alcoholics Anonymous* (New York: Alcoholics Anonymous World Wide Services) (accessed at http://www.alcoholics-anonymous.org/en_pdfs/p-42_abriefguidetoaa.pdf).

Alzheimer's Disease International (April 1999). *Factsheet: The Prevalence of Dementia* (London: Alzheimer's Disease International).

Amato, L., Minozzi, S., Davoli, M., Vecchi, S., Ferri, M., and Mayet S. (2004). 'Psychosocial and Pharmacological Treatments versus Pharmacological Treatments for Opioid Detoxification', *Cochrane Database of Systematic Reviews*, Issue 4, Art. No.: CD005031. DOI: 10.1002/14651858.CD005031.

American Psychiatric Association (APA) (2000). *Diagnostic and Statistical Manual of Mental Disorders* (4th edn.—Text Revision) (Washington, DC: APA).

——— (2001). *Practice Guideline for the Treatment of Patients with Borderline Personality Disorder* (Washington, DC: APA).

——— (2002). *Practice Guidelines for the Treatment of Psychiatric Disorders Compendium* (Washington, DC: APA).

Anderson, J. and Mangels, N. (2006). 'Helping Victims: Social Services, Health Care Interventions in Elder Abuse', in R. Summers and A. Hoffman (eds.). *Elder Abuse: A Public Health Perspective* (Washington, DC: American Public Health Association).

Andreae, D. (2002). 'Canadian Values and Ideologies and Social Work Practice', in F.J. Turner (ed.), *Social Work Practice: A Canadian Perspective* (Toronto: Prentice-Hall).

Antai-Otong, D. (2007). 'The Art of Prescribing: Pharmacologic Management of Posttraumatic Stress Disorder', *Perspectives in Psychiatric Care,* 43(1): 55–9.

——— (2007). 'The Art of Prescribing. Pharmacotherapy of Obsession-Compulsive Disorder: An Evidence-based Approach', *Perspectives in Psychiatric Care,* 43(4): 219–22.

Anthony, W. (1993). 'Recovery from Mental Illness: The Guiding Vision of Mental Health Services in the 1990s', *Psychosocial Rehabiliation,* 16: 11–23.

Antle, B. and Regehr, C. (2003). 'Meta-Ethics in Social Work Research: Beyond Individual Rights and Freedoms', *Social Work,* 48(1): 135–44.

Appelbaum, P. (1985). 'Tarasoff and the Clinician: Problems in Fulfilling the Duty to Protect', *American Journal of Psychiatry,* 142: 425–9.

——— (1991). 'Advance Directives for Psychiatric Treatment', *Hospital and Community Psychiatry,* 42: 983–4.

——— (1994). *Almost a Revolution* (New York: Oxford University Press).

Arai, M. (2006). 'Elder Abuse in Japan', *Educational Gerontology,* 32(1): 13–23.

Armour, M.P. (2002). 'Experiences of Covictims of Homicide: Implications for Research and Practice', *Trauma, Violence, & Abuse,* 3(2): 109–24.

Arseneault, L., Cannon, M., Witton, J., and Murray, R.M. (2004). 'Casual Association between Cannabis and Psychosis: Examination of the Evidence', *British Journal of Psychiatry,* 184: 110–17.

Arturo, S. (in press). 'Forensic Psychiatry: Neuroscience and the Law', *Journal of American Academy of Psychiatry and the Law.*

Auton (Guardian ad litem of) v. British Columbia (Attorney General) (2004). SCC 78, 3 S.C.R. 657.

B.H. v. Alberta (Director of Child Welfare) (2002). 329 A.R. 395 (Alta. Q.B.).

Bachrach, L. (1993). 'Continuity of Care and Approaches to Case Management for Long-Term Mentally Ill Patients', *Hospital and Community Psychiatry,* 44(5): 465–8.

Backman, L. (2008). 'Memory and Cognition in Preclinical Dementia: What We Know and What We Do Not Know', *Canadian Journal of Psychiatry,* 53(6): 354–60.

Badding, N. (1989). 'Client Involvement in Case Recording', *Social Casework,* 70(9): 539–48.

Bagby, M. (1987). 'The Effects of Legislative Reform on Admission Rates to Psychiatric Units of General Hospitals', *International Journal of Law and Psychiatry,* 10: 383–94.

———, Thompson, J., Dickens, S., and Nohara, M. (1991). 'Decision-making in Psychiatric Commitment: An Experimental Analysis', *American Journal of Psychiatry,* 48: 28–33.

Ballard, C., Waite, J., and Birks, J. (2006). 'Atypical Antipsychotics for Aggression and Psychosis in Alzheimer's Disease', *Cochrane Database of Systematic Reviews,* Issue 1, Art. No.: CD003475. DOI: 10.1002/14651858.CD003476.pub2.

Bandura, A. (1977). 'Self-Efficacy: Toward a Unifying Theory of Behavioral Change', *Psychological Review,* 84(2): 191–215.

Barcia, D. (2000). 'Delirium, Dementia, and Amnesic and Other Cognitive Disorders', in M.G. Gelder, J.J. Lopez-Ibor Jr, and N.C. Andreasen (eds), *New Oxford Textbook of Psychiatry* (Oxford: Oxford University Press).

Bates, J., Boote, J., and Beverley, C. (2004). 'Psychosocial Interventions for People with Milder Dementing Illness: A Systematic Review', *Journal of Advanced Nursing,* 45(6): 644–58.

Bateson, G., Jackson, D.D., Haley, J., and Weakland, J.H. (1956). 'Toward a Theory of Schizophrenia', *Behavioral Science,* 1: 251–64.

Bay, M. (2004). '1933–2003: Lessons from 70 Years of Experience with Mental Health, Capacity and Consent Legislation in Ontario', *Health Law in Canada,* 24(3): 36–43.

———, Fram, S., Silberfeld, M., Shushelski, C., and Bloom, H. (1996). 'Capacity and Substitute Decision-Making for Personal Care', in H. Bloom and M. Bay (eds), *A Practical Guide to Mental Health, Capacity and Consent Law of Ontario* (Toronto: Carswell).

BC Mental Health and Addiction Services (2008). *BC Mental Health Timeline* (accessed at http://www.bcmhas.ca/AboutUs/History.htm).

Bearden, C.E., Thompson, P.M., Dalwani, M., Hayashi, K.M., Lee, A.D., Nicoletti, M., et al. (2007). 'Greater Cortical Gray Matter Density in Lithium-treated Patients with Bipolar Disorder', *Biological Psychiatry*, 62(1): 7–16.

Beaton, R.D., Murphy, S.A., Pike, K.C., and Corneil, W. (1997). 'Social Support and Network Conflict in Firefighters and Paramedics', *Western Journal of Nursing Research*, 19(3): 297–313.

Beck, A. (1967). *Depression: Clinical, Experimental, and Theoretical Aspects* (New York: Hoeber Press).

———, Rush, J., Shaw, B., and Emery, G. (1979). *Cognitive Therapy of Depression* (New York: Guilford Press).

——— and Freeman, A. (1990). *Cognitive Therapy of Personality Disorders* (New York: Guilford).

Belmaker, R.H. and Agam, G. (2008). 'Major Depressive Disorder Mechanisms of Disease', *New England Journal of Medicine*, 358(1): 55–67.

Bentley, K. and Walsh, J. (2006). *The Social Worker and Psychotropic Medication: Towards Effective Collaboration with Mental Health Clients, Families and Providers* (Belmont, CA: Thomson)

———, and Farmer, R. (2005). 'Social Work Roles and Activities Regarding Psychiatric Medication: Results of a National Survey', *Social Work*, 50(4): 295–303.

Berenbaum, H., Boden, M., Baker, J., Dizen, M., Thompson, R., and Abramowitz, A. (2006). 'Emotional Correlates of the Different Dimensions of Schizotypal Personality Disorder', *Journal of Abnormal Psychology*, 115(2): 359–68.

Berglund, N., Vahlne, J., and Edman, A. (2003). 'Family Intervention in Schizophrenia: Impact on Family Burden and Attitude', *Social Psychiatry and Psychiatric Epidemiology*, 38: 116–21.

Bezchlibnyk-Butler, K.Z. and Jeffries, J.J. (2005). *Clinical Handbook of Psychotropic Drugs* (15th edn) (Ashland: Hogrete and Huber).

Bezerra-Flanders, W. and Clark, J. (2006). 'Perspectives on Elder Abuse and Neglect in Brazil', *Educational Gerontology*, 32(1): 63–72.

Bhugra, D. and Bhui, K. (2001). *Cross-Cultural Psychiatry: A Practical Guide* (London: Arnold).

Billick, S. (1986). 'Developmental Competency', *Bulletin of the American Academy of Psychiatry and the Law*, 14: 301–8.

Binks, C.A., Fenton, M., McCarthy, L., Lee, T., Adams, C.E., and Duggan, C. (2006). 'Psychological Therapies for People with Borderline Personality Disorder', *Cochrane Database of Systematic Reviews*, Issue 1, Art. No.: CD005652. DOI: 10.1002/14651858.CD005652.

Birks, J. (2006). 'Cholinesterase Inhibitors for Alzheimer's Disease', *Cochrane Database of Systematic Reviews*, Issue 1, Art. No.: CD005593. DOI: 10.1002/14651858. CD005593.

Bisson, J., Ehlers. A., Matthews, R., Pilling, S., Richards, D., and Turner, S. (2007). 'Psychological Treatments for Chronic Post-traumatic Stress Disorder: Systematic Review and Meta-analysis', *British Journal of Psychiatry*, 190: 97–104.

———, Jenkins, P.L., Alexander, J., and Bannister, C. (1997). 'Randomized Controlled Trial of Psychological Debriefing for Victims of Acute Burn Trauma', *British Journal of Psychiatry*, 171: 78–81.

Blackstock, C. (2009). 'When Everything Matters: Comparing the Experiences of First Nations and Non-Aboriginal Children Removed from Their Families in Nova Scotia from 2003–2005', PhD thesis, Faculty of Social Work, University of Toronto.

———, Brown, I., and Bennett, M. (2007). 'Reconciliation: Rebuilding the Canadian Child Welfare System to Better Serve Aboriginal Children and Youth', in I. Brown, F. Chaze, D. Fuchs, J. Lafrance, S.McKay, and S. Thomas-Prokop (eds), *Putting a Human Face on Child Welfare: Voices from the Prairies* (Toronto: Centre of Excellence for Child Welfare).

Blanchard, E.B., Hickling, E.J., Mitnick, N., Taylor, A.E., Loos, W.R., and Buckley, T.C. (1995). 'The Impact of Severity of Physical Injury and Perception of Life Threat in the Development of Post-traumatic Stress Disorder in Motor Vehicle Accident Victims', *Behaviour Research and Therapy*, 33(5): 529–34.

Bledsoe, S. and Grote, N. (2006). 'Treating Depression During Pregnancy and the Postpartum: A Preliminary Meta-analysis', *Research on Social Work Practice*, 16(2): 109–20.

Bleich, A., Gelkopf, M., and Solomon, Z. (2003). 'Exposure to Terrorism, Stress-related Mental Health Symptoms, and Coping Behaviors among a Nationally Representative Sample in Isreal', *JAMA*, 290(5): 612–20.

Blier, P. (2008). 'Do Antidepressants Really Work?' *Journal of Psychiatry and Neuro Science*, 33(2): 89–90.

Bocchetta, A., Fadda, D., Satta, G., Del Zompo, M., Gessa, G.J., and Cocco, P. (2007). 'Long-Term Lithium Treatment and Survival From External Causes Including Suicide', *Journal of Clinical Psychopharmacology*, 27(5): 544–6.

Bocking, C., Spinhoven, P., Schene, A., Koeter, M., Wouters, L., Huyser, J., et al. (2005). 'Preventing Relapse/Recurrence in Recurrent Depression with Cognitive Therapy: A Randomized Controlled Trial', *Journal of Consulting and Clinical Psychology*, 73(4): 647–57.

Bohn, D. (2003). 'Lifetime Physical and Sexual Abuse, Substance Abuse, Depression and Suicide Attempts among Native American Women', *Issues in Mental Health Nursing*, 24: 333–52.

Bomba, P. (2006). 'Use of a Single Page Elder Abuse Assessment and Management Tool: A Practical Clinician's Approach to Identifying Elder Mistreatment', in J. Mellor and P. Bownell (eds), *Elder Abuse and Mistreatment: Policy, Practice and Research* (Birmingham, NY: Haworth Press).

Bonnano, G.A., Galea, S., Bucciarelli, A., and Vlahov, D. (2007). 'What Predicts Psychological Resilience after Disaster? The Role of Demographics, Resources and Life Stress', *Journal of Consulting and Clinical Psychology*, 75(5): 671–82.

Bowlby, J. (1979). *The Making and Breaking of Affectional Bonds* (London: Tavistock Publications).

——— (1980). *Attachment and Loss*, vol. 3 (New York: Basic Books).

Bowman, M.L. (1999). 'Individual Differences in Posttraumatic Distress: Problems with the DSM-IV Model', *Canadian Journal of Psychiatry*, 44(1): 21–33.

Bradley, R., Greene, J., Russ, E., Dutra, L., and Weston D. (2005). 'A Multi-dimensional Meta-analysis of Psychotherapy for PTSD', *American Journal of Psychiatry*, 162(2): 214–27.

Bradley, S. (2003). 'The Psychology of the Psychopharmacology Triangle: The Client, Clinicians, the Medications', *Social Work in Mental Health*, 1(4): 29–50.

Bradshaw, W. (2003). 'Use of Single System Research to Evaluate the Effectiveness of Cognitive-behavioural Treatment of Schizophrenia', *British Journal of Social Work*, 33(7): 885–9.

Brady, K.T., Tolliver, B.K., and Verduin, M.L. (2007). 'Alcohol Use and Anxiety: Diagnostic and Management Issues', *American Journal of Psychiatry*, 164(2): 217–21.

Bramness, J. and Kornor, H. (2007). 'Benzodiazepine Prescription for Patients in Opioid Maintenance Treatment in Norway', *Drug and Alcohol Dependence*, 90(2–3): 203–9.

Brent, D. and Mann, J. (2005). 'Family Genetic Studies, Suicide and Suicidal Behaviour', *Journal of Medical Genetics*, Part C Semin. Med. Genet. 133C: 13–24.

Brewin, C.R., Andrews, B., and Valentine J.D. (2000). 'Meta-analysis of Risk Factors for Post-traumatic Stress Disorder in Trauma-exposed Adults', *Journal of Consulting and Clinical Psychology*, 68(5): 748–66.

Briere, J. (2000). 'Treating Adult Survivors of Severe Childhood Abuse and Neglect: Further Development of an Integrative Model', in J.E.B. Myers, L. Berliner, J.N. Briere, C.T. Hendrix, T.A. Reid, and C.A. Jenny (eds), *The APSAC Handbook on Child Maltreatment* (2nd edn) (Thousand Oaks, CA: Sage Publications).

Brom, D., Kleber, R.J., and Defares, P.B. (1989). 'Brief Psychotherapy for Post-traumatic Stress Disorders', *Journal of Consulting and Clinical Psychology*, 57(5): 607–12.

Brown, A. S. (2006). 'Prenatal Infection as a Risk Factor for Schizophrenia', *Schizophrenia Bulletin*, 32(2): 200–2.

Brown, G.W. and Harris, T. (1978). *Social Origin of Depression* (London: B Press).

Bryant, R.A. and Harvey, A.G. (1996). 'Post-traumatic Stress Reactions in Volunteer Firefighters', *Journal of Traumatic Stress*, 9(1): 51–62.

Bryant, R.A., Sackville, T., Dang, S.T., Moulds, M., and Guthrie, R. (1999). 'Treating Acute Stress Disorder: An Evaluation of Cognitive Behavior Therapy and Supportive Counselling Techniques', *American Journal of Psychiatry*, 156: 1780–6.

Budney, A.J., Vandrey, R.G., Hughes, J.R., Moore, B.A., and Bahrenburg, B. (2007). 'Oral Delta-9-tetrahydrocannabinol Suppresses Cannabis Withdrawal Symptoms', *Drug and Alcohol Dependence*, 86(1): 22–9.

Burgess, A. and Holstrum, L. (1974). 'Rape Trauma Syndrome', *American Journal of Psychiatry*, 131: 981–6.

Burke, B., Arkowitz, H., and Menchola, M. (2003). 'The Efficacy of Motivational Interviewing: A Meta-analysis of Controlled Clinical Trials', *Journal of Counselling and Clinical Psychology*, 71(5): 843–61.

Burlington Post (17 Oct. 2001). 'Brian's Law Broadens Criteria for Treatment of Mentally Ill'.

Buxton, J.A., and Dove, N.A. (2008) 'The Burden and Management of Crystal Meth Use', *Canadian Medical Association Journal,* 178(12): 1537–9.

Calderwood, K., O'Brien, A., and MacKenzie Davies, J. (2007). *Report of the OASW Mental Health Survey: Who We Are, Where We Work, What We Do* (Toronto: OASW).

Calhoun, K.S. and Atkeson, B.M. (1991). *Treatment of Rape Victims: Facilitating Psychosocial Adjustment* (Toronto: Pergamon Press).

Canada Health Act, R.S.C. 1985, c. C-6 (accessed at http://www.canlii.org).

Canadian Alliance on Mental Illness and Mental Health (2006). *Framework for Action on Mental Illness and Mental Health: Recommendations to Health and Social Policy Leaders of Canada for a National Action Plan on Mental Illness and Mental Health* (accessed at http://www.camimh.ca/frameworkforaction.htm).

Canadian Association of Social Workers (CASW) (2001). *The Role of Social Work in Mental Health* (Ottawa: CASW).

——— (2005a). *Code of Ethics* (Ottawa: CASW).

——— (2005b) *Guidelines for Ethical Practice* (Ottawa: CASW).

——— (2007). *Informed Consent and Confidentiality: CASW Guidelines* (Ottawa: CASW).

Canadian Charter of Rights and Freedoms (1982). Part 1 of the Constitution Act, 1982, Being Schedule B to the Canada Act (U.K.). 1982, c. 11.

Canadian Mental Health Association (CMHA) (2004). 'Mental Health Diversion' (accessed at http://www.cmha-tb.on.ca).

——— (2008). *Back to Basics: Enhancing our capacity to promote consumer participation and inclusion: Discussion Guide on Recovery* (accessed at http://www.cmha.ca).

Canterbury v. Spence (1972). 464 F.2d 772 (D.C.Cir.).

Caplan, G. (1964). *Principles of Preventive Psychiatry* (New York: Basic Books).

Capponi, P. (2003). *Beyond the Crazy House* (Toronto: Penguin).

Carballo, J., Harkavy-Friedman, J., Burke, A., Sher, L., Baca-Garcia, E., Sullivan, G., Grunenbaum, M., Parsey, R., Mann, J., and Oquendo, M. (2008). 'Family History of Suicidal Behaviour and Early Traumatic Experiences: Additive Effect on Suicidality and Course of Bbipolar Illness?' *Journal of Affective Disorders,* 109: 57–63.

Cardno, A., Marshall, E., Coid, B., Macdonald, A., Ribchester, T., Davies, N., et al. (1999). 'Relationships Symptom Dimensions and Genetic Liability to Psychotic Disorders: Maudsley Twin Psychosis Series', *Archives of General Psychiatry,* 56: 162–8.

Carey, K., Scott-Sheldon, L., Carey, M., and DeMartini, K. (2007). 'Individual Level Interventions to Reduce College Student Drinking: A Meta-analytic Review', *Addictive Behaviors,* 32(11): 2469–94.

Carlisle, J. (1996). 'Duty to Warn: Report from Council', *Canadian Medical Association*, Members' Dialogue, July/August: 21.

Carpenter, L. (2002). 'Mental Health Recovery Paradigm: Implications for Social Work', *Health and Social Work,* 27(2): 86–94.

Carrasco, J. and Lecic-Tosevski, D. (2000). 'Specific Types of Personality Disorder', in M.G. Gelder, J.J. Lopez-Ibor Jr, and N.C. Andreasen, *New Oxford Textbook of Psychiatry* (Oxford: Oxford University Press).

CBC (2002). 'Suicide Stalks Manitoba Reserve' (accessed at http://www.cbc.ca/canada/story/2002/07/25/shamattawa020725.html).

Chadwick, P. and Trower, P. (1996). 'Cognitive Therapy for Punishment Paranoia: A Single Case Experiment', *Behavioural Research and Therapy,* 34(4): 351–6.

Chaimowitz, G. and Glancy, G. (2002). 'The Duty to Protect', *Canadian Journal of Psychiatry,* 47: 1–4.

———, Glancy G., and Blackburn, J. (2000). 'The Duty to Warn and Protect: Impact on Practice', *Canadian Journal of Psychiatry,* 45: 899–904.

Chapman, K., Tarter, R., Kirisci, L., and Cornelius, M. (2007). 'Childhood Neurobehavior Disinhibition Amplifies the Risk of Substance Use Disorder: Interaction of Parental History and Prenatal Alcohol Exposure', *Journal of Developmental and Behavioral Pediatrics,* 28(3): 219–24.

Chien, W., Chan, W., and Thompson, D. (2006). 'Effects of a Mutual Support Group for Families of Chinese People with Schizophrenia: 18 Month Follow-up', *British Journal of Psychiatry,* 189: 41–9.

Ciarlariello v. Schacter (1993). 2 S.C.R. 119.

Ciraulo, A.M., Alpert, N., and Franko, K.J. (1997). 'Naltrexone for the Treatment of Alcoholism', *American Family Physician,* 56(3): 803–6.

Ciraulo, D.A., Dong, Q., Silverman, B., Gastfriend, D., and Pettinati, H. (2008). 'Early Treatment Response in Alcohol Dependence with Extended-release Naltrexone', *Journal of Clinical Psychiatry,* 69(2): 190–5.

Clark, S. and Goldney, R. (1995). 'Grief Reactions and Recovery in a Support Group for People Bereaved by Suicide', *Crisis,* 16(1): 27–33.

Cleary, M., Hunt, G., Matheson, S., Siegfried, N., and Walter, G. (2008). 'Psychosocial Interventions for People with Both Severe Mental Illness and Substance Misuse', *Cochrane Database of Systematic Reviews,* Issue 1, Art. No.: CD001088. DOI: 10.1002/14651858.

Cochrane-Brink, K., Lofchy, J., and Sakinofsky, I. (2000). 'Clinical Rating Scales in Suicide Risk Assessment', *General Hospital Psychiatry,* 22: 445–51.

Coelho, H., Canter, P., and Ernst, E. (2007). 'Mindfulness-based Cognitive Therapy: Evaluating Current Evidence and Informing Future Research', *Journal of Consulting and Clinical Psychology,* 75(6): 1000–5.

Cohen, D. (2002). 'Research on the Drug Treatment of Schizophrenia: A Critical Appraisal and Implications for Social Work Education', *Journal of Social Work Education,* 38(2): 217–39.

College of Physicians and Surgeons of Nova Scotia (2006). *Guidelines for Medical Record Keeping* (accessed at http://www.cpsns.ns.ca/guidetomedrec.html#31).

Compton, M., Weiss, P., West, J., and Kaslow, N. (2005). 'The Associations Between Substance use Disorders, Schizophrenia-spectrum Disorders, and Axis IV Psychosocial Problems', *Social Psychiatry and Psychiatric Epidemiology,* 40: 939–46.

Consensus Panel (2004). 'Consensus Development Conference and Antipsychotic Drugs and Obesity and Diabetes', *Diabetes Care,* 27: 596–601.

Consent to Treatment and Health Care Directives Act, S.P.E.I. 1996, c. 10 (accessed at http://www.canlii.org).

Coodin, S., Staley, D., Cortens, B., Derochers, R., and McLandress, S. (2004). 'Patient Factors Associated with Missed Appointments in Persons with Schizophrenia', *Canadian Journal of Psychiatry,* 49(2): 145–8.

Cooper, J., Carty, J., and Creamer, M. (2005). 'Pharmacotherapy for Posttraumatic Stress Disorder: Empirical Review and Clinical Recommendations', *Australian and New Zealand Journal of Psychiatry,* 39(8): 674–82.

Corey, G., Corey, M.K.S., and Callanan, P. (1998). *Issues and Ethics in the Helping Professions* (5th edn) (Pacific Grove, CA: Brooks/Cole).

Cox, B. and Taylor, S. (1999). 'Anxiety Disorders: Panic and Phobias', in T. Millon, P. Blaney, and R. Davis (eds), *Oxford Textbook of Psychopathology* (New York: Oxford University Press).

Craik, F.I. (2008). 'Memory Changes in Normal and Pathological Aging', *Canadian Journal of Psychiatry,* 53(6): 343–5.

Cumming, S., Covic, T., and Murrell, E. (2006). 'Deliberate Self-harm: Have We Scratched the Surface?' *Behaviour Change,* 23(3): 186–99.

DaCosta, J.M. (1871). 'On the Irritable Heart: A Clinical Study of a Form of Functional Cardiac Disorder Following Natural Disaster', *American Journal of Medical Sciences,* 61: 17–52.

Daubert v. Merrell Dow Pharmaceuticals (1993). 509 U.S. 579.

Davis, K.L. (2005). 'Delirium, Dementia, and Amnestic and Other Cognitive Disorders and Mental Disorders to a General Medical Condition', in B.J. Sadock and V.A. Sadock (eds), *Comprehensive Textbook of Psychiatry* (8th edn) (Philadelphia: Lippincott Williams & Wilkins).

de Mello, M., de Jesus, M., Bacaltchuk, J., Verdeli, H., and Neugebauer, R. (2005). 'A Systematic Review of Research Findings on the Efficacy of Interpersonal Therapy for Depressive Disorders', *European Archives of Psychiatry and Clinical Neuroscience,* 255(2): 75–82.

Deegan, P. (1996). 'Recovery and the Conspiracy of Hope', paper given at the Sixth Annual Mental Health Services Conference of Australia and New Zealand.

Delaney, R. (2009). 'The Philosophical and Value Base of Canadian Social Welfare', in J. Turner and F. Turner (eds), *Canadian Social Welfare* (6th edn) (Toronto: Pearson Education Canada).

Department of Health (2003). *Delivering Race Equality: A Framework for Action* (London: Department of Health) (accessed at http://www.dh.gov.uk/en/Consultations/Closedconsultations/DH_4067441).

Deshauer, D., Moher, D., Fergusson, D., Moher, E., Sampson, M., and Grimshaw, J. (2008). 'Selective Serotonin Reuptake Inhibitors for Unipolar Depression: A Systematic Review of Classic Long-term Randomized Controlled Trials', *CMAJ*, 178(10): 1293–1301.

Detera-Wadleigh, S.D., Liu, C-Y, Maheshwari, M., Cardona, I., Corona, W., and Akula, N. (2007). 'Sequence Variation in DOCK9 and Heterogeneity in Bipolar Disorder', *Psychiatric Genetics*, 17(5): 274–86.

Dickens, B. (2002). 'Informed Consent', in J. Downie, T. Caulfield, and C. Flood (eds), *Canadian Health Law and Policy* (Toronto: Butterworths).

Dickerson, F. (2000). 'Cognitive-behavioural Psychotherapy for Schizophrenia: A Review of Recent Empirical Studies', *Schizophrenia Research*, 43: 71–90.

Dilling, H. (2000). 'Classification', in M. Gelder, J. Lopez-Ibor, and N. Andreasen (eds), *New Oxford Textbook of Psychiatry* (New York: Oxford University Press).

Dixon, L. (1999). 'Dual Diagnosis of Substance Abuse in Schizophrenia: Prevalence and Impact on Outcomes', *Schizophrenia Research*, 35(supp.): s93–s100.

Downie, J., Caulfield, T., and Flood, C. (eds) (2002). *Canadian Health Law and Policy* (Toronto: Butterworths).

Duffin, J. (2000). *History of Medicine: A Scandalously Short Introduction* (Toronto: University of Toronto Press).

Durkheim, Emile (1951). *Suicide: A Study in Sociology*, trans. J.A. Spaulding and G. Simpson (New York: The Free Press).

Dykeman, M.J. (2000). *Canadian Health Law Practice Manual* (Toronto: Butterworths).

Eaton, W., Kalaydjian, A., Scharfstein, D., Mezuk, B., and Ding, Y. (2007). 'Prevalence and Incidence of Depressive Disorder: The Baltimore ECA Follow-up, 1981–2004', *Acta Psychiatrica Scandanavica*, 116(3): 182–8.

Edginton, B. (2002). *Early Treatment of the Insane in Ontario*, paper given at the meetings of the Canadian Society for the History of Medicine in Toronto.

Ehlers, A. and Clark, D. (2003). 'Early Psychological Interventions for Adult Survivors of Trauma: A Review', *Biological Psychiatry*, 53(9): 817–26.

Eisenman, D.P., Gelberg, L., Liu, H., and Shapiro, M.F. (2003). 'Mental Health and Health-related Quality of Life among Adult Latino Primary Care Patients Living in the United States with Previous Exposure to Political Violence', *JAMA*, 290(5): 627–34.

Ekselius, L., Tillfors, M., Furmark, T., and Fredrikson, M. (2001). 'Personality Disorders in the General Population: *DSM*-IV and *ICD*-10 Defined Prevalence as Related to Sociodemographic Profile', *Personality and Individual Differences*, 30: 311–20.

Elkin, I., Shea, M.T., Watkins, J.T., Imber, S.D., Sotsky, S.M., Collins, J.F., et al. (1989). 'National Institute of Mental Health Treatment of Depression Collaborative Research Program: General Effectiveness of Treatments', *Archives of General Psychiatry*, 46(11): 971–82.

Eschweiler, G., Vonthein, R., Bode, R., Huell, M., Conca, A., Peters, O., et al. (2007). 'Clinical Efficacy and Cognitive Side Effects of Bifrontal versus Right Unilateral Electroconvulsive Therapy (ECT): A Short-term Randomized Controlled Trial in Pharmaco-resistant Major Depression', *Journal of Affective Disorders*, 101(1–3): 149–57.

Etchells, E., Sharpe, G., Walsh, P., Williams, J., and Singer, P. (1996). 'BioEthics for Clinicians: 1. Consent', *Canadian Medical Association Journal*, 155: 177–80.

Evans, S., Ferrando, S., Findler, M., Stowell, C., Smart, C., and Haglin, D. (2008). 'Mindfulness-based Cognitive Therapy for Generalized Anxiety Disorder', *Journal of Anxiety Disorders*, 22(4): 716–21.

Faggiano, F., Vigna-Taglianti, F., Versino, E., and Lemma, P. (2003). 'Methadone Maintenance at Different Dosages for Opioid Dependence', *Cochrane Database of Systematic Reviews*, Issue 3, Art. No.: CD002208. DOI: 10.1002/14651858.CD002208.

Faris, R.B.L. and Dunham, H.W. (1939). *Mental Disorders in Urban Areas, an Ecological Study of Schizophrenia and other Psychoses* (New York: Hafner Publishing).

Farkas, M., Gagne, C., Anthony, W., and Chamberlin, J. (2005). 'Implementing recovery-oriented evidence-based programs: Identifying the critical dimensions', *Community Mental Health Journal*. 41(2): 141–58.

Faulkner Schofield, R. and Amodeo, M. (1999). 'Interdisciplinary Teams in Health Care and Human Service Settings: Are they Effective?' *Health and Social Work*, 24(3): 210–19.

Fearon, P., Kirkbride, J., Morgan, C., Dazzan, P., Morgan, K., Lloyd, T., et al. (2006). 'Incidence of Schizophrenia and Other Psychoses in Ethnic Minority Groups: Results from the MRC AESOP Study', *Psychological Medicine*, 36: 1541–50.

Fehm, L., Beesdo, K., Jacobi, F., and Fiedler, A. (2008). 'Social Anxiety Disorder Above and Below the Diagnostic Threshold: Prevalence, Comorbidity and Impairment in the General Population', *Social Psychiatry and Psychiatric Epidemiology*, 43(4): 257–65.

Fergusson, D., Boden, J., and Horwood, J. (2007). 'Recurrence of Major Depression in Adolescence and Early Adulthood, and Later Mental Health, Educational and Economic Outcomes', *British Journal of Psychiatry*, 191: 335–42.

Ferry, J. (2000). 'No Easy Answer to High Native Suicide Rates', *The Lancet*, 355(9207): 906.

Field, N.P., Nichols, C., Holen, A., and Horowitz, M.J. (1999). 'The Relation of Continuing Attachment and Adjustment in Conjugal Bereavement', *Journal of Consulting and Clinical Psychology*, 67(2): 212–18.

First Nations Child and Family Caring Society of Canada (2008). *Joint Declaration of Support for Jordan's Principle* (accessed at http://www.fncaringsociety.com/more/jordansPrinciple.php).

Fisher, M. (1995). 'Group Therapy Protocols for Persons with Personality Disorders Who Abuse Substances: Effective Treatment Alternatives', *Social Work with Groups*, 18(4): 71–89.

Fitzgerald, P., Oxley, T., Laird, A., Kulkarni, J., Egan, G., and Daskalakis, Z. (2006). 'An Analysis of Functional Neuroimaging Studies of Dorsolateral Prefrontal Cortical Activity in Depression', *Psychiatry Research: Neuroimaging*, 148(1): 33–45.

Floersch, J. (2003). 'The Subjective Experience of Youth Psychotropic Treatment', *Social Work in Mental Health*, 1(4): 51–69.

Follette, V.M., Ruzek, J.I., and Abueg, F.R. (eds) (1998). *Cognitive-behavioural Therapies for Trauma* (New York: Guilford Press).

Forde, S. and Devaney, C. (2006). 'Postvention: A Community-based Family Support Initiative and Model of Responding to Tragic Events Including Suicide', *Child Care in Practice*, 12(1): 53–61.

Foreman, M.D., Mion, L.C., Trygstad, L., and Fletcher, K. (2003). 'Delirium: Strategies for Assessing and Treatment', in M. Mezey, T. Fulmer, I. Abraham, and D.A. Zwicker (eds), *Geriatric Nursing Protocols for Best Practice* (2nd edn) (New York: Springer).

Fournier, J., DeRubeis, R., Shelton, R., Gallop, R., Amsterdam, J., and Hollon, S. (2008). 'Antidepressant Medication *v.* Cognitive Therapy in People with Depression with and without Personality Disorder', *British Journal of Psychiatry*, 192: 124–9.

Fowler, L. (2004). *Powers of Attorney* (Toronto: Law Society of Upper Canada).

Foy, D., Glynn, S., Schnurr, P., Jankowski, M., Wattenberg, M., Weiss, D., et al. (2000). 'Group Therapy', in E.B. Foa, T.M. Keane, and M.J. Friedman (eds), *Effective Treatments for PTSD: Practice Guidelines for the International Society for Traumatic Stress Studies* (New York: Guilford Press).

Freedy, J.R., Resnick, H.S., Kilpatrick, D.G., Dansky, B.S., and Tidwell, R.P. (1994). 'The Psychological Adjustment of Recent Crime Victims in the Criminal Justice System', *Journal of Interpersonal Violence*, 9(4): 450–68.

Freud, S. (1957 [1917]). 'Mourning and Melancholia', in J. Strachey (ed. and trans.). *The Standard Edition of the Complete Psychological Works of Sigmund Freud*, vol. 14 (London: Hogarth Press).

Friday, S. (Nov. 2005). 'Informed consent and Mental Health Legislation: The Canadian Context', *Vancouver/Richmond Mental Health Network Society* (accessed at http://francais.ccamhr.ca/communications/Informed_Consent.pdf).

Frye v. United States (1923). 293 F.1013 (D.C.Cir.).

Fulmer, T., Guadagno, L., Bitondo, C., and Connolly, M. (2004). 'Progress in Elder Abuse Screening and Assessment Instruments', *Journal of the American Geriatrics Society*, 52(2): 297–304.

Furukawa, T., McGuire, H., and Barbui, C. (2003). 'Low Dosage Tricyclic Antidepressants for Depression', *Cochrane Database of Systematic Reviews*, Issue 3, Art. No.: CD003197. DOI: 10.1002/14651858.CD003197.

Furukawa, T.A., Cipriani, A., Corrado, B., and Geddes, J.R. (2007). 'Long-term Treatment of Depression with Antidepressants: A Systematic Narrative Review', *Canadian Journal of Psychiatry*, 52(9): 545–52.

Galea, S., Acierno, R., Ruggiero, K., Resnick, H., Tracy, M., and Kilpatrick, D. (2006). 'Social Context and Psychobiology of Posttraumatic Stress', *Annals of New York Academy of Science*, 1071: 231–41.

Geddes, J. and UK ECT Review Group (2003). 'Efficacy and Safety of Electroconvulsive Therapy in Depressive Disorders: A Systematic Review and Meta-analysis', *The Lancet*, 361(9360): 799–808.

Gelman, S. (1992). 'Risk Management Through Client Access to Case Records', *Social Work*, 37(1): 73–9.

Gibbons, R.D., Hur, K., Bhaumik, D.K., and Mann, J. (2005). 'The Relationship between Antidepressant Medication Use and Rate of Suicide', *Journal of the American Medication Association*, 62: 165–72.

Gibbs v. Gibbs (1985). 1 W.D.C.P. 6 (Ont. S.C.).

Gibbs, L.E. and Gambrill, E. (2002). 'Evidence-Based Practice: Counterarguments to Objections', *Research on Social Work Practice*, 12(3): 452–76.

Gilbert, J. (2008). 'Interprofessional Primary Care Teams: Observations on Realism', plenary presentation given at the meetings of Accelerating Primary Care, Edmonton, AB, 13 Feb. 2008.

Gillespie, N., Kendler, K., Prescott, C., Aggen, S., Gardner, C., Jacobson, K., et al. (2007). 'Longitudinal Modeling of Genetic and Environmental Influences on Self-reported Availability of Psychoactive Substances: Alcohol, Cigarettes, Marijuana, Cocaine and Stimulants', *Psychological Medicine*, 37: 947–59.

Glancy, D. and Glancy, G. (2009). 'The Case That Has Psychiatrists Running Scared: Ahmed v. Stefaniu', *Journal of the American Academy of Psychiatry and the Law*, 37(2): 1–7.

Glancy, G. and Knott, T. (2002). 'Part I: The Psychopharmacology of Long-Term Aggression—Toward an Evidence-Based Algorithm', *Bulletin of the Canadian Psychiatric Association*, 34(6): 13–18.

——— (2003). 'Psychopharmacology of Violence—Part V', *American Academy of Psychiatry and the Law Newsletter*, 28(3): 8–9.

——— (1998). 'Confidentiality in Crisis: Part II—Confidentiality of Treatment Records', *Canadian Journal of Psychiatry*, 43(12): 1006–11.

Gleser, G.C., Green, B.L., and Winget, C.N. (1981). *Prolonged Psychosocial Effects of Disaster: A Study of Buffalo Creek* (New York: Academic Press).

Goel, R. (2000). 'No Women at the Center: The Use of the Canadian Sentencing Circle in Domestic Violence Cases', *Wisconsin Women's Law Journal*, 15: 293–334.

Goering, P., Wasylenki, D., Lancee, W., and Freeman, S.J. (1984). 'From Hospital to Community: Six-Month and Two-Year Outcomes for 505 Patients', *Journal of Nervous and Mental Disease*, 172(11): 667–73.

Goffman, I. (1961). *Asylums: Essays on the Social Situation of Mentally Ill and Other Inmates* (Chicago: Aldine).

Gold, N. (2002). 'The Nature and Function of Social Work Assessment', in F. Turner (ed.), *Social Work Practice: A Canadian Perspective* (Toronto: Prentice-Hall).

Goldberg, D. and Murray, R. (2006). *The Maudsley Handbook of Practical Psychiatry* (New York: Oxford University Press).

Goldstein, R.B., Compton, W.M., Pulay, A.J., Ruan, W.J., Pickering, R.P., Simon, F.S., et al. (2007). 'Antisocial Behavioural Syndromes and DSM-IV Drug Use Disorders in the United States: Results from the National Epidemiologic Survey on Alcohol and Related Conditions', *Drug and Alcohol Dependence*, 90(2–3): 145–58.

Gong-Guy, E., Cravens, R., and Patterson, T. (1991). 'Clinical Issues in Mental Health Service Delivery to Refugees', *American Psychologist*, 46(6): 642–8.

Gonzalez-Salvador, M., Arango, C., Lyketsos, C., and Barba, A. (1999). 'The Stress and Psychological Morbidity of the Alzheimer Patient Caregiver', *International Journal of Geriatric Psychiatry*, 14: 701–10.

Gordon, R. and Verdun-Jones, S. (1983). 'The Right to Refuse Treatment: Commonwealth Developments and Issues', *International Journal of Law and Psychiatry*, 6: 57–73.

Gore-Felton, C., Gill, M., Koopman, C., and Spiegel, D. (1999). 'A Review of Acute Stress Reactions among Victims of Violence: Implications for Early Intervention', *Aggression and Violent Behaviour*, 4(3): 293–306.

Government of Canada (2002). *Romanow Report Promises Sweeping Changes to Medicare* (accessed at http://www.hc-sc.gc.ca/english/care/romanow/hcc0403.html).

——— (2008). *1957—Advent of Medicare in Canada: Establishing Public Medical Care Access* (accessed at http://www.canadianeconomy.gc.ca/English/economy/1957medicare.html).

Government of Saskatchewan (2002). *Adult Guardianship Manual* (accessed at http://www.justice.gov.sk.ca).

Gray, J., Shone, M., and Liddle, P. (2000). *Canadian Mental Health Law and Policy* (Toronto: Butterworths).

Green, B.L., Grace, M.C., and Gleser, G.C. (1985). 'Identifying Survivors at Risk: Long-term Impairment Following the Beverley Hills Supper Club Fire', *Journal of Consulting and Clinical Psychology*, 53(5): 672–8.

Green, B.L., Krupnick, J.L., Stockton, P., Goodman, L., Corcoran, C., and Petty, R. (2001). 'Psychological Outcome Associated with Traumatic Loss in a Sample of Young Women', *American Behavior Scientist*, 44(5): 817–37.

Greenberg, D.E. and Muraca, M. (2007). 'Guideline for Cognitive Impairment: Is this Dementia? Symptoms to Management', in D.E. Greenberg and M. Muraca (eds), *Canadian Clinical Practice Guidelines* (Toronto: Elsevier Canada).

Grote, N. and Bledsoe, S. (2007). 'Predicting Postpartum Depressive Symptoms in New Mothers: The Role of Optimism and Stress Frequency During Pregnancy', *Health and Social Work*, 32(2): 107–18.

Gruber, E., Kajevic, M., Aguis, M., and Martic-Biocina, S. (2006). 'Group Psychotherapy for Parents of Patients with Schizophrenia', *International Journal of Social Psychiatry*, 52(6): 487–500.

Gwynn, R., McQuistion, H., McVeigh, K., Garg, R., Frieden, T., and Thorpe, L. (2008). 'Prevalence, Diagnosis, and Treatment of Depression and Generalized Anxiety Disorder in a Diverse Urban Community', *Psychiatric Services*, 59(6): 641–7.

Haberstick, B., Timberlake, D., Smolen, A., Sakai, J., Hopfer, C., Corley, R.P., et al. (2007). 'Between and within Family Associations of Dopamine Receptor D2 TaqIA Polymorphism and Alcohol Abuse and Dependence in a General Population Sample of Adults', *Journal of Studies of Alcohol and Drugs*, 68(3): 362–70.

Hajek, T., Kozeny, J., Kopecek, M., Alda, M., and Hoschl, C. (2007). 'Reduced Subgenual Cingulated Volumes in Mood Disorders: A Meta-analysis', *Journal of Psychiatry: Neuroscience*, 33(2): 91–9.

Haley, J. (1976). *Problem-Solving Therapy* (San Francisco: Jossey-Bass Inc.).

Hall, W. and Degenhardt, L. (2007). 'Prevalence and Correlates of Cannabis Use in Developed and Developing Countries', *Current Opinion Psychiatry*, 20(4): 393–7.

Hardin, H. (2 July 1993). 'Uncivil Liberties: Far from Respecting Civil Liberties, Legal Obstacles to Treating the Mentally Ill Limit or Destroy the Liberty of the Person', *Vancouver Sun* (accessed at http://www.psychlaws.org).

Harriss, L. and Hawton, K. (2005). 'Suicide Intent in Deliberate Self-harm and Risk of Suicide: The Predictive Power of the Suicide Intent Scale', *Journal of Affective Disorders*, 86: 225–33.

Hart, P.M., Wearing, A.J., and Headley, B. (1995). 'Police Stress and Well-being: Integrating Personality, Coping, and Daily Work Experiences', *Journal of Occupational and Organizational Psychology*, 68(2): 133–56.

Hartford, K., Schrecker, T., Wiktorowicz, M., Hoch, J., and Sharp, C. (2003). 'Four Decades of Mental Health Policy in Ontario, Canada', *Administration and Policy in Mental Health*, 31(1): 65–73.

Harvey, A.G., Bryant, R.A., and Tarrier, N. (2003). 'Cognitive Behaviour Therapy for Post-traumatic Stress Disorder', *Clinical Psychology Review*, 23(3): 501–22.

Hasey, G. (2001). 'Transcranial Magnetic Stimulation in the Treatment of Mood Disorder: A Review and Comparison with Electroconvulsive Therapy', *Canadian Journal of Psychiatry*, 46(8): 720–7.

Health Canada (1996). *Canada's Drug Strategy* (Ottawa: Health Canada) (accessed at http://www.caw.ca).

——— (1999). *Toward a Healthy Future: Second Report on the Health of Canadians* (accessed at http://www.phac-aspc.gc.ca/ph-sp/phdd/report/subin.html).

——— (2002). *Canada Health Act Overview* (accessed at http://www.hc-sc.gc.ca).

——— (2004). *First Nations and Inuit Health: Improved Health of Aboriginal Ppeoples* (accessed at http://www.hc-sc.gc.ca).

——— (2005a). *Canadian Addiction Survey* (Ottawa: Health Canada).

——— (2005b). 'Intentional and Unintentional Injury Profile for Aboriginal Peoples in Canada' (accessed at http://www.hc-sc.gc.ca).

——— (2006). *Fetal Alcohol Spectrum Disorder* (accessed at http://www.hc-sc.gc.ca).

Health Care Consent Act, S.O. 1996, c. 2 (accessed at http://www.e-laws.gov.on.ca).

Hebebrand, J., Hennighausen, K., Nau, S., Himmelmann, G., Schulz, E., Schafer, H., and Remschmidt, H. (1997). 'Low Body Weight in Male Children and Adolescents with Schizoid Personality Disorder or Asperger's Disorder', *Acta Psychiatrica Scandinavica*, 96(1): 64–7.

Heller, N. and Northcut, R. (1996). 'Utilizing Cognitive-behavioural Techniques in Psychodynamic Practice with Clients Diagnosed as Borderline', *Clinical Social Work Journal*, 24: 203–15.

Hembree, E.A. and Foa, E.B. (2003). 'Interventions for Trauma-related Emotional Disturbances in Adult Victims of Crime', *Journal of Traumatic Stress*, 16(2): 187–99.

Herman, J. (1992). *Trauma and Recovery* (New York: Basic Books).

——— and van der Kolk, B. (1987). 'Traumatic Antecedents of Borderline Personality Disorder', in B. van der Kolk (ed.), *Psychological Trauma* (New York: American Psychiatric Press).

Herrmann, N. and Lanctot, K.L. (2007). 'Pharmacologic Management of Neuropsychiatric Symptoms of Alzheimer Disease', *La Revue Canadienne de Psychiatrie*, 52(10): 630–46.

Hettema, J., Prescott, C., and Kendler, K. (2004). 'Genetic and Environmental Sources of Covariation Between Generalized Anxiety Disorder and Neuroticism', *American Journal of Psychiatry*, 161(9): 1581–7.

Hick, S. (2006). *Social Work in Canada: An Introduction* (Toronto: Thompson Educational Publishing).

Hiltz, D. and Szigeti, A. (2004). *A Guide to Consent and Capacity Law in Ontario* (Toronto: LexisNexis Canada).

Hobfoll, S.E. (2001). 'The Influence of Culture, Community and the Nested-self in the Stress Process: Advancing Conservation of Resources Theory', *Applied Psychology: An International Review*, 50(3): 337–421.

Hoek, H., Susser, E., Buck, K., Lumey, L., Lin, S., and Gorman, J. (1996). 'Schizoid Personality Disorder after Prenatal Exposure to Famine', *American Journal of Psychiatry*, 153: 1637–9.

Hoffman, D.L., Dukes, E.M., and Wittchen, H. (2008). 'Human and Economic Burden of Generalized Anxiety Disorder', *Depression and Anxiety*, 25(1): 72–90.

Hoffman, R. and Putnam, L. (2004). *Not Just Another Call: Police Response to People with Mental Illnesses in Ontario* (Toronto: Centre for Addiction and Mental Health).

Hogarty, G. (1997). 'Three Year Trials of Personal Therapy Among Schizophrenic Patients Living Independent of Family', *American Journal of Psychiatry*, 154: 1504–13.

Hollingshead, A.B. and Redlich, F.C. (1954). 'Schizophrenia and Social Structure', *American Journal of Psychiatry*, 110: 695–701.

Hopmeyer, E. and Werk, A. (1994). 'A Comparative Study of Family Bereavement Groups', *Death Studies*, 18: 243–56.

Hopp v. Lepp (1980). 112 D.L.R. (3d) 67 (S.C.C.).

Horne, R., Graupner, L., Frost, S., Weinman, J., Wright, S., and Hankins, M. (2004). 'Medicine in a Multi-cultural Society: The Effect of Cultural Background on Beliefs about Medication', *Social Science & Medicine*, 59: 1307–13.

Horowitz, M. (1991). *Person Schemas and Maladaptive Interpersonal Patterns* (Chicago: University of Chicago Press).

Howland, R.H. and Thase, M.E. (1999). 'Affective Disorders: Biological Aspects', in T. Millon, P.H. Blaney, and R.D. Davis (eds), *Oxford Textbook of Psychopathology* (New York: Oxford University Press).

Humphrey, G.M. and Zimpfer, D.G. (1996). *Counselling for Grief and Bereavement* (London: Sage Publications).

Hurley, S., Jolley, D., and Kaldor, J. (1997). 'Effectiveness of Needle Exchange Programs for Prevention of HIV Infection', *The Lancet*, 349: 1797–1800.

Hurst, R., Nelson-Gray, R., Mitchell, J., and Kwapil, T. (2007). 'The Relationship of Asperger's Characteristics and Schizotypal Personality Traits in a Non-clinical Adult Sample', *Journal of Autism Developmental Disorders*, 37: 1711–20.

Hux, M.J., O'Brien, B.J., Iskedjian, M., Goeree, R., Gagnon, M., and Gauthier, S. (1998). 'Relation between Severity of Alzheimer's Disease and Costs of Caring', *Canadian Medical Association Journal*, 159(5): 457–65.

Hwang, W., Myers, H., Abe-Kim, J., and Ting, J. (2008). 'A Conceptual Paradigm for Understanding Culture's Impact on Mental Health: The Cultural Influences on Mental Health Model', *Clinical Psychology Review*, 28: 211–27.

Hyde, C., Glancy, G., Omerod, P., Hall, D., and Taylor, G. (1978). 'The Abuse of the Indigenous Mushroom: A New Fashion and Some Psychiatric Complications', *British Journal of Psychiatry*, 132: 602–4.

Incompetent Persons Act, 1989, R.S., c. 218, s. 1. (accessed at http://www.gov.ns.ca).

Ingram, R.E., Scott, W., and Siegel, G. (1999). 'Depression: Social and Cognitive Aspects', in T. Millon, P.H. Blaney, and R.D. Davis (eds), *Oxford Textbook of Psychopathology* (New York: Oxford University Press).

International Federation of Social Work (2009). 'Definition of Social Work' (accessed at http://www.ifsw.org).

Involuntary Psychiatric Treatment Act, 2005, R.S.N.S., c. 42. (accessed at http://www.gov.ns.ca).

Ishikawa, S., Okajima, I., Matsuoka, H., and Sakano, Y. (2007). 'Cognitive Behavioural Therapy for Anxiety Disorders in Children and Adolescents: A Meta-Analysis', *Child and Adolescent Mental Health*, 12(4): 164–72.

Jablensky, A. (2000). 'Epidemiology of Schizophrenia: The Global Burden of Disease and Disability', *European Archives of Psychiatry and Clinical Neuroscience*, 250: 274–85.

———, Schwartz, R., and Tomov T. (1980). 'WHO Collaborative Study of Impairments and Disabilities Associated with Schizophrenic Disorders', *Acta Psychiatrica Scandinavica Supplementum*, 285: 152–63.

Jacobs, M. and Fehr, K. (1987). *Drugs and Drug Abuse: A Reference Text* (2nd edn) (Toronto: Addiction Research Foundation).

Janicak, P., Davis, J., Gibbons, T., Ericksen, S., Chang, S., and Gallagher, P. (1985). 'Efficacy of ECT: A Meta-analysis', *American Journal of Psychiatry*, 142(3): 297–302.

Janik, J. (1992). 'Addressing Cognitive Defenses in Critical Incident Stress', *Journal of Traumatic Stress*, 5(3): 497–503.

Jensen, C. (1994). 'Psychosocial Treatment of Depression in Women: Nine Single-Subject Evaluations', *Research on Social Work Practice*, 4(3): 267–82.

Jobe, T.H. and Harrow M. (2005). 'Long-term Outcome of Patients with Schizophrenia: A Review', *Canadian Journal of Psychiatry*, 50: 892–900.

Jones, S. (2004). 'Psychotherapy of Bipolar Disorder: A Review', *Journal of Affective Disorders*, 80(2–3): 101–14.

Kaltman, S. and Bonanno, G.A. (2003). 'Trauma and Bereavement: Examining the Impact of Sudden and Violent Deaths', *Anxiety Disorders*, 17(2): 131–47.

Kaplan, H. and Sadock, B. (1996). *Concise Textbook of Clinical Psychiatry* (Baltimore: Williams and Wilkins).

Kardiner, A. (1941). *Traumatic Neuroses of War* (New York: Hoeber).

Kaslow, N. and Aronson, S. (2004). 'Recommendations for Family Interventions following a Suicide', *Professional Psychology: Research and Practice*, 35(3): 240–7.

Kasper, S., Wehr, T.A., Bartko, J.J., Gaist, P.A., and Rosenthal, N.E. (1989). 'Epidemiological Findings of Seasonal Changes in Mood and Behavior: A Telephone Survey of Montgomery County, Maryland', *Archives of General Psychiatry*, 46(9): 823–33.

Kelsoe, J.R. (2005). 'Mood Disorders: Genetics', in B.J. Sadock and V.A. Sadock (eds), *Comprehensive Textbook of Psychiatry* (8th edn) (Philadephia: Lippincott Williams & Wilkins).

Kendall, P.C., Hudson, J.L., Gosch, E., Flannery-Schroeder, E., and Suveg, C. (2008). 'Cognitive-behavioral Therapy for Anxiety-disordered Youth: A Randomized Clinical Trial Evaluating Child and Family Modalities', *Journal of Consulting and Clinical Psychology*, 76(2): 282–97.

Kendell, R. and Zealley, A. (1983). *Companion to Psychiatric Studies* (New York: Churchill Livingstone).

Kendler, K.S, Prescott, C., Myers, J., and Neale, M. (2003). 'The Structure of Genetic and Environmental Risk Factors for Common Psychiatric and Substance Use Disorders in Men and Women', *Archives of General Psychiatry*, 60(9): 929–37.

———, McGuire, M., Gruesberg, A.M., Ohare, A., Spellman, M., and Walsh, D. (1993). 'The Roscommon Family Study 1: Methods, Diagnosis of Probands, and Risk of Schizophrenia in Relatives', *Archives of General Psychiatry*, 50: 527–40.

Kessler, R., Berglund, P., Demler, O., Jin, R., Merikangas, K., and Walters, E. (2005). 'Lifetime Prevalence and Age of Onset Distributions of *DSM*-IV Disorders in the National Comorbidity Survey Replication', *Archives of General Psychiatry*, 62: 593–602.

———, Sonnega, A., Bromet, E., Hughes, M., and Nelson, C.B. (1995). 'Post-traumatic Stress Disorder in the National Comorbidity Survey', *Archives of General Psychiatry*, 52(12): 1048–60.

Ketchum v. Hislop (1984). 54 B.C.L.R. 327 (B.C.S.C.).

Kho, K.H., Zwinderman, A.H., and Blansjaar, B.A. (2005). 'Predictors for the Efficacy of Electroconvulsive Therapy: Chart Review and Naturalistic Study', *Journal of Clinical Psychiatry*, 66(7): 894–9.

Kinderman, P. and Bentall, R. (1996). 'Self-Discrepancies and Persecutory Delusions: Evidence for a Model of Paranoid Ideation', *Journal of Abnormal Psychology*, 105(1): 106–13.

Kirby, M. (2008). 'Mental Health in Canada: Out of the Shadows Forever', *Canadian Medical Association Journal*, 178(10): 1320–2.

Kirmayer, L., Brass, G., Holton, T., Paul, K., Simpson, C., and Tait, C. (2007). *Suicide Among Aboriginal People in Canada* (Ottawa: Aboriginal Healing Foundation).

Kirmayer, L., Simpson, C., and Cargo, M. (2003). 'Healing Traditions: Culture, Community and Mental Health Promotion with Canadian Aboriginal Peoples', *Australian Psychiatry*, 11(supp.): S15–S23.

Kish, S. (2008). 'Pharmacologic Mechanisms of Crystal Meth', *Canadian Medical Association Journal*, 178(13): 1679–82.

Koenen, K.C. (2006). 'Developmental Epidemiology of PTSD: Self-regulation as a Central Mechanism', *Annals New York Academy of Science*, 1071: 255–66.

König, J. and Leembruggen-Kallberg, E. (2006). 'Perspectives on Elder Abuse in Germany', *Educational Gerontology*, 32(1): 25–35.

Kosok, A. (2006). 'A Moderation Management Program in 2004: What Type of Drinker Seeks Controlled Drinking', *International Journal of Drug Policy*, 17(4): 295–303.

Kraepelin, E. (1904). 'Vergleichende Psychiatric', *Zentralblatt für Nervenheilkunde und Psychiatrie*, 27: 433–7 [English translation: Wright, J. (1974). 'Comparative Psychiatry', in S.R. Hirsch and M. Shepherd (eds), *Themes and Variations in European Psychiatry* (Bristol: John Wright & Sons)].

Kübler-Ross, E. (1969). *On Death and Dying* (New York: Macmillan).

Kuipers, E. (2006). 'Family Interventions in Schizophrenia: Evidence for Efficacy and Proposed Mechanisms of Change', *Journal of Family Therapy*, 28(1): 73–80.

———, Garety, P., Fowler, D., Dunn, G., Bebbington, P., Freeman, D., et al. (1997). 'London-East Anglia Randomized Controlled Trial of Cognitive-Behavioural Therapy for Psychosis. I: Effects of the Treatment Phase', *British Journal of Psychiatry*, 171(10): 319–27.

Kutchins, H. and Kirk, S. (1997). *Making Us Crazy: DSM—The Psychiatric Bible and the Creation of Mental Disorders* (New York: Free Press).

LaFave, H., de Sousa, H., and Gerber, G. (1996). 'Assertive Community Treatment of Severe Mental Illness: A Canadian Experience', *Psychiatric Services*, 47(7): 757–9.

Lai, D. (2004). 'The Impact of Culture on Depressive Symptoms of Elderly Chinese Immigrants', *Canadian Journal of Psychiatry*, 49(12): 820–7.

Lamb, H.R. (1998). 'Deinstitutionalization at the Beginning of the New Millennium', *Harvard Review of Psychiatry*, 6: 1–10.

——— and Weinberger, L.E. (1998). 'Persons with Severe Mental Illness in Jails and Prisons: A Review', *Psychiatric Services*, 49: 483–92.

Lanier, R.K., Umbricht, A., Harrison, J.A., Nuwayser, E.S., and Bigelow, G.E. (2007). 'Evaluation of a Transdermal Buprenorphine Formulation in Opioid Detoxification', *Addiction*, 102(10): 1648–56.

Lara-Cinisomo, S. and Griffin, B. (2007). 'Factors Associated with Major Depression in Mothers in Los Angeles', *Women's Health Issues*, 17(5): 316–24.

Larkin, M. (1994). 'Reality Orientation', *Alzheimer's Outreach* (accessed at http://www.zarcrom.com/users/alzheimers/t-02.html).

Leenaars, A. (2000). 'Suicide Prevention in Canada: A History of a Community Approach', *Canadian Journal of Mental Health*, 19(2): 57–73.

Levander, E., Frye, M.A., McElroy, S., Suppes, T., Grunze, H., Nolen, W.A., et al. (2007). 'Alcoholism and Anxiety in Bipolar Illness: Differential Lifetime Anxiety Comorbidity in Bipolar I Women with and without Alcoholism', *Journal of Affective Disorders*, 101(1–3): 211–7.

Lieberman, J.A., Stroup, T.S., McEvoy, J.P., Swartz, M.S., Rosenheck, R.A., Perkins, D.O., et al. (2005). 'Effectiveness of Antipsychotic Drugs in Patients with Chronic Schizophrenia', *New England Journal of Medicine*, 353(12): 1209–23.

Lieff, S. and Fish, A. (1996). 'Financial Capacity, Contracts and Property', in H. Bloom and M. Bay (eds), *A Practical Guide to Mental Health, Capacity and Consent Law of Ontario* (Toronto: Carswell).

Lilienfeld, S., Van Valkenburg, C., Larntz, K., and Akiskal, H. (1986). 'The Relationship of Histrionic Personality Disorder to Antisocial Personality and Somatization Disorders', *American Journal of Psychiatry*, 143(6): 718–22.

Lima, M.S., Moncrieff, J., and Soares, B. (2005). 'Drugs Versus Placebo for Dysthymia', *Cochrane Database of Systematic Reviews*, Issue 2, Art. No.: CD001130. DOI: 10.1002/14651858.CD001130.

Lindauer, R.J., Olff, M., van Meijel, E.P., Carlier, I.V., and Gersons, B.P. (2006). 'Cortisol, Learning, Memory and Attention in Relation to Smaller Hippocampal Volume in Police Officers with Post-traumatic Stress Disorder', *Biological Psychiatry*, 59(2): 171–7.

Lindemann, E. (1944). 'Symptomatology and Management of Acute Grief', *American Journal of Psychiatry*, 101: 141–8.

Linehan, M., Armstrong, H., Suarez, A., Allmon, D., and Heard, H. (1991). 'Cognitive Behavioural Treatment of Chronically Parasuicidal Borderline Patients', *Archives of General Psychiatry*, 48: 1060–4.

Link, B., Phelan, J., Bresnahan, M., Stueve, A., and Pescosolido, B. (1999). 'Public Conceptions of Mental Illness: Labels, Causes, Dangerousness, and Social Distance', *American Journal of Public Health*, 89(9): 1328–33.

Links, P.S., Steiner, M., Boiago, I., and Irwin, D. (1990). 'Lithium Therapy for Borderline Patients: Preliminary Findings', *Journal of Personality Disorder*, 4: 173–81.

Lis, E., Greenfield, B., Henry, M., Guile, J.M., and Daugherty, G. (2007). 'Neuroimaging and Genetics of Borderline Personality Disorder: A Review', *Journal of Psychiatry and Neuroscience*, 32(3): 162–73.

Lisanby, S.H. (2007). 'Electroconvulsive Therapy for Depression', *New England Journal of Medicine*, 357(19): 1939–45.

Livesley, J. (2005a). 'Behavioural and Molecular Genetic Contributions to a Dimensional Classification of Personality Disorder', *Journal of Personality Disorders*, 19(2): 131–55.

——— (2005b). 'Principles and Strategies for Treating Personality Disorder', *Canadian Journal of Psychiatry*, 50(8): 442–50.

——— (2007). 'An Integrated Approach to the Treatment of Personality Disorder', *Journal of Mental Health*, 16(1): 131–48.

Longhofer, J., Floersch, J., and Jenkins, J. (2003). 'Medication Effect Interpretation and the Social Grid of Management', *Social work in Mental Health*, 1(4): 71–89.

Loo, C., Sheehan, P., Pigot, M., and Lyndon, W. (2007). 'A Report on Mood and Cognitive Outcomes with Right Unilateral Ultrabrief Pulsewidth (0.3 ms) ECT and Retrospective Comparison with Standard Pulsewidth Right Unilateral ECT', *Journal of Affective Disorders*, 103(1–3): 277–81.

Lovestone, S. (2000). 'Dementia: Alzheimer's Disease', in M.G. Gelder, J.J. Lopez-Ibor Jr, and N.C. Andreasen (eds), *New Oxford Textbook of Psychiatry* (Oxford: Oxford University Press).

Luhrmann, T. (2007). 'Social Defeat and the Culture of Chronicity: Or, Why Schizophrenia Does So Well Over There and So Badly Here', *Culture, Medicine and Psychiatry*, 31: 135–72.

Luo, L. and Craik, F.I. (2008). 'Aging and Memory: A Cognitive Approach', *Canadian Journal of Psychiatry*, 53(6): 346–53.

Lurie, S. (2005). 'Comparative Mental Health Policy: Are there Lessons to be Learned?' *International Review of Psychiatry*, 17(2): 97–101.

Luty, J. and Carnwath, T. (2008). 'Specialised Alcohol Treatment Services Area Luxury the NHS Cannot Afford', *British Journal of Psychiatry*, 192: 245–7.

Lynch, T., Chapman, A., Rosenthal, Z., Kuo, J., and Linehan, M. (2006). 'Mechanisms of Change in Dialectical Behavior Therapy: Theoretical and Empirical Observations', *Journal of Clinical Psychology*, 62(4): 459–80.

Lyons, M., True, W., Eisen, S., Goldberg, J., Meyer, J., Faraone, S., Eaves, L., and Tsuang, M. (1995). 'Differential Heritability of Adult and Juvenile Antisocial Traits', *Archives of General Psychiatry*, 52(11): 906–15.

MacKenzie, J. (1920). 'The Soldier's Heart and War Neurosis: A Study in Symptomology', *British Medical Journal*, 1(3093): 491–4.

MacMaster, S. (2004). 'Harm Reduction: A New Perspective on Substance Abuse Services', *Social Work*, 49(3): 356–63.

MacNeil, M.S. (2008). An Epidemiologic Study of Aboriginal Adolescent Risk in Canada: The Meaning of Suicide', *Journal of Child and Adolescent Psychiatric Nursing*, 21(1): 3–12.

Magliano, L., Fiorillo, A., De Rosa, C., Malangone, C., and Maj, M. (2005). 'Family Burden in Long-term Disease: A Comparative study in Schizophrenia vs. Physical Disorders', *Social Science and Medicine*, 61(2): 313–22.

Malla, A.K., Norman, R.M.G., and Joober, R. (2005). 'First Episode Psychosis, Early Intervention and Outcome: What Have We Learned?' *Canadian Journal of Psychiatry*, 50(14): 881–91.

Mandell, D., Ittenbach, R., Levy, S., and Pinto-Martin, J. (2007). 'Disparities in Diagnosis Received Prior to Autism Spectrum Disorder', *Journal of Autism Developmental Disorder*, 37: 1795–1802.

Mann, J., Waternaux, C., Haas, G., and Malone, K. (1999). 'Toward a Clinical Model of Suicidal Behaviour in Psychiatric Patients', *American Journal of Psychiatry*, 156(2): 181–9.

Maple, M. (2005). 'Parental Bereavement and Youth Suicide: An Assessment of the Literature', *Australian Social Work*, 58(2): 179–87.

Markowitz, J., Bleinberg, K., Pessin, H., and Skodol, A. (2007). 'Adapting Interpersonal Psychotherapy for Borderline Personality Disorder', *Journal of Mental Health*, 16(1): 103–16.

Marlatt, G. and Witkiewitz, K. (2002). 'Harm Reduction Approaches to Alcohol Use: Health Promotion, Prevention and Treatment', *Addictive Behaviors*, 27(6): 867–86.

Marmar, C.R., Weiss, D.S., Metzler, T.J., Delucchi, K.L., Best, S.R., and Wentworth, K.A. (1999). 'Longitudinal Course and Predictors of Continuing Distress Following Critical Incident Exposure in Emergency Services Personnel', *Journal of Nervous and Mental Disorders*, 187(1): 15–22.

Marshall v. Curry (1933). 3 D.L.R. 260 (N.S.S.C.).

Marshall, J. (2000). 'Alcohol Dependence and Alcohol Problems', in M.G. Gelder, J.J. Lopez-Ibor Jr, and N.C. Andreasen (eds), *New Oxford Textbook of Psychiatry* (Oxford: Oxford University Press).

Martens, W. (2000). 'Antisocial and Psychopathic Personality Disorders: Causes, Course, and Remission—A Review Article', *International Journal of Offender Therapy and Comparative Criminology*, 44(4): 406–30.

Martin, B. and Cheung, K. (1985). 'Civil Commitment in Ontario: The Effect of Legislation on Clinical Practices', *Canadian Journal of Psychiatry*, 30(4): 259–64.

Martin, J., Barbanoj, M., Schlaepfer, T., Thompson, E., Perez, V., and Kulisevsky, J. (2003). 'Repetitive Transcranial Magnetic Stimulation for the Treatment of Depression: Systematic Review and Meta-analysis', *British Journal of Psychiatry*, 182: 480–91.

Marziali, E. and Munroe-Blum, H. (1994). *Interpersonal Group Psychotherapy for Borderline Personality Disorder* (New York: Basic Books).

Mathew, S., Price, R., and Charney, D. (2008). 'Recent Advances in the Neurobiology of Anxiety Disorders: Implications for Novel Therapeutics', *American Journal of Medical Genetics*, Part C Semin. Med. Genet. 148C: 89–98.

May, R. (1950). *The Meaning of Anxiety* (New York: The Ronald Press Company).

Mayfield, D., McLeod, G., and Hall, P. (1974). 'The CAGE Questionnaire: Validation of a New Alcoholism Screening Instrument', *American Journal of Psychiatry*, 131(10): 1121–3.

Mayou, R., Ehlers, A., and Hobbs, M. (2000). 'Psychological Debriefing for Road Traffic Accident Victims', *British Journal of Psychiatry*, 176: 589–93.

McDowell, D. and Clodfelter, R. (2001). 'Depression and Substance Abuse: Considerations of Etiology, Comorbidity, Evaluation and Treatment', *Psychiatric Annuals*, 31: 244–51.

McFarlane, A. and Yehuda, R. (1996). 'Resilience, Vulnerability and the Course of Post-traumatic Reactions', in B. van der Kolk, A. McFarlane, and L. Weisaeth (eds), *Traumatic Stress: The Effects of Overwhelming Experience on Mind, Body and Society* (New York: Guilford Press).

McFarlane, A.C. (1988). 'The Aetiology of Post-traumatic Stress Disorder Following a Natural Disaster', *British Journal of Psychiatry*, 152(1): 116–21.

McInerney v. MacDonald (1992). 2 S.C.R. 138.

McNeill, T. and Nicholas, D. (2009). 'Our System of Health Care', in J. Turner and F. Turner (eds), *Canadian Social Welfare* (6th edn) (Toronto: Pearson Education Canada).

Mental Health Act, C.C.S.M. c. M110 (accessed at http://www.canlii.org).

Menzies, R. (1995). 'The Making of Criminal Insanity in British Columbia: Granby Farrant and the Provincial Mental Home, Colquitz, 1919–1933', in H. Foster and J. McLaren (eds), *Essays in the History of Canadian Law: British Columbia and the Yukon* (Toronto: University of Toronto Press).

Miller, J., Campbell, K., and Pilkonis, P. (2007). 'Narcissistic Personality Disorder: Relations with Distress and Functional Impairment', *Comprehensive Psychiatry*, 48: 170–7.

Miller, W.R. and Rollnick, S. (1991). *Motivational Interviewing* (London: Guilford Press).

——— (2002). *Motivational Interviewing* (2nd edn) (New York: Guilford Press).

Min, M., Farkas, K., Minnes, S., and Singer, L.T. (2007). 'Impact of Childhood Abuse and Neglect on Substance Abuse and Psychological Distress in Adulthood', *Journal of Traumatic Stress*, 20(5): 833–44.

Ministry of Health and Long-Term Care (2000). *Brian's Law, Mental Health Legislative Reform* (accessed at http://www.health.gov.on.ca).

——— (2002). *The Time Is Now: Themes and Recommendations for Mental Health Reform in Ontario* (accessed at http://www.health.gov.on.ca).

Minozzi, S., Amato, L., Davoli, M., Farrell, M., Lima Reisser, A.A., Pani, P.P., et al. (2008). 'Anticonvulsants for Cocaine Dependence', *Cochrane Database of Systematic Reviews*, Issue 2, Art. No.: CD006754. DOI: 10.1002/14651858.CD006754.pub2.

Mintz, D. (2005). 'Teaching the Prescribers Role: The Psychology of Psychopharmacology', *Academic Psychiatry*, 29 (2): 187–94.

Mishna, F., Antle, B., and Regehr, C. (2002). 'Social Work with Clients Contemplating Suicide: Complexity and Ambiguity in the Clinical, Ethical and Legal Considerations', *Clinical Social Work Journal*, 30(3): 265–280.

Mishna, F., Regehr, C., and Antle, B. (2003). 'Canadian Legal and Ethical Parameters for Working with Suicidal Clients', *Canadian Social Work*, 5(1): 17–28.

Mitchell, R. (2003). 'Ideological Reflections on the *DSM*-IV-R (or pay no attention to that man behind the curtain, Dorothy)', *Child and Youth Care Forum*, 32(5): 281–98.

Moeller, F.G., Schmitz, J.M., Steinberg, J.L., Green, C.M., Reist, C., Lai, L.Y., et al. (2007). 'Citalopram Combined with Behavioral Therapy Reduces Cocaine Use: A Double-Blind, Placebo-Controlled Trial', *American Journal of Drug and Alcohol Abuse*, 33(3): 367–78.

Mojtabai, R. (2005). 'Culture-Bound Syndromes with Psychotic Features', in B.J. Sadock and V.A. Sadock (eds), *Kaplan and Sadock's Comprehensive Textbook of Psychiatry* (8th edn) (Philadelphia: Lippincott Williams and Wilkins).

Moll, J., Oliveira-Souza, R., Eslinger, P., Bramati, I., Mourao-Miranda, J., Andreiuolo, P., and Pessoa, L. (2002). 'The Neural Correlate of Moral Sensitivity: A Functional Magnetic Resonance Imaging Investigation of Basic and Moral Emotions', *Journal of Neuro Science*, 22: 2730–6.

Mollica, R.F., McInnes, K., Poole, C., and Tor, S. (1998). 'Dose-effect Relationships of Trauma to Symptoms of Depression and Post-traumatic Stress Disorder among Cambodian Survivors of Mass Violence', *British Journal of Psychiatry*, 173: 482–8.

Monahan, J., Bonnie, R., Appelbaum, P., Hyde, P., Steadman, H., and Swartz, M. (2001). 'Mandated Community Treatment: Beyond Outpatient Commitment', *Psychiatric Services*, 52(9): 1198–1205.

Moos, I. and Bjorn, A. (2006). 'Use of the Life Story in the Institutional Care of People with Dementia: A Review of Intervention Studies', *Ageing and Society*, 26(3): 431–54.

Morgan, C., Kirkbride, J., Leff, J., Craig, T., Hutchinson, G., et al. (2007). 'Parental Separation, Loss and Psychosis in Different Ethnic Groups: A Case Control Study', *Psychological Medicine*, 37: 495–503.

Morgan, C.A., Wang, S., Rasmusson, A., Hazlett, G., Anderson, G., and Charney, D.S. (2001). 'Relationship among Plasma Cortisol, Catecholamines, Neuropeptide Y, and Human Performance during Exposure to Uncontrollable Stress', *Psychosomatic Medicine*, 63: 412–22.

Morris, J., Ferguson, M., and Dykeman, M. (1999). *Canadian Nurses and the Law* (2nd edn) (Toronto: LexisNexis Canada).

Mott, F.W. (1918). 'War Psychoneurosis. Neurasthenia: The Disorders and Disabilities of Fear', *The Lancet*, 1: 127–9.

Muhlbauer, S. (2002). 'Navigating the Storm of Mental Illness: Phases in the Family Journey', *Qualitative Health Research*, 12(8): 1076–92.

Mur, M., Portella, M.J., Martinez-Aran, A., Pifarre, J., and Vieta, E. (2007). 'Persistent Neuropsychological Deficit in Euthymic Bipolar Patients: Execute Function as a Core Deficit', *Journal of Clinical Psychiatry*, 68: 1078–86.

Murman, D.L., Chen, Q., Powell, B.S., Kuo, S.B., Bradley, C.J., and Colenda, C.C. (2002). 'The Incremental Direct Costs Associated with Behavioural Symptoms in AD', *Neurology*, 59: 1721–9.

Murphy, S.A., Johnson, C., Cain, K.C., Das Gupta, A., Dimond, M., and Lohan, J. (1998). 'Broad-spectrum Group Treatment for Parents Bereaved by the Violent Deaths of Their 12 to 28 Year Old Children: A Randomised Controlled Trial', *Death Studies*, 22: 209–35.

Murray, A.M. and Castle, D.J. (2000). 'Genetic and Environmental Aetiological Factors', in M.G. Gelder, J.J. Lopez-Iber, and N. Andreasen (eds), *New Oxford Textbook of Psychiatry* (Oxford, UK: Oxford University Press).

Myers, L. and Thyer, B. (1997). 'Should Social Work Clients Have the Right to Effective Treatment?' *Social Work,* 42(3): 288–98.

Najarian, L.M., Goenjian, A.K., Pelcovitz, D., Mandel, F., and Njarian, B. (2001). 'The Effect of Relocation after a Natural Disaster', *Journal of Traumatic Stress,* 14(3): 511–26.

Narveson, J. (1986). 'Moral Philosophy and Suicide', *Canadian Journal of Psychiatry,* 31: 104–7.

Nathan, P.E., Skinstad, A.H., and Langenbucher, J.W. (1999). 'Substance Abuse: Diagnosis, Comorbidity, and Psychopathology', in T. Millon, P.H. Blaney, and R.D. Davis (eds), *Oxford Textbook of Psychopathology* (Oxford: Oxford University Press).

National Association of Social Workers (NASW) (2009). *Mental Health* (accessed at http://www.socialworkers.org/pressroom/features/issue/mental.asp).

National Institute for Health and Clinical Excellence (2007). 'Anxiety (Amended). Management of Anxiety (Panic Disorder, with or without Agoraphobia, and Generalised Anxiety Disorder) in Adults in Primary, Secondary and Community Care' (accessed at http://www.nice.org.uk/CG22).

National Institute of Mental Health (1991). *Caring for People with Severe Mental Disorders: A National Plan of Research to Improve Services,* DHHS Publication No. ADM 91 1762 (Washington, DC: US Government Printing Office).

Native Women's Association of Canada (NWAC) (2004). background paper given at Aboriginal Health Canada: Aboriginal People's Roundtable, Health Sectoral Session (Ottawa: NWAC).

Nava, F., Premi, S., Manzato, E., Campagnola, W., Lucchini, A., and Gessa, G.L. (2007). 'Gamma-Hydroxybutayrate Reduces both Withdrawal Syndrome and Hypercortisolism in Severe Abstinent Alcoholics: An Open Study vs. Diazepam', *American Journal of Drug and Alcohol Abuse,* 33(3): 379–92.

Neill, R. (1994). 'Social Work, Helping the Family to Cope with Schizophrenia: Psychoeducational Programs in the Community', *The Social Worker,* 62(2): 89–92.

Nelson, E. (2002). 'The Fundamentals of Consent', in J. Downie, T. Caulfield, and C. Flood (eds), *Canadian Health Law and Policy* (Toronto: Butterworths).

Nelson, F.L. (1984). 'Suicide: Issues of Prevention, Intervention, and Facilitation', *Journal of Clinical Psychology,* 40(6): 1328–33.

Nelson, G. (2006). 'Mental Health Policy in Canada', in A. Westhues (ed.), *Canadian Social Policy: Issues and Perspectives* (Waterloo, ON: Wilfrid Laurier University Press).

———, Aubry, T., and Lafrance, A. (2007). 'A Review of the Literature on the Effectiveness of Housing and Support, Assertive Community Treatment, and Intensive Case Management Interventions for Persons with Mental Illness Who Have Been Homeless', *American Journal of Orthopsychiatry,* 77(3): 350–61.

Nestadt, G., Romanoski, A., Chahal, R., and Merchant, A. (1990). 'An Epidemiological Study of Histrionic Personality Disorder', *Psychological Medicine,* 20(2): 413–22.

Neugroschl, J.A., Kolevzon, A., Samuels, S.C., and Marin, D.B. (2005). 'Dementia. In Delirium, Dementia, and Amnestic and Other Cognitive Disorders and Mental Disorders due to a General Medical Condition', in B.J. Sadock and V.A. Sadock (eds), *Comprehensive Textbook of Psychiatry* (Philadelphia: Lippincott Williams & Wilkins).

Newman, B., Clemmons, V., and Dannenfelser, P. (2007). 'The Diagnostic and Statistical Manual of Mental Disorders in Graduate Social Work Education: Then and Now', *Journal of Social Work Education,* 43(2): 297–307.

Nierenberg, A., Alpert, J., Gaynes, B., Warden, D., Wisniewski, S., Biggs, M., Trivedi, M., Barkin, J., and Rush, J. (2008). 'Family History of Completed Suicide and Characteristics of Major Depressive Disorder: A STAR*D (Sequenced Treatment of Alternatives to Relieve Depression) Study', *Journal of Affective Disorders,* 108: 129–34.

Nordt, C., Muller, B., Rossler, W., and Lauber, C. (2007). 'Predictors and Course of Vocational Status, Income and Quality of Life in People with Severe Mental Illness: A Naturalistic Inquiry', *Social Science and Medicine,* 65(7): 1420–9.

Norris, F.H., Friedman, M.J., and Watson, P.J. (2002). '60,000 Disaster Victims Speak: Part II. Summary and Implications of the Disaster Mental Health Research', *Psychiatry,* 65(3): 240–60.

Norton, P.J. and Price, E.P. (2007). 'A Meta-analytic Review of Cognitive-behavioral Treatment Outcome across the Anxiety Disorders', *Journal of Nervous and Mental Disease,* 195: 521–31.

Nwulia, E.A., Zandi, M.K., MacKinnon, D.F., DePaulo Jr, J.R., and McInnis, M.G. (2007). 'Genome-wide Scan of Bipolar II Disorder', *Bipolar Disorders*, 9(6): 580–8.

O'Reardon, J.P. (2007). 'Efficacy and Safety of Transcranial Magnetic Stimulation in the Acute Treatment of Major Depression: A Multisite Randomized Controlled trial', *Biological Psychiatry*, 62(11): 1208–16.

O'Reilly, R., Keegan, D., and Elias, J. (2000). 'A Survey of the Use of Community Treatment Orders by Psychiatrists in Saskatchewan', *Canadian Journal of Psychiatry*, 45: 79–81.

Offord, D., Boyle, M, Campbell, D., Cochrane, J., Goering, P., et al. (1994). *Mental Health in Ontario: Selected Findings from the Mental Health Supplement of the Ontario Health Survey* (Toronto: Ministry of Health).

Ogloff, J.R.P. (2006). 'Psychopathy-antisocial Personality Disorder Conundrum', *Australian and New Zealand Journal of Psychiatry*, 40(6): 519–28.

Olfson, M., Shaffer, D., Marcus, S.C., and Greenberg, T. (2003). 'Relationship Between Antidepressant Medication Treatment and Suicide in Adolescents', *American Medical Association*, 60: 978–82.

Ontario Association of Social Workers (OASW) (2006). *Role of Social Work in Mental Health* (Toronto: OASW).

Ontario College of Social Workers and Social Service Workers (OCSWSSW) (2005). *Privacy Toolkit for Social Workers and Social Service Workers: Guide to the Personal Health Information Protection Act, 2004 (PHIPA)* (Toronto: OCSWSSW) (accessed at http://www.ocswssw.org).

Ontario Health Care Consent Act (1996). S.O. 1996, c. 2, Sch. A (accessed at http://www.e-laws.gov.on.ca).

Ontario Ministry of Health (1991). *The Road to Reform: Final Report of the Implementation Strategy Sub-Committee* (Toronto: Ontario Ministry of Health).

Oppenheimer, B.S. and Rothschild, M.A. (1918). 'The Psychoneurotic Factor in the "Irritable Heart of Soldiers"', *British Medical Journal*, 2(3002): 29–31.

Orcutt, H.K., Erickson, D.J., and Wolfe, J. (2002). 'A Prospective Analysis of Trauma Exposure: The Mediating Role of PTSD Symptomatology', *Journal of Traumatic Stress*, 15(3): 259–66.

Oswald, P., Souery, D., Kasper, S., Lecrubier, Y., Montgomery, S., and Wyckaert, S. (2007). 'Current Issues in Bipolar Disorder: A Critical Review', *European Neuropsychopharmacology*, 17(11): 687–95.

Ott, A., Breteler, M., van Harskamp, F., Claus, J., van der Cammen, T., Diederick, E., et al. (1995). 'Prevalence of Alzheimer's Disease and Vascular Dementia: Association with Education. The Rotterdam Study', *British Medical Journal*, 30: 970–3.

Owen, F. and Simpson, M.D.C. (1995). 'The Neurochemistry of Schizophrenia', in S.R. Hirsch and D.R. Weinberger (eds), *Schizophrenia* (Oxford: Blackwell Science).

Owens, D. and Johnstone, E. (2006). 'Precursors and Prodromata of Schizophrenia: Findings from the Edinburgh High Risk Student and their Literature Context', *Psychological Medicine*, 36(11): 1501–14.

Oyane, N.M., Bjelland, I., Pallesen, S., Holsten, F., and Bjorvatn, B. (2007). 'Seasonality Is Associated with Anxiety and Depression: The Hordaland Health Study', *Journal of Affective Disorders*, 105(1–3): 147–55.

Ozer, E.J. and Weiss, D.S. (2004). 'Who Develops Post-traumatic Stress Disorder?' *Current Directions in Psychological Science*, 13(4): 169–72.

P. (L.M.) v. F. (D.) (1994). 22 C.C.L.T. (2d) 312 (Ont. Gen. Div.).

Page, H. (1885). *Injury of the Spinal Cord without Apparent Legion and Nervous Shock, in Their Surgical and Medico-legal Aspects* (London: J & A Church).

Page, S. (1980). 'New Civil Commitment Legislation: The Relevance of Commitment Criteria', *Canadian Journal of Psychiatry*, 25: 646–50.

Papastavrou, E., Kalokerinou, A., Papacostas, S., Tsangari, H., and Sourtizi, P. (2007). 'Caring for a Relative with Dementia: Family Caregiver Burden', *Journal of Advanced Nursing*, 58(5): 446–57.

Paris, J. (1994). 'The Etiology of Borderline Personality Disorder: A Biopsychosocial Approach', *Interpersonal Biological Processes*, 57(4): 316–25.

——— (1999a). 'Borderline Personality Disorder', in T. Millon, P.H. Blaney, and R.D. Davis, *Oxford Textbook of Psychopathology* (Oxford: Oxford University Press).

——— (1999b). *Nature and Nurture in Psychiatry: A Predisposition Stress Model of Mental Disorders* (Washington, DC: American Psychiatric Press).

——— (2005). 'Recent Advances in the Treatment of Borderline Personality Disorder', *Canadian Journal of Psychiatry*, 50(8): 435–41.

Parker, G. (2000). 'Diagnosis, Classification, and Differential Diagnosis of the Mood Disorders', in M.G. Gelder, J.J. Lopez-Ibor Jr, and N.C. Andreasen (eds), *New Oxford Textbook of Psychiatry* (New York: Oxford University Press).

Parrish, M. and Tunkel, J. (2005). 'Clinical Challenges Following an Adolescent's Death by Suicide: Bereavement Issues Faced by Family, Friends, Schools and Clinicians', *Clinical Social Work Journal*, 33(1): 81–102.

Patton, G.G., Coffey, C., Lynskey, M.T., Reid, S., Hemphill, S., Carlin, J.B., et al. (2007). 'Trajectories of Adolescent Alcohol and Cannabis Use into Young Adulthood', *Addiction*, 102(4): 607–15.

Paul, M., Foreman, D., and Kent, L. (2000). 'Outpatient Clinical Attendance Consent from Children and Young People: Ethical and Practical Considerations', *Clinical Child Psychology and Psychiatry*, 5(2): 203–11.

Peteet, J.R. and Gutheil, T.G. (1979). 'The Hospital and the Borderline Patient: Management Guidelines for the Community Mental Health Center', *Psychiatric Quarterly*, 51: 106–18.

Picchioni, M. and Murray, R. (2007). 'Schizophrenia', *British Medical Journal*, 335(7610): 91–5.

Pihl, R.O. (1999). 'Substance Abuse: Etiological Considerations', in T. Millon, P.H. Blaney, and R.D. Davis (eds), *Oxford Textbook of Psychopathology* (Oxford: Oxford University Press).

Plassman, B.L., Langa, K.M., Fisher, G.G., Heeringa, S.G., Weird, D.R., Ofstedal, M.B., et al. (2007). 'Prevalence of Dementia in the United States: The Aging, Demographics, and Memory Study', *Neuroepidemiology*, 29: 125–32.

Pole, N. (2007). 'The Psychophysiology of Post-traumatic Stress Disorder: A Meta-analysis', *Psychological Bulletin*, 133(5): 725–46.

Porta, M. (2004). 'Is There Life After Evidence-based Medicine?' *Journal of Evaluation in Clinical Practice*, 10(2): 147–52.

Powers, M.B. and Emmelkamp, P. (2008). 'Virtual Reality Therapy for Anxiety Disorders: A Meta-analysis', *Journal of Anxiety Disorders*, 22: 561–9.

President's New Freedom Commission on Mental Health (2003). *Achieving the Promise: Transforming Mental Health in America. Final Report* (accessed at http://www.mentalhealthcommission.gov/reports/FinalReport/downloads/FinalReport.pdf).

Prigerson, H.G., Shear, M.K., Jacobs, S.C., Reynolds, C.F., Maciejewski, P.K., Davidson, J.R., et al. (1999). 'Consensus Criteria for Traumatic Grief: A Preliminary Empirical Test', *British Journal of Psychiatry*, 174: 67–73.

Prochaska, J. and DiClemente, C. (1982). 'Transtheoretical Therapy: Towards a More Integrated Model of Change', *Psychotherapy Research and Practice*, 19(3): 276–88.

Proctor, E. and Rosen, A. (2004). 'Precise Standards for Developing Evidence-based Practice Guidelines', in A. Roberts and K. Yeager (eds), *Evidence Based Practice Manual: Research and Outcome Measures in Health and Human Services* (New York: Oxford University Press).

Prudich, J., (2005). 'Electroconvulsive Therapy', in B.J. Sadock and V. Sadock (eds), *Kaplan & Sadock's Comprehensive Textbook of Psychiatry* (8th edn) (Philadelphia: Lippincott Williams & Wilkins).

Public Health Agency Canada (2001). *Harm Reduction and Injection Drug Use: An International Comparative Study of Contextual Factors Influencing the Development and Implementation of Relevant Policies and Programs* (accessed at http://www.phac-aspc.gc.ca).

——— (2002). *A Report on Mental Illnesses in Canada* (Ottawa: Health Canada) (accessed at http://www.phac-aspc.gc.ca).

——— (2008). 'What Determines Health?' (accessed at http://www.phac-aspc.gc.ca).

R. v. J.(J.-L.) (1999). 130 C.C.C. (3d) 541 (Que. C.A.).

R. v. Mills (1997). A.J. 891 (Alta. Ct. Q.B.).

R. v. O'Connor (1995). 4 S.C.R. 411.

Rabi, K. (2006). 'Israeli Perspectives on Elder Abuse', *Educational Gerontology*, 32(1): 49–62.

Raging Spoon (2008). 'About Us: History' (accessed at http://www.ragingspoon.com/history.htm).

Rapp, R., Siegal, H., and DeLiberty, N. (2003). 'Demographic and Clinical Correlates of Client Motivation among Substance Abusers', *Health and Social Work*, 28(2): 107–15.

Ravitz, P., Maunder, R., and McBride, C. (2008). 'Attachment, Contemporary Interpersonal Theory and IPT: An Integration of Theoretical, Clinical and Empirical Perspectives', *Journal of Contemporary Psychotherapy*, 38(1): 11–21.

Re: T.D.D. (1999). 171 Dominion Law Reports (4th) 761 (Sask. Q.B.).

Reese, D. and Sontag, M. (2001). 'Successful Interprofessional Collaboration on the Hospice Team', *Health and Social Work,* 26(3): 167–75.

Regehr, C. (2000). Cognitive-behavioural Therapy', in P. Lehmann and N. Coady (eds), *Theoretical Perspectives in Direct Social Work Practice: An Eclectic-generalist Approach* (New York: Springer).

——— (2001). 'Crisis Debriefing Groups for Emergency Responders: Reviewing the Evidence', *Brief Treatment and Crisis Intervention,* 1: 87–100.

———, Alaggia, R., Lambert, L., and Saini, M. (2008). 'Victims of Sexual Violence in the Canada Criminal Courts', *Victims & Offenders,* 3(1): 99–113.

——— and Antle, B. (1997). 'Coercive Influences: Informed Consent in Court Mandated Social Work Practice', *Social Work,* 42(3): 300–6.

——— and Antle, B. (1997). 'Coercive Influences: Informed Consent in Court Mandated Social Work Practice', *Social Work,* 42(3): 300–6.

——— and Bober, T. (2005). *In the Line of Fire: Trauma in the Emergency Services* (New York: Oxford University Press).

——— and Bober, T. (2005). *In the Line of Fire: Trauma in the Emergency Services* (New York: Oxford University Press).

———, Bryant, A., and Glancy, G. (1997). 'Confidentiality of Treatment for Victims of Sexual Violence', *The Social Worker,* 65(3): 137–45.

——— and Glancy, G. (1999). 'Paranoid Disorders', in F. Turner (ed.), *Adult Psychopathology: A Social Work Perspective* (2nd edn) (New York: Free Press).

——— and Kanani, K. (2006). *Essential Law for Social Work Practice in Canada* (Toronto: Oxford University Press).

——— and Kanani, K. (2009). *Essential Law for Social Work Practice in Canada* (2nd edn) (Toronto: Oxford University Press).

——— and Marziali, E. (1999). 'Response to Sexual Assault: A Relational Perspective', *Journal of Nervous and Mental Disease,* 187(10): 618–23.

———, Marziali, E., and Jansen, K. (1999). 'A Qualitative Analysis of Strengths and Vulnerabilities in Sexually Assaulted Women', *Clinical Social Work Journal,* 27(2): 171–84.

———, Stern, S., and Shlonsky, A. (2007). 'Operationalizing Evidence Based Practice: The Development of a Research Institute in Evidence Based Social Work', *Research on Social Work Practice,* 17(3): 408–16.

——— and Sussman, T. (2004). 'Intersections Between Grief and Trauma: Towards an Empirically Based Model for Treating Traumatic Grief', *Brief Treatment and Crisis Intervention,* 4(3): 289–309.

Regier, D.A., Farmer, M.E., Rae, D.S., Locke, B.Z., Keith, B.J., Judd, L.L., et al. (1990). 'Comorbidity of Mental Health Disorders with Alcohol and Other Drug Abuse', *Journal of the American Medical Association,* 264(19): 2511–8.

Regier, D.A., Narrow, W.E., Rae, D.S., Manderscheid, R.W., Locke, B.Z., and Goodwin, F.K. (1993). 'The De Facto US Mental and Addictive Disorders Service System: Epidemiologic Catchment Area Prospective 1-year Prevalence Rates of Disorders and Services', *Archives of General Psychiatry,* 50(2): 85–94.

Reibl v. Hughes (1980). 2 S.C.R. 880.

Reich, James H. (1990). 'Comparisons of Males and Females with DSM-III Dependent Personality Disorder', *Psychiatry Research,* 33(2): 207–14.

Reichborn-Kjennerud, T., Czajkowski, N., Torgersen, S., Neale, M., Orstavik, R., Tambs, K., and Kendler, K. (2007). 'The Relationships Between Avoidant Personality Disorder and Social Pphobia: A Population-based Twin Study', *American Journal of Psychiatry,* 164(11): 1722–8.

Reinecke, M. (2000). 'Suicide and Depression', in F. Dattlilio and A. Freeman (eds), *Cognitive-Behavioural Strategies in Crisis Intervention* (New York: Guilford Press).

Resick, P.A. (2000). *Stress and Trauma* (Philadelphia: Taylor & Francis).

Resnick, H.S., Kilpatrick, D.G., Best, C.L., and Kramer, T.L. (1992). 'Vulnerability-stress Factors in Development of Post-traumatic Stress Disorder', *Journal of Nervous and Mental Disease,* 180(7): 424–30.

Reynolds, L. (2008). 'Wave of Suicides Hits Troubled First Nation', *Winnipeg Free Press,* 9 May 2008 (accessed at http://www.canada.com/topics/news/national/).

Riedel-Heller, S.G., Busse, A., Aurich, C., Matschinger, H., and Angermeyer, M.C. (2001). 'Prevalence of Dementia According to DSM-III-R and ICD-10', *British Journal of Psychiatry*, 179: 250–4.

Riemersma-van der Lek, R.F., Swaab, D.F., Twisk, J., Hol, E.M., Hoogendijk, W.J., and Someren, V. (2008). 'Effect of Bright Light and Melatonin on Cognitive and Noncognitive Function in Elderly Residents of Group Care Facilities', *Journal of the American Medical Association*, 299(22): 2642–55.

Rihmer, Z. and Angst, J. (2005). 'Mood Disorders: Epidemiology', in B.J. Sadock and V.A. Sadock (eds), *Kaplan & Sadock's Comprehensive Textbook of Psychiatry* (8th edn) (Philadelphia: Lippincott Williams & Wilkins).

Ritchie, J., Sklar, R., and Steiner, W. (1998). 'Advance Directives in Psychiatry: Resolving Issues of Autonomy and Competence', *International Journal of Law and Psychiatry*, 21(3): 245–60.

Roberts, A. and Everly, G. (2006). 'A Meta-anaysis of 36 Crisis Intervention Studies', *Brief Treatments and Crisis Intervention*, 6(1): 10–21.

Roberts, A.R. (2000). *Crisis Intervention Handbook: Assessment, Treatment and Research* (New York: Oxford University Press).

Robins, C. and Chapman, A. (2004). 'Dialectical Behaviour Therapy: Current Status, Recent Developments, and Future Directions', *Journal of Personality Disorder*, 18: 73–9.

Rock, P. (1998). *After Homicide: Practical and Political Responses to Bereavement* (Oxford: Oxford University Press).

Rosen, A. and Proctor, E. (2002). 'Standards for Evidence-Based Social Work Practice', in A. Roberts and G. Greene (eds), *Social Worker's Desk Reference* (New York: Oxford University Press).

Rosenberg, H. and Phillips, K. (2003). 'Acceptability and Availability of Harm-reduction Interventions for Drug Abuse in American Substance Abuse Treatment Agencies', *Psychology of Addictive Behavior*, 17(3): 203–10.

Rosenthal, N., Sack, D., Gillin, J., Lewy, A., Goodwin, F., Davenport, Y., et al. (1984). 'Seasonal Affective Disorder: A Description of the Syndrome and Preliminary Findings with Light Therapy', *Archives of General Psychiatry*, 41(1): 72–80.

Rothbaum, B. and Foa, E. (1996). 'Cognitive-behavioural Therapy for Post-traumatic Stress Disorder', in B.A. van der Kolk, A.C. McFarlane, and L. Weisaeth (eds), *Traumatic Stress: The Effects of Overwhelming Experience on Mind, Body, and Society* (New York: Guildford Press).

———, Riggs, D.S., Murdock, T., and Walsh, W. (1992). 'A Prospective Examination of Post-traumatic Stress Disorder in Rape Victims', *Journal of Traumatic Stress*, 5(3): 455–75.

Rothbaum, B., Meadows, E., Resick, P., Foy, D. (2000). 'Cognitive Behavioural Therapy', in E. Foa, T. Keane, and M. Friedman (eds), *Effective Treatments for PTSD: Practice Guidelines from the International Society for Traumatic Stress Studies* (New York: Guilford Press).

Rouget, B. and Aubry, J. (2007). 'Efficacy of Psychoeducational Approaches on Bipolar Disorders: A Review of the Literature', *Journal of Affective Disorders*, 98(1–2): 11–27.

Royal Commission on Aboriginal Peoples (1996a). *Breaking the Silence* (Ottawa: Supply and Services Canada).

——— (1996b). *Bridging the Cultural Divide: A Report on Aboriginal People and the Criminal Justice System in Canada* (Ottawa: Supply and Services Canada).

Rozovsky, L. (2003). *The Canadian Law of Consent to Treatment* (Toronto: Butterworths).

Rutter, M. (1993). 'Resilience: Some Conceptual Considerations', *Journal of Adolescent Health*, 14(8): 626–31.

———, Champion, L., Quinton, D., Maughan, B., and Pickles, A. (1995). 'Understanding Individual Differences in Environmental Risk Exposure', in P. Moen, G.H. Elder, and K. Luscher (eds), *Examining Lives in Context* (Washington, DC: APA).

Ryder, A., Yang, J., Heine, S., Zhu, X., Yao, S., Yi, J., and Bagby, M. (2008). 'The Cultural Shaping of Depression: Somatic Symptoms in China, Psychological Symptoms in North America?' *Journal of Abnormal Psychology*, 117: 300–13.

Saarni, S. and Gylling, H. (2004). 'Evidence-based Medicine Guidelines: A Solution to Rationing or Politics Disguised as Science?' *Journal of Medical Ethics*, 30(2): 171–5.

Sackett, D., Rosenberg, W., Gray, J., Haynes, R., and Richardson, W. (1996). 'Evidence-based Medicine: What It Is and What It Isn't', *British Medical Journal*, 312(7023): 71–2.

Salyers, M. and Tsemberis, S. (2007). 'ACT and Recovery: Integrating Evidence-based Practice and Recovery Orientation on Assertive Community Treatment Teams', *Community Mental Health Journal*, 43(6): 619–41.

Samuels, J., Eaton, W., Bienvenu, O., Brown, C., Costa, P., and Nestadt, G. (2002). 'Prevalence and Correlates of Personality Disorders in a Community Sample', *British Journal of Psychiatry*, 180: 536–42.

Sass, H. (2007). 'Conceptual History of Psychopathology', paper given to the American Academy of Psychiatry and the Law Annual Meeting, 24 Oct. 2007.

Schaefer, H.S., Putnam, K.M., Benca, R.M., and Davidson, R.J. (2006). 'Event-related Functional Magnetic Resonance Imaging Measures of Neural Activity to Positive Social Stimuli in Pre-and Post-treatment Depression', *Journal of Biopsychology*, 60(9): 974–86.

Schlesinger, A. and Silk, K. (2005). 'Collaborative Treatment', in J. Oldham, A. Skodol, and D. Bender, *Textbook of Personality Disorders* (Washington, DC: American Psychiatric Publishing).

Schneider, R. (1988). *Ontario Mental Health Statutes* (Toronto: Carswell).

Schnurr, B. (2004). *Court Appointment of Guardians for Mentally Incapable Persons* (Toronto: Law Society of Upper Canada).

Schoenfeld, F.B., Marmar, C.R., and Neylan, T.C. (2004). 'Current Concepts in Pharmacotherapy for Post-traumatic Stress Disorder', *Psychiatric Services*, 55(5): 519–31.

Schreiber, S., Peles, E., and Adelson, M. (2008). 'Association Between Improvement in Depression, Reduced Benzodiazepine (BDZ) Abuse, and Increased Psychotropic Medication Use in Methadone Maintenance Treatment (MMT) Patients', *Drug and Alcohol Dependence*, 92(1–2): 79–85.

Schuter, S.R. and Zisook, S. (1993). 'The Course of Normal Grief', in M.S. Stroebe, W. Stroebe, and R.O. Hansson (eds), *Handbook of Bereavement: Theory, Research and Intervention* (New York: Cambridge University Press).

Scott, J., McNeill, Y., Cavanagh, J., Cannon, M., and Murray, R. (2006). 'Exposure to Obstetric Complications and Subsequent Development of Bipolar Disorder: Systematic Review', *British Journal of Psychiatry*, 189: 3–11.

Seivewright, N. (2000). 'Disorders Relating to the Use of Amphetamine and Cocaine', in M.G. Gelder, J.J. Lopez-Ibor Jr, and N.C. Andreasen (eds), *New Oxford Textbook of Psychiatry* (Oxford: Oxford University Press).

Seligman, M., and Garber, J. (1980). *Human Helplessness* (Toronto: Academic Press).

Selten, J., Cantor-Graae, E., and Kahn, R. (2007). 'Migration and Schizophrenia', *Current Opinions in Psychiatry*, 20: 111–15.

Selye, H. (1936). 'A Syndrome Produced by Diverse Nocuous Agents', *Nature*, 138: 32.

Seow, D. and Gauthier, S. (2007). 'Pharmacotherapy of Alzheimer Disease', *La Revue Canadienne de Psychiatrie*, 52(10): 620–9.

Sevels v. Cameron [1995] O.J. No. 381 (Ont. Ct. J. Gen. Div.).

Shaffer, A., Cairney, J., Cheung, A., Veldhuizen, S., and Levitt, A. (2006). 'Community Survey of Bipolar Disorder in Canada: Lifetime Prevalence and Illness Characteristics', *Canadian Journal of Psychiatry*, 51(1): 9–16.

Shalev, A. (2002). 'Acute Stress Reactions in Adults', *Biological Psychiatry*, 51(7): 532–43.

Shea, A., Walsh, C., MacMillan, H., and Steiner, M. (2004). 'Child Maltreatment and HPA Axis Dysregulation: Relationship to Major Depressive Disorder and Post-Traumatic Stress Disorder in Females', *Psychoneuroendocrinology*, 30(2): 162–78.

Shear, M.K., Frank, E.F., Foa, E., Cherry, C., Reynolds, C.F., Vander Bilt, J., et al. (2001). 'Traumatic Grief: A Pilot Study', *American Journal of Psychiatry*, 158: 1506–8.

Shera, W., Aviram, U., Healy, B., and Ramon, S. (2002). 'Mental Health Systems Reform: A Multi Country Comparison', *Social Work in Health Care*, 35(1–2): 547–5.

Shiloh, R., Nutt, D., and Wizeman, A. (2005). *Clinical Handbook of Psychotropic Drugs* (15th edn) (Ashland: Hogrefe and Huber).

Silva de Lima, M., Farrell, M., Lima Reisser, A.A., and Soares, B. (2003). 'Antidepressants for Cocaine Dependence', *Cochrane Database of Systematic Reviews*, Issue 2, Art. No.: CD002950. DOI: 10.1002/14651858.CD002950.

Sireling, L., Cohen, D., and Marks, I. (1988). 'Guided Mourning for Morbid Grief: A Controlled Replication', *Behavior Therapy*, 19(2): 121–32.

Skelton, M. (1996). 'Social Work', in E. Shorter (ed.), *TPH: History and Memories of the Toronto Psychiatric Hospital, 1925–1966* (Toronto: Wall & Emerson).

Slade, M. and Hayward, M. (2007). 'Recovery, Psychosis and Psychiatry: Research Is Better Than Rhetoric', *Acta Psychiatrica Scandinavica*, 116: 81–3.

Sluzki, C.E., Beavin, J., Tarnopolsky, A., and Veron, E. (1967). 'Transactional Disqualification: Research on the Double Bind', *Archives of General Psychiatry,* (4): 494–504.

Smith, L.A., Cornelius, V., Warnock, A., Bell, A., and Young, A.H. (2007). 'Effectiveness of Mood Stabilizers and Antipsychotics in the Maintenance Phase of Bipolar Disorder: A Systematic Review of Randomized Controlled Trials', *Bipolar Disorders,* 9(4): 394–412.

Smoller, J. and Faraone, S. (2008). 'Genetics of Anxiety Disorders: Complexities and Opportunities', *American Journal of Medical Genetics,* Part C Semin. Med. Genet. 148C: 85–8.

Smoller, J., Gardner-Schuster, E., and Covino, J. (2008). 'The Genetic Basis of Panic and Phobic Anxiety Disorders', *American Journal of Medical Genetics,* Part C Semin. Med. Genet. 148C: 118–26.

Sneiderman, R., Irvine, J., and Osborne, P. (2003). *Canadian Medical Law* (3rd edn) (Toronto: Thompson).

Snowdon, L. (2007). 'Explaining Mental Health Treatment Disparities: Ethnic and Cultural Differences in Family Involvement', *Cultural and Medical Psychiatry,* 31(3): 389–402.

Sobell, M. and Sobell, L. (1995). 'Controlled Drinking after 25 Years: How Important was the Great Debate?' *Addiction,* 90: 1149–53.

Soloff, P. (2005). 'Somatic Treatments', in J. Oldham, A. Skodol, and D. Bender, *Textbook of Personality Disorders* (Washington, DC: American Psychiatric Publishing).

Solomon, R. and Visser, L. (2005). *A Legal Guide for Social Workers* (Toronto: Ontario Association of Social Workers).

Solomon, S.D. and Johnson, D.M. (2002). 'Psychosocial Treatment of Post-traumatic Stress Disorder: A Practice-Friendly Review of Outcome Research', *Journal of Clinical Psychology,* 58(8): 947–59.

Southward, E. (1919). *Shell Shock* (Boston: W.M. Leonard).

Sowers, W. (2005). 'Transforming Systems of Care: The American Association of Community Psychatrists Guidelines for Recovery-oriented Services', *Community Mental Health Journal,* 41(6): 757–74.

Special Senate Committee on Euthanasia and Assisted Suicide (1995). *Of Life and Death* (accessed at http://www.parl.gc.ca).

Spector, A., Orrell, M., Davies, S., and Woods, B. (2000). 'Reality Orientation for Dementia', *Cochrane Database of Systematic Reviews,* Issue 3, Art. No.: CD001119. DOI: 10.1002/14651858.CD001119. pub2.

Spiegel, D.A. and Barlow, D.H. (2000). 'Generalized Anxiety Disorders', in M.G. Gelder, J.J. Lopez-Ibor Jr, and N.C. Andreasen (eds), *New Oxford Textbook of Psychiatry* (New York: Oxford University Press).

Stahl, S.M. (2000a). 'Anxiety Disorders and Anxiolytics', in S.M. Stahl, *Essential Psychopharmacology: Neuroscientific Basis and Practical Applications* (3rd edn) (Cambridge: Cambridge University Press).

——— (2000b). 'Dementia and Its Treatment', in S.M. Stahl, *Essential Psychopharmacology: Neuroscientific Basis and Practical Applications* (3rd edn) (Cambridge: Cambridge University Press).

——— (2008). *Essential Psychopharmocology* (New York: Cambridge Press).

Standing Senate Committee on Social Affairs, Science and Technology (The) (2002). *The Health of Canadians—The Federal Role* (Ottawa: Senate Canada) (accessed at http://www.parl.gc.ca).

——— (2006). *Out of the Shadows at Last: Transforming Mental Health, Mental Illness and Addiction Services in Canada* (Ottawa: Senate Canada) (accessed at http://www.parl.gc.ca).

Statistics Canada (2001a). *The People: Equity Groups* (accessed at http://www43.statcan.ca).

——— (2001b). *2001 Census Aboriginal Profile* (accessed at http://www12.statcan.ca).

——— (2002). *Family Violence in Canada: A Statistical Profile* (Ottawa: Statistics Canada).

Statutes of Canada (1997). c. 30 (Bill C-46, 1996). An Act to Amend the Criminal Code (production of records in sexual offence proceedings).

Steele, L.S., Dewa, C.S., Lin, E., and Lee, K.L. (2007). 'Education Level, Income Level and Mental Health Services Use in Canada: Associations and Policy Implications', *Healthcare Policy/Politiques de Santé,* 3(1): 96–106.

Stein, D.J., Ipser, J.C., and Seedat, S. (2005). 'Pharmacotherapy for Post-Traumatic Stress Disorder (PTSD)', *Cochrane Database of Systematic Reviews,* Issue 4, Art. No.: CD002795. DOI: 10.1002/14651858. CD002795.pub2.

Stein, L. and Test, M. (1980). 'Alternative to Mental Hospital Treatment. I. Conceptual Model, Treatment Program, and Clinical Evaluation', *Archives of General Psychiatry,* 37(4): 392–7.

Stern, A. (1938). 'Psychoanalytic Investigation of and Therapy in the Borderline Group of Neuroses', *Psychoanalytic Quarterly*, 7: 467–89.

Stroebe, M., Schut, H., and Finkenauer, C. (2001). 'The Traumatization of Grief? A Conceptual Framework for Understanding the Trauma-bereavement Interface', *Israel Journal of Psychiatry and Related Sciences*, 38(3–4): 185–201.

Subramanian, K. (1991). 'Structured Group Work for the Management of Chronic Pain: An Experimental Investigation', *Research on Social Work Practice*, 1(1): 32–45.

Sussman, T. (2006). 'Negotiating Community Care as a Stress: The Experience of Spousal Caregivers', paper given at the 4th Annual National Gerontological Social Work Conference, Chicago, Illinois.

Sussman, T. and Regehr, C. (2009). 'The Influence of Community Based Services on the Burden of Spouses Caring for Their Partners with Dementia.' *Social Work in Health Care*. 34(1) 29–39.

Szasz, T. (1963). *Law, Liberty and Psychiatry* (New York: Macmillan).

Talbot, N. and Gamble, S. (2007). 'IPT for Women with Trauma Histories in Community Mental Health Care', *Journal of Contemporary Psychotherapy*, 38(1): 35–44.

Tarasoff v. Regents of University of California (1976). 17 Cal.3d 425.

Tarrier, N., Pilgrim, H., Sommerfield, C., Faragher, B., Reynolds, M., Graham, E., et al. (1999). 'A Randomized Trial of Cognitive Therapy and Imaginal Exposure in the Treatment of Chronic Posttraumatic Stress Disorder', *Journal of Consulting and Clinical Psychology*, 67(1): 13–18.

Tauriac, J. and Scruggs, N. (2006). 'Elder Abuse Among African Americans', *Educational Gerontology*, 32(1): 37–48.

Teicher, M. (1952a). 'The Role of the Psychiatric Social Worker', *Canadian Welfare*, 27(8): 14–20.

——— (1952b). 'Let's Abolish Social Service Exchange', *Social Work Journal*, 33(1): 28–31.

Test, M. (2002). 'Guidelines for Assertive Community Treatment Teams', in A. Roberts and G. Greene (eds), *Social Worker's Desk Reference* (New York: Oxford University Press).

Thara, R. (2004). 'Twenty-Year Course of Schizophrenia: The Madras Longitudinal Study', *Canadian Journal of Psychiatry*, 49(8): 564–9.

Thomlison, R. and Bradshaw, C. (2002). 'Canadian Political Processes and Social Work Practice', in F. Turner (ed.), *Social Work Practice: A Canadian Perspective* (Toronto: Prentice-Hall).

Thompson, M.P., Norris, F.H., and Ruback, R.B. (1998). 'Comparative Distress Levels of Inner-city Family Members of Homicide Victims', *Journal of Traumatic Stress*, 11(2): 223–42.

Tjepkema, M. (2004). 'Alcohol and Illicit Drug Dependence', *Supplement to Health Reports*, 15: 9–51 (accessed http://www.statcan.ca).

Torrey, E. and Kaplan, R. (1995). 'A National Survey of the Use of Outpatient Commitment', *Psychiatric Services*, 46: 778–84.

Toseland, R., Zaneles-Palmer, J., and Chapman, D. (1986). 'Team Work in Psychiatric Settings', *Social Work*, 31: 46–52.

True, W., Xian, H., Scherrer, J., Madden, P., Bucholz, K., Heath, A., et al. (1999). 'Common Genetic Vulnerability for Nicotine and Alcohol Dependence in Men', *Archives of General Psychiatry*, 56(7): 655–61.

———, Rice, J., Eisen, S.A., Heath, A.C., Goldberg, J., Lyons, M.J., et al. (1993). 'A Twin Study of Genetic and Environmental Contributions to Liability for Post-traumatic Stress Symptoms', *Archives of General Psychiatry*, 50(4): 257–65.

Trueman, S. (2003). 'Community Treatment Orders in Nova Scotia—The Least Restrictive Alternative?' *Health Law Journal*, 11: 1.

Turnbull, G.J. (1998). 'A Review of Post-traumatic Stress Disorder. Part 1: Historical Development and Classification', *Injury*, 29(2): 149–67.

Turner, E., Matthews, A., Linardatos, E., Tell, R.A., and Rosenthal R. (2008). 'Selective Publication of Antidepressant Trials and its Influence on Apparent Efficacy', *New England Journal of Medicine*, 358(3): 252–60.

United Nations (1948). *Universal Declaration of Human Rights* (accessed at http://www.un.org).

——— (1990). *Convention on the Rights of the Child* (accessed at http://www.unhchr.ch).

US Department of Labor (2009). *Occupational Outlook Handbook, 2008–2009 Edition: Social Workers* (accessed at http://www.bls.gov/oco/ocos060.htm).

van der Kolk, B.A. (1997). 'The Psychobiology of Post-traumatic Stress Disorder', *Journal of Clinical Psychiatry*, 58(supp. 9): 16–24.

——— and van der Hart, O. (1989). 'Pierre Janet and the Breakdown of Adaptation in Psychological Trauma', *American Journal of Psychiatry*, 146(12): 1530–40.

van Laar, M., van Dorsselaer, S., Monshouwer, K., and de Graaf, R. (2007). 'Does Cannabis Use Predict the First Incidence of Mood and Anxiety Disorders in the Adult Population?', *Addiction*, 102(8): 1251–60.

Vanyukov, M.M., Maher, B.S., Devlin, B., Kirillova, G.P., Kirisci, L., Yu, L.M, et al. (2007). 'The MAOA Promoter Polymorphism, Disruptive Behaviour Disorders, and Early Onset Substance Use Disorder: Gene-environment Interaction', *Psychiatric Genetics*, 17(6): 323–32.

Vasilaki, E., Hosier, S., and Cox, M. (2006). 'The Efficacy of Motivational Interviewing as Brief Intervention for Excessive Drinking: A Meta-analytic Review', *Alcohol and Alcoholism*, 41(3): 328–35.

Vayda, E. and Satterfield, M. (1997). *Law for Social Workers* (Toronto: Carswell).

Veling, W., Susser, E., van Os, J., Mackenbach, J., Selten, J., and Hoek, H. (2008). 'Ethnic Density of Neighbourhoods and Incidence of Psychotic Disorders among Immigrants', *American Journal of Psychiatry*, 165: 66–73.

Vocci, F.J. and Appel, N.M. (2007). 'Approaches to the Development of Medications for the Treatment of Methamphetamine Dependence', *Addiction*, 102(supp. 1): 96–106.

Vonk, R., van der Schot, A.C., Kahn, R.S., Nolen, W.A., and Drexhage, H.A. (2007). 'Is Autoimmune Thyroiditis Part of the Genetic Vulnerability (or an Endophenotype) for Bipolar Disorder?' *Biological Psychiatry*, 62(2): 135–40.

Vulnerable Persons Living with a Mental Disability Act, (The) SM. 1993, c. 29 (accessed at http://www.gov.mb.ca).

Walker, E.F., Savoie, T., and Davis, D. (1994). 'Neuromotor Precursors of Schizophrenia', *Schizophrenia Bulletin*, 20(3): 441–51.

Walker, L. (1979). *The Battered Woman* (New York: Harper & Row Publishers).

Wall, A.E. and Kohl, P.L. (2007). 'Substance Use in Maltreated Youth: Findings from the National Survey of Child and Adolescent Well-being', *Child Maltreatment*, 12(1): 20–30.

Wang, J. (2007). 'Group Reminiscence Therapy for Cognitive and Affective Function of Demented Elderly in Taiwan', *International Journal of Geriatric Psychiatry*, 22: 1235–40.

Webb, S. (2001). 'Some Considerations on the Validity of Evidence-based Practice in Social Work', *British Journal of Social Work*, 31(1): 57–79.

Weerasekera, P. (1993). 'Formulation: A Multiperspective Model', *Canadian Journal of Psychiatry*, 38: 351–8.

Weinshenker, D. and Schroeder, J. (2007). 'There and Back Again: A Tale of Norepinephrine and Drug Addiction', *Neuropsychopharmacology*, 32: 1433–51.

Widiger, T. and Clark, L. (2000). 'Toward DSM-V and the Classification of Psychopathology', *Psychological Bulletin*, 126(6): 946–63.

Williams, C. and Collins, A. (1999). 'Defining New Frameworks for Psychosocial Intervention', *Psychiatry*, 62: 61–78.

——— (2002). 'The Social Construction of Disability in Schizophrenia', *Qualitative Healthy Research*, 12(3): 297–309.

Williams, J., Alatiq, Y., Barnhofer, C., Fennell, M., Duggan, D., Hepburn, S., et al. (2008). 'Mindfulness-based Cognitive Therapy in Bipolar Disorder: Preliminary Evaluation of Immediate Effects on between Episode Functioning', *Journal of Affective Disorders*, 107(1–3): 275–9.

Wilson, M., Hayward, R., Tunis, S., Bass, E., and Guyatt, G. (1995). 'Users' Guides to the Medical Literature: VIII. How to Use Clinical Practice Guidelines: B. What Are the Recommendations and Will They Help You in Caring for Your Patients?' *JAMA*, 274(20): 1630–2.

Winstock, A.R. and Strang, J. (2000). 'Opiates: Heroin, Methadone, and Buprenophrine', in M.G. Gelder, J.J. Lopez-Ibor Jr, and N.C. Andreasen (eds), *New Oxford Textbook of Psychiatry* (Oxford: Oxford University Press).

Witkiewitz, K. and Marlatt, G. (2006). 'Overview of Harm Reduction Treatments for Alcohol Problems', *International Journal of Drug Policy*, 17(4): 285–94.

Witkin, S.L. (1998). 'The Right to Effective Treatment and the Effective Treatment of Rights: Rhetorical Empiricism and the Politics of Research', *Social Work*, 43(1): 75–80.

Wolff, S., Townhend, R., McGuire, R., and Weeks, D. (1991). 'Schizoid Personality in Childhood and Adult Life', *British Journal of Psychiatry*, 159: 620–9.

Woods, B., Spector, A., Jones, C., Orrell, M., and Davies, S. (2005). 'Reminiscence Therapy for Dementia', *Cochrane Database of Systematic Reviews*, Issue 2, Art. No.: CD001120. DOI: 10.1002/14651858.CD001120.pub2.

Worden, J.W. (1991). *Grief Counseling and Grief Therapy: A Handbook for the Mental Health Practitioners* (New York: Springer).

World Health Organization (2002). *Toronto Declaration on the Global Prevention of Elder Abuse* (accessed at http://www.who.int).

——— (2004). *Global Status Report on Alcohol* (Geneva: World Health Organization).

——— (2007). *Suicide Prevention* (accessed at http://www.who.int/mental_health/prevention/suicide/suicideprevent/en/).

Wu, L.T. and Howard, M.O. (2006). 'Psychiatric Disorders in Inhalant Users: Results from the National Epidemiologic Survey on Alcohol and Related Conditions', *Drug and Alcohol Dependence*, 88(2–3): 146–55.

Yang, J., Law, S., Chow, W., Andermann, L., Steinberg, R., and Sadavoy, J. (2005). 'Assertive Community Treatment for Persons with Severe and Persistent Mental Illness in Ethnic Minority Groups', *Psychiatric Services*, 56(9): 1053–5.

Yatham, L.N., Kennedy, S.H., O'Donovan, C., Parikh, S.V., MacQueen, G., McIntyre, R., et al. (2005). 'Canadian Network for Mood and Anxiety Treatments (CANMAT) Guidelines for the Management of Patients with Bipolar Disorder: Consensus and Controversies', *Bipolar Disorders*, 7(supp. 3): 5–69 (accessed at http://www.canmat.org/resources/PDF/Bipolar_Guidelines.pdf).

——— (2006). 'Canadian Network for Mood and Anxiety Treatments (CANMAT) Guidelines for the Management of Patients with Bipolar Disorder', *Bipolar Disorder*, 8(6): 721–39.

Yearwood-Lee, E. (2008). *Mental Health Policies: Historical Overview* (Victoria, BC: Legislative Library of British Columbia).

Yehuda, R. (1999). 'Biological Factors Associated with Susceptibility to Post-traumatic Stress Disorder', *Canadian Journal of Psychiatry*, 44(1): 34–9.

——— (2002). 'Clinical Relevance of Biologic Findings in PTSD', *Psychiatric Quarterly*, 73(2): 123–33.

——— and McFarlane, A.C. (1995). 'Conflict between Current Knowledge of Post-traumatic Stress Disorder and its Original Conceptual Basis', *American Journal of Psychiatry*, 152: 1705–13.

Index

Note: Terms not included in the index may be found in the glossary. Page numbers in italics indicate illustrations.

About Oxford University Press Canada

OUP Canada's first home, at 25 Richmond Street West in Toronto.

The Canadian branch of Oxford University Press was established in 1904. It was the first overseas branch to be set up after an office was established in New York in 1896. Although the branch did not open until 1904, the first book published for the Canadian market actually appeared eight years earlier—a hymnal for the Presbyterian Church of Canada.

Before the twentieth century, the main suppliers of books to the trade in Canada were the Copp Clark Company, the W.J. Gage Company, and the Methodist Bookroom (in 1919 renamed The Ryerson Press after its founder, Egerton Ryerson). These three firms acted as 'jobbers' for other lines that were later to be represented either directly by branches of their parent houses or by exclusive Canadian agents. Prior to 1904, Oxford books had been sold in Canada by S.G. Wilkinson, who, based in London, England, travelled across Canada as far west as Winnipeg. Wilkinson did a large trade with S.B. (Sam) Gundy, the wholesale and trade manager of the Methodist Book-room. When Oxford University Press opened its own branch in Canada, Gundy, already familiar with Oxford books, was invited to become its first manager. The premises were at 25 Richmond Street West and, lacking an elevator of any kind, were hardly ideal for a publishing house.

An etching of Amen House on University Avenue, created by Stanley Turner.

The original reception area and library at 70 Wynford Drive. The library was later removed to make room for offices.

In 1929, the branch moved to Amen House, located at 480 University Avenue, and in 1936, after Gundy's death, the branch became closely allied with Clarke, Irwin and Company under W.C. Clarke. This association continued until 1949 when Clarke, Irwin moved to a separate location on St Clair Avenue West. In 1963, the Press moved to a new building at 70 Wynford Drive in Don Mills, which served it well for the next 46 years. By 2009, however, the branch had outgrown the 70 Wynford site. An extensive search process culminated in the move that November to a split-site configuration. The offices relocated to new premises at the Shops at Don Mills, an innovative retail/office/residential development, while the warehouse moved to a site in Brampton that not only offered more affordable rent and carrying charges but also provided a modern high-bay space much closer to major customers and Pearson International Airport.

Today OUP Canada is a major publisher of higher education, school, and English-as-a-second-language textbooks, as well as a significant trade and reference publisher. The Higher Education Division publishes both introductory and upper-level texts in such disciplines as sociology, anthropology, social work, English literature and composition, geography, history, political science, religious studies, and engineering. The division publishes more than 60 new Canadian texts and 150 student and instructor supplements each year, and derives about 60 per cent of its total sales from books and other learning materials written, edited, and published in Canada.

Some of the many books recently published by Oxford University Press Canada.

Highlights in the History of Oxford University Press Canada

1904 Canadian branch office opened at 25 Richmond Street West, Toronto
1913 First Canadian title published: *The Oxford Book of Canadian Verse*
1925 First Canadian educational title published: *Canadian High School Arithmetic*
1929 OUP Canada moves to new offices at 480 University Avenue, Toronto
1936 Canadian branch founder Sam Gundy dies
1939 OUP Canada opens its own sheet music department
1941 Two OUP titles win Governor General's Awards: Emily Carr's *Klee Wyck* for non-fiction, and Alan Sullivan's *Three Came to Ville Marie* for fiction
1944 *The War: Fourth Year* by historian Edgar McInnis wins Governor General's Award for non-fiction
1946 *Poems*, by Robert Finch, receives Governor General's Award for poetry
1947 *Haida* by William Sclater wins Governor General's Award for non-fiction
1947 Paul Hiebert's *Sarah Binks* published; wins Stephen Leacock Memorial Award for Humour
1957 First edition of the *Canadian Oxford School Atlas* published
1957 Jay Macpherson's poetry collection *The Boatman* wins Governor General's Award for poetry
1958 Joyce Hemlow's *The History of Fanny Burney* wins Governor General's Award for non-fiction
1960 Robert Weaver's anthology *Canadian Short Stories* published as part of the Oxford World's Classics series
1960 *Canadian Oxford School Atlas* becomes first atlas to be entirely manufactured in Canada
1962 Kildare Dobbs' *Running to Paradise* wins Governor General's Award for fiction
1963 Branch moves to 70 Wynford Drive, Don Mills
1967 Norah Story's *Oxford Companion to Canadian History and Literature* published; wins Governor General's Award for non-fiction
1968 Margaret Atwood's first book with Oxford published—*The Animals in That Country*
1969 William Toye appointed editorial director
1970 Margaret Atwood's *Journals of Susanna Moodie* published
1971 John Glassco's *Selected Poems* wins Governor General's Award for poetry
1973 Canadian music department closes
1973 First edition published of Dennis Reid's *A Concise History of Canadian Painting*
1976 *The Writing of Canadian History* by Carl Berger wins the Governor General's Award for non-fiction
1978 Branch publishes first edition of bestselling high school history text, Cruxton and Wilson's *Flashback Canada*—it goes on to sell more than 100,000 copies in its first year
1978 Patrick Lane's *Poems New and Selected* wins Governor General's Award for poetry
1979 Maria Tippett's *Emily Carr: A Biography* wins Governor General's Award for non-fiction
1983 First edition of Bennett and Brown's *An Anthology of Canadian Literature in English* is published
1983 Branch publishes first edition of *Oxford Companion to Canadian Literature*, edited by William Toye
1989 *The Oxford Companion to Canadian Theatre*, edited by Eugene Benson and L.W. Conolly, is published
1990 Paul Morin's *The Orphan Boy* wins Governor General's Award for children's book illustration
1991 William Toye retires
1992 First edition of William Norton's *Human Geography* is published; by the time of the seventh edition (2010), it becomes the most widely adopted human geography book in Canadian universities

1998 *Canadian Oxford Dictionary* is published, becomes national bestseller
1999 First edition of Robert Bone's *Regional Geography of Canada* is published and quickly becomes the most widely used text in post-secondary Canadian geography courses (fifth edition, 2010)
2004 Branch celebrates centenary with publication of *The Oxford Companion to Canadian History*
2004 First edition of *Sociology: A Canadian Perspective* by Lorne Tepperman and James Curtis is published
2008 Canadian titles account for more than half of branch revenues for the first time
2009 Margot Northey's post-secondary writing guide *Making Sense* celebrates its 25th anniversary with more than a quarter-million copies in print
2009 Ninth edition published of the *Canadian Oxford School Atlas*, bringing total sales since 1957 to more than 3 million copies
2010 Branch offices relocate to 8 Sampson Mews at the Shops at Don Mills
2010 *The Oxford Companion to Canadian Military History* by J.L. Granatstein and Dean F. Oliver is published in association with the Canadian War Museum
2011 Second edition of William Toye's *Concise Oxford Companion to Canadian Literature* is published
2011 Higher Education Division publishes two major psychology texts, Rutherford's *Child Development* and Chaudhuri's *Fundamentals of Sensory Perception*